# Finally Organized, Finally Free
# For the Office

# FINALLY
## ORGANIZED
# FINALLY
## *Free*

### FOR THE OFFICE

## MARIA GRACIA

Published by **BlueMoon Publishing.**

Copyright © 2006 by Maria Gracia.

This publication is designed to provide accurate and authoritative information in regard to the subject matter covered. It is sold with the understanding that the publisher and the copyright owner are not engaged in rendering legal, accounting or other professional service. If legal advice or other expert assistance is required, the services of a competent professional person who specializes in that particular field should be sought.

While due care has been exercised in the compilation of this guide, we are not responsible for errors or omissions. This reference is intended to assist in providing information to the public, and the information is delivered as accurately as possible.

Senior Executive Editor: Joseph Gracia, Laura Sherman

Executive Editor: Maribel Ibrahim

Index: WordCo Indexing Services

Cover Design: Cathi Stevenson of Book Cover Express

Please direct any comments, questions or suggestions regarding this book to:

BlueMoon Publishing
611 Arlington Way
Watertown WI 53094
USA

**Library of Congress Cataloging-in-Publication Data**

Gracia, Maria
    Finally Organized, Finally Free for the Office/by Maria Gracia
    ISBN # 0-9779777-0-6 $34.95

    Library of Congress Control Number 2006923864

    Includes Index.

    Reference: Office Organization, Goals, Self-Help, Business Resources, Time Management, Planning, Achievement.

ISBN # 0-9779777-0-6

Printed in the United States of America.

# Dedication

*This book is dedicated to my husband and best friend, Joe.*
*You are the most intelligent, logical and persistent*
*person I've ever known.*
*When you have a goal, you stop at nothing to reach it.*
*Since I've known you, I've never, ever seen you give up—on anything.*
*That's why you have reached so many goals in your life.*
*You're an inspiration to me and I love you for*
*your never ending support*
*and for a thousand other reasons.*

# Acknowledgements

*Thanks to all of you from the bottom of my heart*
*for all your positive influence and support.*

*My daughter, Amanda Grace*

*My father and mother, Mike and Margie*

*My sister and her family, Jude, Ed and Mary Elizabeth*

# Table of Contents

# Chapter 1

# Introduction

"I've got to get organized!"

When did you last utter these words? Was it when you realized that the raging, paper beast had taken complete control of your office?

Maybe it was when you were late for a staff meeting . . . yet again.

Perhaps it was when you looked at all the clutter on your desk, computer center, bookcase, credenza and everyplace else. You may have even contemplated tossing everything out the window!

Was it when you desperately searched for that missing client folder?

It could have been when you missed that important appointment. Or when that deadline crept up on you.

Maybe it was when you had to work late again because you couldn't finish everything on your list.

Perhaps it was when you realized that you have enough tasks on your To Do list to last the next ten years and you've given up on ever catching up with it all.

Or even worse, it may have happened when you found out you had no time left for yourself, your family, your friends, that needed vacation or anything else you love to do.

You're not alone. Those words have been expressed over and over again by thousands of people throughout the world.

Disorganization can actually trap you into living a life filled with stress, frustration and chaos. It can rob you of the precious time you should be spending enjoying your life.

By overcoming disorganization, you will be set free to live the kind of life you've always dreamed of.

## Teeny-Tiny tips equal big changes

For some reason, many people equate being organized with achieving an enormous and impossible feat—something only lucky people are capable of having.

If this is your thinking, then let me ease your mind.

Being organized does not require you to perform time-consuming, complicated systems.

It is not rocket science.

It is not something that's going to take you years of soul-searching to start.

And it's not something that only lucky people are capable of having.

Just a few small organizing tips—a few little, teeny-tiny tips, applied with a positive attitude—can help you be more organized today, than you were yesterday.

As you apply them to your life and those teeny-tips become habits that you do each day, you will become more and more organized.

Your goal should never be to get totally organized.

That is a difficult, overwhelming, frightening, major, impossible goal and something I would never recommend you try to take on.

No one can ever be totally organized. Even professional organizers are occasionally late for appointments or have a messy desk!

Your goal should be to apply small organizing tips today that will make your life just a little more organized tomorrow. Those teeny-tiny tips can help make big changes in your life.

And you'll get all the teeny-tiny tips you need and more, as you read *Finally Organized, Finally Free for the Office.*


**Venturing outside your comfort zone**

We are faced with making choices throughout our lives. If you had to choose between comfort and risk, which would you take?

Most people would choose comfort. We do this because we find comfort in the familiar. We each have a "comfort zone"—our own personal area of thoughts and actions where we feel safe and relaxed.

Anything we haven't thought or done—something new—lies outside the parameters of our comfort zone. When we think about these things, it may make us feel uncomfortable.

And, after feeling uncomfortable, we often feel discouraged and tend to give up before ever trying something new.

You can get organized. But you have to believe it and you have to step outside your comfort zone to begin.

## Start off on the right foot

Right now, I'm going to ask you to determine exactly what it is you're trying to accomplish by reading this book.

The more specific you are in your description, the easier it will be for you to succeed in achieving your objectives.

For example, stating, "I'd like to eliminate clutter," is too broad.

It would be better to say, "I'd like to remove every piece of paper from my desk and create an effective filing system so that I can find anything I need in 30 seconds or less."

Or how about, "I'd like to be able to accomplish a minimum of 4 tasks on my To Do List each day, without having to work late to complete them."

Take a moment right now to think about and write down your personal objectives.

My objectives are:

1. _____
   _____
   _____
   _____
   _____

2. _____
   _____
   _____
   _____
   _____

3. _____
   _____
   _____

4. _____

_____

_____

_____

_____

5. _____

_____

_____

_____

_____

The next critical step is to set a practical deadline to accomplish each of these objectives. Go back to each one of your goals and assign a specific date for when you want each one to be completed. Saying, "as soon as possible" is too broad. It must be a calendar date, such as September 26th or July 7th.

Setting objectives and deadlines gives you something to aim for. If you don't meet your goals by your deadlines, it doesn't mean that you have failed. It just means you need to re-adjust your deadlines and work on them until you've reached your objectives.

## You'll benefit from my organizing experience

What qualifies me to help you get organized? I worked for ten years with Dun and Bradstreet's Nielsen Media Research in New York City as an organizing and management specialist. Throughout my tenure, I managed the data analysis department, worked with hundreds of television stations and advertising agencies, and developed effective, productive systems for my clients and staff.

In 1996, I moved to Wisconsin and founded Get Organized Now! My husband and I both run our business at home, while raising our daughter Amanda. Our home is very organized. Everything has a place where it belongs. We can welcome unexpected guests without having to pick things up before we answer the doorbell. I don't just teach the organizing techniques you will find in this book, I use them myself. I guarantee you that they all work beautifully!

I have literally helped thousands of individuals and businesses get organized. I teach "real life organizing." In fact, my Get Organized Now! web site is visited by over a million people each year and my Get Organized Now! Newsletter is read by hundreds of thousands of people every week.

I have appeared on, written for and have been interviewed by hundreds of international, national and local media and organizations such as:

Fox 6 News WITI-TV Milwaukee

World Talk Radio

KNEV Radio: The New Mix 95.5 Morning Show

11 Alive News WXIA-TV Atlanta

Fox 6 News WOWT-TV: Discover Omaha

WJR Radio 760 AM: The Internet Advisor

FM 89.3 KPCC Nat'l Public Radio, Talk of the City

WQIK-FM 99.1 Radio, Jacksonville, FL, Morning Show

WKZK Radio, Augusta, Marilyn Joyce Motivational Talk Show

Woman's Day Magazine

Country Living Magazine

First for Women Magazine

Parenting Magazine

Woman's World

Kitchen and Bath Ideas Magazine

Milwaukee Business Journal

Barnes and Noble, Milwaukee, WI

Staples Office Supplies Stores Business Expert

Delta Connections Magazine

Lifestyles Magazine of Orlando

Venice Gulf Coast Living

The News-Sun and The Evening Star

Access Magazine

**What you won't find in this book**

There are volumes of organizing books on the market. Believe me, bookstore and library shelves are full of them. This book, however, is unique.

You won't find a whole lot of philosophy, theories, difficult-to-understand concepts or fluff. You won't have to read dozens of pages before you get to the meat. You won't have to read the entire book to begin to get organized. The second you hit Chapter One, you'll find tips and ideas you can apply—immediately!

**How to use this book**

*Finally Organized, Finally Free for the Office* is categorized into individual topics applicable to anyone who works in an office setting. There are tips, ideas and real life question/answer sessions throughout to help you save time. Some can help you save a few minutes, some a few hours. All of them will help you get and stay better organized.

Choose a few tips and ideas at a time. Don't try to implement too many at once. Realize that effective organization is an ongoing process. Once you begin to execute the tips I will share with you, continue to practice them over and over again. Before long, each tip or idea that you implement will become a habit.

By the way, studies show only after you do something repetitively—a total of 21 consecutive times—does it become a habit and part of your everyday routine.

Each idea, tip, technique and system you utilize will bring you another step closer to achieving organizational success.

This is not something to be accomplished in a day. Getting organized requires knowledge, implementation, practice and motivation just as it does to master other skills like riding a bike, playing golf or cooking a meal. Taking it one step at a time, while maintaining an "I can do it" attitude, will get you organized before you know it.

I wish you the greatest success in getting organized, so that you can be *Finally Organized, Finally Free.* You can do it. I know you can!

# Chapter 2

# Creating a comfortable, productive environment

- **Determine your needs.** An office does not need to be elaborate. Many people can get by with less than they think. Others have more advanced needs. Seek office furniture and office equipment as the need arises—not just because a business colleague of yours has something.

  Anne, a home-based entrepreneur, gets by with nothing more than a laptop. She doesn't have any need to rent an office each month, which means she doesn't need any office furniture. Plus, she is able to "carry" her business wherever she goes.

  Gary, an accountant, needs a more elaborate set up, as he has clients who visit his office each day. He rents his office in a business development. He has a desk and chair, a 4-drawer filing cabinet, a credenza, a guest chair, a computer, printer, fax machine, answering machine and copy machine.

  Sue, a jewelry expert, is satisfied with her simple office made up of a desk, a chair and a small 2-drawer filing cabinet. She doesn't have a need for a computer or any additional office furniture.

  While viewing *Designer's Challenge* on HGTV, I saw a work-at-home couple's office. The couple worked together in the same office. The wife had her computer station on one of the walls; the husband had his computer setup on the opposite wall. A very large work surface was positioned in the center of the room so that when either of them needed a writing surface, he or she simply rotated their chair to it. In other words, one office served two people beautifully!

- **Think before you do.** If you are involved in the very beginning stages of setting up a new office, make sure you give considerable planning to the placement of electrical outlets. Think about where your equipment should be located to enhance your workflow. Give function and safety top priority. Use surge protectors. Place electrical equipment where it will be most efficiently used and where wires aren't exposed to cause a safety risk.

  Equipment to remember: fax machine, printers, computers, scanners, photocopiers, external CD-ROMS, external hard drives, electric pencil sharpener and telephone systems.

It's also a very good idea to prepare in advance for placement of telephone lines, not only for your phone system, but also for your fax machine and data lines for your computers.

- **Look for the bare necessities .** Create a list of the "bare minimum" amount of furniture you need. This will help you avoid the purchase of duplicate items that serve the same purpose. You will always have the option to add furniture later as the need arises.

  For example, Steve, a web site designer, got started in his home with nothing more than a computer on a table in his bedroom. Later, as his business began to take off, he began to accumulate more projects than his small table could handle and he went out and purchased a nice computer workstation.

- **Be a good matchmaker.** Take your time when making a decision about your office furniture. The furniture that will serve you best will depend on your needs, personality, style and available space.

  My husband, Joe, and I each have an office in our home. Joe has an open computer desk with a hutch, plus a very large desk, a bookcase and a lateral 2-drawer filing cabinet. The scale of the furniture is perfect for the size of his office and the look of the furniture matches his style and personality. There is a swivel chair between the computer desk with the hutch, and his large desk, so he can easily switch from using the computer at one desk to writing at the other desk.

  I have a large computer armoire in my office, but my office is also an occasional guestroom. I selected a unit that has doors, so I can "close shop" when we have visitors. My armoire has a pullout keyboard shelf, plus a second pullout shelf that I use as a writing surface when I'm not using the keyboard.

  In addition to my computer armoire, which has plenty of storage and filing space, I also have a 2-drawer lateral filing cabinet that holds all of my files. A five-shelf bookcase holds my business books and books for reading pleasure when guests visit. There is a large sofa, which converts to a queen-size bed. It's the perfect set for my style and personality. I enjoy using it each day.

  The bottom line is, before spending money on new office furniture, take time to determine your needs, personality, space and style. Chances are, you're going to have your office furniture for a long time and it won't be easy to replace if months later you decide you're not really happy with it.

- **Leave plenty of time.** Make sure you leave plenty of time for your decision process and actual purchase. Ideally, you should begin your search for furniture a few months in advance. Delivery can take anywhere from six to twelve weeks depending on the type of furniture and the size of your order.

If you're in a rush, again, buy the "bare minimum" until you're able to take your time and better determine your needs.

- **A bunch of bids.** Furniture is a big investment. Make sure you obtain two to three bids. All bids should include installation fees, hardware expenses and delivery fees.

Alan, a systems analyst, visited his local office furniture store and purchased an entire set of office furniture. He was quite disappointed when he was in a large office store a few weeks later and saw the same set he had just purchased for 25% less than what he originally paid.

Bottom line—it pays to shop around.

## Organizing Clinic

### Question

I am in the process of renovating my office. I'm building a business office to seat four employees with computer workstations and file cabinets, book shelves and if possible a small conference table. The room is 13' x 13'. Any suggestions?

Animal Medic

### Answer

Dear Animal Medic,

Good for you on renovating your office and building a business office. Here are three simple ideas that come to mind immediately:

- Ensure each employee has his or her own personal space. Perhaps dedicate one corner to each person, centralizing the file cabinets and bookshelves to provide some privacy for greater productivity.

- If you have two lateral filing cabinets, they can be set up back to back. This will provide each person with easy access to the files, plus the tops of these low filing cabinets can be used as a work surface or as a small conference table.

- Finally, since this room is 13' x 13', you don't want to overpower it with lots of furniture. Be sure not to forget about your wall space for shelving, wall pockets to collect incoming mail and corkboards for incoming phone messages.

- **Save a few bucks.** If possible, try to take advantage of volume purchasing power. Consider the possibility of combining your order with other offices or departments. As the size of your purchase increases, your discount should increase.

- **Measure, measure, measure.** Then measure once more. I can't stress this enough. Don't purchase anything for your office before determining if it's going to fit comfortably with breathing room. Make sure you have enough room to reach electrical sockets and phone/cable jacks. Also, take air ducts into account.

When Joe and I were first purchasing items for our offices, we had a designer help us with the scale of the furniture. The designer measured once and determined that a particular executive chair, plus two bookcases, should fit just fine in addition to Joe's other office furniture.

When the furniture was delivered, the delivery person said, "We have a bit of a problem." We discovered that only one bookcase would fit and the chair was way too large for the room. We had to return one of the bookcases and we had to exchange the chair for something more fitting for Joe's office. Luckily, we purchased from a very reputable store and did not have a problem with the exchange. But it's obvious the designer didn't measure as accurately as she should have.

Also, if you shop in a very large store or gallery, furniture may appear much smaller than it actually is, so don't rely on a guess. Joe's office chair, which looked normal size in the huge furniture store when we originally saw it, suddenly looked enormous in Joe's office!

- **Don't skimp with office equipment.** This is not where you should try to save money. Your most important pieces of office equipment will likely be your computer and printer. Purchase a computer with extensive memory, a good size hard drive and high-speed capabilities. Buy a high-speed, high-resolution printer.

You might also need a scanner, answering machine, fax machine, photocopier, a CD burner and other equipment depending upon your needs.

My recommendation is to invest in the best equipment you can afford, rather than trying to save a few bucks here and there. Often, the lowest priced equipment is being discontinued, which means you might not be able to get support from the manufacturer or store if you need it. Plus, in nine out of ten cases, the cheapest is not going to come close in reliability and lifespan to higher quality models. The small amount you save by purchasing less than great equipment, is rarely worth as much as the time you're likely to waste replacing it in the future.

- **You don't have to spend tons to get good equipment.** When considering new computer equipment (add-ons, rebuilds or peripherals) do some comparison-shopping at smaller retail and repair outlets. Often you will find a "mom and pop" or "college buddies" store that will build you the system of your dreams from scratch with the features you desire for a very competitive price.

These stores usually offer personalized service and customer incentives like free help or consultation, complete upgrade and repair services and small rebates on items being replaced or upgraded as a way of creating a loyal customer base.

Building this sort of relationship can be invaluable to you in the future as your business grows and expands. Having immediate access to personalized service in the midst of a computer crisis can also save you valuable time and needless stress.

## Organizing Clinic

### Question

I work in a two-story office building that was built as a house in 1919. The copy room lacks work surfaces to the point the typewriter is not always usable because people place files on it. What are your tips for obtaining additional work surface area in a busy copy room?

Paul Harmon

### Answer

Dear Paul,

It definitely sounds like this room needs to be revamped a bit to handle modern equipment.

I would highly recommend you consider adding shelving for anything that is currently being placed on the typewriter or the copy machines. Very often, wall space is forgotten about. It's amazing what a few shelves can do to increase your available space.

I would also advise that people don't lay their files down on the typewriter. If they need a temporary place to lay files down for a few minutes, you might consider getting a few pocket holders, which can be attached to the wall. If staff members need a more permanent place for their files, a filing cabinet is a must.

If possible, you can place a mobile workstation in your office. The typewriter can sit on top of it, which will give staff members a place to work while they're waiting for their copy projects to be completed.

- **Or go with a big name.** My husband and I both purchased our computer systems from Dell. We went to their web site, checked the features that were important to us, placed our order and both computers were delivered and running within a few days. We haven't had any problems, so we consider them a wonderful investment.

- **Think form and function.** Be sure your furnishings complement your working style and workflow or they can be a liability instead of an asset. Buy furniture and equipment that will encourage productivity *and* that you will enjoy looking at. I love my office furniture and equipment and am thrilled to be using it each day.

- **Give yourself some elbow room.** A small, cramped workspace is difficult to work in. Create enough space for you to do your daily work—a sufficient writing surface, enough space to spread out papers when you work on projects, sufficient storage space for your office supplies and so on.

  Remove anything from your office that doesn't belong there. Archive old files in a storage area, basement or outside storage facility if necessary. If you work in a tiny office, don't forget about the wall space. Shelving can often solve many space problems.

  Janet works in a corporate office three days a week and works from home two days each week. She doesn't have much space in her small apartment, so she installed a homemade flip-up table. It's simply a board that is attached to her wall with hinges. When she needs the table, she flips it up. When she doesn't need it, she flips it down—the perfect solution for her needs!

- **Roll-top or Regular?** Many people I know love roll-top desks. In fact, I also think they're lovely. Unfortunately, most offer little to no work area and limited storage space.

  Roll-top desks are first for beauty and second for function. I always try to find office furniture that is equally beautiful and functional. Even after reading this though, you may decide to get a roll-top desk anyway. Maybe it's very nostalgic for you, but I just wanted to warn you about the drawbacks.

- **Get a comfy chair.** If you're sitting on the wrong chair all day long, you're bound to get a backache. Test several chairs before you buy. Adjustable, swivel-style chairs, especially those with wheels, are often the best. You can raise or lower them to the proper height for you and maneuver them easily. Make sure you get a comfortable chair that offers good back support and set the height appropriately.

- **Be sure you can glide.** If you have thick, plush carpeting in your office, you may need an acrylic chair mat, so you can slide your chair easily. Standard size mats are sold at major office supply stores. If you need a custom size, speak with someone at your local office furniture or office supply store. They should be able to accommodate you.

I have carpeting in my office, but it's low carpeting, so my chair moves around easily without a mat.

- **A place for your books.** If you have lots of books, you need a bookcase. These come in a variety of finishes and styles. The one I have matches the furniture in my office, nearly reaches the ceiling, is about thirty inches wide and has five shelves. I store my business books and several personal books in the one bookcase and there is room to spare for future books.

  Most bookcases are open, which means you can see the books readily.

  Barrister-type bookcases hold books enclosed behind smoky glass doors. These have a very regal look and are often seen in lawyer's offices. Two drawbacks: you have to open the glass doors every time you need a book and the height of the shelves doesn't always accommodate larger books.

  Other bookcases have doors that allow you to hide your books. These are great if you prefer to keep your books hidden, but bookcases with doors are difficult to find.

  Your decision needs to be based on what type of bookcase meets your personal needs, style and budget.

- **Every office needs a filing cabinet.** No matter what type of work you do, you're going to need a filing cabinet for your paperwork. Before you purchase a filing cabinet, you should decide the type that will suit you best.

  The most common filing cabinets available are a) the vertical cabinet and b) the lateral filing cabinet. I've detailed some notes on each below to help you with your decision.

  No matter which type you purchase, be sure it's a full-suspension unit. This means that the drawers will pull out all the way for easy filing and file retrieval and that the unit won't fall forward when the drawers are open—even if they're filled to the max with heavy file folders.

- **Vertical filing cabinet notes.** The vertical filing cabinet, the more traditional style, has anywhere from two to five drawers. Letter or legal-sized files are stored facing the front of the drawers.

  - ❖ Since these cabinets are built up, rather than wide, they take up very little side-to-side wall space and make good use of floor-to-ceiling space.
  - ❖ They are ideal for tiny offices that don't have enough room for wide cabinets.
  - ❖ They're less expensive than lateral cabinets.
  - ❖ They come in a variety of sizes, finishes and styles.

❖ When the drawers are pulled out they can take up a large amount of space and may block passage. This is a safety hazard and can cause problems in a busy office.

❖ It can sometimes be a little awkward for shorter people to find a file in the top drawer of a 4-drawer vertical filing cabinet. Therefore, for shorter people, the top drawer(s) of tall vertical filing cabinets are best suited for long-term storage or less frequent reference.

- **Lateral filing cabinet notes.** The lateral filing cabinet is a much wider cabinet that allows files to be stored either front to back or side to side. Units for home office or small business use are generally two drawers high, but some steel units for larger businesses can be four or more drawers high.

  ❖ They're not as deep as vertical cabinets, which means they require less floor space, specifically when the drawer is open.

  ❖ They can often hold legal and letter-sized files in the same drawer, while vertical designs must choose one or the other in each drawer.

  ❖ Lateral drawers are bigger. They hold about one-third more files than a standard vertical unit.

  ❖ They're wide enough to accommodate two people filing at the same time.

  ❖ They often keep wall space free for items like shelving units and bulletin boards.

  ❖ Because they're wide, they can actually be used as credenzas or partitions, which makes them work double-duty for you.

  ❖ Lateral filing cabinets take up more horizontal wall space than a vertical, which may cause a space issue for some users.

  ❖ Lateral filing cabinets are almost always more expensive than their vertical counterparts.

- **Final filing cabinet thoughts.** Here are just a few other points to consider before purchasing your filing cabinet:

  ❖ Beware of the very inexpensive ones. They almost always pose a nuisance, can be hazardous and often are a waste of money.

  ❖ Decide how many filing cabinets you need and what size. A small two-drawer one may be fine now, but if you are going to accumulate more files in the future—and you probably will—buy a larger size than what you need right now. Always plan for the future.

  ❖ Make sure the drawers slide in and out easily. Be sure your cabinet comes with hanging file guides so that hanging file folders can be stored in them.

Many filing cabinets come with them, but some don't. If the one you're considering does not, be sure to buy the separate attachments.

❖ Think sturdy. Ensure the cabinet doesn't fall forward when the drawers are open and a little bit of weight is applied. Be sure it's a full-suspension cabinet.

❖ Buy a design, style and color that you'll always be happy with. It will probably be in your office for years to come. Keep in mind that if you work in a home office, you might want to invest in a nice wood cabinet that looks more like furniture than like commercial office equipment.

❖ Consider a lock feature if you store confidential files now or if you may in the future.

❖ I've come across filing cabinets stuffed with shoes, purses, lunch bags, software, candy, raincoats—I can go on and on. Your filing cabinet should be thought of as *high-rent space* to be used for the specific purpose of filing away your most important papers. I'll say no more.

- **Remember ergonomics.** Give consideration and attention to the health and safety of your employees by investigating comfort and ergonomics. The wrong desk and chair will make everyone in the office susceptible to disorders such as backaches, headaches and eyestrain.

- **Check your distance.** According to the Cornell University Ergonomics web site, the recommended angle of a chair back should be 100 to 110 degrees for the most comfort.

  Your eyes should line up approximately two to three inches below the top of your computer screen and be 24-36 inches away from the screen.

  Your elbows should be at an angle of 90 degrees or more to avoid elbow nerve compression.

  It is recommended that when looking at a computer for a period of fifteen minutes, you should take an eye break and then look away from the computer screen to let your eyes relax.

- **Color your world.** Do you have a say about the color of your office? If so, choose one of your favorite colors and buy some paint. A new, fresh coat will give you a new, fresh feeling and the color you choose will reflect your style and personality. You can even paint your metal filing cabinets to match your decor!

- **Shelves for the sentimental.** Enjoy having photos of loved ones and inspirational doodads adorning your office? Install hanging shelves to display your personal items so they don't take over your desk and credenza.

## Organizing Clinic

### Question

I want to rearrange my office. Any suggestions on where to place things so I'm more productive?

Anna

### Answer

Dear Anna,

The way you arrange your office is a very personal decision that must be made based on your specific needs and styles. But here are a few points to consider before you spend the time rearranging.

- Put things where you use them. If you answer your telephone with your left hand, put your phone on the left side of your desk. If you're always spending time walking across the room to retrieve a file folder, put your filing cabinet right behind your desk so you can swivel around and retrieve a file without having to get up.

- Consider the amount of light in your room. You would not want your computer facing the window if the light causes a lot of glare on the screen.

- If you position your desk so that you're looking outside of your office, rather than at the wall, you'll be able to see if visitors are standing at your door waiting to speak with you, rather than having to twist your neck around if you suspect someone is there.

Before you begin arranging, make a list of your needs. Then lay out some possibilities on graph paper. When making your diagrams, keep in mind that some furniture requires extra room for opening drawers and doors that swing out.

Once you do this, you should be able to see if your new arrangement allows enough room for you and your office visitors to easily get around the room. You're basically looking for a layout that will be comfortable, allow you easy access to the items you use each day and is both tasteful and pleasing to you.

- **Meet me in my office.** If you regularly have clients or customers in your office, you will need chairs for your guests. Office chairs can take up a large amount of space. Choose carefully to ensure the chairs fit nicely so the office won't be cramped. Comfortable chairs with wheels are best.

During a visit to an accountant's office, I sat on this huge wicker guest chair. It was extremely uncomfortable, too big for her small office and it squeaked every time I moved. I left with an impression that was not good.

- **Add some life.** A few plants can greatly enhance the look of any office. If you think you'll remember to water them, get some live ones. If not, artificial ones work well.

  The artificial ones are great for me, as I don't feel like spending the time having to care for plants each day. A colleague of mine has an office that looks like a botanical garden—well, maybe that's a bit of an exaggeration, but she does have beautiful plants that add charm and that she enjoys.

> ### Great idea!
>
> My tax forms and information, receipts, bank and credit card statements and other important papers are kept in a four-drawer filing cabinet with color-coded file folders.
>
> I use this often because it is only a spin in my chair away from the desk. With the different colored file folders, I am able to find what I need in seconds.
>
> Jason Michael Gracia
> www.motivation123.com

- **Screen it off.** Some home offices do double-duty. My office is also a guest room. When I have guests staying in the guest room, I'm able to "close shop" by closing the doors of my computer armoire.

  A friend of mine has a home office set-up in her family room. Each evening, she closes shop by hiding her desk behind a decorative screen.

- **Be inspired.** Working in an office each day that is not very inspiring can zap your productivity and energy. If your spouse or kids inspire you, you may want to hang a family photograph on your wall.

  Or, perhaps you enjoy inspirational framed art or a photo of a vacation spot you want to visit soon. Include things in your office that will motivate you and make you happy to be there every day.

- **Don't bring me down.** It can be aggravating to walk into your office each day and have to look at a piece of furniture or an accessory that you don't particularly like.

  If you work at home, trade in that old piece for something you do like or if your budget is an issue, consider refurbishing or reupholstering to make the piece look better.

  If you work for someone else, redecorating and refurbishing may not be possible, but ask your boss anyway. It won't hurt to ask—especially if you promise that your productivity will surely rise if your office is a more pleasant place to work.

- **Match accessories to your décor.** If you've gone out of your way to buy expensive-looking office furniture, don't destroy the look with cheap-looking office accessories. Purchase accessories that are functional and that you'll enjoy using each day.

  By the way, you don't have to break the bank to have nice things. Shop around and you'll find many beautiful, yet reasonably priced, file holders, trays, baskets, supply organizers and so on.

### Great idea!

In my office, I have created activity stations so that like items are stored together and nearest the point of use. For example, all computer related books, disks and information is filed by category and near my computer.

I have set up an area for all my office supplies. Each supply has a "home" and it is easy for me to access and also see when I need more of a particular item.

I have followed through in the same manner in all areas including telephone information, bills, checkbook items and files.

Barb Friedman
Organize IT
www.organizeitbiz.com

- **Add a fragrance.** Your office should be a place that is pleasant and enjoyable to work in. One way to make the environment more pleasant is to add a room freshener or potpourri or burn a fragrant candle. By the way, never leave a burning candle unattended. It should not take up too much space and the smell should not be overpowering.

  Of course, you may need to reconsider this when sharing office space with others. Perhaps you can speak with your co-workers and agree on a fragrance you can all enjoy.

- **Moving from a work office to a home office.** Your first step should be to locate an area in your home to use as a home office. It is best if the room is not used for anything else. However, for many of us that is not practical and you must make do with whatever space you have.

- **Make changes if necessary.** Once you change or rearrange furniture and equipment in your office, spend a minimum of one week in that setting to ensure it's working for you. It will take at least a week or two to get a good feel for any changes needed.

- **What's your position?** Are you right-handed or left-handed? If right-handed, you may want to position your phone on your left side, which will leave your right hand free for note taking. The reverse is true if you're left-handed.

- **Move the computer.** If your computer is on your desk and you have no space for writing or spreading out a project, consider moving your computer to a portable computer desk or rear credenza.

- **When shopping for a desk,** some things to consider are:
  - ❖ Drawers that easily slide open and shut
  - ❖ A front panel to block legs from view if the front of the desk is not placed against a wall
  - ❖ A side extension for a computer, fax machine or other piece of equipment
  - ❖ File space for your daily files
  - ❖ At least one shallow drawer for supplies
  - ❖ A pull-out surface for additional writing space
  - ❖ A locking mechanism if you have confidential material or kids/pets if you work in a home office
  - ❖ A large work area for spreading out your papers

- **When shopping for a computer armoire**, the above points apply, plus
  - ❖ Doors that close when you want to be able to "close shop"
  - ❖ Ample space for your computer hard drive and monitor
  - ❖ Additional shelving for paper, labels and reference material
  - ❖ Built-in storage space for CDs and diskettes

- **Let the music set you free.** I don't know how I would be able to work each day without my dual radio/CD player in my office. When I'm working on detailed work, I put on the classical station.

When I need an energy pick-up, I insert a rock or country CD. When I'm working on tasks that don't require too much thought, I turn on the news or a radio talk show.

## Great idea!

We basically follow the 4-D rule (Do it, Delegate it, Delay it, Dump it) whether in our office/administration end of the business or in the actual manufacturing end of the business.

Mail is sorted over the recycle bin for example. Email is answered within 48 hours of receipt Monday to Friday. Phone calls are returned within 24 hours Monday to Friday. We label all files, folders, materials, sewing directions and products. We use consistency in our labeling system and have assigned product numbers, account numbers, supplier labels and more to all of our items. We use the Golden Rule and all items go back to where they belong immediately.

At the end of every day all areas are picked up and readied for the next day's work. On Friday all areas are completely cleaned and reorganized where needed for the following Monday.

Kate Lozier
KRLCP, Inc. / TuffBaggs ®
P.O. Box 387, East Greenbush, New York 12061- 0387
518-479-4052
Main Web site: www.tuffbaggs.com
Article Center: www.tuffbaggs.com/artnew.htm

- **Stretch your space.** If you feel cramped, you're going to feel anything but productive. Even if you have a small office, there are always ways to stretch your space. Buy compact furniture. Add shelves to the walls. Take the door off a closet and use the space for a small desk, filing cabinet or bookcase. A little bit of creativity can go a long way.

- **Tame those wires.** It can be very distracting to have computer, lamp or other equipment wires sitting on your desk. Consider drilling a hole in your desktop and feeding the cords through the hole to a power source. Or, at minimum, use a wire-taming mechanism. If possible, have an electrician install an outlet in the floor, rather than on the wall. This way, wires aren't stretched across your office.

- **Think wireless.** There is so much available in wireless styles these days. You can have a wireless laptop and still be able to connect to the Internet. Keyboards don't have to be attached to your computer tower anymore. You can use a wireless mouse. You can use a wireless headset while you walk and talk. There is no doubt that Wi-Fi (wireless fidelity) is going to be a staple in many offices. The fewer wires you have, the less cluttered your office will be and the more mobile you can be.

- **You've got it pegged.** Install a pegboard on one wall. Display office essentials on a hook right on the pegboard. Hang baskets on the hooks to store smaller items. The pegboard concept is wonderful because you can have a huge amount of storage that can be easily customized to fit your needs and style. Plus, you can keep loose items off your desk. It will be a cinch for you to stay organized and productive.

- **Keep it clean.** Being organized is important to productivity and professionalism, but so is cleanliness. Make it a point to keep your office dust-free, grime-free, vacuumed and otherwise clean. Keep the inside and outside of any windows clean. If necessary, hire a cleaning service to do a thorough cleaning job. It should look clean and smell fresh.

- **Add a painting.** In my office, I have a painting of a Spanish countryside. The warm, deep tones look wonderful against the soft yellow paint of my decorating scheme and it's a pleasure to look at each day.

  As I'm thinking up new ideas, pondering a decision or seeking some creativity, I relax my eyes by gazing on my painting. I imagine I'm walking through that lovely countryside. It's relaxing, comforting and I consider it one of the nicest touches in my office.

- **Other neat amenities.** You may want to have a small refrigerator for beverages and food, a microwave oven to heat up your breakfast and lunch, a coffee machine—maybe even a bathroom with a shower. Try to make your office as comfortable as possible, as you're likely to spend eight hours or more there each day.

# Chapter 3

# Office supply savvy and storage

- **It doesn't stand alone.** Organizing tools can help, but don't be misled that any organizing tool, product, supply or piece of equipment will automatically get you organized.

It's simply not true. A great set of golf clubs may help you improve your game, but they will not take the place of dedication and practice to learn how to use them properly. The same is true of organizing tools.

Mary, an insurance agent, had a very cluttered office. She went out and purchased tons of plastic containers, figuring they would help her get organized. But these containers sat in a corner of her office for months—empty. She came to the conclusion that the containers were not a good solution for her. Bad conclusion. It wasn't the containers that were the problem. It was Mary's failure to put them to use.

## Organizing Clinic

### Question

I would like to buy my office supplies in bulk, but I just don't have the space. Any ideas?

Gary Cranton

### Answer

Dear Gary,

Are you certain you don't have the space? Take a look at your walls. Are they completely bare? If so, shelves, wall cabinets or pegboards can provide extra storage space. Place several see-through, plastic containers on shelves and group similar supplies together.

Peek under your desk. If you can include some plastic boxes for your supplies underneath, that would be wonderful. Just be sure you still have enough legroom for comfort.

Do you have empty space on top of a bookshelf or cabinet to store some baskets with extra supplies?

Of course, in the end, if putting anything else in your office would make you feel truly cramped, don't worry about buying in bulk. Just be sure to make your office supply purchases from a company that delivers within 24 hours, so you'll have the supplies you need the very next business day.

- **Don't go on a buying frenzy.** Don't go out and start shopping just because you now have an office, otherwise you're going to end up with tons of things you don't need. First determine your needs. Then buy based on those needs.

- **Bulk supplies.** Once you know for sure that you use certain office supplies often, if you have room to store extra office supplies, buy in bulk. You may be able to save money in volume discounts by doing so, plus you'll eliminate unnecessary trips back and forth to the office supply store.

- **Buy online.** The Internet has made it so easy to buy online these days. No more trips to the office supply store. Everything can be delivered right to your door. I like using Office Max. They're fast and they have free shipping and handling for orders over $25.00. I get nothing by recommending them to you. I just like them and have been using them for years. Their web site address is: www.officemax.com

- **Order together.** Get office supplies from one company whenever possible and order several supplies at the same time. You'll be better able to keep track of what was purchased and from whom.

If you order supplies from a web site or catalog, be sure you physically check the inventory when it arrives for accuracy and quality. Immediately ask for a refund on anything that doesn't meet your needs.

### Great idea!

My favorite office supplies are pens and markers of all colors and varieties. You can use them in so many ways to keep yourself organized and on task.

I meet with my boss on a biweekly basis. I prepare an agenda prior to each meeting. As we go through each item, I make notes and use different colored fine tip markers to indicate what needs to done for each. For instance, blue indicates tasks I need to perform and green are items to be handled at a future meeting.

I also work on projects that involve others in the organization. I keep a log of progress of the project and highlight duties of other employees in different colors (one for each other person) to keep track of who is responsible for what task.

Beth Dennik is the Office Assistant for Gilles Frozen Custard. She is married to Bob and they have two children, Richard and Libby. They live in Wauwatosa, WI.

- **Give them a home.** Depending on your space situation, decide where you're going to store your office supplies. I keep enough supplies in my office to last me a month or two. The rest are stored in the basement. I like to buy in bulk, so I don't waste time ordering supplies every week.

The steel office supply cabinet we have in our basement is about six feet tall with four shelves and doors that keep everything out of sight and dust-free. If you don't have a closet in your office, you may want to invest in an office supply cabinet.

### Great idea!

My favorite office supply of all time is the lowly but incredibly versatile binder clip. Sorting, filing and storing any type of paper becomes a breeze when paper clips of any size are replaced with heavy-duty binder clips.

Available in various sizes, shapes and colors, it is capable of holding anywhere from a few individual pieces of paper to reports over an inch thick! When a stack of papers is waiting to be dealt with, I can quickly clip them all together without worrying about a single paper clip flying off and the pages becoming separated.

While the handles are designed to fold down neatly over documents, you can also flip one handle up, making the clip equally useful for hanging papers from a cork bulletin board or from a nail or hook. For permanent binding, the handles can be easily removed from most brands of clips.

Jane Ellen, Associate Editor of *Finally Organized, Finally Free for the Office*

- **Containerize the small stuff.** If you just toss a tiny box of paper clips in your supply cabinet, chances are it's going to make its way to the back of the cabinet and get buried behind something larger. Instead, get yourself a bunch of plastic boxes with lids—shoebox size—and keep your smaller items inside these boxes in your supply cabinet.

- **Map it out.** Don't put supplies in your cabinet haphazardly. Each shelf should have similar items on it. For instance, desk-type supplies like paper clips and fasteners on the top shelf, paper on the second shelf, filing supplies on the third shelf and computer-related items like toner and disks on the bottom shelf.

- **Shoe organizers are not just for shoes.** Use clear, plastic, hanging shoe organizers with divided pouches to store office supplies. They can be hung over a door and are excellent for storing paper clips, stamps, rubber bands and more.

You can find them in dollar stores, mail order catalogs and housewares stores. They're perfect for keeping everything organized and visible.

- **Dump those old pens.** A business associate of mine had a desk organizer on his desk, stuffed with pens, markers and pencils. When I needed him to sign some papers, he had to go through four pens in his organizer to find one that worked.

  And then what do you think he did with those old pens? He put them right back in his organizer!

  I couldn't bear to watch this, so I helped him go through all his pens and markers and tossed all those no longer in commission. Do yourself the same favor. Only keep writing instruments that work. And while you're at it, sharpen those dull pencils too!

- **Use an Office Supply Checklist.** Make yourself an Office Supply Checklist or make a few copies of the one in this book. As you find you're running low on a particular supply, check off the item on your checklist. When it comes time to buy, you won't forget anything. Bring the list when you go shopping or use it as a reference as you shop online or through a catalog.

- **Use drawer organizers.** When storing office supplies in your desk drawers, use a drawer organizer which will allow you to separate push pins, paper clips, binder clips, postage stamps and other small items into their own individual compartments. Measure first to be sure your organizer will make good use of your drawer space.

  I have an expandable drawer organizer that fits perfectly in my desk drawer without leaving an inch of empty, unusable space. It stretches and shrinks to fit the drawer beautifully and has eleven compartments. My supplies are divided into each of the eleven compartments as follows:

  - ❖ Compartment 1:   ruler, calculator
  - ❖ Compartment 2:   jumbo paper clips
  - ❖ Compartment 3:   regular size paper clips
  - ❖ Compartment 4:   liquid correction fluid
  - ❖ Compartment 5:   Post-it Notes
  - ❖ Compartment 6:   pens and pencils
  - ❖ Compartment 7:   highlighters and markers
  - ❖ Compartment 8:   scissor and X-acto knife
  - ❖ Compartment 9:   binder clips
  - ❖ Compartment 10: adhesive tape
  - ❖ Compartment 11: postage stamps and address labels

## Great idea!

Have an ongoing "To Buy" list for a small office—a piece of paper taped inside an upper cabinet door works well. Each person must be taught to write an item on this list as soon as it is down to the last one or two on the shelf. Do not wait until you use the last one. Buy extras beforehand to save last minute headaches of running out of supplies.

Linda Richards
Organize and More
352-373-1086
Linda@organizeandmore.net
www.organizeandmore.net

- **Hide those supplies.** Rollaway and portable office carts can be stocked with office supplies and other necessary items and stored out of sight. They come in all shapes and sizes, so you can make use of those tight spaces that are usually left unused.

## Great idea!

For many of us, office supply stores are like candy shops. It's fun to browse and fill our basket with striped paperclips and jewel-toned sticky notes. But just like with a candy shop, we usually don't need as much as we buy. It's tempting to buy bulk paper because the cost per sheet is a little less or the multi-pack of colored pens when you only need red. But think of this: If there's no space left in your desk drawer for new supplies, your options are to buy another drawer unit costing you money and floor space or let it overflow onto your desk costing you productivity.

Be mindful about bringing things into your space. Ask yourself: What do I really need? How long will I have to store it and how much space will it take? A few fun and functional office supplies can bring a little joy to your workday. The occasional bulk bargain can also reap a benefit when weighed against the amount of space it will take up in your office. Stop and think when shopping for office supplies and base your purchase decisions more on logic than on emotions.

Kerry Crocker, Professional Organizer
Space Cadette
Chapel Hill, NC
919-928-9825
kerry@space-cadette.com
www.space-cadette.com

- **Slip in a reordering sheet.** Place a colored sheet of paper to flag reordering of standard forms, stationery and so on. You'll never be caught short. For example, insert a colored sheet of paper into your stationery pile about fifty pages up from the bottom. Once you reach the colored sheet, you'll know it's time to reorder more.

- **Inventory Pull System.** When you approach a low quantity of an item, add it to your reorder list. The reorder quantity can be determined in advance, based on how long it takes to refill the order and how fast the supplies are used. If you order from a catalog or online company, you can keep a standing order that your office supply manager can send in once a month.

- **Label office supply cabinets.** Once you have organized office supply cabinets, be sure to label the outside drawers with short, descriptive names. This will speed up the search for supplies.

- **Avoid office supply theft.** Some offices have the problem of staff members taking office supplies home for personal use. This can cost companies hundreds or thousands of dollars each year. To avoid this:

  ❖ Put a lock on the office supply cabinet.

  ❖ Put one person in charge of the office supplies and inventory.

  ❖ Have staff members sign out supplies so you know who is taking what and how much.

Make it known to staff members that supplies are for in-office use only and that taking supplies for personal use is considered theft.

## Great idea!

I have two favorite office supplies:

- **Alphabetical Sorter Book**: This book helps me with my filing every week. Some weeks my filing load is too much to handle. While I don't have time to get the paperwork into each individual case file, I have it sorted alphabetically in a book, ready to go. If I have a few extra minutes before the end of the day, I'll take two letters worth and file just those sections. If the boss calls, asking for a particular case, I can quickly locate the documents!

- **3-Ring Binders or Book Rings**. I have many 3-ring binders for various areas that I need to maintain in an organized fashion. If I don't have enough room for binders, I use book rings to hold my documents. They save space and are considerably less expensive.

Jodi Arrowsmith, Associate Editor of *Finally Organized, Finally Free for the Office*

# Office Supplies Checklist

### Audio/Visual
___ laser pointer
___ presentation pointer
___ replacement bulbs
___ transparency film
___ _____
___ _____
___ _____
___ _____

### Binders & Accessories
___ ½" binder
___ 1 ½" binder
___ 2" binder
___ 3" binder
___ ready index tabs
___ sheet lifters
___ hanging binders
___ _____
___ _____

### Binding
___ binder clips-large
___ binder clips-medium
___ binder clips-small
___ bulldog clips
___ fasteners
___ glue
___ glue sticks
___ reinforcements
___ staples
___ _____

### Break Room
___ coffee
___ napkins
___ non-dairy creamer
___ paper cups
___ paper towels
___ Styrofoam cups
___ sugar
___ stirrers
___ trash bags
___ _____

### Computer/Printer
___ 3.5" disks
___ CD-ROMs (read/write)
___ mouse pad
___ toner cartridges
___ zip disks
___ _____
___ _____
___ _____
___ _____
___ _____

### Desk
___ desk pad
___ Rolodex
___ Rolodex cards
___ stacking trays
___ wire basket
___ blotter_____
___ _____
___ _____
___ _____
___ _____
___ _____

### Fax/Copy/Adding Machine
___ adding machine paper
___ fax paper
___ ink cartridge/toner
___ copy paper
___ _____
___ _____
___ _____
___ _____
___ _____

### Filing
___ accordion folders
___ hanging folders
___ hanging file holder
___ index dividers
___ magazine box
___ manila file folders
___ pocket folders
___ tabs
___ sorters
___ _____
___ _____

### General Supplies
___ ink for stamp pad
___ paper clips-large
___ paper clips-small
___ rubber bands
___ scotch tape
___ ruler
___ scissors
___ letter opener
___ glue stick

### Hanging
___ corkboard
___ hooks
___ map pins
___ push pins
___ thumbtacks
___ _____
___ _____
___ _____
___ _____

### Identification
___ colored circle labels
___ name badges
___ price tags
___ wide labels
___ file labels
___ media labels
___ _____
___ _____
___ _____

### Mailing
___ bubble wrap
___ catalog envelopes
___ disk mailers
___ letter envelopes
___ padded envelopes
___ sealing tape
___ shipping labels
___ shipping paper
___ assorted boxes

### Pads
___ legal pads
___ phone message pads
___ pocket notebook
___ Post-it notes-small
___ steno pad
___ spiral notebook
___ _____
___ _____

### Paper
___ 3-hole loose-leaf paper
___ cardstock
___ glossy paper
___ graph paper
___ index cards
___ ink jet paper
___ laser paper
___ photo paper

### Stationery
___ award certificates
___ gift certificates
___ report covers
___ sheet protectors
___ business cards
___ letterhead
___ envelopes
___ postage stamps

### Specialty
___ biz card blanks
___ fancy paper
___ fancy envelopes
___ letter envelopes
___ dictation cassettes
___ routing slips
___ _____
___ _____

### Time Tracking
___ calendar
___ planner
___ planner refills
___ scheduling forms
___ time cards
___ _____
___ _____

### Writing
___ erasers
___ highlighters
___ markers
___ pencil refills
___ pencils
___ pens
___ clipboard
___ correction fluid
___ _____

### Other
___ _____
___ _____
___ _____
___ _____
___ _____
___ _____
___ _____
___ _____

### Other
___ _____
___ _____
___ _____
___ _____
___ _____
___ _____
___ _____
___ _____

## Organizing Clinic

### Question

My co-worker, Sandy, is constantly stealing my office supplies. She takes them from my desk without asking. Last week, I went on vacation. When I returned, more than half of the office supplies I had recently purchased had mysteriously vanished. I know Sandy took them and I am so frustrated. Please help.

Gena, Dubuque, IA

### Answer

Dear Gena,

I'm guessing that you haven't spoken to Sandy about this problem. Definitely give her information on how she could obtain the office supplies she needs when she needs them or give her an office supply requisition form and offer to order the supplies she needs when you place an order for your supplies. Hopefully, she will get the message.

If the problem persists, kindly tell her that your desk and office supplies are off-limits. If you feel it's still a problem after that, speak with your boss. Of course, know that this may cause some friction between you and Sandy.

If possible, get yourself a lock and lock everything up when you're not at your desk. This is a less stressful alternative and will most definitely end the problem.

---

- **Can it!** No office is complete without a wastepaper basket. If you don't have one, papers are going to end up all over the place. Having one in your office discourages clutter.

  Be sure the basket is not too small. It should be large enough to hold papers for at least a week before recycling day.

- **Make it a match.** When purchasing desk accessories, buy pieces that match. The more matching items you have, the more uniform your office will be. Many office supply stores carry wood, mesh, wire, acrylic and plastic choices in a variety of colors. Look for a set that meets your needs.

- **In and out.** Rather than buying both an inbox and an outbox, buy one stackable sorter. They take up less space and can stack many levels high to accommodate different categories. Typical levels are Inbox, Outbox, Incoming mail, Outgoing mail and To Be Filed.

- **Use a pen/pencil caddy.** Include a handy pen/pencil caddy on your desk to store your favorite writing instruments. Some have several compartments that allow you to hold pens, pencils, scissors, Post-it notes and other common everyday supplies.

- **Where to buy?** Here is a listing of some of my favorite online office tool and supply stores:

    - ❖ Staples      www.staples.com
    - ❖ Organize-Everything      www.organize-everything.com
    - ❖ The Container Store      www.thecontainerstore.com
    - ❖ Stacks and Stacks      www.stacksandstacks.com
    - ❖ Lillian Vernon      www.lillianvernon.com
    - ❖ Office Max      www.officemax.com
    - ❖ Office Depot      www.officedepot.com

# Organize your office supply cabinet

Here's a simple, 7-step system to get your office supply cabinet organized and eliminate the stress:

1. **Too many cooks spoil the pot.** Put one person in charge of the supplies, whether taking supplies out or putting supplies back in. This person is either going to be you or someone to whom this responsibility is delegated.

2. **Divide and conquer.** One of the reasons that it's so difficult to find things is because everything is just stacked, one item on top of another and one item in front of another. Try dividing supplies, especially the smaller ones, into labeled organizing containers. Covered, plastic Rubbermaid containers work well here, especially the ones you can see through. They stack nicely on top of each other, without the risk of toppling. Make sure each container is labeled not on top, but in front, so you can identify the contents at a glance.

3. **Empty it out.** In order to truly organize that cabinet, it's going to have to be emptied out completely.

4. **Plan and designate.** If you have a mix of supplies, you might consider designating each shelf a different category:

5. **Take inventory.** As you're putting the supplies back into the cabinet, make a running list of everything inside. Do this on your computer, alphabetically within each section A, B and C. While you're at it, create a list of what you currently have. For instance:

| **Shelf A** | **Shelf B** | **Shelf C** |
|---|---|---|
| Disks (3.5 HD) – 10 | Pens – 20 boxes | Binders (1 inch) - 12 |
| Disk Mailers – 50 | Pencils – 25 boxes | Binders (1½ inch) - 14 |
| Toner Cartridges – 4 | Paper Clips – 15 boxes | Binders (2 inch) - 9 |
|  | Scotch Tape – 18 rolls |  |

When you're done, you should have a pretty good idea of what's inside and where to find it.

6. **Giving out supplies.** When others need supplies, they should ask you for them. Give them what they need, while adjusting your inventory list. (Example: If there were 12 one-inch binders and someone just took 5, then there are 7 left.) Indicate this on your list. By the way, if you're using the computer for this list, it will be easier to update.

7. **Keeping track.** Always arrange your office supplies so that the newest are in the back and the oldest are up front. This way, you'll use up the older supplies first. Once you notice that a particular office supply is running low, you can re-order without having to take a physical inventory of the cabinet.

# Chapter 4

# Neat storage ideas

- **Start a reference library.** Keep your own reference library, such as a dictionary, thesaurus, almanac, style and grammar book and phone book, on your credenza or a wall shelf. This will keep everything organized and you'll have an excellent reference source.

- **Hook it.** Rather than throwing your coat, bag and umbrella onto a table or chair in the office, install a few hooks on the back of the door or on the wall. When you get to your office, hang these things up and they'll be out of the way.

- **Where's my pen?** Always losing your pens to customers and staff members who inadvertently pick them up and then walk away with them? Stop losing pens by using a mounted coil pen—just like you find in banks and post offices. These have adhesive backing and stretch cords that can be mounted on your desk or telephone.

## Organizing Clinic

### Question

I hate those large boxes that computer software arrives in. They're so bulky!

Nadine Naylor, Lisbon, WI

### Answer

Dear Nadine,

I rarely keep my computer software boxes. I remove the CD-ROMs and instructions and recycle the box. Instructions are kept in a file folder in my filing system labeled Computer Software Instructions. The CDs, in their cases, are kept in CD-slots in my desk. If you don't have CD-slots you can use a CD holder instead.

This saves tons of space. Since you can't return most computer software once it's opened, there's no reason to keep the original box.

- **Raise your monitor.** It's not easy to work efficiently when your desk is being taken over by your computer monitor. Consider using a monitor stand, which allows you extra storage space underneath it.

If you're in the market for a new monitor, consider one of the new flat-screen LCD's—these take up a third of the typical computer monitor's space!

- **Put a pocket on your wall.** Affix Lucite wall pockets to your wall. Clearly label each one to identify the contents. For instance, one can be for Incoming Mail and another can be for Outgoing Mail.

If you regularly give paperwork to or receive paperwork from various people in your office, you might have a wall pocket on your wall for each person.

The person can come into your office and pick up papers or drop off papers without disturbing you.

Jack, an office manager, uses a Lucite wall pocket for each of his five employees. He instructed them to drop off any paperwork for him twice each day, at 9:00am and 3:00pm. He also asked them to pick up any paperwork from the pockets twice each day, at 11:00am and 4:00pm.

It's a very efficient system, since Jack enforces it well. He doesn't allow any paperwork to be dropped off any place else in his office and he doesn't accept paperwork at any time other than the assigned drop-off times. He is never disturbed and papers never get misplaced.

## Organizing Clinic

### Question

I use a laptop on my desk, which is the typical "L" type. Consequently the corner space that is typically filled with a large monitor is now wasted space. How do you recommend utilizing that space effectively?

Avi

### Answer

Dear Avi,

Actually, you have a problem that most people only dream of: extra storage space!

This space can be used for a number of things. Perhaps you can use it for a portable file holder, where you hold all of your Action files. Or maybe a To Read basket can be stored there. Use this area to display a planning calendar or you can use it for a desk lamp.

Also, don't be afraid of having empty space. If you don't have a need for something additional in your office, leave the space empty for the future and enjoy the airy feeling. The possibilities are endless.

- **What's on the agenda?** Attach a large, erasable planning calendar to your office wall. If you're good about recording events and information regularly, everyone in your office can look at your calendar and know your schedule without having to ask you.

  If you work alone, it will give you a large, visible picture of your days ahead.

  When I worked for Nielsen Media Research in New York as a manager, I had one of these large calendars attached to my office wall. It indicated where I would be throughout the month—meetings, vacation, outings— so my staff members were always aware.

  I also indicated staff member vacations and other time off, dates we had to work on important projects, staff member birthdays and more.

### Great idea!

For things not normally filed, such as books, binders and tapes, I use a large four-shelf storage closet. I like it because everything I need is in plain sight and easy to get to. Plus, it is only a turn away from my desk.

Jason Michael Gracia
www.motivation123.com

- **Don't cause a media frenzy.** Use floppy disk, zip disk and CD-ROM organizers. They keep disks off your desk and handy when you need them. Plus, you can better organize them by subject and/or alphabetically.

- **Label binder spines.** Have lots of binders in your office? Hang a shelf and store the binders on the shelf. You should be able to identify the contents of each binder without taking it off the shelf by labeling the spines and/or color-coding the binders.

- **Store by height.** Never store a short item behind a tall item. Tallest items should always be stored behind shorter items so everything is visible.

- **Keep a card table on hand.** Set up a card table or a banquet table for additional workspace when needed. It can easily be folded and stored when not in use.

- **Use a folding screen.** Folding screens are especially handy if you work in a home office. Put one up and you'll be able to easily disguise a work area or convert one work area into two!

- **Cube it.** I have a cube set in one of my closets that includes four cubes of various shapes and sizes. These are perfect for storing tons of stuff and the closed doors and drawers ensure the closet remains neat and organized.

## Great idea!

Here's an idea for the home office that lacks space for archive storage.

Every business is required to retain records and documentation for seven years. This can cause a storage dilemma for the home office where space is always at a premium. Rather than pay monthly to rent space off site, why not buy a pre-fabricated garden shed from your local home improvement center?

Pre-fab garden sheds are available in wood, metal or resin building materials. Weatherproof and secure, you can choose from a variety of styles and sizes to suit your needs and outdoor decor. Size, construction and style will determine cost, but you can easily determine the value to you based on storage facility rental rates and the convenience of having your records close at hand.

Be careful not to use your new storage for other stuff, like garden tools and kids' toys. Plan the space so that you can be taking year seven out as you put the most current year in. Store your trade show booth and materials here. Businesses like event/wedding planners can use the space for storing larger, bulky items.

In keeping with the principle of "like things together," this storage solution will prevent the scattering of your business materials to every spare corner in your home.

Stacy Walker
Gettin' Around To It Professional Organizing
780-717-1745
Edmonton, Alberta, Canada
info@gettinaroundtoit.ca
www.gettinaroundtoit.ca
"Customized, sustainable organizing solutions"

- **Shut the doors, please.** While utility shelves and other open storage units can store a large volume of paper, supplies and other office items, they can sometimes look unsightly or cluttered in a nice office. Definitely consider the option of storage units with doors that close shut and hide everything when not in use.

- **Subscription storage.** Magazine boxes are excellent if you like to keep business magazines in your office for yourself or your visitors.

  Another option is a magazine ladder basket. These attach to your wall and display several magazines in three to four compartments. You've probably seen them in waiting rooms.

- **Don't like filing cabinets?** Have no fear. You also have the option of getting file carts, file boxes, wicker file baskets, stackable file boxes, cardboard banker boxes and more. Plenty of options, so no excuses for not filing!

- **Here's my card.** If you regularly have clients and customers in your office, get yourself a business card holder and place it on the edge of your desk, near and facing your guest chair. If your guest needs a card, it will be visible and handy.

- **One step up.** Desktop step file holders allow you to keep important files at your fingertips where they will easily be seen. Each compartment is graduated—one step up.

- **You can rent space.** Tiny office with no space to store inventory? No problem. There are many storage warehouses that would be happy to store your things for a fee. They're not as expensive as you may think and many have several options such as heated facilities or 24-hour service.

- **Archive old files.** Use cardboard banker boxes to store old files you need to keep, rather than allowing them to take up unnecessary space in your daily filing cabinet. Store these boxes in a storage area, basement or outside storage facility.

  Tom, a frozen custard stand owner, has two filing cabinets in his office. These cabinets hold all vendor, management, financial and employee paperwork for the current year and back one year. He then stores all older paperwork, up to seven years back, in large banker boxes in a separate storage area.

  Each year, he hires a paper shredding service to come in and shred the oldest year's worth of archived paperwork.

- **Get a hide-away chair.** The office furniture company I shop from in Wisconsin sells office chairs with a neat feature. The chairs look like normal office swivel chairs when open, but the backs of these chairs actually fold down for storage in a closet, under a shelf or in an armoire in the area where you stretch your legs.

  If you like the idea of tucking the chair away when you're done with it, this may be an option for you. Ask your local office furniture store if they carry these.

- **Use a paper organizer.** Have lots of paper in different weights, colors and designs? Get yourself a paper organizer. These come in various sizes and have individual slots for each type of paper to keep everything neat and organized.

- **Make it visible.** Large, plastic, see-through containers are perfect for providing extra storage space. Plus, they can be stacked one on top of the other for maximum storage capacity in a small space.

- **Sort that mail.** Lots of employees in your company? Keep mail separated for easy retrieval with a mail sorter that has a separate slot for each staff member.

- **Slide it under.** Slide your computer keyboard out of the way when not in use with a sliding keyboard tray. It attaches under your desk and slides back and forth as needed. Additionally, it provides you with additional workspace on the desk.

- **Make it homey.** Your office doesn't have to look like a corporate office. Make it homey by using a large flowerpot as a trashcan, a water glass to hold pens and pencils or a hatbox to store office supplies.

- **You've got a magnetic personality.** Buy a few magnetic strips and attach them to your wall. Use them to hang items like scissors, envelope openers, paper clips and other metal tools.

- **Who's knocking?** Sand and paint an old door and use it as a desktop. You can use two 2-drawer filing cabinets as legs. Instant desk and file storage!

- **Roll it.** Buy a rolling storage cabinet. You'll be able to store all your supplies and roll them anywhere at any time.

- **Use up that empty space.** Closets are notorious for not having enough shelves, but you have the option of adding additional shelf space. Stacking shelves can be placed in your closet—no assembly required—and they are perfect for organizing the inevitable odds and ends you accumulate.

- **Add a hutch.** If you have a tiny desk with little storage space, consider creating a customized work center by using a desktop hutch. They lock onto your desk with fasteners and provide you with extra compartments for paper and accessories.

- **Use decorative baskets.** Baskets are sold everywhere these days. Get several for your shelves, closets and credenza to keep things easily accessible, but nicely separated and organized.

- **Don't underestimate dollar stores.** Plastic storage items and inexpensive supplies can be purchased at dollar stores. This is especially good if you only need small lots.

I don't recommend purchasing high-use equipment, such as staplers or hole punches at dollar stores.

However, items like cubes, baskets, bins, pens, notebooks, index cards and similar supplies are often available at dollar stores at a great price.

## Great idea!

Use a binder to store manuals, warranties and receipts. You'll need a 3-ring binder and page protectors. When you make major purchases, staple the receipt to the manual and tuck it into a page protector sheet. If you have a lot of "stuff," make several binders divided by categories such as electronics, furniture and tools.

Allison Carter
The Professional Organizer & Speaker
770-579-9866
organizer@theprofessionalorganizer.com
www.theprofessionalorganizer.com

- **Put it on wheels.** While viewing *Designer's Challenge* on HGTV, I saw an excellent idea. This work-at-home couple had wheels put on the base of their 2-drawer filing cabinet. When they were done working at night, they simply wheeled the cabinet under the desk.

- **Drape it.** Drape an end table with a pretty quilt or tablecloth that hangs all the way to the floor. You'll have under-the-table storage that will be invisible to anyone visiting your office.

- **Buy furniture that serves double duty.** A table with built-in drawers or a bench with a hinged seat can be perfect for storage. Since items would be stored inside, your office guests will never know!

- **Say cheese.** Acid-free photo boxes are perfect for storing photographs related to your business. For instance, a deck contractor I know takes photos of all his completed decks and stores them in a photo box organized by customer address.

  A landscaper in town takes before and after photos. She stores all her photos in photo boxes, organized by project location. The best thing is, she is able to store 1000 photos in one small box.

- **Hang a plant basket.** A 3-tiered plant basket is not just for plants. Use it to store swatches, samples, office supplies, magazines, disks and more.

- **It doesn't have to be conventional.** Ice cube trays, muffin tins or baby food jars provide great storage for small items like office supplies, small fabric swatches, tiny promotional items like magnets and more.

- **Add a bedside table.** A bedside table with drawers is the perfect accessory for an office. It doesn't have that real-office look, but has more of an at-home feel. It's wonderful for storing supplies, paper, media and other office items.

### Great idea!

Make sure that what you are storing is something that really needs to be stored. For instance, many businesses must adhere to and comply with, government legislative statutes and rules. Most of these rules are kept updated on public databases and are available online.

Instead of continually updating large binders holding the statutes or rules that apply to your business or office, see if the resource is available to you online. Get rid of the binders and access the info online only when you need it. This ensures you are always referencing the most recent versions of any documentation.

Judy Brown, Associate Editor of *Finally Organized, Finally Free for the Office*

- **Hang shelves in your office closet.** Most office closet space is poorly utilized. It's no wonder, being that most only have a rod for coats and the rest is empty space. Instead, add some drawers, shelves and hooks to make the most efficient use of that space.

- **Get a merry-go-round.** That is, a merry-go-round for your keys. If you have lots of office keys, a key carousel may be the perfect tool for you. Some are even cleverly disguised as books so others won't know you're storing keys inside. Many can hold up to 50 keys and include identification for each.

- **Office in a closet.** An associate of mine has her office in her closet! When she begins her day, she opens the doors and goes to work. At the end of the day, the doors are closed and nobody even knows there's an office inside.

- **Invest in a custom closet system.** If you're ready to go up to "the next level" with closet storage, consider investing in a custom closet system. Joe and I had California Closets install closet storage systems in our home and we feel it was an excellent investment that increased our closet storage space by more than 70%! There is no longer any "dead space" in our closets, as there are shelves and drawers from floor to ceiling. If it's within your budget, keep this thought in mind for your home and office closets.

# Chapter 5

# Conquering clutter

- **Neat versus organized.** Being neat and being organized are not the same. Neat refers to an uncluttered "appearance," but just because you have a neat stack of boxes in the corner of your office, doesn't necessarily mean you can easily find what you need in those boxes. Just because you have all your papers in a filing cabinet, does not always mean you can find a piece of paper inside within a few seconds. Aim to be both neat *and* organized.

- **Start with the most recent.** If you have boxes of old papers in your office to organize in addition to current papers, start with the most recent and work your way backwards.

  So many people make the mistake of starting with the oldest papers in the pile. The truth is, many of those older papers can probably be discarded or archived, but having the more current papers organized will help you keep your current work up to date.

### Great idea!

Decide immediately when you get a piece of "potential clutter" whether you're keeping it or not. If you're not keeping it, throw it away. Don't add it to a pile of stuff or put it somewhere out of the way where you'll get to it later. Just get rid of it. If you plan to keep it, make sure there is a place for it.

Scott Gracia
Owner of The Great Throwzini
www.throwzini.com

- **Have a place to toss nearby.** How many times have you set paperwork on your desk, because there wasn't a wastepaper basket nearby? Or maybe the little, teeny one you do have is overflowing?

  Always keep a large wastepaper basket in your office, right near or under your desk. You'll be able to immediately dump the junk mail and any other papers you don't need.

- **No more homeless stuff.** Every item in your office should have a home—a specific place to store that item when it's not in use. If it doesn't have a specific home, it's homeless—and it's just contributing to the clutter.

- **Don't keep them if they don't work.** Dump your pens that are out of ink and your pencils that have dwindled to minuscule bits. Sharpen your usable pencils.

- **Hang it up.** Your desk is your main work area. If it's cluttered with photographs, papers, books, directories and other paraphernalia, you're not going to have sufficient room to work.

Instead, make use of wall space. Affix Lucite wall pockets for incoming and outgoing mail and papers. Install wall shelves for reference books and directories. Pin large planning calendars to the wall. Hang framed pictures and other inspirational decorations. Install a hook on the back of your office door for your coat, hat and umbrella.

---

## Organizing Clinic

### Question

It appears that my desk area is constantly filled with piles of paper. We produce and receive a lot of correspondence that accumulates on my desk. Any ideas on how to organize my desk area so the papers are neat and orderly?

Raymond Cervantes
Business Development Specialist
U.S. Dept. of Commerce
Minority Business Development Agency

### Answer

Dear Raymond,

Have you considered using plastic wall pockets? These are carried at most office supply stores.

You can purchase a number of them, one for each of your paper categories. As paper is delivered to your office, each sheet can be immediately placed in the proper pocket. Since everything will be sorted and your desk will be clear, it will be easy for you to work on what you need to at any time during the day.

A similar system can be done with trays. A stackable tray system is recommended to minimize desk space needed.

Of course, it will be very important for you to keep the papers in the pockets or trays moving from day to day. In other words, hopefully by the end of each day, the pockets or trays will be emptied out and ready for tomorrow's papers.

---

- **Use air space.** Air space is that space you'll find on walls, ceilings and under furniture—space that often goes unused. A decorative tablecloth draped over a table can create instant storage space inside.

  Grace, an Avon representative, has a 3-tiered fruit basket hanging from her office ceiling. The top basket stores office supplies, the middle basket stores company samples and the bottom basket holds promotional items.

- **A clear desk is a sure sign of a sick mind.** This little saying was always meant to be funny. It was certainly never meant to be a mantra you should follow.

  A clear desk is a reflection of you and a sign that you have everything under control. It is impossible to be productive when you're working among piles of paper and other desk clutter. Clear off your desk and stop working in chaos.

- **Schedule a "15-minute Tidy Session."** My first recommendation is to put things away the second you're done using them. This stops clutter in its tracks before it even starts. But as a safeguard, schedule a 15-minute Tidy Session at the end of each day to straighten up and put anything away that is out of place. Never leave your office for the day without doing this. This way, each business day you'll arrive to a nice, organized, clutter-free office.

---

### Messy desk costs company $562,489

According to an article in the November 10, 1998 issue of The Calgary Herald, the Fluor Corporation had a very good chance of overturning a pending $562,489 US judgment. However, they neglected to respond to the lawsuit until well after the deadline had expired.

Apparently, the legal papers were placed on the desk of the person responsible, during a period of time that the person was absent. They became buried under the piles and were not discovered until 38 days later.

The court refused the company's appeal after the judge awarded a Default Judgment and more than a half-million dollars in damages.

This was indeed a costly mistake for a messy desk!

---

- **Don't allow other people to clutter your life.** If you have others regularly dropping off papers, be sure to have wire trays, baskets and/or wall pockets available. When people drop off, instruct them to put the papers in the appropriate areas, so that nothing gets lost.

# Organizing Clinic

## Question

My workspace is disorganized and sometimes I don't work as efficiently and effectively as I could. In other words, my focus isn't exactly razor sharp and I'm afraid it can affect my bottom line. Any advice?

Mark Meyer

## Answer

Dear Mark,

A disorganized workspace breeds disorganized thoughts. That's why you're losing focus. Here are some quick tips for you:

- **Clear off the surface of your desk.** At any one moment, you're working on one project or task. Only papers pertaining to that project or task should be sitting on your desk. When your desk is clear, you're not going to be distracted by business magazines, loose papers and unread mail.

- **Store other projects until you're ready for them.** Projects you're working on should be kept in file folders or pocket folders and stored in a binder or portable file box until you're ready to work on them. Afraid you'll forget where they are? Make a list of your current projects along with their storage location and keep this list on your bulletin board.

- **File daily.** The second you receive a sheet of paper that needs to be filed, do so immediately. Or at minimum, put that paper in a To Be Filed tray and file at the end of each day. If you allow the filing to go unattended for more than one day, you're going to end up with piles of paper that causes a stressful, chaotic environment.

- **Fix things that are a hassle.** Take a look at your office set up and determine what's bothering you. For instance, maybe you have to get up and walk across your office every time you need to fax something. Or maybe your chair isn't comfortable. Perhaps your lighting is too dim. Don't ignore these annoyances. Fix them as soon as possible, so you can focus on your work.

- **Be realistic about your reading goals.** Do you have business magazines and articles piled up all over the place? Most businesspeople are over-ambitious with their reading goals. Use magazine holders to keep recent magazines organized, keep a limited amount of articles to be read in a basket or file folder and then schedule at least 15 minutes of reading time each day to ensure you're keeping up with your reading. Weed out reading material weekly as you're done reading it. Or if it's truly necessary to keep, file it away.

- **Keep the things you use most often close to you.** Is the phone book far away even though you use it frequently? Do you have to stretch pretty far just to reach the phone when it rings? The rule of thumb is, the more often you use it the closer it should be stored to you.

- **Clear off your visitor chair.** Stacks of papers and magazines do not belong on top of your visitor chair. That chair should only be used for what it was meant for—people visiting for meetings or appointments. While you're at it, clear off your credenza surface too. One or two attractive plants look a lot better than tons of papers, computer disks and so on.

- **Clear off your bulletin board.** Old phone lists, ancient memos, letters that are outdated, old business cards, phone numbers and other unnecessary items should not be cluttering your bulletin board. Transfer any necessary information to your To Do list, Rolodex or other contact system and toss all of those papers away. The less cluttered your bulletin board is, the less chaotic your office will look.

- **Organize your software.** CD-ROMs, disks and Zip disks should be organized and stored in holders—not just tossed here and there throughout your office. While you're at it, install some shelving on your walls if possible and store computer manuals on them to save space in your office.

- **Keep it hidden.** What is currently stored out in the open in your office? The more you have out in the open, the more cluttered your office is going to look. For instance, you might consider getting a cabinet with doors to hide loose office supplies. Or, hang a few hooks on the back of your door to hold coats, hats and umbrellas.

- **Make it more comfortable.** If you have the luxury of being able to do what you'd like with your office, make it as comfortable as possible. Give the walls a fresh coat of paint. Make visitor chairs or sofas comfy with a few decorative pillows. Add a nice lamp with comforting lighting. Hang a favorite piece of artwork on the walls. The more comfortable you make your office, the more you'll want to be there and the more productive you will be.

- **File, don't pile.** As you receive papers that need to be filed, do so right away. Or, at minimum, do so before you leave the office. Otherwise, they're just going to keep accumulating into a huge, cluttered pile.

- **Use a new file folder for each new project.** Every time you start a new project, immediately label a new file folder or pocket folder for it. Papers pertaining to that project can immediately be placed in that folder, rather than randomly scattered throughout your office.

- **Get rid of old magazines and newspapers.** Most magazines have a shelf life of about one month or two. If they're older than that, flip through them, tear out any articles you wish to keep for future reference and then get rid of the magazine.

Old newspapers have a shelf life of about a day or two. Same rule applies. The last thing you need is a fire hazard.

- **Store magazines you do need to keep.** Certain professions may require you to keep a year's worth or more of a trade magazine that is regularly referenced. If this is the case, get yourself magazine file boxes to keep them organized. Store one magazine title per box only, with each magazine in chronological order.

---

### Great idea!

Surfaces can be the enemy in your efforts to get organized. In fact, the more surfaces you have, the more clutter you are likely to collect. To see what I mean, look around your office. Maybe you've set up an extra "work" table, but it's covered with papers and other items that don't belong there. Can you actually work there? Wouldn't it be great to display a beautiful object on that table or maybe even get rid of it altogether and free up some floor space?

First, separate papers from the other items that have accumulated. Put non-paper items back in their homes: office supplies back in the cabinet, placemats near your dining table and so on. Now, take a closer look at the papers. Tax-related receipts go into your Current Year file; last year's taxes? Put into the file drawer.

Return business-related papers to your office or into the trash. Miscellaneous addresses go into a stack until you enter them into your address book.

Keep going until you've defined and dealt with every piece of paper. Now relax and decide what you really want to do with that table!

Ann Bingley Gallops
The Organized Life — Professional Organizing in New York City
"Making Life More Livable, Every Day"
917 President St. #2, Brooklyn, NY 11215
ann@theorganizedlife.net
www.theorganizedlife.net

---

- **You're not working on everything.** So many people say, "I need to keep all of these papers on my desk because I'm working on tons of tasks and projects." While you may be working on lots of different things each day, at any one moment you're only working on one thing—you're certainly not working on everything on your desk. You'd need a clone to do that.

  The only papers on your desk at any given moment should be those pertaining to the one thing you're working on this very second and nothing else. Put the other papers in a project binder or file folder until you're ready to tackle that particular task or project. You will find simple instructions for creating a project binder in this book.

- **Make it useful.** If you have a credenza, treat it with respect. Get rid of any clutter on top of it. It's not meant to be piled with things like papers, books and computer disks—and if there's a dead plant on it, please get rid of that too!

A credenza can be a wonderful place to store attractive baskets for business magazines or catalogs, a place to store your favorite business books between bookends or it can even be used as an additional work area.

### Great idea!

As an educational assistant for Kindergarten, it is imperative that the teacher is organized to ensure efficiency in a classroom of five-year-old students. I have folders labeled Monday, Tuesday, Wednesday, Thursday and Friday; I keep the class work for the students in each folder and the teacher pulls from those folders when she is teaching. I have an Educational Assistant Assignment Sheet, similar to lesson plans. It follows the teacher's lesson plans. It gives me pages to copy on the copy machine and projects to do. I complete the tasks on Friday for the next week and organize them in the M-F folders.

At the end of the school year, I compiled a box of "Beginning of School Year" items to begin In-Service and the first week of school. This box contains work for students, decorations, calendar, bulletin board materials, labels for students folders, address labels for students and parents, notes to go home for the first week of school and other pertinent information that will save the teacher time and effort and will cut down on stress. This box is stored in a prominent place in the classroom so that it is accessible.

The teacher compiles a scrapbook for each student. Each student has a file with a zippered plastic bag stapled on the inside of the folder. This bag will hold photographs for scrapbooking purposes. A clip art file box has been made to hold clip art pages and pictures, stickers and other things pertaining to scrapbooking throughout the school year activities. Copies of clip art pages are saved on the computer so additional copies can be printed off at any given time.

Jodi Williams
Collierville, TN
Jodi has three adult children who are married. She loves to write Christian poetry and short stories and play the mountain dulcimer.

- **Keep your bulletin board clutter-free.** Bulletin boards are wonderful, as long as everything on the bulletin board is in clear view and current. This means that, once each week, you should toss anything outdated and arrange anything left so that you can easily see it without having to look behind other papers. If you can't see everything at a glance, you have too much posted on your bulletin board.

I once assisted Aaron, a grade school teacher, with organizing his bulletin board. We found student notices from more than 5 years ago, memos for last year's field trips, random phone numbers with no names indicated, invitations for upcoming school events—it's really too much to even list here. Aaron never actually looked at his bulletin board because it was so full of outdated papers that he could not actually find anything.

We cleared it off and Aaron's new rule is that he weeds old papers off the board weekly on Fridays before he leaves school for the day. His bulletin board has been clutter-free ever since and he's a much better role model for his students.

- **Move infrequently used items.** Take a quick scan of your office and you're bound to see things that you rarely use cluttering your space. You certainly don't need five reams of copy paper stacked in a corner or ten pads of sticky paper taking up space in your desk. Move items you don't use every day to another storage area, closet or basement.

- **Give it breathing room.** Your computer is an expensive and useful piece of equipment. Don't surround it with paper, soda cans, diskettes and other apparatus. Make it a point to remove the clutter and give your computer room to breathe.

- **Box them.** Place CD-ROMs in their jewel cases so they don't get ruined. Floppy disks and CDs should be stored in holders. There are plenty of inexpensive ones on the market. If they're just tossed in a box, there's a good chance you're going to lose or damage them.

## 10 easy steps to a happy, organized, clutter free desk

Your desk is lost! It has mysteriously been confiscated by articles, magazines, memos, letters, pink phone message slips, yellow sticky notes, mail, pads of paper, file folders and a multitude of papers in all shapes, colors and sizes. You think your desk was once somewhere near your chair, which also seems to be quickly disappearing. You think to yourself, "Gee, I could have sworn it was here yesterday."

What can you do to find your desk? Here is a simple 10-step system:

1. Grab your calendar and schedule two hours of uninterrupted time for Desk Day. When the date and time rolls around, keep that appointment with yourself. If you must, get to work early, stay a little bit late or do it on the weekend.

2. Pick up the following supplies before Desk Day:

   -- A shallow desk drawer organizer with several compartments for daily office supplies

-- 4 wire baskets. Label them as follows: To Do-Today, To Do-Future, To Delegate, To File

-- a large recycling container or cardboard box

-- a large plastic trash bag

3. When Desk Day arrives, wear casual, comfortable clothes. Things can get messy!

4. Close your door. All calls should be directed into your voicemail or to your assistant. Turn on your favorite music. Grab a cup of water or coffee. Eliminate any chance that you might leave your office and get sidetracked, by getting everything you need ahead of time.

5. Here's a secret. Your desk is under all those papers. Bet you thought you'd never see it again. Pull every sheet of paper, all folders, office supplies, magazines—basically everything—off your desk and put everything in a pile on the floor in a corner of your office or workspace or into a large box on the floor. This may seem drastic, but I promise you'll feel a lot better later.

6. Open each desk drawer. Remove the contents and put everything into a large plastic trash bag. Don't worry about sorting right now. That's going to take too much time. Just toss everything into the bag. If there are loose papers in or on your desk, add them to the paper pile on the floor. *Just a side note: One time when I was helping one of my customers empty out her desk we found over $52.00 worth of loose change!*

7. Now that you've found your desk and it's totally clear, dust and/or wipe it off. Take a good look at it. This is how your desk should look at the end of each day—clear, clutter-free and ready for you to be as creative and productive as possible.

8. You're now ready to tackle papers you've removed from your desk and everything in your large plastic trash bag. Grab those wire baskets and put them on the floor. Sit comfortably on the floor. Pick up each paper one by one and decide whether or not it can be dumped. Remember, if you haven't needed it since it has been buried somewhere on your desk then that paper is a good candidate for dumping, unless it has tax or legal implications.

If you decide it absolutely cannot be dumped, then put it into one of your wire baskets. Do not put everything in the To Do – Today basket. Whatever goes in that basket must be done before you leave the office—today. Be realistic.

Here are some guidelines that will help you decide which wire basket each paper should be sorted into:

**To Do – Today:** These papers require action and need to be handled today before you leave the office.

**To Do – Future:** These papers require action, but don't need to be handled today.

**To Delegate:** These papers are to be given to someone else.

**To File:** These papers are for reference. There is no action required, except to file them.

**To Read:** These papers are those you wish to read. Be discerning here. You don't have 20 hours each day to read.

Do this until you've gone through every piece of paper. If you can't get through it today, continue for an hour or two tomorrow. Once everything is off the floor and in one of these baskets, the baskets can be moved to your office credenza or placed on a shelf. Once they're empty, you can make them part of your daily paper handling system. Then, start going through the stuff in your plastic bag.

Desk supplies should be organized into your desk drawer organizer and then stored in your desk.

Loose change should be brought to your bank and cashed in.

Gadgets and things you can't identify should be tossed.

Loose keys should be gathered and put on a key ring, unless you no longer need them in which case they should be dumped.

Floppy disks and CD-ROMS need proper storage. Once you determine how much you have, pick up an organizer for them.

Don't keep anything in your desk that should not be there. I once worked with someone who kept an assortment of soy sauce and duck sauce in his top desk drawer! Really, food does not belong in your desk.

9. Schedule 15-20 minutes per day to go through all of those papers in your baskets—although, hopefully, you've done a lot of dumping by now.

➤ Remember to work on all papers in your To Do – Today basket before you leave the office.

➤ Papers in your To Do – Future basket should be filed into your Tickler File.

➤ Papers in your Delegate basket should be hand-delivered or mailed to the appropriate people.

➤ Papers in your To File basket should be filed in your filing cabinet.

➤ Papers in your To Read basket should be read, for at least 15 minutes each day so you can get through them all. Get rid of them or file them when you're done reading.

10. By now, you should be enjoying a clutter-free desk. Straighten up for approximately 20 minutes each day before you leave work and you won't run the risk of ever losing your desk again!

- **Weed out your files.** Overflowing file drawers are an avoidable office affliction. Go through your files and remove all outdated information—anything you haven't referred to in the past year qualifies. This will most likely only take a couple hours and is an excellent investment of time considering the extra space you'll be gaining.

## Organizing Clinic

### Question

My office has 4 computers and 2.5 people. I have a home office and contract with two different hospitals whose computer systems are not compatible—thus, 2 computers on my desk. My partner has her own computer and my daughter (6 years old) has her own computer. There are three desks in the room as well. I have a lot of reference books that I use daily, some on my desk and some on the floor. I know that there is a better way to organize this mess. I am just not a creative person. I would like to use my wall space better but I need the shelves in reach?

Kate Ann Lews

### Answer

Dear Kate,

It would be more ideal if you can find a computer for yourself with the ability to access the software systems from both hospitals. You didn't mention what wasn't compatible, but contact a computer technician to determine how this need can be met. If this is not possible or is out of your budget, increase the space on your desk by storing the computer towers under the desk and just have the monitors on top. The monitors can sit on risers, generally referred to as clear acrylic monitor/keyboard stands, which will allow you to use the space under the monitor to hold the keyboard out of the way when it's not in use and to provide a little bit of extra storage space.

If having three desks in your office takes up too much space, consider getting a long table that will hold all four or arrange your computers along one wall. Then, just pick up four under-desk keyboard holders and attach them to the table. You'll have an instant multi-computer workstation, with room to spare on the other side of the room. Is it possible for your daughter's computer to be moved to her bedroom or the family room? This would free up space in your office, plus would provide your daughter with some privacy. Since your daughter is very young, you'll want to monitor what she's doing on the computer and you'll want to learn a bit about parental blocks if she is surfing the Net.

Regarding your reference books, definitely add some simple wall shelving. Your books should be neatly organized and out of the way when not being used. Books should not be on your desk and definitely not on your floor. Your local hardware store should have what you need to create a wall shelf or two. Use one for manuals and another to hold trays for things like computer paper and supplies.

- **Shelve it.** Place frequently used computer manuals on a shelf so they're easily accessible. Rarely used computer manuals should be stored in an out-of-the-way storage area, perhaps in a box in the closet or in another room. Don't take up valuable real estate with things you rarely, or never, use.

By the way, I would generally recommend you toss things you rarely or never use, but as long as you have your computer or the software installed on it, it's probably safer to keep the manuals just in case you need to refer to them. If you have to call someone for assistance, you might have to pay an hourly consultation fee—too much money when you can access the information right from your manual. Of course, if the manual is for something you no longer have, by all means get rid of it.

- **Banish old software.** There is absolutely no reason to keep software that you don't plan on ever using again. If you're not going to use it or it's out of date, either toss it or donate it.

  By the way, it is legal to donate software only if you give the original disks, license and manual to the individual or organization, you certify you have no other copies of the software you are donating and you are actually the owner of the software. Try local schools, local libraries or an online auction service.

  Of course, the older the software is, the less of a chance anyone is going to want it. The same is true if you're using software that isn't a common or popular one.

- **Toss bulky boxes.** Most computer software cannot be returned once you have opened it. Therefore, there is no reason to keep the bulky boxes that software normally comes in. Store the disks or CDs in a holder.

  Store the manual near your computer if you plan to refer to it often or in a storage area if you rarely use it. Toss the box and any additional paperwork you no longer need, including advertising and old registration cards.

- **Toss dated publications.** Don't hold onto dated publications that you no longer need. Recycling them will clear space in your office. If you're concerned about needing to refer back to important articles, simply remove the articles and file them appropriately for easy future retrieval.

  Create a file to store new publications as soon as they arrive. Store in wall-mounted magazine racks and set aside time on a regular basis to read so you get the most out of them.

- **Manage your time.** What does managing your time have to do with clutter? A lot! When you don't manage your time properly, you end up doing things in a rush. Papers get tossed on the desk. Appointments are scribbled on desk blotters. Magazines and mail gets piled on the credenza. Manage your time well, however, and you will be less likely to be so haphazard.

- **Flat-world thinking.** The second you start piling one thing on top of another, you end up with a mountain.

- **Limit personal items.** While some personal items like photographs or mementos can be inspirational, too many can clutter your office. Only display very special things or at least rotate personal items every so often. Keep some on display and others in storage, rather than having everything out at once.

- **Don't wait until later.** Clutter is often the result of postponed decisions. You're not sure if you want to keep something, so you put it aside "just for now." Those "just for now" items may sit in that "temporary" spot for months or years. When you're finished using something, no matter what it is, put it back in its assigned home the second you're done with it.

- **Survey your workspace.** Take a few moments to survey your workspace and you will probably find a surprising number of items that you rarely or never use. Files that need to be placed in storage, knick-knacks that get in your way and collect dust, the desk lamp that you never turn on, the pens that no longer work or leak. Keep only items worth keeping—items you actually utilize— within arm's reach and remove everything else.

  No one needs dozens of message pads on their desk—keep office supplies in your supply closet and retain only a few of each item in your work area. Maintain this environment by reviewing your workspace on a regular schedule, perhaps every Friday.

- **Take baby steps.** If your office is filled with lots of clutter, it probably didn't get that way in a day. So, chances are, you're not going to be able to get it under control in a day. Set aside fifteen minutes each day that is specifically dedicated to getting rid of the clutter. If you spend a short amount of time each day on this, your clutter will be under control in no time.

- **Where do I start?** Not sure where to start? It really doesn't matter. The important thing is that you get started somewhere. Just by getting started, you're halfway there!

- **What's bothering you the most?** This is usually the best place to begin. If you hate that pile of papers on your desk, start there. If you're getting stressed because you can't fit another item on the credenza, then you've found the perfect starting point.

# Chapter 6

# Saving time with your computer

- **Keep an eye out for enhancements.** Upgrade your current computer software whenever new features are added. Doing so will help make your job easier, less time consuming and more productive.

- **Don't waste time or space using old, outdated equipment.** If your computer or computer equipment was purchased more than ten years ago, you most likely need to upgrade. While it may cost you a few bucks to do so, the time you're wasting on outdated equipment should be just as precious to you. Plus, newer equipment is generally sleeker—and more compact.

### Great idea!

Sometimes I get too busy or just don't take the time to back up my computer, so one way I save time with my computer is to automate my backups. I have an external hard drive that is connected to my computer with a USB connection.

The software I use allows me to make a complete image of my hard drive, so I have this scheduled to run automatically at 9:00PM, Monday through Friday. I never have to remember to take the time to do it manually.

I can also make a backup at any time with the click of a button. If my hard drive ever fails I've always got a complete copy to restore from.

Jean Hanson
16212 Miles Circle, Brainerd, MN 56401
218-855-1854
jean@vaofficesolution.com
VA Office Solution, www.VAOfficeSolution.com
Virtualize Your Business!, www.VirtualizeYourBiz.com

- **Get comfortable.** Your keyboard should be at elbow level, preferably on a keyboard pullout tray under your desk or computer table.

  The top of the computer screen should be at or just below eye level.

  Turn your computer away from the sun if possible or get an anti-glare cover.

  Don't sit at your computer for more than an hour at a time. Get up and stretch or take a walk to prevent strain and fatigue.

- **Don't harbor computer clutter.** Just like paper clutter reduces your productivity, the same goes for computer clutter. Get rid of computer programs and files you no longer use and organize the ones you do use.

- **The name game.** When naming files, come up with names that will help you remember what is in that file. For instance, if you have an Excel spreadsheet file that contains sales for March, name the file something like: sales-mar.xls

- **Create computer folders.** Computer folders can help you organize your computer files. A main folder might be named "Customers." Sub-folders of that category might be customer names, such as Jones_Frank, Donaldson_ Harvey and Anderson_Wade.

- **Don't overdo it.** Be cautious of creating too many folders. It is better to come up with a few major categories and keep your computer files in them, rather than having a hundred different categories and wasting time looking through each folder for the computer file you need.

- **Back it up.** Back up your computer files on a regular basis—and this doesn't mean every few years. I can't stress enough how important it is to have back-ups of your files once a month at minimum or even more often. You won't think it's that important until you have to reenter information and recreate files after a power surge or drive breakdown. Speak with your computer technician to find out about the easiest and most reliable back-up system for your needs.

- **Keep one copy of your backup off the premises.** In case of a fire or some other unforeseen emergency that can damage your backup information, keep one backup copy in a safe deposit box, at home or somewhere else off the premises.

- **Make a list.** Keep a word processing file in each of your computer folders that lists 1) the name of the files in that folder and 2) a short description of each file. Later, when you're looking for a file, you can open up your word processing document, do a quick search using your find feature and locate the file you're looking for in an instant.

- **Stop duplicating your efforts.** Rather than keeping Master Lists and To Do Lists on paper, keep these on your computer. The information can be easily changed when necessary and never needs to be completely re-written.

- **Order online.** Need stamps? They're just an online connection and a few keystrokes away. The same goes for office supplies, computer software, flowers for staff members and a wealth of other things.

- **Save your work often.** One of the easiest ways to save time on your computer is to save your work often. Just in case your computer crashes in the middle of whatever you're working on, you won't have to start over again from the beginning. When I'm working on a computer document, I make it a point to save the file at 5-10 minute intervals.

## Organizing Clinic

### Question

I work in an office, but often like to take some of my files home to work on them. The way I do this is, I copy my file(s) from my work computer to floppy disks, copy them on to my home computer and then copy then again to floppy disks and finally copy them back on to my work computer. This is so time consuming and I'm afraid I'm going to lose my floppy disks in transit. Help!

Mark Green, Parts Manager

### Answer

Dear Mark,

The way you're doing it now is the way most people would do it. Unfortunately, floppy disks are prone to get corrupted from age, they can get easily damaged if you're not very careful, they may get lost in transit since they're so tiny and they have limited storage capacity. Instead of working with floppy disks, you may want to email the files from work to home. Of course, this will only save time if you have a speedy connection like a cable line or a DSL line. But it can be a very effective system if you do.

Another idea is to invest in a laptop if you don't have one already. You can carry your laptop back and forth from home to the office and the files you work on can be permanently stored on your laptop—no copying data anymore. Plus, your laptop will allow you the opportunity to work on your files not only at work or home, but also in the park, on a bus or in the library.

A third idea is to use PC Anywhere software, which allows for remote access between your work computer and your home computer. Telecommuting instantly becomes a reality.

Of course, I should mention that you re-think working on your work files at home in the first place. If you're at work eight hours each day, wouldn't you prefer to spend your time at home relaxing? If you can't get all your work done at work, you may be asking the wrong question. Instead, you may need to ask how you can better manage your time so you can complete all of your tasks at work and not have to take work home.

- **Say it again, the same way.** Come up with answers to common staff or customer questions and keep them in a computer file. When the need arises, copy the information and paste it into a document.

I have to respond to many customer and media questions each month. I have a directory on my computer called "Common Responses." Each file in that directory is named appropriately, so that I can find a response quickly when I need it. For instance, when someone asks me a question about becoming a professional organizer, I open the file entitled po-start.txt, highlight the text, copy the text (CTRL-C) and paste the text (CTRL-V) into the email or letter I'm responding to.

There's no sense in having to re-think, re-word and re-type something that is already done.

- **Take a shortcut.** Get familiar with some of the common keyboard shortcuts that work with most word processing and email programs and you'll save tons of time. Here are just a few . . .

  - ❖ **Quickly go to the beginning of a line:** Press Home.

  - ❖ **Quickly go to the end of a line:** Press End.

  - ❖ **Go to the beginning of a document:** While holding down your CTRL key, press Home.

  - ❖ **Go to the end of a document:** While holding down your CTRL key, press End.

  - ❖ **Highlight a word:** Hold the cursor over it and click twice.

  - ❖ **Copy a word, phrase, sentence, paragraph or large selection:** Highlight it. Then, while holding down your CTRL key, press C.

  - ❖ **Paste or insert text somewhere else:** Click the appropriate area. Then while holding down your CTRL key, press V.

  - ❖ **Move your cursor one word at a time to the right:** While holding down your CTRL, press your right arrow key repeatedly until you get to the appropriate word. Use the left arrow key to go left one word at a time.

- **Alternate between applications.** In Windows, when you have two or more applications open, you can easily switch from one application to the next using your ALT-TAB keys simultaneously.

  This is especially helpful when you're working in between two programs, such as Excel and PowerPoint. In other words, you don't have to completely shut down Excel to work in PowerPoint and vice versa. You can easily switch between these applications in seconds.

- **Add shortcuts to your desktop.** A shortcut is an icon (or graphic) on your desktop that allows you to open an application upon clicking on it. Just like you have shortcuts on your desktop to open common applications such as Word and Excel, you can also create shortcuts to open commonly used files.

For instance, I do a particular Excel report called report.xls weekly and I have a shortcut icon on my desktop that opens this report.

## Organizing Clinic

### Question

I've always heard that I should back up my computer files more often, but it takes so long to do and it wastes a whole bunch of floppy disks. Besides, my computer has never crashed before. I think I'm going to forego backing up and take my chances.

Janet Greenberg, Brooklyn, NY

### Answer

Dear Janet,

I beg you not to take your chances if you're at all concerned about losing any files on your computer. The time it takes to back up for most people, is way better than the time, cost and aggravation of a computer crash that takes all your files with it.

I don't recommend you back up your files on floppy disks. You might consider getting yourself a CD-ROM drive that can burn CD-ROMS. You can fit lots more information on a CD-ROM than you can on a floppy disk.

Or, you can get an external hard drive and back up your entire hard drive once each week with little or no effort at all.

Another thought is to use an online file storage service, which charges a fee based on the number and size of the files you ask them to store.

Again, if you don't really care about your files, then don't bother backing up. But, if it will hurt at all to lose them, I suggest you change your mind.

- **Sort it automatically.** Excel, Word and other common software applications allow you to sort a list alphabetically, numerically and chronologically with the click of a mouse. This can save an enormous amount of time with tasks such as alphabetizing a list of employee names or organizing account numbers numerically.

Emma, a senior manager, uses her sort feature almost every single day. First, she sorts her spreadsheet by employee birthday, so she knows employee birthdays coming up. She announces these birthdays in the employee newsletter. Second, she sorts by date hired, so she can determine who has been employed for six months or more. This helps her determine who is eligible for health insurance. Third, she sorts by employee number, since the payroll accountant makes out payroll checks based on this number.

- **Use formulas.** Why use your calculator to manually add numbers when you can easily perform the task in a computer spreadsheet or even a word processing program? Learn to use the mathematical functions you have available to automatically do your calculating tasks for you.

- **Record a macro.** If you find you're performing lots of repetitive tasks in your spreadsheet or word processing program, record automatic macros to do those tasks for you.

  For instance, I have a spreadsheet that, each week, needs to be sorted, blank lines need to be deleted and certain numbers need to be added. Rather than doing this manually each time, I worked on recording a macro to do these tasks for me. The task, when done manually, used to take about ten minutes or so. Now that the macro is in place, the task only takes me about five seconds—big time saver indeed!

- **Use your thesaurus.** Looking for the perfect word to use? Programs like Word come with a built-in thesaurus ready for you to use when writing letters and other correspondence.

- **Fill it in.** Need to type the months January through December into your spreadsheet? Just type January and let the "fill series" feature fill in the rest for you. The fill series feature is also useful for filling in a series of numbers or letters automatically.

- **Count your words and characters.** When you need to type an article that is a specific length such as 500 words long or 2000 characters long, you don't have to manually count each word or each letter to determine if you're coming close to your limit. Word, Textpad and many other applications give you a word count and character count feature to automatically count for you.

- **Use your "Find" feature.** If you can't remember where you stored a file on your computer, look in your file index. Or, use the "Find" feature on your computer that automatically searches for certain files.

  If you're not sure of the entire filename, you can often use wildcards in your search. For example, when looking for a file you think you may have named "vendor-contracts," you can usually type *vendor* (with the asterisks) in the search field and your system should find any file that has the word "vendor" somewhere in the filename.

- **Find and replace.** You've just finished typing a 50-page document and just realized that for every time you put "Kerry Smith" in your document, it should have been listed as "Keri Smythe." Don't look for every instance manually. If your computer program has a "find and replace" feature, use that instead and all incidents will be changed in a jiffy.

## Great idea!

While on the phone, take notes in an email in Outlook, rather than taking paper notes. For instance, if the caller is suggesting you send out a communication, type the notes into an actual email.

You can fine-tune them later, but you won't have to re-write them and you won't have to find a place to put the notes you wrote down.

When using Outlook, just by hitting CTRL-S it saves a copy of your email in the Drafts folder.

You can return to it later or drag it into your Tasks folder and set a reminder of the action needed.

If the communication needs to be mailed, rather than emailed, it can be cut and pasted into a document when you're ready to work on it. For now, it's just a task, but you have saved the time it would have taken to copy it from longhand.

Likewise, type the address or phone number a caller gives you into your Contacts folder as they are giving it to you. We create so much duplicate work by writing things on pieces of paper before transferring them to the computer.

Tracy Wyman
The Clutter Buster
Tallahassee, Florida
850-205-5279
solutions@clutterbuster.org
www.clutterbuster.org

- **Check spelling and grammar.** Most common computer word processing programs, databases and spreadsheets come with a function that will spell check your documents. Many programs also come with a grammar check function. These features can save hours of manual editing time.

  Of course, these functions do not replace manual editing completely. If you do a spell-check on the word "there" and the correct form of the word should have been "their" the spell check will not catch it.

- **Arrange and line up your icons.** Does your computer desktop look like a jumbled mess of icons? On your desktop, right click your mouse and use the "arrange icons" or "lineup icons" function to organize everything for you.

- **Never print before previewing.** Always preview your documents before printing them out. You'll save time and paper by having the opportunity to make any corrections beforehand.

## Great idea!

I always maintain separate folders for each person that I work for. Once a document is complete it goes straight to that folder. If I need to retrieve that document or refer to it, I know exactly what folder to go to.

Also, I keep email folders. Once I've read an email I either put it in its designated folder or I trash it. That way my email box stays clear and I don't have to go back later on and clean it out. Plus, if I need to retrieve an old email later on, I can put my hands on it very quickly.

Lynne Poindexter, Associate Editor of *Finally Organized, Finally Free for the Office*

- **Find a technician.** If you're not a computer technician yourself, be sure you have one available that you can call in a moment's notice. If your computer crashes, your productivity will depend on you getting the machine working again quickly. The technician should be someone you trust and someone who will respond to your service-call quickly.

  The computer guy that my husband and I use is available during evening and weekend hours—very, very convenient. Also, he doesn't take up time during the day that we should be using to work on our business.

- **Get involved.** If you have someone set up your folders and sub-folders for you, be involved in the decision-making. The system has to be organized in a way in which you will be able to easily find your files.

- **Use an optimization program.** Optimization programs can help you gain maximum capacity and speed out of your computer.

  I use Norton SystemWorks for my optimization program and for anti-virus reasons. It's easy to use and I can log on to the Internet to download software updates and virus definitions often.

- **Label your disks and CDs.** If you use diskettes and CD-ROMS to store data, be sure to label each clearly. If you label your CDs by writing directly on them, make sure you only use a standard permanent ink marker, as other writing utensils may cause damage and render your CD useless.

- **Use folders when you burn CDs.** You can fit a large capacity of files on a CD-ROM. Use folders and sub-folders just as you would on your hard drive when storing your files on this type of media.

- **Keep them safe.** Keep CD-ROMS and diskettes in their storage cases. Keep them out of high-heat areas and away from magnets.

- **Take classes or read your manuals.** It's generally better to take a class or read a manual for a new software program you're unfamiliar with, than just trying to poke around the system.

- **Be sure it's saving you time.** Sometimes the allure of using "cool" software overshadows the fact that a particular task may be done more quickly by simply using a pen and paper or a calculator.

  For example, for very simple projects, purchasing sophisticated Project Management Software may be going overboard. The bottom line is, it has to have a benefit, like saving time or preventing errors.

- **Network.** Do several people in your office need to work on common files or share printers or know each other's schedules? If so, you may want to investigate a computer network for your company. Networks allow many people to access information simultaneously. Basically, files and software are stored on a network server versus individual hard drives.

> ### Great idea!
>
> I like to sort through my email every day, this way it doesn't overwhelm me.
>
> I have my accomplishments, expenses and goals in my computer and try and check them every day so I stay on top of things in my life.
>
> Diana Romagnano, Associate Editor of *Finally Organized, Finally Free for the Office*

- **Customize your toolbar.** Most software will allow you to customize your toolbars for your needs. For instance, if you regularly include drawings in your Word documents, you probably want the Drawing toolbar to be visible all the time. If you regularly use charts in Excel, you may want the Charts toolbar to be visible all the time. Customize your toolbars as you see fit. You don't have to settle for the standard.

- **Don't start from scratch.** If you want to create a document or spreadsheet, first determine if you have a similar one available. If so, you just have to open the old file, save it as a new name and update that file with the new information. No sense starting from scratch if most of the work is already done.

- **Keep contacts organized.** Keep all of your customers and prospective customers in a contact management program, such as ACT! This will help you stay on top of your contacts and be a great help when you wish to send them offers and incentives.

- **Are you addicted?** Most computers come with fun games like Solitaire and these can offer you a needed break during your workday. However, if you're addicted to these games and you can't get any work done, it might be best to remove them from your hard drive so you're not tempted to play all day.

- **Learn how to type.** You'll save tons of time if you aren't spending all of it typing with one or two fingers. Learn how to type. Take a class or buy a typing program.

  I can type at 70-80 words per minute. With some practice, you can too. Typing is a skill that almost anyone can learn. A little effort will save you a lot of time.

- **Get acquainted.** Familiarize yourself with common computer applications, like word processing documents, spreadsheets and databases. Here's a super-quick breakdown:

  - ❖ Word processing document: Used to type letters and reports.

  - ❖ Spreadsheets: Used to keep track of numerical data. Includes ability to include formulas so calculations are done automatically.

  - ❖ Databases: Used to organize records, such as an address book or records of all your customers.

- **Keep it clean.** Don't spend your day working on a grimy computer. Be sure you clean your computer tower, monitor, keyboard and mouse at least once every few weeks. Make sure you use appropriate cleaners for computer peripherals. Water or other liquids in the wrong place, such as your keyboard, can do a lot of damage.

  Also, remember never to spray other cleaners, such as window cleaner and furniture polish, near your computer or keyboard. They can inadvertently get into places you don't want them to when you are simply cleaning something near your computer.

- **Run virus scan automatically.** A computer virus can delete all of the files and programs on your hard drive. Avoid getting a computer virus by running virus scan automatically each and every night. Most virus protection software allows you to schedule these scans at a specific time each day.

- **Center it.** I once watched Kelly, an administrative assistant, hitting her spacebar while she tried to center a title in her report. I couldn't take watching this for very long. It was hurting my brain! I quickly showed her how to use the "center" feature in her document to center the title automatically.

Learn how to use features such as center, left align, right align, justify and set tabs, rather than trying to eyeball where you want your text to go.

- **Empty your Recycle Bin weekly.** When you delete a file on a computer that uses the Windows operating system, it stores these files in an area called the Recycle Bin. These files remain in this area until you restore or delete them. It is recommended that you delete these files regularly, such as once each week. No sense taking up unnecessary space on your computer.

- **Run scandisk.** As you save, erase and move files, your computer begins to cause unwanted interaction between programs and files. This interaction may cause your computer to run very slowly. Run the scandisk utility every once in awhile, to find and correct errors in your programs and files.

- **Defrag.** When you save files, they're sometimes stored in random places on your hard drive. It's a lot of work on your hard drive to open one file that has pieces of it scattered everywhere. Running your Defrag utility places scattered files together so that disk access time is reduced and it increases the life of your hard drive. You can run defrag right from Windows. Search in your Windows help menu for more information.

- **Zip it.** When you want to save a file on your hard drive to a floppy disk, but it's too large to do so, you can often zip the file or compress the file down to a much smaller size. WinZip is the program I use to do this.

  Later, when you want the file decompressed, you can copy the zipped file back to your hard drive and run the WinZip utility again.

  This utility is also a lifesaver if you want to send a large file to someone via email. A compressed file, versus a huge uncompressed file, is both uploaded and downloaded very quickly.

- **Get a CD burner.** If you store lots of large computer files, such as those that contain photographs or graphics, definitely consider getting yourself a CD burner, if there's not one already installed in your computer system.

  My husband and I use ours regularly to store large files for our business, such as our books, business photographs and old financial files.

- **Do something while you're waiting.** It takes a few minutes for most computers to boot up. As soon as you walk into your office, turn on your computer. As you're waiting for it to boot up, have your breakfast, make a phone call or do some business reading. Don't just sit there and wait.

# Chapter 7

# Staying organized with email

- **Delete, delete, delete.** When you retrieve your email, quickly scan the subject lines of each. Often, email can be immediately deleted unopened.

- **Email it.** When you send a letter or computer file through the US Mail, the earliest it can arrive at its destination is the next day. Send it by email—your letter and your attached computer file—and it should reach its destination within minutes.

- **Be wary of attachments.** Opening up an email attachment can infect your computer with a virus—some are minor, some can completely wipe out your hard drive as well as all of your programs and files.

  Never open email attachments from people you don't know. Before opening them from people you do know, realize that these can also contain viruses. It's not likely that your best friend would purposely send you a virus, but the attachment he or she is sending may have been obtained from someone else— and that file can potentially contain a virus.

  As a rule of thumb, I would highly recommend you only open attachments that you're virtually 99.999% sure do not contain a virus. This excludes most jokes, chain letters, scares, unsolicited advertising or other similar messages that are forwarded liberally to many people. The chance of getting a virus from opening one of these types of messages is pretty high. Also, always use an email protection program that will flag potential viruses.

- **Set up email folders.** Much of the email received on a daily basis can be deleted immediately after it's read—some immediately after you've responded to it. However, in some cases you'll probably want to save an email for a set amount of time.

  Rather than printing out your email, set up email folders. You can then drag your email from your email inbox into the email folders you set up. You'll have to check with your email provider (ATT, Charter, AOL, Hotmail, etc.) or email management program (Outlook, Outlook Express, Eudora, etc.) to determine how to do this.

  Let's say you're working on a project and you can't delete the email correspondence until it's finished. Instead of printing all that email out, create a virtual folder called "Project-Budget" or whatever the project is and then drag all email related to the budget project into the budget project folder.

- **Use email filters.** Spam is basically email sent to a large group of people—who never asked to receive it. It is unsolicited email that is nothing more than virtual clutter. Very often, spam comes from passing your email address out, posting your email address on the Web, joining discussion groups and so on. It clogs your email inbox.

  Unethical companies send automatic robots throughout the Internet to steal your email address. They then spam you and many sell or share your email address with other companies who also send out spam.

  According to CRN Canada (July, 2003), provider of e-business statistics, nearly 76 billion spam emails were delivered over the Internet in 2003 alone.

  Many email programs and email managers give you the ability to automatically filter out email. Some programs prevent the email from ever getting through at all. Others allow you to automatically send certain emails directly into your Deleted Mail folder.

  Contact your email company or look at your email manager manual to determine how to set up your own filters. When email is automatically filtered, you spend less time having to delete them manually and there is a lot less aggravation.

- **Automatically send mail into categorized folders.** Email filters can help you organize your email. Many programs give you the option of automatically moving email from your email inbox into an email folder based on the criteria you set up.

  For instance, you can filter all email from a particular customer or a specific employee into a Jane Doe or John Doe folder. Or, you can filter all email with the word "report" in the subject line into a Reports folder.

  While I would not recommend you set up tons of filters which may turn out to be confusing—you don't want to be searching through email folders for email—when used sparingly, filters can be extremely helpful.

- **Don't use all caps.** When sending email to others, never type the entire subject line and/or the entire body of the email in all UPPERCASE letters. It's difficult for the recipient to read, all capital letters represents SHOUTING and many people are now filtering out email they receive that arrives in all capital letters.

- **Tell them what it is.** Email subject lines help recipients scan their email quickly and find messages easily. If you leave out the subject line, your email may be inadvertently deleted.

Always include a subject line and make it as descriptive as possible. This is a courtesy for the person receiving it. The subject line will also serve as a reference in your own Sent Mail folder.

Subject lines such as "Retirement Party," "Company Picnic," or "Budget Report" are a whole lot more descriptive than "Hi," "Hello," or "Stuff."

### Great idea!

I get a ton of email at work, which I used to save in folders by topic, such as project or committee. However, I found that if I didn't get an email for a while on a topic, I'd make a new folder with a different name. After awhile, I had so many folders I couldn't find anything. I started to notice that when I wanted to find something, I thought about what else was happening at the time. So, I reorganized all email by month including sent items. I keep a rolling year and clean out next month's about midway through each month (e.g. about mid-April I start looking at my May email.)

If there is something I feel I still want to keep, I put it into one of two folders:

Old Mail: which I prune often

Keepers: there's not a lot in there, but while I could lose the "Old Mail" folder with just a small pang wondering what I've lost, I'd be very upset about losing something in "Keepers."

I try to delete things right away that I know I don't need. I also move anything that's not an action item into the current month right away. I love having an inbox with only about a dozen items.

I've been working with my boss to help him get his email under control. We found that the monthly timeframes don't work for him. When looking for something, he tends to think about who sent it to him, so we're working on organizing his email by person.

Louise Morganti, Quincy, MA

- **Your email address book.** If you've been using email for a while, hopefully you're using your email address book to store email addresses of people you contact regularly. If you're not using the email address book, it's a good time to start.

  Keep your email address book organized and up to date and back it up. Take a peek at it at least quarterly to ensure you're not saving unnecessary addresses.

  If someone changes his or her email address, update your address book the same day so you don't forget. As an extra precaution, also keep important email addresses in your Rolodex or other contact management system.

- **Don't check every 5 minutes.** Checking for email too frequently can soak up your time, especially when you have other tasks and projects to do. I used to check email several times throughout the day. However, I was getting sidetracked too often and it was taking me longer to complete other projects.

Now, I check for email twice each day and that works very well for me. If your email reminder bell chimes in every time you get email, it may be very distracting. Stop the reminder or close your email software while you're working on other things.

## Great idea!

Email is my main communication tool. To start with, I use the best email client, Outlook and the best spam-fighting product, SpamNet.

To make email management easy, I am extremely organized and can find answers fast. I have a routine of checking email twice a day when I'm busy. I do something with each one the first time I open it. I save only what I really need into a subject-based filing system, using broad categories with subcategories. I make a point of always being able to see the bottom of my Inbox without scrolling.

Peggy Duncan is a productivity trainer and author of *Conquer Email Overload with Better Habits, Etiquette and Outlook Tips and Tricks*. She offers tips and a free Webzine on her site at www.peggyduncan.com

- **Assign a due date.** Some email software (MS Outlook, for one) allows you to assign a due date to an email and reminds you when that due date is here. If this is the case, you can set up an email *tickler* to help you process your mail. If you cannot respond to the email immediately, set a due date and file the email for processing later.

  Create a specific folder called In-Pending for these scheduled emails. Naming the folder "In_Pending" will put it next to your Inbox folder alphabetically.

- **Kiss: Keep it short and sweet.** Keep your email short and sweet and stay on the subject. Keep your paragraphs short—no more than 5-6 lines each.

- **Number your points.** If you're making more than one point in your email message, number each one. This makes it easier for the recipient to absorb and focus on each individual comment or question.

  Ellen, a business consultant, once typed long email messages to her clients. She was always very detailed and included questions her clients needed to respond to in each message. But she couldn't figure out why her clients always missed responding to some of her questions.

When I told her to number each question, rather than typing everything in one long, boring paragraph, she was able to get each question answered successfully.

It's easier for people to see a list of questions, rather than a long paragraph.

- **FRAT your email.** When you process email in your inbox, you should remember to FRAT:

  ❖ **F**ile the email for reference

  ❖ **R**espond to the email if it can be done in less than 5 minutes or is critical

  ❖ **A**ssign email to another person for follow-up or assign a date when you will follow-up

  ❖ **T**rash the email

### Great idea!

Microsoft Outlook and Outlook Express make it easy to stay organized with email. All you have to do is make folders and subfolders to keep up with email that you want to save for reference.

To create a folder within a folder—a subfolder—just right-click on the existing folder where you want the new folder to be, then type the new folder's name. Once the new folder is created, you can drag messages from your "inbox" or "sent items" folder into the new folder you've created, so that your "inbox" and "sent items" folders remain uncluttered.

For instance, I like to separate all of my business and personal email, so I've created subfolders for each of those categories under the "Local Folders" heading. Within my "personal" folder, I have a folder called "correspondence" which holds all of the email I exchange with friends. Within the "correspondence" folder, each of my friends has their own subfolder named after them.

In addition to keeping your "inbox" and "sent items" folders uncluttered, folders also allow you to keep all of your correspondence with a particular person in one place.

Mike Logan
Logan's Logic
256-348-7485

- **60 characters please.** Never type more than 60 characters per line or there's a good chance your email will arrive looking messy and unprofessional to your recipient—even if it looks perfectly fine on your end.

When Charlie, an Internet marketer, first began sending out email updates to his prospects, he didn't realize that some computer programs cannot properly read more than 60 characters to a line. He just began typing and allowed the lines to wrap automatically at 80 characters.

Some people saw this:

*Important Note: If you didn't get a chance to read the last issue of our marketing newsletter – which featured the article "Learn How to Get Your Site Higher in the Search Engines" – then I highly recommend that you read it today. This article caused quite a stir, so I decided to spend some time this issue discussing your questions and comments.*

Others unfortunately saw this:

*Important Note: If you didn't get a chance to read the last*
*>>issue of our*
*marketing newsletter – which featured the article "Learn*
*>>How to Get Your*
*Site Higher in the Search Engines" – then I highly*
*>>recommend that you read it*
*today. This article caused quite a stir among everyone, so I*
*>>decided to spend*
*some time this issue discussing your questions and comments.*

To prevent this, always type 60 characters or less and then press Enter or Return at the end of each line.

- **Know what to keep, what to delete.** Just as you have to keep your everyday paperwork under control, the same is true for your email. That's why it's so important to determine which email can be deleted immediately.

  For example, if someone sends you a note about an upcoming meeting, jot the meeting information in your calendar, send back your comments and get rid of the original email message. The only email messages you may want to save are: 1) those awaiting your reply and 2) those you need for future reference. Everything else should be deleted.

- **Store the email you need to refer to later.** Some people prefer printing out email that they need to refer to later, while others choose to store the message electronically in an appropriately titled folder within their email software.

  The same goes for electronic folders. For example, if you need to store email from Human Resources, the Graphics Department and your vendors, you should have three electronic folders named: HR, Graphics and Vendors.

- **Remove yourself from unnecessary lists.** If you're constantly receiving company group email or email subscriptions that you really don't need to get, ask the sender(s) to remove you from his or her list(s).

## Great idea!

Most email programs give us access to organizational tools that help us keep control of the influx of email that we get. Consult your email program's Help to learn how to use the following features.

- **Spam Filtering**: Spam filtering service may be available through your Internet Service Provider. Ask them to activate it for your account or talk to your company's IT department.

- **Custom Mail Boxes**: The inbox alone is usually not adequate. Create boxes where you'll put email relating to specific subjects such as Clients, Receipts, Opportunities or Friends. When you are finished acting on a message in your inbox, drag it to the appropriate box. Religiously file your email and your inbox will become your Action File. Each email left there denotes something to take action on.

- **Filters**: Filters automatically file messages regarding a common subject or from a specific sender into specified boxes. This cuts down on the clutter in your inbox. If a filtered mail needs to be acted upon, don't close it. Minimize it so you'll see it even when your custom box is closed.

- **Trash**: Don't forget to trash old or unnecessary email on a regular basis.

Kerry Crocker, Professional Organizer
Space Cadette
Chapel Hill, NC
919-928-9825
kerry@space-cadette.com
www.space-cadette.com

- **Think before adding someone.** Not everyone in your company typically needs to receive every message you send out. Only include the people on your outgoing lists that truly need to receive those particular messages.

  When I worked in the corporate world, I used to hate getting messages that had nothing to do with me. They were sent only because I happened to be on the management team.

  Come up with a few different email address lists for different purposes. Perhaps only Department A needs to receive certain email and maybe Department B only needs to receive certain email.

- **Respond to email quickly.** This avoids a pile up in your inbox. Most email can be answered with a few simple words within a minute or two.

- **Reduce the time-waster email.** There are a lot of jokes, poems, chain letters, scares and other email that are sent to an entire list of people at once. While it's okay to read one or two of these every once in awhile, it's not a good use of your time to read dozens each day.

Kindly ask your family and friends to limit or refrain from sending these types of email, especially to your work email address. Also, avoid sending these types of email to a laundry list of recipients—many probably don't want to receive them in the first place, but are too polite to ask you to stop.

- **Make use of your Drafts folder.** Many email programs, such as Outlook Express, automatically provide a Drafts folder for you to temporarily hold messages you've begun, but haven't finished, writing. Once you've had a chance to complete them, you can then easily send them off.

### Great idea!

Inside my email client, I have written out several standard responses to questions that I get asked frequently. I save these as "templates," so that I only have to think about and write the information one time, instead of every time someone sends me an inquiry. It is quite the time and labor saver.

Monica Ricci, owner of Catalyst Organizing Solutions, has been an organizing specialist since 1999. She helps her clients declutter, organize and streamline their lives both at home and at work. She is also a speaker and appears regularly in various magazines, newspapers and online publications. Contact Monica at www.CatalystOrganizing.com or 770-569-2642.

- **Beware of urban legends.** Ever hear about the woman who decided to try a famous Neimann-Marcus cookie? She asked a waitress how much she could buy the recipe for and the waitress told her "two fifty; it's a great deal!"

Thirty days later, upon receiving her credit card statement, this woman discovered she had been charged $250.00, not $2.50 as she originally thought the waitress said. When she complained to Neiman's Accounting Department, they refused to budge telling her they would not refund her because they couldn't possibly be responsible for what a waitress said and how it was interpreted.

In the end, the woman was so upset that she decided to give out Neiman-Marcus's famous cookie recipe for free to everyone she knew.

Sounds like an interesting story, but it's simply not true. Yet, it has been passed to hundreds of thousands of people via email for years now.

Needless to say, beware of urban legends and hoaxes. This particular one was not very harmful, except perhaps to the reputation of Neiman-Marcus, but this is just one of the many being passed on.

The last thing you want to do is pass on lies to other people. A few good web sites to verify email hoaxes are: http://hoaxbusters.ciac.org, http://urbanlegends.about.com and www.snopes.com/

## Great idea!

Resist the urge to "cc" yourself on email you send. A copy of this email will automatically be stored in your "Sent" folder. Once per week or once per month depending on the volume of email you send, refer to your sent file.

Sort the file alphabetically by the person you emailed. You can do this by clicking on the "To" field.

Be sure to use a descriptive "subject" line so that you can quickly look at the email you sent and determine if you need to:

1. Delete the email

2. File it for future reference

3. Open it and follow up with the person you have not yet received a response from

By using descriptive subject lines, you can accomplish this task quickly because you will remember the email without having to open each one in order to decide what to do with it.

Using this technique, it will give you the opportunity to manage your email from the sent file without creating duplicate email to process.

Laura Leist
Eliminate Chaos, LLC
425-670-2551
laura@eliminatechaos.com
www.eliminatechaos.com
Author of *Organizing and Customizing with Microsoft Outlook*

---

- **Don't badmouth others, especially in email.** Whenever you badmouth someone, you run the risk of putting yourself in an uncomfortable situation if the person you badmouth finds out. With email, badmouthing is even more of a risk. Many companies now have the ability to review email staff members send back and forth. Plus, what if the email you send ends up in the wrong hands?

  Sally, a systems analyst, was writing an email to her friend John about a frustrating situation she just experienced with her boss, also named John. In her email, she described her boss as "a tyrant" and "a bother."

  Sally later found out to her dismay that she sent the email to John, her boss, rather than John, her friend, in error. Can you even imagine what kind of a relationship Sally and her boss had after this mishap?

  A word to the wise, don't badmouth others verbally or in writing, especially in an email—after all, it's now in writing.

- **Always include your name with your messages.** Not everyone is going to recognize your email address and be able to identify who you are. Always include your name in your email, just as you would in a hard copy letter.

- **Use the http.** If you are including a link to a web site within an email, type the URL in the form of "http://…" (e.g., http://www.getorganizednow.com). This will ensure that most recipients will be able to click on the URL to go to the web site.

- **Use plain text.** There are hundreds of different email clients. To ensure that anyone you send email to can read your message, use plain text and leave out elaborate formatting such as italics, bold and fancy fonts.

- **Put it in the body.** When possible, it is better to send information in the body of a message than to send an attached file because the attached file may be in a form that is unreadable by the recipient. Many people are reluctant to open email attachments these days due to potential viruses.

- **When you must send an attachment.** If sending an attachment is a must, try the following suggestions for the greatest chance of your recipient being able to successfully view the file:

  - ❖ For best readability, save attached files in RTF (Rich Text Format) with no spaces in the file name. RTF is readable by most word processing programs.

  - ❖ If you need to ensure that all formatting remains as is, save attached files in PDF (Portable Document Format). Your recipient will need Acrobat Reader to open this type of file.

  - ❖ When possible send the link for a web site instead. This will keep the size of your message to a minimum.

- **Spell-check it or not.** Do you always use the spell-check feature before sending out your email? If so, set your email program to spell-check automatically before your message is sent. If you don't use the spell-check feature before sending out your email, proof carefully and be sure this feature is turned off.

- **Consider the difficulty level.** When you choose an email address, choose something memorable and simple. For example, an address like x2hyws@yahoo.com is much more difficult to remember than joe5@yahoo.com.

- **Are you preventing others from getting your email?** With the amount of spam today, many ISPs are automatically blocking email from getting through. When you send out an email, be careful of using words and subject lines that have a high chance of being filtered.

## Great idea!

Here are some of my favorite tips for staying organized with email:

- Handle email on a schedule, taking the time to reply immediately when possible.

- Don't let yourself be interrupted each time a message arrives.

- Change the subject line when replying if it's no longer appropriate.

- Send separate messages for separate subjects.

- Always include your name and contact information at the end of the message.

- Keep messages short.

- Use bullet points and if asking questions, number them.

- Keep your inbox clear by deleting messages no longer needed and by moving those to be saved to subject folders.

Susan Kousek
Balanced Spaces, LLC ®
PO Box 3204, Reston, VA 20195
703-742-9179
skousek@balancedspaces.com
www.balancedspaces.com

---

- **Don't save all mail in your Deleted Items folder.** In most email programs, when you put email into your Deleted Items folder, it is not automatically truly deleted until you issue the delete command.

  Keep deleted mail for a week, just in case you need to retrieve something you didn't mean to get rid of. Then, empty out your Deleted Items folder weekly to free up space.

- **Set up group mail.** If you regularly send directives or memos to specific people in your organization, set up email groups. For instance, all the people in the marketing department can be in one group, all the people in the billing department in another group.

  Each group only contains the email addresses in that particular department.

  When you're ready to send an email, just put the group name in the To: field and your email will only reach those people.

  This is much better than having to send out email individually or even having to look up everyone's email address every time you send something out.

## Great idea!

I use folders and filters to keep my email organized. I have several clients, so each client has a folder in my email program. Within that folder I have an inbox, an outbox and a To Do Box.

I use filters (or rules, in Outlook) to colorize and organize my email. For example, all email from clients automatically downloads with a red color so that I can pick them out immediately.

From there I can drag the email to the appropriate folder or have them all moved to the appropriate folder with a click of a button.

Email I send to clients is automatically filtered into the appropriate outbox so I can find them easily. Email that I need to take action on gets dragged to the To Do Box.

The search feature also makes finding a particular email quick and easy. Simply type in keywords and you're presented with a list of email messages that have those keywords.

Jean Hanson
16212 Miles Circle, Brainerd, MN 56401
218-855-1854
jean@vaofficesolution.com
VA Office Solution, www.VAOfficeSolution.com
Virtualize Your Business!, www.VirtualizeYourBiz.com

- **Check your email from the road.** As long as you have an Internet connection, it is generally not too difficult to check your email from the road. Some Internet providers give you the ability to login to their site and check your email there.

I set up Outlook Express on my laptop to access my regular email account. To do this, you will have to ask your email service provider for their Incoming Mail POP3 and Outgoing Mail SMTP settings.

Once these are saved in Outlook Express (which only has to be done once), I'm able to connect my laptop phone line into a data line at any hotel and simply dial up and access the Internet using my spare AOL account.

I then open Outlook Express and receive, and even send, my mail from the road. This may sound a bit difficult, but once it's set up, it's a breeze. Your email service provider should be able to assist you in getting this set up.

If you use AOL, all you have to do is connect your laptop phone line into a hotel data line and sign on to your AOL account. Even if you don't have the AOL software on your laptop, you can go to the www.aol.com web site and access your mail from there.

Of course, you don't want a relaxing vacation to be soaked up with email to answer. Generally when I'm away, I check and respond to my email for no more than 30 minutes each day.

- **Ask for a read receipt.** If you use Outlook or Outlook Express, you can ask for a read receipt. Basically, this means that when you send someone an email, when that person gets your email he or she can choose to let you know whether or not it was received. If this person accepts, you will get an email back letting you know that your message was received, on what date and at what time.

- **Set up signatures.** If you always want specific information to be included with your outgoing email, you can set up signatures. After typing up a note, just tell your email program to add the signature(s) you have set up and your information will automatically be pasted in. For example, at the end of my outgoing email messages, I usually include the following signature line:

Maria Gracia
Get Organized Now!
www.getorganizednow.com

# Chapter 8

# Organizing your web surfing

- **Make your favorite page your home page.** Most web browsers, such as Microsoft Explorer, allow you to set up a specific web page as your home page—the page you automatically go to when you go on the web.

  For example, you can set up our www.getorganizednow.com as your home page so that when you open your web browser, our site is the site you see.

- **Save your favorite sites.** When you find a web site you really like, most web browsers will allow you to save these sites in a "Favorites" area so you don't have to search for the web site address or type the entire web site address in every time you wish to visit that site.

  On my computer I have my Favorites area organized with folders such as Marketing, Travel and Educational. All my marketing sites are stored in my Marketing folder; all my travel related sites are stored in my Travel folder and so on.

---

### Great idea!

One thing that I discovered that helps me navigate the Internet and my computer faster and easier is a Trackball Optic Mouse. This is the kind of mouse that is ergonomically designed to fit your hand and rather than moving your hand all over the mouse pad to move your cursor, you simply move your cursor with a trackball controlled by your thumb.

Not only that, but the center of the mouse has a scrolling wheel to allow you to quickly scroll up and down screen with just the touch of your index finger and instead of having only a right and left mouse button, there are four places to click in total. The two extra buttons can be programmed to do any number of functions, depending on what you use most often. I have mine set to go "back" a page when I'm surfing the Internet and I have the other one set to "copy" highlighted text.

This little invention takes a few days to get your hand muscles accustomed to, however, it is worth its weight in gold in regard to speed and wrist comfort!

Monica Ricci, owner of Catalyst Organizing Solutions, has been an organizing specialist since 1999. She helps her clients declutter, organize and streamline their lives both at home and at work. She is also a speaker and appears regularly in various magazines, newspapers and online publications. Contact Monica at www.CatalystOrganizing.com or 770-569-2642

---

- **Use your folders!** Don't make the mistake of setting up and organizing sub-folders in your favorite sites area, without taking the time to use them. It only takes an extra second to place a newly discovered link into its appropriate folder, as opposed to spending time reorganizing links into folders at a later date.

- **Know what you're saving.** Many browser links have complicated names when you save them in your Favorites. Don't be afraid to rename links titles. Keeping your list of Favorites as short and compact as possible will help you find what you need more quickly.

- **Save space by "storing" your reference books on the web.** If you often refer to a dictionary, thesaurus or other reference book, why not save premium desk or shelf space by using some of the free resources available on the Internet? Create a folder marked "Reference" in your browser's favorites and then add links to free online references. Some popular free resources are:

  - ❖ www.yourdictionary.com
  - ❖ www.merriam-webster.com
  - ❖ www.refdesk.com
  - ❖ www.encyclopedia.com

- **Save links to office software.** Another time-saver is to set up a folder for links to software vendors. Whether it's the free text editor you downloaded last week or the expensive accounting package purchased last year, having immediate access to online help, technical support or customer service pages can save you needless worry in case of a software crisis.

- **Use search tools.** There are hundreds of sites that allow you to conduct free searches for the information you need. Three of the popular ones are:

  - ❖ www.google.com
  - ❖ www.yahoo.com
  - ❖ www.askjeeves.com

- **Narrow your search.** When you visit the search engines, be sure to read the specific searching instructions for each. Most of them will allow you to truly define and refine your search, so the only results that come up are the ones that will best help you.

For example, let's say you want to do a search on "bargain office supplies." If you just type in the words bargain office supplies the search engine will find every web site with the word "bargain" in it, every site with the word "office" in it and every site with the word "supplies" in it. In other words, it will probably come up with millions of results—most of which have nothing to do with bargain office supplies.

However, if you type in: +"bargain office supplies" it will then find only sites that contain the complete phrase "bargain office supplies." If that is too narrow, you may want to expand it a bit by typing: + "bargain"+ "office supplies." It will then find only sites that contain both the word "bargain" and the phrase "office supplies."

The above instructions work well for www.google.com, but each search engine has its own criteria for narrowing your search, so be sure to read the instructions before you begin.

**Great idea!**

It seems like you have to login to almost every web site nowadays and each site requires different password formats, so you can't always use the same password. Your list of passwords and user names can get to be very long. Make an Excel spreadsheet of all of your usernames and passwords. Laminate it and keep it under your keyboard or in your top desk drawer for quick reference.

Suzanne M. Keezel
The Organized Planet, Inc.
Organizing Solutions for Your World!
Located in Central Florida
www.theorganizedplanet.com

- **Use search site directories.** If you're not sure what you're searching for, most search engines contain categorized directories. For example, on Yahoo, you can click on the Business and Economy category. That will then lead you to other business categories to help you see everything available.

- **Leave out the http and the www.** When you type a web page address, most of the time you can just type the name and then the .com For instance, instead of typing in www.getorganizednow.com try typing in just getorganizednow.com in your web browser. In most browsers, this works just fine. Every second saved can be used for something else!

- **Try the obvious.** Many companies and organizations have chosen the name of their business as their web site address. Before searching for a company name, first try the obvious. If you're looking for Barnes and Noble or JC Penney or the FBI, the business or organization name is often the name of the web site. For example:

  ❖ www.barnesandnoble.com

  ❖ www.jcpenney.com

  ❖ www.fbi.gov

## Organizing Clinic

### Question

I have to search the web each day for my business, but it takes me forever to access the sites that interest me. Why do some pages take so long to load and is there any way to make them load faster? I'm currently using a 3-year-old computer with a dial-up connection.

Margaret Corning
Dunedin, FL

### Answer

Dear Margaret,

The loading speed of web pages includes a number of factors including the amount of text and graphics on the particular page, the quality and speed of your connection and the number of people on the Internet when you're surfing.

A no-cost solution for you is to attempt to surf the net during off-peak hours. A cost-based solution may be to upgrade your dial-up connection to DSL or Cable, which should increase the loading time dramatically. This can save you tons of time.

Check to be sure your Internet cache is cleared out. Otherwise, an overload in your cache could be causing some delays. Check with your Internet service provider to determine how to do this.

Finally, you mentioned that your computer is three years old. That's a pretty young computer, but once a computer is 5 years old or more, you might have to consider upgrading your computer. Check with your local computer technician to determine if your computer is equipped to handle what you need to do on it each day.

---

- **Clear your cache.** Laura, one of my loyal web site visitors, visited my site and could not find the most recent information she just read about in my newsletter. She thought I hadn't uploaded the new information yet. But the problem was on her end. You see, every time you visit a web page, your computer stores that page on your hard drive.

  Why? Because if you leave that page for a moment and want to return, it's quicker for the computer to read the page from your hard drive, rather than to retrieve it from the Internet again. As a result, there's a chance you're not seeing any updates made since your last visit to that page.

  Try clicking your "Refresh" icon to temporarily solve the problem. But, if your browser doesn't do so automatically, be sure to clean out these temporary Internet files once each day. Check with your Internet provider to determine the best way to do this—especially if you use AOL.

- **Knowing web site extensions can help.** The letters at the end of a web site are usually indicative of the nature of that particular site.

  While this is not true in all cases, generally the following extensions indicate:

  - ❖ **.com**  a commercial web site
  - ❖ **.biz**  a business web site
  - ❖ **.net**  a network site
  - ❖ **.org**  a non-profit group site
  - ❖ **.edu**  an education site
  - ❖ **.gov**  a government site

- **Reload and refresh.** If a page doesn't load the first time you enter a web site, try using your browser's Reload/Refresh button a few times before giving up. This can help sometimes.

## Organizing Clinic

### Question

I surf the Net all day and I can't get any of my work done. I'm addicted. Please help or I'm liable to lose my job!

Alvin Alderidge
Washington DC

### Answer

Dear Alvin,

Surfing during business hours for reasons other than those associated with your job can have dire consequences. Even if your boss can't see you surfing, your company may have a program in place that allows management to see what you're doing on your computer each day.

I'm sure your boss expects you to be "working" and not "surfing" during business hours, especially when she or he is paying you for that time.

If your company allows it, limit your web surfing time to before hours, during lunch and/or after hours. Try setting a timer.

For instance, if you wish to surf from 8:30AM to 9:00AM, set your timer at 8:30AM to sound off in 30 minutes. When the timer sounds, it's time to get off the Net and get back to work.

You say you're addicted, but if you want to keep your job, you have to find the willpower within yourself to control your web surfing time better.

- **Avoid peak times.** From about 11:00AM EST to 6:00PM PST, the information superhighway is super-crowded with users. Similar to physical highways, as traffic increases, speed decreases.

  If you are having trouble visiting busy sites or if your browser is creeping along, try again earlier in the morning or later in the evening.

- **Get the latest browser.** The latest versions of both Internet Explorer and Netscape can be downloaded for free, so make sure you have them. To get one or the other, visit www.microsoft.com or www.netscape.com

- **Be sure viewing is comfortable.** Increase or decrease the size of your browser's font for better viewing. If you have poor vision, you will probably want to increase it. However, a smaller font size allows for more page text area when viewing.

- **Use your browser's find feature.** Find the information that you need without scrolling through bulky pages, by using the "find" feature within your browser. For both Netscape and Explorer, go to Edit/Find in Page and type in the word(s) you are looking for. It will find it for you.

- **Buy from safe sites.** Always verify that a server is secure when submitting any credit card information. To do this, look for the lock symbol in the lower-right corner of your browser window.

  A locked lock means it's secure and that it's safe to enter your credit card number. You'll usually find this only on the page of the site where you would enter your credit card number. Also, the URL name will start with https:// when it is a secure page.

- **Get firewall protection.** If you're using a cable connection, getting a firewall is an absolute must. Otherwise, a hacker may break into your system. Once this occurs, the consequences can be dire, such as your entire hard drive being erased. You can get firewall software in your local office supply store. Try Norton Firewall or search the web for free firewall software like Zone Alarm.

  When I first switched from a phone line to a cable line, I wasn't aware of firewall software. The very first day on the new cable line, I learned that my computer had been hacked and I could not get into any of my programs. Thank goodness, it wasn't a major hack attack. I was able to contact Microsoft to get the problem resolved. But who knows if I would have been that lucky if it happened again. Needless to say, that afternoon I had firewall software protecting my computer.

## Great idea!

Because some web sites are particular about the login ID you use, as well as specific in directing an appropriate password (combination of letters and numbers or requiring a certain number of digits to be acceptable), I quickly realized using the same IDs and passwords was not always possible and I soon became overwhelmed.

My solution has worked well for over the past several years. I started jotting everything down in my address book—something I keep handy in my briefcase and small enough to drop in my purse, because portability is a must.

Think about it. We don't always have access to the same computer for all our transactions. Using the address book has been incredibly beneficial for me. The information is alphabetized and I include the web site address, login and password.

I have referred to it time and time again. As long as I consistently add the information as soon as I set it up, I'm good to go. This works great for email and web site addresses for business contacts, friends and family, too.

Dawn Gepfer
dawngepfer@aol.com

- **Schedule time to surf.** Need to research the web for your job or business but can't find the time to do so? You won't find the time. You have to make the time. Set a consistent web-researching schedule each week, such as Mondays, Tuesdays and Thursdays from 3:00PM to 4:00PM. When that time rolls around, be sure you use it for your scheduled web research.

- **Keep a site notepad.** When reading newspapers or magazines, listening to the radio or watching television, you're bound to learn about web sites you would like to visit. Whenever you want to try out a site, jot the URL (web address) into your notepad. During your scheduled web research time, just open your notepad and the addresses will be right there waiting for you.

- **Go back in history.** Can't remember the helpful business site you were on the other day? Many web browsers allow you to go back in time. If your browser has a "history" option, it will list links to pages you recently visited.

- **Get a good view.** Some browsers allow you to hide one, or all, of the toolbars. This is especially helpful if you have a small monitor and want to see more of a particular web site. For example, in Windows Explorer, you can click F11 to make your toolbar disappear and F11 again to make it reappear.

## Great idea!

In my home office, I use a small notebook for my Internet passwords. It's a tiny binder that I can take paper in and out of and it keeps all my passwords in one place. If you're one to put your passwords on little pieces of paper and lose them on your desk, this system can work well for you.

Start with a little notebook (mine is 4" x 6 ½"), dividers (A - Z) and lined paper (this comes with the notebook and refills can be purchased where you bought it). Then when you register on a web site, simply log your user name and password under the name of the web site in the correct section of your binder, making sure to write it exactly as you typed it. Most user names and passwords are case sensitive.

Add more pages as needed. I use the front and back of each sheet and usually put about 3 or 4 web site names on one side.

I recommend that you do not keep your notebook out for all to see. Passwords are meant to protect your security on the computer and you wouldn't want someone having access to your information without your authorization.

Tammy Burke
Organize it all, LLC
368 North Pleasant Avenue, Dallastown, PA 17313
tburke@organizeitall.biz
Visit my web site at www.organizeitall.biz/ for other great organizing tips.

- **Surf with your keyboard.** You don't have to always use your mouse. Keyboard keys such as PageUp and PageDown allow you to navigate up and down a web page.

- **Like a page? Print it!** While I certainly would not recommend you print every single web page you land on, sometimes information is really worthwhile to print, such as troubleshooting instructions, driving directions or an article you'd like to pass on to an employee or customer.

  Just use your print icon to print the page. Some browsers even allow you to highlight a portion of the page and just print that selection.

- **Forget the http and the .com.** Tired of typing the http and .com every time you want to access a web site? Just type in the site name and hit CTRL-Enter. For example, if you want to go to my site, www.getorganizednow.com. just type "getorganizednow" (no quotes) into your address line and hit CTRL-Enter. The www and .com will be added for you. This generally works for Internet Explorer users.

## Great idea!

It's so easy to fly off on a tangent when web surfing. Suddenly you've forgotten what subject matter you were researching and you've lost 3 hours. Stay on track by using a tree structure to surf.

From the first page you are browsing, do not simply left-click a link that interests you. Right-click the link and then select Open in New Window or New Tab. A new browser window or tab will open. If you have determined that this page is of no use, close it by clicking its Close box. Your surfing starting point will become visible once again.

Right-click the next link of interest and open it in a new window or tab. This new page may also have a link of interest. Right-click-open it. Each time you have exhausted the usefulness of a page, close it. The page you just came from will always be displayed as you move up and down through the tree branches, keeping you on track and not letting you stray far from the roots of your starting point.

Kerry Crocker, Professional Organizer
Space Cadette
Chapel Hill, NC
919-928-9825
kerry@space-cadette.com
www.space-cadette.com

- **Use your wheel.** If you use Internet Explorer, you can use the wheel on your mouse to increase or decrease the font size on a web page. Just hold down your CTRL key and roll the wheel on your wheel mouse. This is especially helpful if the web site you're visiting has very small type.

# Chapter 9

# Paying your bills and keeping finances organized

- **Develop a consistent system.** If you're in charge of bill paying in your office, one of the keys to paying your bills on time is to develop a system to do so.

  For our business, my husband usually takes care of the bill paying. He prefers not to let invoices pile up and would rather take care of them as he receives them. Some people may prefer to choose one day a week or two days each month to pay bills. Whatever you choose, it should be consistent and easy so that you stick with it.

## Organizing Clinic

### Question

I'm in charge of organizing and making out checks for the various invoices our company receives. My boss is then in charge of signing these checks and mailing them out. I make out the checks weekly and pass then on to my boss. Unfortunately, they stay on his desk for weeks before getting mailed, which often results in unnecessary late fees. Any suggestions?

Eric Timberfield
Akron, OH

### Answer

Dear Eric,

First, is your boss aware of the late fees and how much money they're costing him? Chances are, if he's not aware and if you let him know, he will be more conscientious about taking care of them sooner.

Rather than just leaving these checks to be signed on your boss's desk, I suggest that you bring them in, wait for him to sign them and then take care of the mailing for him. This may turn out to be a much more efficient system, even if you have to wait a few minutes in his office while he signs the checks.

In addition, get him a signature stamp so he can stamp each check, rather than having to sign each one.

Another possibility is for your boss to give you authorization to sign and mail the checks yourself. You can always then provide him with a weekly report of what you paid for his records.

- **Sort it out.** As soon as your mail arrives or at your designated mail sorting time, sort through the mail, separating your pending bills from all of your other mail. When you're finished sorting, immediately place your pending bills in a bill paying system, envelope, pocket folder or pending bills basket.

- **Do not separate each pending bill into a separate area.** Whatever you do, don't put your business insurance bill in one folder, your printing invoices in another folder and your company magazine membership dues bill in another. All pending bills should be together so they can be paid without having to search 10 different places to find them.

- **Keep bill-paying supplies together.** Keep all bill paying supplies—your checkbook, check register, postage stamps, pens, envelopes, a calculator and an address stamp or address labels—in one place.

---

### Great idea!

Use a binder for all bill paying needs. Use a monthly checklist as the front page with all bills due and their due date. Check them off as you pay them.

At the end of the month it will be easy to see (at a glance) that all of your bills have been paid and on time.

The second page should be your written budget.

In the following pages of the binder add separate folders to hold the following: address labels and stamps, payment coupons (car loans, mortgage payments, etc.) envelopes and pocket calculator.

Add additional folders to suit your individual needs.

Keeping these items in a binder makes it easy to transport to another room (if need be) or wherever it is most convenient to pay your bills.

Claudette Alburger
Organize and Beyond
Riverview, FL
813-236-4087
claudette@organizeandbeyond.com
www.organizeandbeyond.com

---

- **Store your statements.** Every time you pay a bill, write the check number, date and amount on the enclosed statement. That statement then needs to be filed away. Use a binder with several pocket folders—one for each company—to store each statement for the year.

Or, if you have lots of statements, make a labeled manila file folder for each payee and file them in a "Paid Bills" section in your filing cabinet, alphabetically by payee.

The statements should be filed so that the most current statements are in the front of the file folder and oldest in the back.

- **File statements immediately.** As soon as you're done paying the bills, file the receipts in their respective file folders. This way, if you need to reference them in the near future, you'll be able to find them easily.

- **Immediately record your paid bills.** As soon as you've paid the bills, immediately record the payments in your check register or computer software register. Don't wait until later because if you do, there's a good chance you will forget.

- **Use a reminder system.** For recurring bills you don't normally get statements for, indicate deadlines on your calendar or get an automatic system such as Quicken to remind you when due dates are coming up.

- **Use an electronic system.** If you're writing out many checks each month, it is recommended that you use commercially available software. We use Quicken, but some other popular names are QuickBooks and Peachtree Accounting.

  These software programs allow you to print your checks out, calculate totals automatically, keep a check register, develop a budget and analyze expenses and lots more.

  If you're computer savvy and enjoy using computers, once you get the hang of using one of these systems, you'll never go back to using a calculator, pen and paper again for paying your bills.

- **Automatic payment.** Some companies give you the option of paying your bills directly from the company checking account or credit card account.

  This is a convenient option for many people. It cuts down on check writing, the bills are always paid on time and you don't have to spend time stamping or mailing out envelopes.

- **Online Bill Payment.** Most banks now have online bill payment available for free with a current bank account. This method of bill payment gives you another easy way to speed up payments.

  The advantages of online bill payment is that you can schedule payments in advance, schedule recurring payments and automatic payments. This option is excellent for when you will be away for a while and best of all— no more checks or stamps.

Additionally, payments will be processed faster and the information will be included in your bank statement.

The latest Internet browsers ensure the highest level of security with online transactions.

As opposed to Automatic payments, you can still control payments before they go out with online bill payment.

---

## Organizing Clinic

### Question

I'm the owner of a fast-food restaurant. I get tons of invoices each month from my vendors. Some of my vendors require payment upon receipt, some weekly, some monthly and still others offer a discount if I pay their invoices within 10 days.

I don't like paying my bills earlier than I have to. Any suggestions?

John Terrance
San Diego, CA

### Answer

Dear John,

In your case, I suggest you pay your bills weekly on one consistent day each week, such as Wednesdays.

If you do this weekly, everyone should get paid on time with no problem and you can determine if there are certain bills you'd prefer to wait on paying.

As you get your invoices, highlight the due date with a bright yellow highlighting marker. Keep all of your pending bills in one folder.

Each Wednesday, pay the bills you wish to pay based on the due dates or the early pay dates. You should be able to flip through them easily, since all due dates will stand out.

If you choose not to pay a particular vendor that week, just keep that bill in your pending bills folder until the following week.

Hope this helps!

---

- **Pay by phone.** Some companies will allow you to pay your bills right over the phone, using your credit card, debit card or checking account. Make sure you ask if there is any additional charge for this convenience and determine if time saved is worth the fee.

- **Will it post today?** When you pay your bills over the phone or online, there may be a one to two day delay. Some companies take the money out of your bank account and then cut a physical check. This may take a few days, so be sure to pay earlier than the deadline. Other companies make an electronic transfer, which is immediate.

- **Keep a list of payees.** No matter when or how you decide to pay your bills, keeping a list of payees gives you a quick way to verify that you have paid every bill. Sometimes, a bill may get lost in the mail, so this quick check will ensure that you don't unintentionally miss a bill payment. Note: you are still responsible for bills that are lost in the mail!

If you pay bills manually, you can keep your list on an index card or use the automatic lists generated in money management software or online bill payment sites.

A list is also helpful when a co-worker or designee who is not normally responsible to pay the bills has to cover bill-paying responsibilities.

As bills are paid, check off the payees on your list.

### Great idea!

I find that my business runs a whole lot smoother when I know my home bills and finances are being taken care of.

Everyday when I get my mail, I sort through it immediately. I write on each bill the date it's due. I bought a three-drawer plastic desktop container for about five dollars. The top drawer is for my children's saving accounts, along with stamps and return address labels. The middle drawer is for the bills that need to be paid and the bottom drawer is a temporary holder for receipts that need to be filed.

When it's time to pay bills, I pull out the middle drawer, as well as the stamps and address labels and get to work. My husband only gets paid twice a month, on the 15th and 30th, so by having the due dates already on the bills, I know which ones need to be paid during which bill paying session. When I'm finished, I put all the receipts in the third drawer, until I have time to file them in the filing cabinet.

Christine Jahn
P.O. Box 174, Utica, Ky. 42376
270-733-4886
Christine Jahn and Melissa Pogue are Serenity, Inc. They will make your home a sanctuary through organizing, painting and decorating. Visit their site at www.serenityinc.net/

- **Organize your cancelled checks and checking account statements.** Every month you will receive checking account statement(s) and possibly cancelled checks, from your bank. Immediately place them in a folder until your designated monthly date rolls around to reconcile your checking account. Then, keep your statements and cancelled checks all together in a folder for the year. You may need to retrieve them later for your accountant when tax season rolls around.

By the way, any bank statements and/or cancelled checks more than a year old can be stored away in a different area than your current files.

You may also consider checking with your accountant to determine how long he or she suggests you need to keep this information, so you don't end up with 20 year's worth filling up your office.

- **Keep cancelled checks with your donation statements.** Keep cancelled checks with your donation letters or acknowledgements. They will be in one place for tax time and you will be able to get your tax write-off.

- **Prepare envelopes for recurring bills beforehand.** For recurring bills, such as mortgage, rent or loan payments, you'll save a lot of time preparing a bunch of envelopes for each beforehand.

  For example, let's say you have to pay office rent each month. Make out a year's worth of envelopes with your landlord's company name and mailing address, your return address and a stamp. This way, everything will be all set to go each month. You just write out a check, place it in the prepared envelope and mail.

- **Reduce your business credit cards.** Reduce some paper and aggravation in your life by limiting the number of business credit cards you have. Most businesses can get by with one card. Try not to have more than two. Most companies accept Visa, MasterCard and American Express. You'll have fewer checks to make out each month and you'll be better able to control your spending.

- **Get mileage.** Use a business credit card that gives you airline mileage credit or money back for each purchase you make.

  My husband and I have a Midwest Express credit card. We get one mile for every dollar we spend. All of our business expenses, such as meals, business travel, supplies, printing and postage, go on our credit card and we pay the card off each month to prevent having to pay interest.

  Our mileage bonuses result in two to three free airline trips per year for both of us and our daughter.

- **Find an accountant.** If you're responsible for your business taxes, it is recommended that you find a good accountant. So many businesses figure they can save a few bucks and just take care of their own taxes. If you have the time to do this and to focus on the many new tax laws each year, then doing this may be fine for you.

My husband and I found that it's easier to just take it to the professionals. We don't have the time to learn about all the latest tax laws and run and grow our business at the same time. It's an accountant's duty to do so.

Of course, this doesn't alleviate you from staying abreast of your finances.

## Great idea!

Create a master file for all tax related papers. Even before your 1099 papers arrive, start a master file using an expanding red folder and manila files. Label the files with the important tax categories such as W-2 information, interest and dividend income, capital gains and losses, charitable donations, medical and dental expenses, deductible business expenses and miscellaneous deductions (educational expenses, safe deposit boxes, financial planning).

If you file a Schedule C for your business, create files for business expenses like income, advertising, office supplies, office equipment, costs of goods sold, education and auto expenses.

Even before your papers arrive, this file will be their "home" and papers will not get lost!

To prepare for the current year, begin a master file for these documents for the current year, making copies for the file so you will not have to search for them at this time next year.

Ellen R. Delap
Professional-Organizer.com
Personal Organization Solutions for Home, School, Work and Life
281-360-3928
edelap@professional-organizer.com
www.professional-organizer.com

- **Always get a receipt.** Some items are tax deductible such as postage, travel, fuel, office space and more. As you receive receipts for these types of things, keep those receipts organized in #10 envelopes by category, within a file folder or box. Or organize these receipts in file folders.

  Be organized. Your accountant doesn't deserve a shoebox full of disorganized receipts dumped on his desk during the busy tax season.

- **Expense it.** Many companies have a business expense program for staff members to keep track of business expenses for reimbursement. Usually employees are asked to fill out an expense form and then turn it in monthly to be paid back any money they spent on travel, meals, and so on.

  I highly recommend you fill in your expense report line by line as you spend each day and keep all of your receipts in one envelope. As soon as the end of the month rolls around, total everything, make a copy of your expense report and receipts and then turn in your report and receipts for quick reimbursement.

Kara, a sales representative, was nine months behind in filling out her expense reports. It was a nightmare getting all the receipts finally organized into the proper months and in the end, her company would only accept six months back. This meant that Kara lost out on three months of expenses she would have been reimbursed had she been more conscientious about getting them in on time. Don't let this happen to you.

### Great idea!

The bill folder is the answer to keeping all bills together and organized. It consists of a file folder (I chose red, as red is a commanding color to me, but whatever color you choose is up to you) and printed out monthly calendars for every month in the year.

You attach the current month's calendar to the front of the folder and when a bill comes in, you open it, record the due date on the calendar, place the bill in the folder, and it stays there until it is time to pay bills. It's easy to use because you record your bills in the block date they're due and all you have to do on payday is look on the calendar to see what bills need to be paid.

I've also gotten in the habit of clipping postage stamps to the folder and printing off a sheet of address labels for return addressing.

I use the Microsoft Works Program on my computer to print out pre-addressed envelopes for recurring bills, such as car payment and rent. That way you just insert the payment and invoice in the envelope, stamp it and send.

Charity Wilt
Ms.Organized
112 East Race Street, Martinsburg, WV 25401
304-267-6871
organized03@yahoo.com
www.geocities.comorganized03/organize

- **Keep track of your income and expenses.** An easy and efficient way to keep track of your income and expenses is with a spreadsheet program. For each year, assign 12 columns listing each month, Jan, Feb, etc. Then, use the rows to include common income categories (client sales, affiliate sales, commission checks) and common expense categories (wages, printing, postage). Each month, indicate how much money you made or spent on each category. This information will be extremely helpful when tax time rolls around.

- **Verify expenses.** As you receive credit card and bank statements, verify that all expenses listed match with your expense log.

- **Keep business expenses separate.** It's a good idea to have a separate credit card just for business expenses so credit statements will reflect only business-related charges. This simplifies expense reporting and record keeping for tax purposes. It also allows you to easily monitor business expenses.

- **Start a tax folder.** As you file receipts throughout the year, it is helpful to start a tax folder. This folder can be placed in your tickler file at the time you plan to start filing your taxes.

  Keep receipts or copies of receipts for big-ticket items that have tax implications as you process paperwork year round. Once tax season comes, you will have all your paperwork in one place, ready for action!

- **Let one person pay the bills.** Rather than delegating this responsibility to whoever is available, it is best to assign one person to take care of paying the bills. As the old saying goes, "Too many cooks spoil the stew."

- **Avoid late fees.** Read your statements carefully and follow the payment guidelines. Use the envelope from the company if provided. Make sure your checks are legible and accurate. Send in your payment at least five days prior to the due date, if not earlier.

- **Pay more than the minimum.** If possible, pay off your credit card bills each month. This will avoid you having to pay interest charges. If you cannot afford to pay the entire bill, at least pay more than the minimum. In doing so, you will actually be making a dent in the amount you owe.

- **Know basic accounting.** If you are a business owner, it is crucial for you to understanding basic accounting. Being aware of the cash in and the cash out of your business and having the ability to understand Profit and Loss Statements, Balance Statements, etc. will help you to better run your business.

  While you may feel this is your accountant's job, not understanding basic finances can be detrimental. Most accountants are not going to care if your labor is at 50% or if your business is losing money each month. It's up to you to understand your numbers and to keep your business running at a profit.

- **Work up a monthly tax plan.** To avoid paying a huge amount of money at year-end, if you pay estimated taxes each quarter, determine how much money needs to be put aside.

# Chapter 10
# Collecting payment with ease

- **Charge an upfront deposit.** In most cases, charging an initial deposit upfront before you start work for a customer will help you determine if the customer is willing and capable of paying his or her bills. If you provide products instead of services, always get paid before you provide the product to the customer to avoid payment collection hassles.

## Organizing Clinic

### Question

I spend quite some time each month writing out invoices to my customers. Each invoice requires me to itemize on several lines. I then have to total each invoice with a calculator. I don't have a computer and don't want one. Do you have any ideas to make this chore easier?

Dawn Coulter
El Cajon, CA

### Answer

Dear Dawn,

Although you mentioned you don't want a computer, it would definitely make this task easier and less time-consuming. With a computer, you wouldn't have to re-type the same names over and over each month, you would be able to copy and paste itemized lines from previous invoices, and you can even set it up to calculate totals automatically. Definitely reconsider.

In the meantime, I suggest you make a standard form with all possible line items and prices on it. Each month, just write in the appropriate person's contact information at the top and check off the services or products purchased. This would help alleviate writing out all the itemizations.

- **Get a signed contract.** In some businesses, it may be worthwhile for you to have a customer sign a contract stating they will pay their invoice within a certain length of time.

Janie, a landscape contractor, once had some difficulties getting her customers to pay for their landscaping projects. Now, she asks her customers to sign a contract stating that 50% of payment must be made before the job is started and the remaining 50% must be paid upon completion of the project. This way, she always gets paid at least half of the project price before the job is even started and most of her customers pay the second half upon completion according to the contract.

- **Same day each month.** Send invoices out to your clients on the same day each month. For example, January 26, then February 26, then March 26, etc. Your clients will know exactly when to expect your bill and you won't get confused as to when you've sent a request for payment.

- **Clearly mark your invoices.** Mark every invoice you send with a unique invoice number, the name of the person who authorized the purchase and their company order number. Also include the payment due date.

- **Offer an incentive.** You might want to offer an incentive for paying earlier like a 5% discount if paid within seven days. This encourages customers to pay sooner.

- **Keep on top of payments.** If someone misses a payment, immediately send out a friendly reminder. Don't let too much time pass or you'll waste hours agonizing over how difficult it's going to be to collect payment.

- **Know the accounts payable rep.** Determine who pays the bills at your customer's company and send the invoice directly to that person.

- **Give them a friendly call.** Before approaching a customer with collection letters, first call (or have someone call) the customer to find out if they received the bill and if they sent out payment. Sometimes a friendly reminder is all it takes.

- **Keep detailed records.** If you don't receive payment and you speak to someone inquiring about this matter, be sure you keep accurate notes for your records. Include the person you spoke to, the current date and the date he tells you the payment will be made. Also, keep track of any special payment arrangements, such as a customer paying half this month and half next month.

- **Include a SASE.** Always include a self-addressed, stamped envelope with your invoices. If your customer has to take the time to search for an envelope or stamp, it may delay payment.

- **Record as you receive.** As soon as you receive payment, record that payment in your record book or computer file.

Jane, an answering service owner, collects payment from her customers on a weekly basis. Sometimes she gets so busy with other projects that she doesn't record customer payments immediately. At the end of the week, she searches for all the checks on her desk and then records payment.

This ended up very unfortunately for her. At one point she didn't record payment immediately from one of her top customers and the payment her customer sent was misplaced under other papers on her desk. When she looked at her record book, it appeared this customer had not yet paid.

Jane sent a collection letter out, which infuriated her customer. He was so annoyed with her that he cancelled his service and switched to another company.

This was a mistake Jane never made again.

- **Cash checks quickly.** It is in your best interest to cash checks quickly after you receive them. Since it generally takes 10 business days for checks to clear, deposit them within one week.

- **Take credit cards.** Avoid having to wait for checks by accepting credit cards. The minimal fee you have to give to the credit card companies is almost always worth it.

  First, you will get more customers and sales when you have this additional payment option. Second, no more having to worry about bounced checks or waiting for payments. Third, the money goes right into your bank account automatically.

  Just an additional incentive . . . my web site sales quadrupled the second I began accepting credit cards!

- **Charge automatically.** If you charge your customers for a service monthly, you might consider automatically charging that amount to your customer's credit card or debit card each month—with no additional work on the customer's part.

- **Give a receipt.** If a customer pays you in cash, she is going to expect a receipt verifying payment. Create your own receipts or buy pre-made ones at an office supply store.

- **Be realistic.** The longer a customer debt is outstanding, the less likely it's going to be paid at all. Don't be afraid to ask for payment and get to the bottom of why payment has not been made. Tell the customer you will work with her if she's willing to work with you. She must begin making payments immediately or she will have made the decision to force you to contact a collection agency.

- **Send collection letters when necessary.** Unfortunately, in some instances you may need to send out collection letters for payment after you've attempted to contact your customer(s) by telephone. The following templates are samples you can use for every step of your collection process:

## <u>First</u> Past Due Notice

Dear (Contact Name),

Bills sometimes get misplaced or overlooked and we have not yet received your payment of (amount due) for our invoice (invoice number) due on (due date). A copy of the original invoice is attached.

Please check your records and if payment has not gone out, please mail payment today in the enclosed, self-addressed, stamped envelope. If you're confused about this charge or you'd like to discuss this matter, please call us today at (your phone number).

If your payment was recently mailed, please disregard this notice. Thank you for your prompt attention to this matter. We appreciate your business.

Sincerely,

(Your Signature)

(Your Name)

(Your Company Name)

## <u>Second</u> Past Due Notice

Dear (Contact Name),

We still have not received your payment of (amount due) for our invoice (invoice number), which was due on (due date). Your account is now (# of days past due) days past due. A copy of the original invoice is attached.

Please mail payment within the next 5 days in the enclosed, self-addressed, stamped envelope.

If, for some reason, you need to discuss this matter, please contact us at (your phone number) to avoid further collection action.

If your payment was recently mailed, please disregard this notice. Thank you for your immediate attention to this matter. We appreciate your business.

Sincerely,

(Your Signature)

(Your Name)

(Your Company Name)

# <u>Third</u> Past Due Notice

Dear (Contact Name),

We still have not received your payment of (amount due) for our invoice (invoice number), which was due on (due date). Your account is now (# of days past due) days past due. A copy of the original invoice is attached.

It is rare for someone to order one of our products and then keep it without paying for it or to receive a service and not pay for it.

In the few instances when this has happened in the past, we've found it is the result of one of the following:

1. Our customer never received our invoice or has misplaced it. No problem. We've enclosed another invoice—our fourth.

2. Our customer has a question about the invoice or needs to arrange payments. If you have any question about our invoice or need to arrange payments, please call us at (your phone number). If we don't receive payment or hear from you within 5 days, we will call you.

3. The person is unprofessional, dishonest and unethical. We believe that this type of person, although extremely rare, takes advantage of honest people whenever possible. He or she has no intention of paying for products or services that he/she orders. We turn these rare people over to our collection agency and/or our attorney to pursue legal remedies.

We are assuming that you fall into either #1 or #2. Please mail in your payment immediately or call us within five business days to discuss your seriously past due account.

If your payment was recently mailed, please disregard this notice. Thank you for your immediate attention to this matter. We appreciate your business.

Sincerely,

(Your Signature)

(Your Name)

(Your Company Name)

# <u>Final</u> Past Due Notice

Dear (Contact Name),

We still have not received your payment of (amount due) for our invoice (invoice number), which was due on (due date). Your account is now (# of days past due) days past due. A copy of the original invoice is attached.

Your seriously past due account is about to be forwarded to our collection agency.

You should know that we intend to pursue this claim and reserve the right to report this matter to the TRW Credit Bureau, as well as pursue other remedies.

This can include litigation.

The process of litigation has not yet been instituted. If it happens, it will be pursued through a local attorney in accordance with (your state) statutes.

Should a Judgment be issued against you as a result of this process, you may also be charged with court costs and attorney fees.

After a Judgment is issued a Creditor has a number of methods available to recover a claim.

It might be valuable for you to check the laws in your state pertaining to the satisfying of a Judgment.

It is not our intent to threaten or alarm you about this matter. We would hope, that you take a moment and seriously consider the consequences of your non-payment.

You can prevent further action by submitting full payment within five business days.

If you have any questions about our invoice, please call us at (your phone number).

Sincerely,

(Your Signature)

(Your Name)

(Your Company Name)

# Chapter 11

# Records retention

- **Can you find it elsewhere?** A large percentage of what we file is never looked at again. Think about whether you really need to keep documents before you file them. Don't retain anything you can easily find or duplicate somewhere else.

---

## Great idea!

"What do you save?" A corporate Records Retention Schedule tells you how long to keep information for financial or historical reasons, but general information still overflows the paper and email filing systems. To manage your files, ask yourself these five questions before saving any information:

Is it a W-A-S-T-E™?

**W – Is it WORTHWHILE?** Is the information worthwhile? If it's not worthwhile, toss it. If it is, go on to question A.

**A – Will I use it AGAIN?** Would you use this information again? If not, toss it. If yes, go on question S.

**S – Can I easily find it SOMEWHERE ELSE?** If you can easily find the information, then it's a WASTE. If not, go on to question T.

**T – Will anything happen if I TOSS it?** Is it historical or financially needed? Is it critical for the project? If not, toss it and move on to the final question, E.

**E - Do I need the ENTIRE item?** Do you need the entire document or just part of it? If you answered yes, then save it. If you answered no, save just the part you need. If the information didn't pass all five questions, it's a WASTE™.

Eileen Roth is a professional organizer, speaker and author of Organizing For Dummies®.
Contact her at Everything in its Place® in Scottsdale AZ, 602-788-4141
www.everythinginitsplace.net or email EileenRoth@aol.com

---

- **Give it a discard date.** When you do decide to file a document, note a discard date on it. Consistently use a colored pen/pencil in one of the corners and write the expiration date on the material. Whenever you are unsure about the expiration date, add three to six months onto the date.

The next time you are in that file and find one with an expiration date that has passed, toss it! Don't re-read the document or re-analyze your decision. This is precisely what you are trying to avoid by noting the date in the first place.

- **Mark it on all four sides.** When using storage boxes, make sure the contents are indicated on all four sides as well as on the top of the lid. This will facilitate retrieval of these records by making the contents visible from any angle.

- **The 7-year rule.** Save tax records and other important documents for a minimum of seven years. When storing tax information, be sure to include credit card billings, receipts, check registers, bills and any other documentation used in calculating your deductions. Also include copies of your tax forms.

  Keep in mind that certain types of businesses and professions are required by law to maintain records longer than 7 years. Check with your accountant or attorney regarding your individual circumstances.

- **Protect against damage.** If you need to store records in your basement, make sure there is clearance between the floor and the boxes to protect your files against potential flooding.

  Check the storage area's climate, especially if you're storing records that have been transferred onto microfilm or other media formats. Extreme temperatures and/or humidity will deteriorate microfilm and media images over time.

  Also, be sure your business files are safe from rodents.

- **Shred it.** When the retention period for certain records expires, you'll want to destroy them safely. Shredders can be utilized to not only destroy paper, but some will also handle computer disks, CDs and credit cards.

  Straight-cut shredders will cut your documents into long strips, while crosscut shredders cut up your records into small pieces of paper, similar to confetti.

  If you decide a shredder is right for you, make sure you purchase one that is large enough and fast enough to manage your destruction schedule.

- **Or hire someone else to shred it.** If you can't handle or don't want to handle the shredding, hire a shredding company. Many will come to your office and shred in the truck, right on your premises.

  Chris, owner of a retail store, had boxes and boxes that needed to be shredded, but he kept putting it off. His assistant suggested that he simply hire a shredding company, but he figured that he could do it himself and save himself a few bucks.

Well, as it turned out, he never got around to doing it. When his assistant got sick and tired of looking at all the boxes, she decided to do Chris a favor and called the shredding company herself. Chris was grateful for the gesture and now uses this shredding company annually.

## How long should I keep my records?

According to Jeremy L. White, CPA, PLLC, retaining old records is a burden for many businesses. The following types of records and retention periods are general guidelines and should be tempered by your own business and investment concerns, as well as the advice of legal counsel.

Accident Reports/Claims (Settled Cases) ............................................................ 7 Years

Accounts Payable Ledgers And Schedules ........................................................ 7 Years

Accounts Receivable Ledgers And Schedules .................................................... 8 Years

Audit Reports ...................................................................................................... Permanently

Bank Statements.................................................................................................. 3 Years

Capital Stock And Bond Records (Ledgers, Transfer Registers, Stubs Showing
    Issues, Record of Interest Coupons, Options)............................................ Permanently

Charts Of Accounts ............................................................................................ Permanently

Checks (Cancelled Checks For Important Payments, Special
Contracts, Purchase Of Assets, Payment Of Taxes)
    Note: Checks Should Be Filed With The Papers Pertaining To The
    Underlying Transaction............................................................................ Permanently

Checks (Cancelled Except Those Noted Above)................................................ 7 Years

Contracts And Leases (Expired)......................................................................... 7 Years

Contracts And Leases Still In Effect .................................................................. Permanently

Correspondence, General And Schedules .......................................................... 2 Years

Correspondence, Legal And Important Letters .................................................. Permanently

Correspondence, Routine With Customers/Vendors .......................................... 2 Years

Deeds, Mortgages And Bills Of Sale ................................................................. Permanently

Depreciation Schedules....................................................................................... Permanently

Employee Personal Records (After Termination) .............................................. 7 Years

Employment Applications................................................................................... 3 Years

Financial Statements (Year-end, Other Months Optional) ............................... Permanently

General Ledgers, Year-end Trial Balances......................................................... Permanently

Insurance Records, Policies, etc. ....................................................................... Permanently

Internal Audit Reports (Miscellaneous) ............................................................ 3 Years

Inventory Records .............................................................................................. 7 Years

Invoices to Customers Or From Vendors ............................................................ 7 Years

IRA And Keogh Plan Contributions, Rollovers, Transfers And Distribution ............. Permanently

Minute Books Of Directors, Stockholders, Bylaws & Charter ................................... Permanently

Payroll Records, Summaries And Tax Returns .................................................... 7 Years

Petty Cash Vouchers ................................................................................ 3 Years

Property Records, Including Costs, Depreciation Reserves,
    Year-End Trial Balances, Depreciation Schedules, Blueprints and Plans ........... Permanently

Purchase Orders ..................................................................................... 3 Years

Receiving Sheets .................................................................................... 1 Year

Safety Records ...................................................................................... 6 Years

Sales Records ....................................................................................... 7 Years

Stock And Bond Certificates (Cancelled) ......................................................... 7 Years

Subsidiary Ledgers ................................................................................. 7 Years

Tax Returns, Revenue Agents' Reports and Other Documents
    Relating To Determination Of Income Tax Liability ......................................... Permanently

Time Cards And Daily Reports ...................................................................... 7 Years

Trademark Registrations, Patents and Copyrights ................................................. Permanently

Voucher Register And Schedules .................................................................... 7 Years

Vouchers For Payments To Vendors, Employees, etc.
    (Includes Allowances & Reimbursements Of Employees, Officers, etc.,
    For Travel & Entertainment Expenses) ..................................................... 7 Years

The normal statute of limitations on federal returns is three years. Under some circumstances it is six years and if you fail to file a return or there is fraud involved, the statute of limitations does not close. This means that the Internal Revenue Service under nominal conditions would audit your return any time up through three years.

Since the statute of limitations in some states exceeds the federal statute, you should tailor your years of retention to the longer of the two statutes. For example, Kentucky has a four-year statute of limitations. Therefore, you should keep the above items for four years.

In deciding your own record retention schedule, consider keeping indefinitely records which any other office, institution or governmental unit cannot replicate.

Source: Jeremy L. White, CPA owns an accounting and investment firm specializing in tax, retirement, estate and investment planning for small businesses and individuals. This article and other free information and tips are available at his web site at www.consultcpa.com. He is the writer of *Wealth to Last: Money Essentials for the Second Half of Life* (www.wealthtolast.com) and *Splitting Heirs: Giving Money and Stuff to Your Children without Spoiling Them* (published in Spring 2004).

- **Put someone in charge.** An appropriate person should be assigned to maintain your records room as well as to keep track of which records have been removed and by whom.

- **Out of date?** Throw away any magazines/periodicals you can do without. Most are out of date after six months if not sooner. In addition, often the information is available on the Internet if you need to retrieve it at a later date.

---

## Organizing Clinic

### Question

I've been audited in the past and I'm really gun shy about tossing any of my records—even those that go more than ten years back. I have so many boxes in my office and basement. I feel like I'm working in a warehouse. Any ideas?

Susan Zhurbin
Leonia, NJ

### Answer

Dear Susan,

First, talk to your accountant about the papers you truly need to keep in case of a future audit. She should be able to help you with this.

Second, forget about storing all of these boxes in your office and basement. Instead, find a local storage facility. For a fee each month, you can store all your past records there. Just be sure each box is clearly labeled in case you need to retrieve something later.

This solution will free up your office space for current projects and files.

---

- **Use accordion files for yearly filing.** Each year, you can set up an accordion file for yearly receipts and expenses. Once the year is complete, you can store the file away and start a new one. This makes archiving older records a snap.

# Chapter 12

# The lowdown on filing supplies

- **Tools for setting up your filing system.** To create an efficient filing system, you will need:

  - ❖ Hanging file folders (for your main categories)

  - ❖ Manila file folders (for your sub-categories)

  - ❖ Plastic tabs and inserts for the hanging file folders

  - ❖ File labels for the manila file folders

  - ❖ A fine-point black marker

- **Don't use one without the other.** Never just use regular manila file folders in your filing cabinet without first inserting them into hanging file folders. Otherwise, your files will end up sliding to the bottom of the file drawer making it very difficult to find what you're looking for.

---

### Great idea!

- For hanging file folders, use vinyl tabs that are clear and 1/3 cut (3 1/2 inches wide). You can have longer file names than when using 1/5 cut.

- Use vinyl tabs that slant toward the back rather than stand straight up. They're much easier to read when looking down at a file drawer.

- Use a label maker. Slip the printed label inside the vinyl tab.

- Insert the vinyl tab in the front of the file folder so you can easily pull the folder open and drop papers inside.

- Keep a supply of file folders and vinyl tabs within arm's reach, so you can easily create a new file folder when needed.

Susan Kousek
Balanced Spaces, LLC ®
PO Box 3204, Reston, VA 20195
703-742-9179
skousek@balancedspaces.com
www.balancedspaces.com

---

- **Slip them inside.** It may seem like overkill to use both hanging file folders and regular manila file folders. But the most effective filing systems use both.

Hanging file folders identify the major filing categories. Regular manila file folders identify smaller sub-categories. Several manila file folders can be stored inside each hanging file folder.

Using both also ensures that, when you need a file folder, only the regular manila file folder needs to be removed. This helps later when you need to re-file that folder, because the hanging file folder will still be inside your filing cabinet and you'll be able to see at a glance where to return your file.

---

## Organizing Clinic

### Question

I work at a law firm and our files get quite large. How can I keep everything together? Loose filing is out of the question.

John

### Answer

Dear John,

First, it's important to dedicate 2 separate areas for your files: one area for active cases and one for inactive.

If possible, store any files for the inactive cases in another office or storage area. This will ensure that your space is maximized for your active cases and you'll know where a particular file is located when you need it.

Use red-rope, expanding file folders. They help you keep paperwork organized for each case in one consolidated place.

Then, organize these folders on wall shelves or in filing cabinets, either by case number or alphabetically, whichever is easier for you to find.

---

- **To color-code or not.** Color-coding your file folders can either be very helpful or catastrophic. This depends on your personality.

  For instance, if you choose to use green folders for your financial categories, red for your tax categories and yellow for your customer categories, you'll very easily be able to identify the main file folder category even if you're standing far away. That's a good thing.

  However, to use this system, you have to be very meticulous about keeping extra file folders of each color on hand for additional categories when needed.

Otherwise, you're not going to be able to file until you have the chance to order more file folders or to visit your office supply store.

Or worse, you might actually use one of the other colors you do have available and before you know it, your color-coding system will slowly but surely be destroyed. Know yourself first. Then decide whether or not you should color-code.

- **Clear or colored plastic tabs.** Many colored hanging files come with matching plastic tabs. Although red files can be easy to spot, sometimes it's not as easy to read the file's contents through a red plastic tab. If this poses a problem for your eyes, buy a package of clear plastic tabs for your hanging files. Discard the colored ones without using them.

- **Keep enough on hand.** Maintain a sufficient supply of file folders nearby, in all the colors you use regularly. Not having a file folder available is a bad excuse for falling behind on your filing.

- **Stick it on ahead.** To save time, stick a blank, white file folder label on all your new manila folder tabs. When you need a file folder, you won't have to search for a label and you can write the description on it right away.

  In fact, if you have old file folders that have old descriptions written on them, but are still in good condition, reuse them. Stick blank white file folder labels right over the old categories and the folder will now be ready for your new category.

- **Straight or staggered.** You can either use the manila file folders that have just one tab on the left or the ones that have staggered tabs.

  Many professional organizers now encourage people to use the file folders with just one tab on the left that line up one behind the other. They feel if everything is in one straight line, you'll be able to easily walk your fingers through each file folder to find what you're looking for. Plus your eyes don't have to travel from left to right when searching.

  Other people still like using the staggered tabs so that they don't have to finger through each file folder to find what they're looking for. The problem with staggered tabs is, after you've set up your filing system, they are going to get misaligned. If you've been filing left, center, right, left, center, right and so on, the second you have to place a file folder in between another, your sequence is going to be thrown off.

  In the end, it's really a matter of preference. I don't feel that using one or the other is especially better as far as locating a specific file in your system. But I do feel having one tab on the left is easiest, as you never have to worry about whether you should use a left, center or right tab. In addition, you will also only have to buy one type of manila file folder.

- **An extra left or an extra right.** If you decide to use the staggered filing system and you run out of left tab folders, just fold a right-tabbed file folder inside out and you'll instantly have the left tab folder you need.

- **Letter vs. legal.** Most people should use regular letter size file folders that fit easily inside standard filing systems. Legal size file folders are usually used by lawyers and other legal personnel, hence the name "legal" file folders.

- **Toss ratty file folders.** I once worked with someone whose filing system was atrocious. Not only were the files poorly organized, but the actual file folders were old, ratty, torn, musty, dirty and covered with scribbled writing dating back almost 20 years.

  I later discovered that she just couldn't bring herself to toss these old file folders because she felt that was wasteful. I can appreciate that, but she wouldn't have to toss them. She could place them in the recycling container and those old file folders can be reused to make new file folders or another paper-based product using these recycled materials.

  If your filing system looks terrible, it's going to reflect on your professionalism. The bottom line is, once your file folders begin to look bad, recycle them and use new ones.

- **Keep your folders looking young.** When you begin using a new file folder, just write the description on the label on the tab. Avoid writing anywhere else on the folder. Don't staple or tape papers to it.

  Be sure when you re-file the file folder, that it fits easily into your new filing system. If you have to force it to fit, that new folder is going to look horrible very quickly.

- **Use the creases if necessary.** You'll notice scored lines on the bottom of most manila file folders. These help you increase the amount of space available in a file folder. Simply fold the file folder along the creases and you'll create a box-like effect creating extra support and larger capacity.

- **Use box bottom folders.** For even more file folder space, use expandable box-bottom folders for large volume files.

- **Plastic tabs on the back.** When putting the plastic tabs on hanging file folders, you have the option of putting the plastic tab on the front of the hanging file or the back. Personally, I like putting the tabs on the back of the hanging file, but there's really no right or wrong way. Just do it consistently— either all on the front or all on the back.

## Organizing Clinic

### Question

We create a lot of paper! I need a detailed, creative way of filing documents that pertain to many, many different areas. Help. We can't find anything now!

S. Walker

### Answer

Dear S. Walker,

It's very important to first determine the major categories of paper you have and to separate them (Category A, Category B, Category C, etc.) Once you've done this, dedicate certain file drawers to certain categories and label the file drawers accordingly.

If you must put more than one category in one file drawer, you can use colored, hanging file folders to separate the categories. For instance, a typical business filing system might have financial categories in green hanging folders, management categories in blue, client categories in red and marketing in yellow. This will definitely help to keep everything separated. Plus if you're looking for a file that falls into any of those categories, the color will immediately catch your eye.

---

- **Avoid paper clips.** Paper clips take up unnecessary space. They often fall off the papers and land at the bottom of the filing cabinet. They also tend to get caught on other papers. If your papers are in a file folder, there's little reason to paperclip them. They're not going anywhere. If you really must group papers together, staple them together.

   Another reason to do away with paperclips is that many metallic ones today become magnetized, either because they were sold in a magnetic dispenser or came in contact with one. Anything magnetic can have a disastrous effect on a floppy disc with stored information. Switching to vinyl-covered paper clips only adds more bulk. It's better to keep them out of your files.

- **Don't fold.** Be sure to unfold papers and letters before inserting them into your file folders to save space. Folded paper is bulky.

- **Use a label maker.** If you absolutely must type (perhaps your handwriting isn't the best or there might be a medical reason), then you might wish to invest in a label maker. They're portable and they're definitely better than having to drag out the old typewriter every time you need a label.

- **It's not a scribbling pad.** Except for the tab, don't write other descriptions on the surface of your file folders. If you do, you will never be able to use that file folder for anything else without crossing out whatever was scribbled on it in the first place, eventually causing the file folder to look messy.

### Great idea!

Label your file folders neatly and high on the tab at the top of the folder. That way, you'll be able to read your writing when the folders are full and the filing cabinet is stuffed.

Chad Gracia, President of the Gracia Group
The Gracia Group is a consulting firm specializing in providing services to governments and businesses in the Middle East. Visit: www.graciagroup.com

- **Black marker marks the spot.** Some people like to write out the file folder descriptions on the tab in pencil. They figure that if they wish to change the description later on, that pencil mark can be easily erased. The problem, however, is that pencil tends to smudge. Additionally, pencil is not that easy to see clearly in a filing cabinet, especially if a very fine point pencil is used.

  Since one of the most important aspects of a good filing system is being able to actually see what's written on the label, I would recommend that you write the tab out with a medium-point black marker. It's easier to see in the filing cabinet and if you have to change the description later, you can stick a blank label over the old description and re-identify the contents.

- **Cursive writing is for love letters, not file folders.** When labeling file folders, always print your file description on the tab. It's much easier to read print than cursive writing at a glance and it makes filing easier. This is especially true if other people will also be accessing the filing cabinet. No matter how nice your handwriting is, you'll be making it much easier on everyone if you print.

- **A sticky note won't do.** After seeing various filing systems, I can't stress enough to identify the contents of the file folder either directly on the tab or with a label stuck securely to the tab. Please don't identify your file folder contents by sticking a sticky note on the center of the file folder.

  First, you won't be able to see a sticky note when the file folder is in your filing cabinet. Second, the glue on sticky notes is not meant to be permanent, which means it's eventually going to fall off the folder. When it falls off, there's a good chance that folder is going to be misplaced.

## Great idea!

It pays to buy quality supplies when it comes to file folders, both manila and the hanging type. Manila folders with reinforced tabs not only last longer, they're easier to use than store brands.

First, the reinforcement protects your fingers and cuticles from paper cuts.

In addition, these better quality folders are easier to create new folds when you need to use the expandable feature.

Likewise, the hanging files you purchase should be of high quality. With high-quality supplies, you can set up the bulk of your household or business files once and still use the same system effectively 20 years later.

Tracy Wyman
The Clutter Buster
Tallahassee, Florida
850-205-5279
solutions@clutterbuster.org
www.clutterbuster.org

- **When it just can't get lost.** For file folders containing legal or financial data that would cost the company dearly if lost, use file folders with two-punch fasteners at the top, always placing the most recent papers on top. Use these file folders sparingly and only when very necessary, as they take much more space.

- **Use hanging binders.** Hanging binders are wonderful for keeping large groups of paper together in your filing cabinet. They look like regular 3-ring binders, but they have tabs that actually sit just like hanging file folders in your filing cabinet.

You can fill one with several papers or fill one with pocket folders to keep papers in one place, but separated into categories.

Judy, a training coordinator, uses these hanging binders—one for each training subject in her company. Each binder holds 5 pocket folders for presentation materials, handouts, statistics, questions/answers and trainee worksheets.

# Chapter 13

# Setting up and using your filing system

- **Know your filing system.** Many people have different methods of filing. Some are good systems. Some are disastrous. One person told me that she filed her bank statements under *Jack*. When I asked her why, she nonchalantly told me she did it because Jack was her banker. Not a good reason.

  Anyway, there are a variety of filing systems. The trick is determining which one would work best for the type(s) of information you need to file. Here's a rundown of some of the more basic systems:

  ❖ **Alphabetical:** This is the most basic type of filing system and it's also the most common. It means that you file your file folders in the same sequence as the alphabet (A, B, C, D and so on.)

  Many people file their customer names and employee names using an alphabetical system, because names are generally easiest to find when they're filed this way.

  ❖ **Numerical:** If you choose this type of filing system, you would put your file folders in number order (1001, 1002, 1003, 1004, etc.)

  A common use for numerical filing would be if you have to look up a file by account number.

  ❖ **Chronological:** Chronological filing systems are organized by date (Jan, Feb, Mar or Jan 1, Jan 2, Jan 3, Jan 4, etc.)

  You might use a chronological filing system to locate financial statements or paycheck stubs.

  ❖ **Geographical:** This is filing by geographical location (East Coast, Midwest, West Coast, Canada and so on.)

  This type of filing system may be helpful, for instance, if you have sales managers who cover certain regions of the country.

  ❖ **Combination:** Many filing systems are a combination of two or more of the filing systems I just mentioned.

  For instance, let's say you wish to file geographically by coast (East Coast and West Coast). Within those files, you might file alphabetically by sales representative. Within the sales representative files, you might file numerically by account number. Your system might look like this:

**East Coast**
    Andrews, Mike
        228-2938
        228-2939
        228-2940
    Gleason, Tom
        229-1019
        229-1020
        229-1021
    Palmer, Dennis
        230-8126
        230-8127
        230-8128

**West Coast**
    Abrams, Sheila
        231-4938
        231-4939
        231-4940
    Larrabee, Kathy
        232-9005
        232-9006
        232-9007
    Zabar, Eric
        233-4609
        233-4610
        233-4611

### Great idea!

Color-coding your files by category allows you to find information quickly. The number of different colors you should use will depend on the nature of your business and the type of information you keep in your files, but you will likely need at least five: customers, suppliers, finances, forms and information.

For example, you can use green for your financial records, setting up an individual file folder for each income and expense category and red for your customer files, setting up an individual file for each customer.

Within each category, the folders should be clearly labeled and filed alphabetically.

Janet Barclay, owner of Organized Assistant, is a Time Management Consultant, Professional Organizer and Virtual Assistant. For more information visit www.organizedassistant.com

- **Save your creativity for another time.** The most important thing to determine is the absolute easiest way to find what you're looking for within a few seconds. You should never have to finger through your file folders searching for something endlessly because your filing system is too complicated.

Always ask yourself, "What is the most logical way to file the type of information I have?" If you have to search by name or subject, use an alphabetical system.

If you have to search by account or other number, use a numerical filing system.

If you have to search by day, month, year or another period of time, use a chronological filing system.

And if you have to search by area or region, use a geographical filing system.

These methods are the basic foundation of your filing systems. If you need to further organize your filing system, use a combination of the basic filing systems.

## Great idea!

I discovered a very helpful and professional looking file labeling system in the Smead Viewables Labels for hanging files and file folders. Initially, you purchase a starter kit in which you receive everything needed to begin setting up your files—software to install on your computer as well as tabs, labels and label protectors. You can then purchase refills of anything else you need.

The hanging file labels are attached to a three-sided plastic hanging folder tab. This allows the labels to be read from the front, back or top. Clear adhesive label protectors are attached to each tab for a smooth look.

You can color coordinate your files (very helpful!) with the color labeling system or simply use the black and white labeling system.

The hanging file labels as well as the file folder labels are generated on the computer using a template and then printed on your printer.

Colleen V. Isaac
Executive Secretary
Loyola University Medical Center
2160 South First Avenue, Maywood, Illinois 60153
cisaac1@lumc.edu

- **Keep it short and sweet.** When describing the contents in a file folder, you don't have much room to describe the contents on the tiny label. This means you have to be very concise when determining what to label your file folders.

Ninety-nine percent of the time, you should be able to identify the contents of the folder in three words or less.

## Great idea!

I like to use hanging file folders to separate papers for filing. Sometimes I'll get behind and then discover a big stack of papers waiting to be divided and put away. When that happens, I just drop a few empty hanging file folders into the front of a file cabinet drawer and then start separating the papers by category into the hanging folders.

I make sure that the cabinet drawer is at a comfortable height for me to work. Usually the second drawer up from the bottom is a good one, as it allows me to work from a seated position.

I also sometimes use a portable file box, which allows me to work on filing while seated in a more comfortable chair.

The "hanging file method" also has at least three advantages over dividing my papers on the floor or on my desktop.

It's more comfortable, it allows me to separate my papers into several more categories at the same time and (my favorite) it lets me put my filing project on hold at any time, close the drawer and not have to clean up a mess before moving on to another task.

Mike Logan
Logan's Logic
256-348-7485

- **Be consistent.** While visiting with a friend of mine, she asked me for some advice on her filing system. She said she was having difficulties finding files once she filed them.

A quick glance showed me she was very inconsistent in naming her files. For example, one file was called Jerry Smith (First Name – Last Name), another was called Jacobs, Emily (Last Name-First Name).

It was easy to see why she was having difficulties finding her information.

Consistency is very important. If you start using the Last Name, First Name format on your file folders, continue to use that format throughout your system.

For example:

Jacobs, Andrew

Ponne, Mary

Smith, Mike

In addition, if you have similar file folder categories, keep them in separate file folders, but file them all together in one area. For instance:

Computer Software: Act

Computer Software: Microsoft Excel

Computer Software: Windows

This way, similar items won't be scattered around throughout your filing system. Anytime you need to find one of your computer software folders, you'll find it listed under "C."

- **Miscellaneous is not a file description.** A file labeled Miscellaneous becomes a catch all for everything you're not sure where to file. It's also known as the "lazy man's category."

Every single sheet of paper that is good enough to file away deserves to be placed in a properly categorized file folder. Try to think of the major category this paper falls in. Financial? Employee Related? Marketing? Ideas? There is always, always, always a better file category available than Miscellaneous.

- **Keep the recent stuff in the front.** Some people like to file oldest stuff in the front of the file folder and newest stuff in the back. I prefer just the opposite; newest in the front and oldest in the back. This way, when you open the file folder, you immediately see the most recent information. It's rare when you're going to want to reference the oldest information.

- **Organize within the file folder.** Don't just toss papers in your file folders in any old order. I usually recommend filing the most recent information towards the front and the oldest information in the back. Or, if names in the file folder are more relevant, organize alphabetically.

The contents in each file folder you have should be stored in an organized, systematic manner for easy retrieval later.

- **Use the "two-inch" rule.** If a file folder is filled with more than 2 inches of paper, it should be weeded out. If it's still full after weeding, create another file folder for that subject. Label the first one with an A and the second with a B. For example, Clark, Janice-A and Clark, Janice-B.

- **Write. Don't type.** Unless you have lots of time on your hands, don't type labels for your file folders. Print by hand instead and you'll be done in seconds.

- **Labeling Consistently.** Be consistent when labeling file folder tabs. If you choose a computer-labeling program, you will need to stick with it for the files to have a neat, consistent appearance.

  If you would like to add files quickly, using a black felt tip pen will give you an easy way to create readable files. Whichever option you choose, stay consistent with the labeling or your file system will have a cluttered look and some files may be overlooked.

  Additionally, the format should also be consistent—Title Case is easier on the eyes than all capital letters.

---

### Great idea!

My husband and I have run his home-building business for 14 years (and now my organizing business) out of our home. Keeping files organized and separated is a must!

Any home office should keep household and personal bills separate from business files. Make sure personal and business files are in separate drawers (i.e. top drawer for business and bottom drawer for personal.)

It will also help if you choose different colored hanging file folders for each (i.e. red for business and green for personal).

In our case, three different file drawers and three different colored file folders keep two businesses separate from our household files.

If your filing system is set up like this from the beginning, it makes it much easier to keep bills paid on time and out of the correct checking account for business and home.

Jackie Dunaway
Mind Over Clutter Professional Organizing
7560 Lascassas Pk, Lascassas, TN 37085
615-273-1067 (local to Nashville, TN)
mindoverclutter@msn.com
www.mind-over-clutter.com

---

- **Remember, it's not set in stone.** Just because you have your filing system set up one way, doesn't mean you can't change it. I know, you're probably saying that it's too much of a hassle to re-organize it.

  I'll even admit that it's going to take a little while to get your filing system exactly the way it should be so that you can find what you're looking for in seconds.

  But, believe me, it's worth it. The more organized your filing system is, the less chaotic your life will be. An organized filing system will allow you to use your time productively, rather than wasting time searching for files in a disorganized system.

---

## Organizing Clinic

### Question

My husband and I have taken over a small 35-employee construction company and there is no organization for filing. Is there a standard system that I can implement so we can find the documents we need when we need them? Thank you!

Swamped in Paper

### Answer

Dear Swamped,

Having an organized filing system is a must for all businesses. It's vital to be able to find papers instantly. Otherwise lots of valuable time will be wasted.

First, come up with your 'Major' Filing Categories. For most businesses, these include categories such as Employees, Financial, Legal, Vendors and Marketing.

Once you've done this, it will be easier for you to know where to file your sub-categories.

For instance, in the Employees section, you would have all files that pertain to your employees, probably in alphabetical order.

In the Financial section, you would have Accounts Payable, Accounts Receivable, Overdue Accounts, Bank Accounts, Loans and so on.

Finally, if you're really having difficulties with this, you might want to buy a pre-made filing system in which the categories have already been thought out for you.

---

- **Create a file index.** If you are having trouble deciding how to file, create a file index. On a separate piece of paper (or the computer) create a list of the categories you need to file and the order in which you would like to file them.

  Once you get a general idea, you can create your file system with the blueprint you have established.

  Also, for complicated filing or if others are using your filing system, your file index is an easy way for others to review your system without rummaging through the files.

- **File as you go.** I've found that the very best way to avoid having to spend hours filing, is to file your papers as you go, rather than temporarily putting them in a To File pile.

## Organizing Clinic

### Question

Can't I write my file descriptions directly on the file folder tab, rather than first sticking on a label and then writing the description on the label? It seems that buying labels is a waste of money.

Stan Franklin
Las Vegas, NV

### Answer

Dear Stan,

There's no absolute rule that forces you to use file folder labels, but I will tell you why I like using them.

If I wrote directly on the tab and wanted to change a file description later, I would certainly not mess up the folder by crossing out the old description. What I would do is stick a clean, white label over the old description. I would then have a clear surface for identifying the new contents.

I wouldn't like it if some of my file folders had labels and some did not. Inconsistency gives a disorganized look. Therefore, I suggest using labels right from the beginning.

The more uniform your system looks, the easier it will be to find what you're looking for.

---

- **Or at least do it daily.** If you just can't bring yourself to file as you go, then at least set aside 10 minutes each afternoon to file away your papers. Don't allow the papers to sit more than one day or they're bound to get out of hand.

  Most people hate filing, but it's only because they've allowed their filing to grow instead of just taking care of it every day.

  Veronica, who worked in a mailroom, hated to file. She figured that if she just let the filing pile up all week, she would only have to file once each week.

  As it turned out, the filing pile got so high at the end of the week, she was too overwhelmed to file. And each week, the pile grew taller and taller until it completely fell over on the floor.

  Her boss was furious and hired a temporary employee to catch up on Veronica's filing backlog. He then tossed Veronica's To File tray and instructed her to file immediately, as soon as she received a paper that needed to be filed. This was years ago and Veronica was never caught behind in her filing since!

- **Cross reference when necessary.** If a sheet of paper is appropriate for two different file folders and you are not sure which one to file it in, file it in one of them. Then, open the other file folder and tape a sheet of paper to the left hand side. List the name of the paper to be cross-referenced and what folder it is being stored in. In doing this, you can use the one taped paper for several cross-references, without having to make duplicate copies of every paper you file.

---

### Great idea!

The FILE system will help you decide where you should file, how you should file and how to maintain your files.

Further away. If you are filing files that are only used periodically or possibly never, file them furthest away from your workspace.

Immediate area. Your immediate area of course is your workspace area. So files that are used more than once or twice a week can be filed in your desk draw or in an organizer on your desk. Caution: Do not clutter your desk by placing too many folders on it.

Local area. Files that are used on a monthly basis can be filed in your credenza or a filing cabinet nearby.

Easily accessible. Wherever you are filing your records make sure they are easily accessible. Being easily accessible would include using labeling that has broad titles. They are labeled with titles that are easily retrieved by all in your office or home.

Yvonne Surrey
Y.E.S. Surrey Office Services
181 Hawthorne Street, Suite 1H, Brooklyn, NY 11225
www.sos-organizing.com

---

- **Action, reference or archive?** There are three different kinds of files:
  - ❖ **Action:** Papers that require some sort of action, like calling someone or writing a letter, should be placed in an Action or Active filing system.

    You don't want to put Action papers in your regular filing system where they may be forgotten.

    Instead, it is recommended that you have a portable file holder to temporarily hold papers that require action or that you use a Tickler File or Project Management Binder until the action is completed.

  - ❖ **Reference:** This is your regular filing system that you would use to reference papers on a regular basis or in the near future.

No action is required on these papers, except your reference from time to time.

❖ **Archive:** Depending on what type of work you do, keeping all of your papers year in and year out may grow to be enormous. Plus, keeping old papers in your filing cabinet that you rarely reference is a waste of space.

Any papers or files that you hardly ever look at, but you're required to keep, can be stored in an archived filing system. For example, if you have a home business, you can file all tax related information for previous years in cardboard file boxes in your basement or attic.

If you work for someone, perhaps you can convince him/her to get another filing cabinet to store this type of information or use the cardboard file boxes and store them in your company's basement, separate filing area or outside storage facility.

Be careful not to archive unnecessary papers. Tax and financial types of papers generally need to be kept a long time, but things like old maps and old telephone lists can most likely be tossed so they're not taking up valuable filing space.

## Great idea!

Assign a different color to each project you are working on and get matching supplies like ink pens, hi-liters, paper clips and file folders. That way you can organize each project individually so it will be easy to identify visually. Whenever you need to add a document to a project file or edit an existing document, make sure you identify it with the corresponding color—either by adding a colored paper clip or writing in the corresponding color of ink—and you'll never again come across a loose paper and ask yourself: "Now where does this belong" or "how will I find it later?"

Take your color scheme a step further and use the colors red, yellow and green to create instantly identifiable files—we're used to these colors in our traffic lights and each color has a different meaning we recognize instantly. For example, in a law firm, you could use red for cases lost, green for cases won and yellow for cases pending or in court. Use your imagination and apply it to your work environment. I work in sales and marketing, so red for me is proposals lost/customers at risk, green is for proposals won/customer advocates and yellow is for current or pending proposals/vulnerable customers.

Shari Puddicombe
5-S S.O.S.: Simple Organizing Solutions
1388 Charbonneau, LaSalle, QC, Canada H8N 1M2
Phone: 514-365-5495, Cell: 514-883-4021
5-S S.O.S. helps you create order and harmony out of clutter and chaos!

- **Papers can morph.** An Action paper, once the action is completed, can either become a Reference paper or even an Archive paper. A Reference paper may later turn into an Action paper.

- **Organize the backlog.** If your current filing system is totally out of whack, you will need to spend some time getting it under control. Set aside a few days—preferably a weekend when others aren't around—to work on this project.

  If you find you're having a difficult time figuring out what to keep, what to toss and what category to file under, you should consider one of the pre-fabricated filing systems on the market. Or, consider hiring a professional organizer to help you get a good system in place.

- **Start with the newest.** When getting your filing backlog under control, start with the newest paperwork and work backwards. Chances are, you won't need most of the older paperwork. Chances also are that you will need to look at paperwork that is more recent. The quicker you get the recent papers filed, the better.

- **Here's just a few.** While all office filing systems will differ depending on the type of industry and needs of the business, here are some general office filing categories to get you started:

| | | | |
|---|---|---|---|
| Accounts Payable | Computer | Operations | Sales and Marketing |
| Accounts Receivable | Employees | Overnight Mail | Seminars/Workshops |
| Administrative | Existing Customers | Past Customers | Software |
| Advertising | Expenses | Postal Mail | Stationary |
| Articles | Goals and Plans | Project Files-Current | Suppliers |
| Assets | Human Resources | Project Files-Future | Tax Related |
| Business Forms | Insurance | Prospective Customers | Trade Publications |
| Business Plan | Legal | Public Relations | Training |
| Catalogs | Liabilities | Reference | Travel |
| Company Policies | Office Equipment | Research | Vendors |

# Chapter 14

# Weeding out your files

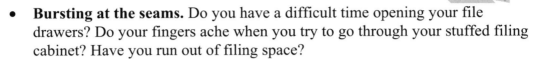

- **Bursting at the seams.** Do you have a difficult time opening your file drawers? Do your fingers ache when you try to go through your stuffed filing cabinet? Have you run out of filing space?

  Is it virtually impossible to retrieve a sheet of paper from your filing cabinet without ripping it or without pulling a stack of other papers along with it? Are your file folders so packed that the folders are tearing apart?

  If you answered yes to any of these questions, it's time to weed out the papers in your filing cabinet.

---

### Great idea!

In an attempt to eliminate duplicate files, weed out unnecessary files, and have a reference for what is in our files, I have created a "File Listing" of all the files in our office.

Each area under my supervisor's span of control has its own tab within a notebook. I then list each hanging file in alphabetical order as well as the file(s) within each one.

This list is on my computer and whenever a new file is needed, I check to be sure there isn't one already made.

If a new hanging file is needed, I put this new file on the list and replace the page in my notebook.

In order to be efficient, I try to devote Friday mornings to doing my filing. This system is helpful to my supervisor as he can pick up the file listing and determine where he would like something filed.

It is also helpful because he can review the file listing periodically and easily eliminate any unnecessary files.

Colleen V. Isaac
Executive Secretary
Loyola University Medical Center
2160 South First Avenue, Maywood, Illinois 60153
cisaac1@lumc.edu

---

- **Leave 3 to 4 inches.** Each of your file drawers should have a minimum of three to four inches of empty space, so you can easily finger through files when you need to find one.

- **How often should I weed?** Just as a garden can get out of hand if you don't weed often, the same goes for your filing system.

  If you're very conscientious about putting only very important papers in your filing cabinet and you don't file tons of papers every day, then you only have to weed out once or twice a year.

  But, if you're constantly stuffing papers in your filing cabinet or you're not that discerning about what you're filing, then you should probably weed out once a month or once every two months at most. This way, you will be able to keep it under control.

- **Weed as you go.** A good system for keeping your system free of papers you don't need is to weed every time you pull out a file folder. Every time you remove a file folder, simply take a few minutes to toss anything inside that is no longer relevant.

- **Archive important files.** There are some files that you may have to keep for a long period of time, such as tax-related documents or old employee files.

  You can't keep all of these old files in your everyday filing cabinet. If you do, you most likely won't have space for your everyday reference files.

  If it's going to be rare that you ever look at these old files, but you're required to keep them by law, they should be archived.

  If you're fortunate enough to have an area in your office basement or another file storage room to place your older files, move them to this area.

  If not, these old files can be boxed up and stored in an out-of-the-way area or an outside storage facility.

- **Use file markers when purging.** The thought of purging files can seem overwhelming. However, there is a way to divide the task so that you can purge a portion of your files periodically, instead of all at one time.

  Set aside a certain amount of time for purging. It can be fifteen minutes or one hour. Starting from the beginning, go through each file and determine if a) it is still needed, b) it should be archived or c) you need to keep the file but some of the outdated papers inside can be trashed.

  At the end of the time period, insert a file marker behind the last file you examined for purging.

  A file marker can be a manila (or colored) file folder inverted perpendicularly so that it sticks up slightly. This will "mark" your purge spot for the next time you resume file purging.

## Organizing Clinic

### Question

What about those of us who just don't like filing and don't want to break ourselves of the piling habit. Is there a way to make piling productive and organized?

Martha Powers
Indianapolis, IN

### Answer

Dear Martha,

My first recommendation to anyone who piles, is NOT to pile. The problem with piling is that it easily gets out of control. When it does, the person is generally too overwhelmed to get the stuff filed away and it has to be filed one way or the other eventually.

When you file as you go, you never have to worry about papers taking over your life. They will be filed and ready to access whenever you need them, without you having to waste time shuffling through hundreds of papers.

It only takes a minute to file one sheet of paper, but it could take hours or days to file piles of paper.

If it's just not convenient to file as you go, like if your filing area is not in your immediate office or you just can't bring yourself to do so, I would recommend that you pile for no more than one day. This is really important. If you let it go for more than one day, you're bound to end up with a mountain.

If you're piling several categories of papers, such as Things to Do, Papers to Delegate, Papers to Mail or Papers to Copy, then I would suggest you get yourself several wire baskets or stackable trays and label them. This way you pile into a basket/tray, but the basket/tray is already categorized for you. This will help you save filing time later.

At the end of each day, schedule 15 minutes for filing and stick to that schedule. Don't leave the office until your entire pile is filed away, either in your filing cabinet if no further action is needed, or your Tickler or Projects file if further action is required.

---

- **Just in time purging.** Another way to purge files is to examine file folders if they start to "grow." If a file folder is more than one inch in width, it may be time to purge.

  Also, as you retrieve files, check a file that has not been touched in a while. This file may be a candidate for archiving or purging. Taking care of a few files here and there may be enough to keep your filing system in control.

## Great idea!

A painless way to purge files for the home office is to simply take one or two files out whenever you watch TV. Weed out unneeded papers during commercials. Put purged folders back in the filing cabinet at the end of the TV show. Do this steadily over a long period of time and before you know it, you will have weeded out your filing cabinet and not even noticed the work!

Linda Richards
Organize and More
352-373-1086
Linda@organizeandmore.net
www.organizeandmore.net

- **Does your company have a file room and staff?** Keep a "Return to File" tray in your office. The file person can then easily collect material from you on a daily basis. If there is no file retrieval person, have the tray anyway. At the end of the day, you can return all necessary materials to the file room for storage.

- **Think before you file.** To keep weeding out your filing system to a minimum, scrutinize every sheet of paper you plan to file. Does it really need to be filed? Do you need to keep it? Is there any chance you're going to need it again? Is it a slim chance? Don't file documents you're never going to look at again.

- **Don't move your files without checking.** If you're planning to move from one location to another, that is the perfect time to give your filing system a good weeding out. Don't move files that are not needed.

- **Institute a File Purging Day.** If you're the boss or the manager, declare a specific date as "File Purging Day." On this day, all of your staff members will be required to purge out their files. This is a good way to help your staff members keep their filing systems up to date.

# Chapter 15

# Paper clutter and
# paper flow management

- **How does it happen?** Most paper piles start innocently. You're not exactly sure where to put a sheet a paper, so you put it down—just for now. Perhaps you are working on a number of projects at once and are afraid that if you put those papers away, you'll forget about them. Maybe you fear if they're out of sight you won't be able to find them later on.

  Of course, leaving everything on your desk—whether in piles or in solitaire card fashion—is not effective. This is how piles start and grow. In addition, piles of paper can easily begin to take over your office until they get so out of hand that you don't know how you'll ever get everything organized again.

- **It's the decision, not the paper.** In general, it's usually not the paper that's causing paper clutter in your life. Most of the time the problem lies in making the "decision" about what to do with the paper.

- **The 4 D's.** Wondering how to begin tackling your paperwork mountain? To make it easy for you, take comfort in the fact that there is only one of four decisions to make with a piece of paper. Pick up each sheet of paper and take one of these actions:

  - ❖ **Do it.** This means that you take appropriate action on this paper today or tomorrow at the very latest.

  - ❖ **Delegate it.** If possible, give this paper to someone else who is capable of performing the appropriate action.

  - ❖ **Delay it.** Also known as File it. Place this paper in your Current Projects file or your permanent files.

  - ❖ **Dump it.** Over eighty percent or more of the paper that enters your office can be discarded immediately. If your company has a recycling program, be sure to dump it in the recycling container.

- **The "Delay it" category.** This is the one "D" that many people have trouble with. The main idea is to have a good holding place for these papers until you're ready to work on them, without having them scattered all over your desk. The Delay it category can be broken up into a few different sub-categories, such as a) Current Projects, b) Future Projects, c) Reference, d) Reading and e) Legal or Tax Related.

**Great idea!**

Do not wait to place important documents in your Tickler file. Put them in immediately, otherwise you may throw out or misplace an important document.

Paul Heller, Research Director, MGM Networks

- **Delay it: Current Projects.** There is a fantastic system for storing these "Delay It" type of papers. It's called the "Current Projects Holding System" and you can set it up within a few minutes:
  - ❖ You will need:
    - o One 2 inch, 3-ring binder
    - o 10 pocket folders: these folders can be purchased at office supplies stores. They are 3-hole punched and fit into any standard 3-ring binder.
    - o Removable file folder labels, approximately 1" to 2" in size
    - o A pen or marker
  - ❖ To assemble:
    - o Insert the pocket folders into your binder.
    - o Put one removable file folder label on each pocket folder, on the bottom right.
    - o On each label, write the name of one of your projects.
    - o When you're done, place all of the papers that pertain to each of your projects in the properly labeled pocket folder.
  - ❖ To use:
    - o Now all of your projects are categorized and ready to be flipped to whenever you're ready to tackle one of them. Work on one project at a time.
    - o Once a project is completed, those papers should be removed from the pocket folder and filed in your filing cabinet for future reference if necessary, discarded if you don't need to keep these papers any longer or passed on to an appropriate recipient.
    - o By the way, you shouldn't have more than a few "current" projects going on at any one time and ten is definitely the absolute maximum.

- **Delay it: Future Projects.** You can use the exact system described above with another binder and call that system your "Future Projects Holding System" if you'd like. Or, you might opt to use the "Tickler System" described below, also referred to as the "31-Day Reminder System":
  - ❖ You will need:
    - o 12 hanging file folders
    - o 31 manila file folders
    - o File folder labels
    - o A pen or marker
    - o A portable file box (only if you don't plan to use your filing cabinet or desk file drawer)
  - ❖ To assemble:
    - o Label 12 hanging file folders by month—Jan, Feb, Mar, etc. all the way to December.
    - o Place these folders in a container that holds hanging file folders, such as a filing cabinet, a portable file box or portable file holder.
    - o Label 31 manila file folders—in a different color than the hanging file folders—1,2,3,4, etc. all the way up to 31. The 31 file folders represent each day of each month.
    - o Place all 31 manila file folders in the hanging folder for the current month. In other words, if the current month is May, put the 31 manila file folders in that month. If the current month is November, put the 31 manila file folders in that month.
  - ❖ To use:
    - o When you have a task or project you're not ready to start right now but would like to start in a few days or a few months from now, no problem! Slip the appropriate documents into the appropriate day—or month—and it will be there later when you need it. For example, if you have to do something on the 14th of the month, put the required documents in folder number 14 and add extra notes as needed.
    - o If you need to start the task before a certain day of the month, put a note in the folder a number of days ahead of the date that it's due. For instance, if a customer's birthday is coming up on August 20th and you want to send him a greeting card ahead of time, put a note or the actual greeting card in your Tickler System in folder number 10, for instance, and your card will make it to your customer on time.

o   For items that are to be started in another month, put a note in the hanging file folder for that particular month. If the current month is December, but the task needs to be done in February, a note pertaining to that task should go in the folder labeled February. Be sure to give each paper a due date.

o   When the current month ends, all 31 manila file folders should be moved to the following month. Any papers that were in the hanging file folder for the month should be moved into specific days, based on the due dates you previously assigned.

o   The first task on your To Do list each day should be to check your Tickler System. The system will not work if you don't get into the habit of checking it daily. If you're having difficulties getting into this habit, set an alarm to go off at a set time each day until you can do it without being reminded. Eventually, it will be very natural.

o   Finally, if you have to reschedule a task or event, move the note from the date it's in, to another month or day in your system.

o   You can also "roll" your tickler file every day. As you check each day, place the empty tickler file at the end of the files. Thus, if today is the 16th, process the papers for the 16th and place the 16 folder at the end of the files. Tomorrow, the 17 folder will be the first folder in the tickler system.

### Great idea!

To avoid piling too many papers in one day's tickler, create a "Free Slot" flag. If you are using hanging folders, this would be a color-coded file tab with the words Free Slot.

As you work your ticklers, if you have a folder with 3 or more items in it, attach the Free Slot tab to the next folder that has less than 3 items in it.

This is an easy way to help you schedule items that don't have a specific due date, without scheduling too much in one day. If you are using manila folders, you can use a piece of colored card stock as the free slot marker.

Maribel Ibrahim, Executive Editor of *Finally Organized, Finally Free for the Office* and owner of www.abundantliving.net

•   **Delay it: Occasional Reference.** The best thing to do with papers that fall into this category is to file them away. Out of sight does not have to be out of mind if you use proper filing techniques:

❖ **Articles:** We have a wonderful system to help you organize your articles in this book in the Chapter titled Magazines and Magazine Articles.

❖ **Recurring reference papers:** These are papers that you have to look at on consistent days, such as the first Tuesday of each month or every quarter. File these papers in your filing cabinet under an appropriate category. Then, using your calendar, mark each day these papers must be referenced so you don't forget. You might consider using an abbreviation on your calendar, such as FLU (File Lookup). Include the File Name and File Location so you know exactly where these papers are the next time you need them.

❖ **All other reference papers:** These papers should be filed in your filing cabinet in categorized file folders. Don't file under the "Miscellaneous" category. Use very specific names, such as Insurance Account #586739 or Tax Write Offs or Meeting Notes.

If you're worried you won't be able to find a sheet of paper after you file it away, you may consider creating an index using your word processing software or better yet, a spreadsheet program like Excel if you know how to use one. Create three columns:

1. **Category:** This might be Taxes, or Payroll, or Finances, or Self-Help

2. **Description:** Describe the papers as specifically as possible. An example might be: *Possible tax write-off*

3. **File Location:** This might be: *green filing cabinet, 2ⁿᵈ drawer, Smith file*

Every time you file a sheet of paper, first type the appropriate information in your Index computer file. In the future, you can use your automatic *find feature* to quickly search for specific words or phrases to help you locate the paper you're looking for.

• **Delay it: Reading Materials:** Your reading pile can easily grow into a mountain if you let the papers pile up for days. First, consider how much you're actually going to be able to read. Most people collect reading material that would take 10 lifetimes to get through. Be selective in the reading material you keep and keep up with it.

❖ **Option 1:** Using your Tickler File, drop the paper you wish to read in a specific day slot. When that day arrives, read the paper you've inserted.

❖ **Option 2:** Create a traveling reading folder to take with you everywhere you go. There are always opportunities to catch up on your reading.

❖ **Option 3:** Keep a shallow basket (no more than 6 inches tall) in your office marked "To Read." Next, grab your calendar and schedule time each day to read the papers in this basket. Each day, during your scheduled time, read the papers in your basket. Rule: If the papers in your basket begin to pile over the rim, it's time to begin recycling some of that reading material. You were probably too ambitious in your original reading goals and if the pile has grown way over the top of the basket, chances are you'll never get to all of it.

## Great idea!

The one idea I use with all my business/home-business clients is the concept of a Business Bible or Business Notebook. This eliminates the many little pieces of papers I find all over my clients' offices and desks. I recommend they keep a running commentary of what goes on in their business, like every phone call that comes in, every phone call that goes out and every action item they need to do.

The unique thing about this notebook is the "key" that I have them use. If they call someone and leave a message, then I have them underline the name. If they call someone and actually connect with them, I have them draw a rectangle around their name. If there is an action item that they need to follow up with, I have them put a little box in the margin next to the item.

Once they have completed the action item, they check off the little box. This way they can quickly flip back through pages and see what they need to do yet or who they need to follow up with. I have many satisfied customers using this system.

Beth Randall
Joe Organizer
Plainfield, Illinois
815-436-1578
www.JoeOrganizer.com

• **Delay it: Keepers for Legal or Tax Reasons.** These papers are generally the most annoying because they take up tons of space and will rarely, if ever, be referenced.

Place them in categorized file folders as usual, keeping the file names as specific as possible. Then, try to keep these files someplace other than your regular, everyday filing cabinet.

Buy a few cardboard file boxes and store them in a separate storage area. Label the boxes and mark them with a discard date so you can trash them later—probably years from now.

- **What to keep? What to toss?** One of the biggest reasons people get overwhelmed with paper is because they're unsure whether or not they need that paper.

  The easy solution may seem to be just tossing it in the paper pile, but this results in mountains of paper.

  Here's a way to determine whether or not you need that paper. Just ask yourself:

  - ❖ **Did I request it?** Very often, the papers we receive each day are the result of automatic computer mailing lists—unsolicited mail. If you did not ask for it, there's an excellent chance you don't need it.

  - ❖ **Is it outdated?** This is a no-brainer. If the paper is outdated, it's of no value to you. Get rid of it.

  - ❖ **Can I get it somewhere else?** Sometimes you might be interested in a sheet of paper that contains information on an upcoming event or it contains informative information on a subject you're interested in.

    If the information you need is easy to retrieve from a web site, book, library, or elsewhere, then it's safe to toss the paper and get the information from the other source if and when you need it.

  - ❖ **What's the worst thing that could happen if I toss it and need it later?** If the answer is that you could lose your job, lose your business thousands of dollars or go to jail, then that's a good enough reason to keep that paper.

    If the answer is that you may have to look the information up on the Internet again or you'll have to call the person to send you another catalog, then obviously that situation wouldn't be too bad—and chances are, you won't need it later anyway.

- **Give it a home.** The majority of time, it will only take a few seconds to recycle or file it in your filing cabinet, Tickler File or Projects Binder. Don't just toss papers on your desk or in a pile. A second or two of thinking now can save an hour or two of searching later.

- **Make small pieces big.** Sometimes it's necessary to keep a small piece of paper, such as a coupon or an invitation. Rather than taking the chance of it getting lost, staple or tape that small piece of paper onto an 8" x 11" sheet and place in a file folder, your Tickler file or inside your planner.

## Great idea!

If you are an "out of sight, out of mind" person, do not feel obligated to change your personality to work within a traditional paper flow system. As new documents and mail enter your office, decide at that point what you will do with it (discard, call today, etc.)

Then, use various colored paperweights on your desk as an Inbox.

For instance, use green, yellow and red weights. When a new document or mail comes into your office decide if it is urgent (red), important (yellow) or To Be Done, but not urgent (green). File the paper under the appropriate weight.

You'll be able to see what has to be done each day and you will have a smaller chance of forgetting about a project. Then, as you begin each day, review what is filed under each weight and move papers as necessary.

What may look like chaos to others is now a flexible paper system specific to your work style!

Towanda L. Long
TimeStylist
P.O. Box 1245, Linden, NJ 07036
www.timestylist.com

- **Getting rid of paper the Lew Wasserman way.** With the constant flow of paperwork landing on your desk, it's imperative to have a simple system for keeping it under control.

  Lew Wasserman, president of MCA, was renowned for being ruthless with his paperwork and that of his executives. He would wander through the company's offices late in the evening looking for loose paper on the desks of others. Anything found would be thrown straight in the trash!

  He worked on the principle that if you couldn't finish whatever you were working on by the end of day or at least put the incomplete project in a proper holding place, then you're not working efficiently or effectively. His tactics, reportedly, resulted in a huge increase of productivity. Of course, before you start waging war on other people's paperwork, first ensure your own desk is under control.

- **Jot a note.** To assist with remembering what is to be done with each paper, write a small note in pencil on the top of the paper. Examples can be where to file the paper, who to delegate paper to or a deadline date for a response. This will speed up the process of assigning these papers to their permanent homes.

  Additionally, from a filing standpoint, you may decide to change the name of the file based on other related papers you encounter further down the pile.

Assigning a name before creating the file folder can eliminate a lot of rework and confusion.

---

## Organizing Clinic

### Question

I would like to organize my desk and get some of the clutter off but I have a problem of "if it's out of sight, then it's out of mind" and I'm afraid if I can't see it I will forget it.

Valerie Dillon

### Answer

Dear Valerie,

If your desk is filled with clutter, then most likely the papers on it are already out of sight and hidden underneath other papers and folders. Your desk should have plenty of room for you to work each day, without you feeling stressed or chaotic. This will give you an environment in which you can be both productive and creative.

If you work on several projects at one time, get yourself a 3-ring binder and insert several 3-hole punched pocket folders. Using removable labels, label each pocket folder with a specific project name. Keep all of your pending projects in your Projects binder until they're completed. You can keep the Projects binder on your desk or in your desk. Either way, all of your projects will be organized and there will be no clutter on your desk.

Keep your office supplies organized in desk caddies and in organizers within your desk drawers. Keep some stacking wire baskets on your desk, to collect incoming mail and outgoing mail. If you get a sheet of paper listing a task you have to work on or an event you will be attending, jot the task or event on your calendar or To Do list to jog your memory. Then, file the paper away until you need it again. It won't be "out of mind" because your calendar or To Do list will remind you of it.

---

- **Handle it here.** The last thing you want to do is handle your paper in several different places.

  For instance, if you have a home office, paper should be handled on one desk or one table in your home office—not in the kitchen sometimes and in the living room at other times.

  If you handle your paper in one single place, your papers will be condensed to one area and will have less of a chance of being misplaced somewhere else. The further away the paper gets from your regular paper handling area, the less of a chance you're going to find it when you need it.

## Great idea!

It won't take much to make you laugh. Two words: paperless society. It's true I shell out my mortgage by automatic withdrawal. Still my "paperless" transaction generates plenty of paper.

Paper organization is daunting. Pick up a ream of printer paper and plop the ream on your desk. Use it as a yardstick.

Notice that you have paperwork higher than those 500 sheets. Busy people close their eyes and add to the stack.

Dealing with the mess is intimidating. Somehow, our mind dictates that the papers must do a Samantha Stephens' bewitched type twist and float alphabetically into folders.

Impossible you say. You're right. Days pass and paperwork accumulates. You're still struggling to sort the early part of last year. Stop.

The way to get organized is to begin with today's mail. File. Act. Toss. Delegate. Or, put it on your calendar. Repeat. It takes 30 days to make a habit.

Imagine, a month where you do not add to your stacks. Next month, add to your habit. Deal with ten items from the old stacks daily.

At month end, you will have dealt with 300 items.

If you ever get discouraged, think paperless society, have a good chuckle and start again.

Lea Schneider, NAPO, is a professional organizer and owns Organize & More in Jackson, TN. Visit www.organize-and-more.com for your office, your home and your life.

---

- **Does your paper have the measles?** The old saying, "never pick up a sheet of paper more than once," is sometimes not an effective mantra. After all, if you're working on something and someone hands you a sheet of paper that requires an action, it's not generally productive to drop everything you're doing to handle the task on that paper.

On the other hand, paper shuffling—constantly moving paper from one pile to another—is not an effective system either.

From now on, every time you pick up a sheet of paper, pencil in a dot on it. When you pick up the paper again, pencil in another dot. Keep doing this each time you pick up that sheet of paper.

If a sheet of paper begins looking like it has the measles, you're just paper shuffling. Try to reduce your dots to no more than two to three dots per paper.

## Great idea!

You know paper clutter has gotten way out of control when a) you can't see the top of your desk and b) you are forever scrambling around to find important papers that you know are "here somewhere."

To start with, get a number of boxes and label them with appropriate names such as Taxes, Bills, Legal and Banking. As you sort through piles of papers they can be just tossed into the correct box. Once everything is sorted into the appropriate box, filing correctly is a breeze. Just continue to categorize. For example bills can be broken down into separate files for Venders, Utilities, and Telephone and dated so that the most recent bill is on top.

TIP: If you don't already own one, consider buying a shredder. It will protect your privacy, plus it makes parting with paper clutter kind of fun. If you work at home, the kids can even help!

Elizabeth Hanley
Coyote Professional Organizing
Hagersville Ontario Canada
Coyote81067@hotmail.com

# Chapter 16

# Handling incoming and outgoing mail

- **Open and dump.** Always open your mail over your recycling container so you can immediately toss the pieces you don't need, such as unsolicited advertising and bulk rate mailings.

  If you do this, junk mail will never have a chance to start building on your desk or credenza. Don't waste time opening junk mail that you don't want or don't need.

- **Record. Then dump.** When you receive mail reminding you of dates for meetings or appointments, immediately jot the date and time on your calendar. Then, toss the reminder mail.

## Great idea!

As soon as you take mail out of the mailbox start sorting it into categories. Make groupings within the pile in your hands: "junk" mail to be tossed can go on the bottom of the pile, important bills or "Do ASAP" items go on top of the stack, etc. Group other items by like categories (i.e. magazines for recreational reading grouped together, all the mail to your spouse or co-workers in another grouping and so forth.)

That way, once you arrive to your desk, most of the sorting work is already done. All you have to do is put each grouping into its appropriate "home" in the office (i.e. bills go in monthly bills-to-pay slot, spouse or co-worker's mail goes into their slot.

Linda Richards
Organize and More
352-373-1086
Linda@organizeandmore.net
www.organizeandmore.net

- **Delegate it.** If you receive mail that should be forwarded to someone else or delegated to a staff member, do so immediately so the mail doesn't end up sitting on your desk for days.

- **Act on it.** Some mail requires a simple phone or email response. If it's only going to take a moment to complete the action necessary, take that action right now and then get rid of that mail. If you have to take action at a later date, file it temporarily in your Tickler file so it's not forgotten about.

- **File it.** Some mail simply needs to be filed away. If your files are in order, it should just take you a moment to place the paper(s) into your filing cabinet.

  Don't allow mail that needs filing to pile up. What will take you a second now, can turn into hours later. If the mail requires some reading, put it in your To Read file or in your traveling To Read file.

- **Save your identity.** With the increase of identity theft, you may decide to shred any junk mail that includes personal information. If so, keep a portable shredder right on a recycling container. As you need to shred, you can do so immediately rather than collecting it all in a box to shred later.

- **Weed it out.** As you get bills you have to pay, keep only the statement and the envelope you have to mail the statement back in. Toss the outer envelope and any unnecessary inserts right away.

- **Contact the DMA.** You can eliminate 50% or more of your junk mail by contacting the Direct Marketing Association. Their Web site address is: www.dmaconsumers.org

  Tell them you wish to have your name, address and telephone number removed from their direct mail lists.

  Another web site that can help you opt out of many mailing lists can be found at: www.opt-out.cdt.org

- **Cancel your subscriptions.** If you get a magazine and you read it every single time, great. That's a keeper subscription. But if you're subscribed to magazines that you never read, cancel those subscriptions. They're just adding to your paper piles.

  On a side note: I once knew someone who subscribed to so many magazines and the stacks of them were so high, that he couldn't even work in his office—he had to work on his kitchen table. The sad thing is, the magazines were clearly crisp and new. In other words—he hadn't read a single issue in months—maybe years! What a waste of money and space.

- **Prevent getting on mailing lists.** Whenever you place a catalog order, subscribe to a magazine, sign up for a new credit card or anything else in which you give out your name and/or address, you can be pretty certain your name will be passed on to other companies who you'll start to receive mail from.

  Always ask the businesses and organizations you're dealing with not to share your contact information and you'll be able to reduce your name getting put on tons of different mailing lists.

If you don't specifically do this, your name and address has a good chance of being sold to 30 or more mailing lists, every time you share your information!

## Organizing Clinic

### Question

Every day, I get about four mail deliveries from our office mail person. By the end of the day, it accumulates to a pile of mail. I can't possibly go through it all with all of my other projects! I can't give this project to my assistant, as she would not know how to handle it. Is there any light at the end of the tunnel for me?

Tad Gleisner

### Answer

Dear Tad,

First, it's important to put a more positive spin on it. It's not that you "can't." It's probably that you "don't want to." Having an "I can" attitude will help you solve this problem much quicker.

Get off of mailing lists, unsubscribe from magazines and newsletters you never read, send a "please remove" letter to companies you no longer deal with—do whatever it takes to reduce the amount of mail coming in.

Then, make a checklist for your assistant, giving her specific instructions on how to sort out your mail. On the checklist, include instructions such as toss all bulk-rate mail and unsolicited advertising, put all bills into a To Be Paid folder and put all correspondence to be answered in a Correspondence folder. If you give your assistant instructions, she will be able to assist you.

Finally, once your mail has been sorted, it's your job to set aside 15 minutes each morning and 15 minutes each afternoon to go through anything your assistant has not tossed. It should not take you longer than this each day and sometimes 15 minutes will even be too long.

If you keep up with the mail each day, you WILL be able to get through it all and it won't have the chance to accumulate to large piles.

- **Remove me, please.** Make a form letter for requesting the removal of your name from mailing lists to send to companies who are sending you mail you don't want. As you receive unwanted mail, drop a form letter in an envelope, address the envelope to the organization sending the mail and mail it out.

- **Use an In Basket and an Out Basket.** In Baskets and Out Baskets are perfect for catching your daily incoming mail and holding your daily outgoing mail. Be sure to tend to them every single day. These baskets should both be empty before you leave for the evening.

- **Start from the bottom.** If, for some reason, you haven't been able to get to your mail for a few days, begin opening the mail at the bottom of your In Basket. By working from the bottom up, you'll give the older mail higher priority.

### Great idea!

I have a simple way to help streamline the mail-sorting process in your home office. Purchase a plastic mail sorter with three slots (the kind you hang on the wall) and a trashcan.

Hang the mail sorter right by the door of your office (or desk if you have no separate home office).

Label each slot as follows: incoming business, incoming household, outgoing. Place the trashcan directly below the mail sorter.

As soon as you bring the mail in, sort it before you have a chance to lay it on the kitchen counter or someplace else.

The trashcan will make it very simple to "file" the junk mail.

If you get in the habit of sorting the mail before it gets "lost" somewhere it will be so much easier to keep your mail separated between household/personal mail, business mail and the junk mail that just wastes your valuable time.

Jackie Dunaway
Mind Over Clutter Professional Organizing
7560 Lascassas Pk, Lascassas, TN 37085
615-273-1067
mindoverclutter@msn.com
www.mind-over-clutter.com

- **Open and sort every day.** Unless you're on vacation, there's really no reason to leave the office without opening and sorting today's mail.

- **Use a letter opener.** Avoid paper cuts by opening all of your mail with a letter opener. It's a quick, neat, safe system.

- **Seal it up.** Stop licking envelopes and use the self-sealing ones instead. They come in a variety of sizes and you'll never have to taste envelope glue again. Yuck!

- **Buy printed envelopes.** If you're still sticking return address labels on your business envelopes, get your printing company to make envelopes with your company name and logo pre-printed on them.

- **Save an envelope format.** Make a computer template and print envelopes directly from your printer. Make custom templates for contacts you mail to all the time so you don't have to keep re-typing the same name and address.

## Organizing Clinic

### Question

Is it worth it for me to try one of those "print postage from your own computer" services?

Candice Clarkson

### Answer

Dear Candice,

With a service like this, for an initial start up fee and regular monthly charges, you can get rate quotes, purchase and print postage using your computer and printer.

Generally, most services require you to first install software.

To get your postage, you have both online and offline options. The online option allows you to store your postage securely online, but requires a connection to the Internet every time you need to print a stamped envelope or label. Or, you can go online just to purchase postage and then work offline by downloading purchased postage into a device plugged into your computer's parallel port.

Your account can hold a maximum of $500. This is a restriction imposed by the United States Postal Service. You can then simply print onto labels or envelopes.

As with anything, there are some drawbacks. For instance, the USPS requires both a destination address and a return address in order to print a label or envelope. This prevents you from being able to keep pre-printed envelopes on your desk if you need to send out a single letter.

Addresses also need to be approved from the USPS, which means you can spend a significant amount of time online (a real inconvenience if you're using a dial-up connection, rather than cable or DSL) or by using a service-provided CD-ROM to verify addresses.

Of course, technology isn't always perfect, so you may run into some snafus along the way.

But there are benefits too. For instance, if you spend at least $50 each month in postage, this option may be one that you should consider. It is usually less expensive to use this type of service, versus a postage meter. Plus, you won't have to run to the post office to fill your postage meter or to buy stamps.

Is this type of service worth it for you? That's an answer you'll have to determine for yourself. You might want to just give it a try to see how you like it and if it saves you time compared to the time you're currently spending getting postage.

- **Get envelopes ready ahead of time.** Prepare several mailing envelopes for people you mail to frequently. For instance, I send a check to one of my affiliate partners every single week. I have about 25 envelopes already made up and ready to go. No need to print out envelopes for this partner for about 25 weeks.

- **Stamp and address it.** As you open your bills, attach a stamp and an address label before filing it away. When you pay the bill, it will be ready to go!

- **Distribute.** If you're handling mail for a number of people, use plastic wall slots. These attach to a wall and allow you to insert papers into open slots. Label each slot or compartment with the appropriate person's name.

  When mail arrives, sort the mail into the unit. Then, each person can pick up his or her mail each day.

- **Set up a mail station.** Set up an area in your office specifically for incoming and outgoing mail and mailing supplies. Include items like envelopes, return address labels, overnight courier service forms, shipping boxes, packing paper, bubble wrap, shipping tape, mailing labels, stamps, a postage meter and anything else you need. With everything in one place, you'll be able to efficiently handle your mailing needs.

- **Find a home for the rest of your mail.** If you've dumped and/or distributed everything from your incoming mail pile, the rest of your mail will either require 1) that you take an action on it or 2) that you file it. If an action needs to be done, schedule time to do it on your calendar and then place that mail in your To Do file or your Tickler file system. If you just need to file it in your filing cabinet, do so now.

- **Have a contingency plan.** If you're going on vacation, before you leave schedule a mail sorting hour for the day you'll be returning to the office—first thing in the morning. This way, you can get it handled before you move on to your other work tasks. If possible, have a trained assistant sort through and handle your mail while you're away.

- **Don't waste time in line.** Avoid visiting the post office during busy hours, such as lunchtime and a few minutes before closing. Find out when your post office is empty and go then.

  The post office in my town is a mad house at lunchtime, so I try to go around 2:00 to 3:00 in the afternoon when there are generally no lines at all.

- **Order stamps and postage supplies.** Rather than waiting in line, order your postage stamps from the United States Postal Service Web site: www.usps.com While there, you can also check rates, zip codes and order supplies for services like Priority Mail.

If you use courier services like UPS or Fed Ex, use their web sites for ordering supplies, scheduling pick-ups and deliveries, checking rates, tracking packages and more. Visit www.ups.com or www.fedex.com

- **Hold personal mail online.** The Post Office now offers the ability to schedule mail holds online. This is a great process for holding your mail while you are away on vacation. Also, you can schedule delivery of this mail for a date that is convenient for you.

- **Get a postage meter.** If you send lots of mail from your office, you may wish to invest in a postage meter. You'll never run out of stamps again, you'll always know the exact postage to affix and you'll get speedier delivery because metered mail takes fewer steps to process.

  Be sure to anticipate your need for postage and order extra in advance. This will ensure that you never run out of postage at an awkward time.

- **Get it picked up.** Rather than waiting in line at the post office or other courier service, have your packages picked up from your office. The post office offers Priority Mail pick-up. UPS and FedEx pick up your ground and air packages.

  When I wrote my first book (the days before I had a fulfillment service), my husband and I went to the post office each day, lugging our book orders with us. This took more than a half hour each day, between getting the books in the car, taking them out of the car and standing in line at the post office.

  We later discovered that the post office picks up Priority Mail boxes weekly for a small fee. The fee was definitely worth all the time and energy we saved.

- **Use courier software.** If you regularly use courier services, see if your favorite courier has software available that will allow you to set up all your packages and shipping labels on the computer to be printed on your printer.

- **Use Internet Shipping.** The major couriers (FedEx and UPS) offer online Internet shipping. This feature is available to anyone with Internet access and an account number. Internet shipping allows you to store frequent recipients in an address book. You may even get a discount for using Internet shipping.

- **To assemble or not to assemble.** If you ship boxes regularly and you have ample space in your office or another area, you may wish to pre-assemble some boxes. When you have something to ship, you can then fill the box, seal it and ship it very quickly.

  The downside of pre-assembling boxes is that they take up lots of space. If your space is tight, you're better of keeping the boxes unassembled until you need them.

- **Use your assistant.** If you have an assistant, have him or her open your mail. Train this person to automatically get rid of junk mail, file and/or delete as needed so it never appears on your desk. Then, this person should only give you mail that needs your personal attention.

- **Ease the passing of mail.** If someone else is handling your mail, have this person sort mail into folders such as:

  ❖ Urgent

  ❖ To Do

  ❖ To Approve or Sign

  ❖ To Read

  You may even want to color code these folders for added clarity, such as using a red file folder for Urgent mail, a green folder for To Do, a purple folder for To Approve or Sign and a blue folder for To Read. If your assistant adds mail to these folders, the oldest information should be stored towards the front of the folder and the newest information towards the back. This way, the oldest mail gets handled first.

- **Determine the best method.** When sending outgoing mail, determine how soon you need the letter or package to be delivered, whether or not you need a signature confirmation and how much you're willing to pay. Check the web site to determine the best method for delivery. When using a courier service, always include the recipient's phone number to expedite deliveries and to avoid delays.

- **Address properly.** The contact name goes on the first line, the company name (if any) goes on the second line, the street address and suite/room number/apartment number go on the third line, the city, state and zip go on the fourth line and the country (if necessary) goes on the fifth line, just like this:

  JANE DOE
  ABC CORPORATION
  1111 WEST MAIN STREET
  JERSEY CITY NJ 07307
  USA

- **Use the recommended layout.** A guideline for addressing a business envelope is to use 11 or 12-point type with a readable font (such as Arial). Also, all uppercase letters are preferred by the post office, as doing so makes it easier to sort mail electronically.

- **Use an Outbox.** All outgoing mail for the regular postal service should be placed in an outbox and mailed once each day. Either you or your mailroom person should do so. All mail for other couriers should have their own designated pick up spot in your office.

- **Fill out forms ahead of time.** Whenever possible, fill out mailing forms ahead of time. When our company ships International orders, we have to fill out Customs forms. We always fill in all our information ahead of time. We then just have to fill in the recipient's address and contents of the box.

  When we order shipping forms from UPS, all of our standard information is pre-printed by UPS right on our shipping form. It's a pleasure not to have to fill out this information each time we have to make a UPS delivery.

- **Get pre-printed company labels.** For business packages, get professional company labels printed up. My company labels have my business name, web site and address on them in a light green border at the top of the label. The rest of the label is white and ready for the recipient's name. They come ten labels to a sheet.

- **Stamp special instructions.** Every once in awhile, you're going to have to mark a letter or package "Urgent," "Confidential," "Do Not Bend," or "Fragile." Determine what special instructions you use regularly. Then, get stamps or stickers made up so you don't have to always write these instructions on your correspondence or boxes.

- **Get a postage scale.** To ensure you're applying the right amount of postage, if you do it yourself, a postage scale is a good investment. You might also consider a postage meter or a service like Stamps.com.

# Chapter 17

# Magazines and magazine articles

- **Buy one subscription for the office.** Most offices have subscriptions to industry magazines to help everybody keep up with the latest trends, technologies and issues. To keep costs down, many companies buy one subscription. They then attach a routing slip to it and hope that it makes its way from one person to the next.

If you have very courteous people in your office, this system may work nicely and magazines won't pile up all over the place. But very often, the magazines end up getting lost or they sit on one person's desk for so long that the issue is three months old before it ever gets passed on.

If this is the case, keep the magazines in a company Reading Room and don't allow staff members to remove the magazines from this room. Set up some comfortable chairs and some tables so staff members can read in the Reading Room during their break or between projects.

## Great idea!

I write a lot of articles on varying subjects and was having a hard time organizing them. If I wanted to submit an article to a magazine that I had already written and it needed to be 500 words, for example, I would have to do five steps:

1. Open up Microsoft Word.
2. Select the document and double-click it to open it.
3. Go to the "tools" menu and scroll down to "word count" and look at the number.
4. Close the document.
5. Repeat the process if the article wasn't the right length.

I finally came up with a terrific way to organize them, which eliminated four of the steps. Now I simply include the word count in the file name. So, for example, if the file name would normally be called OrganizingFiles.doc, I'd just name it OrganizingFiles525.doc. This way, I can see simply by looking at the file name that the word count is 525. It's so simple, yet so incredibly helpful and timesaving.

Monica Ricci, owner of Catalyst Organizing Solutions, has been an organizing specialist since 1999. She helps her clients declutter, organize and streamline their lives both at home and at work. She is also a speaker and appears regularly in various magazines, newspapers and online publications. Contact Monica at www.catalystorganizing.com or 770-569-2642.

- **Use a key person.** If possible, have one person go through the magazines and find the most relevant and interesting articles. That person will usually need to be a boss, manager or trained assistant.

  The designated person—or that person's assistant—can then make a copy of those articles for each person that needs to read them. Now, everybody gets the articles at the same time and nobody gets left behind.

- **Be discerning.** If you're like many business people, you probably have a large number of industry related articles in your To Read pile. Some of those articles are worthwhile to keep for future reference and some aren't. The last thing you need is a stack of magazines piled in a corner.

  You only have so much time in a given day that you can dedicate to reading articles. If you plan to read for 30 minutes each day and you can usually read two to three articles in that amount of time, don't plan on saving enough articles to fill a library.

  Be discerning and keep only those articles that will provide you with the most beneficial information for you and your job.

- **Tear it out.** As you're reading articles in a magazine, tear out the pages that you wish to keep—use an Xacto knife so the edges of the articles are flat and neat.

  Of course, if the magazine is not yours, don't tear out the pages. Instead, make copies of the articles that interest you and save them for your own personal use.

- **Scan it.** Software, such as Scanalog, allows you to scan, store, catalog and retrieve your favorite articles from your favorite magazines. If you're technologically savvy and you need to save magazine articles, software like Scanalog may be for you.

  Annie, an administrative assistant, spends thirty minutes each week checking through three industry magazines. She scans articles that meet certain criteria into her boss's computer for him to review later that day.

  Once her boss reviews the scanned articles, most of them are then deleted and the rest are kept for future reference.

  The nice thing is, no more paper copies!

- **Weed them out.** Articles that are important to you today may not necessarily be important to you later. Weed out articles regularly, at quarterly or 6-month intervals.

## Organizing Clinic

### Question

I work in advertising and there are certain magazines I like to keep in my office for ideas. I'm a very creative person and I get some of my best ideas just by flipping through old magazines. What's the best way to organize them?

Mike Masterson, Detroit, MI

### Answer

Dear Mike,

Get yourself some magazine holders in an office supply store. You can get cardboard, wood or plastic to suit your personality.

Store these magazine holders on shelves in your office. Try to keep just one magazine type in each holder and face the holders so you can see the spines of the magazines for easy access.

Another alternative is to get yourself a filing cabinet, just for your magazine storage. Magazines can be stored spine up in hanging file folders. Organize by title, chronologically within each title.

---

- **Create article storage.** Create labeled, categorized file folders for articles you wish to reference again in the future.

  1. **Make categories.** Let's say you have articles pertaining to marketing, management, goals and customer service. Make four separate folders, one for each category. Label them with codes such as:

     - MK: Marketing
     - MN: Management
     - GL: Goals
     - CS: Customer Service

  2. **Code them.** Code each article by jotting a small code at the top right of the page. For example, for the first marketing article, code it MK-1, for the second marketing article, code it MK-2 and so on in numerical order. Do this for each of your articles within the appropriate category.

  3. **Index them.** Using a word processing file or a spreadsheet, make headings for each of your main categories. Under each heading, type the code for each article you have and a short description. When you're done, your file should look something like this:

**Marketing**

MK-1: Prospecting for gold

MK-2: Cold calls can help

MK-3: Winning ads

**Management**

MN-1: Rewarding employees

MN-2: Hiring tips and tricks

**Goals**

GL-1: Goal setting

GL-2: Obstacles to reaching goals

GL-3: Setting mini-goals

**Customer Service**

CS-1: Handling customer problems

CS-2: The customer is always right

CS-3: Making sure customers are happy

CS-4: Inspiring customer service stories

4. **Store them.** Insert each article into the appropriate folder and store the folders in your filing cabinet. Be sure to weed out articles every now and then, so your files aren't bursting at the seams. If you permanently remove an article, be sure to blank out the description in your computer index. Leave the code there, just blank out the description. When you have another article, use the available code and put the new description in your computer file.

5. **Locate it later.** Now that your articles are all indexed into a word processing file, you have the ability to find exactly what you need whenever you need it. Open up your computer file and peruse your article descriptions. Or, if your computer program has a find feature—which most do—do a search on key words. For instance, if you're looking for articles based on hiring employees, you might do a search on "hiring" so that your cursor hops immediately to the article you're looking for.

# Chapter 18

# Faxing quick tips

- **Create a personal cover sheet.** Prepare and make multiple copies of your own fax transmittal cover sheet to use when sending faxes or create a software template if you wish. It should include:

  - ❖ Your name, company name, phone/fax number and current date.

  - ❖ Space for your recipient's name, company name and fax number.

  - ❖ An area for you to include how many total pages, including the cover sheet, are being sent.

  - ❖ Check boxes for you to mark an appropriate action you'd like your recipient to notice—Urgent, Reply ASAP, Please Comment, Please Review, For Your Information, Confidential.

  - ❖ Ample space for you to write your message.

- **Tip for techies.** If you're good at creating stuff on your computer, you can design your fax as a type-in form, instead of having to write out your fax correspondence. Plus, you can store common fax numbers and program a formula into it so that the date appears automatically.

- **Sometimes you can skip the cover sheet.** For those faxes that don't require a long cover note, office supply stores sell small, adhesive "Fax It" notes instead.

  These small notes—similar to sticky notes, are stuck right on top of the paper you're faxing. They include lines for your name and your recipient's name and fax number. Since there's no need for a cover sheet, you'll save fax transmission time and paper.

- **Keep fax supplies in the faxing area.** Store your fax supplies right near the fax machine so they're handy. Some common supplies include cover sheets, small "fax it" notes, a pen, fax paper, extra fax toner/ink and a staple remover. Keep extra supplies on hand so you don't run out unexpectedly.

- **Catch your incoming faxes.** Make sure your fax machine has something to catch incoming faxes in, or they'll end up all over your floor or behind a cabinet.

- **Use fax software.** If you use fax software on your computer, you'll be able to send a file directly from your computer without using a single sheet of paper and without wasting time at the fax machine. These are best used for sending files directly from your computer though. If you're mostly using your fax for sending actual papers, just use a regular fax machine.

- **Redial automatically.** Use a fax machine that automatically redials when your recipient's line is busy, otherwise you're going to waste time waiting for the line to free up.

> ## Great idea!
>
> Use light colored paper for faxes you are sending out and white paper for incoming faxes. Hang a three tiered pocket organizer on the wall beside the fax for: In, Out and Coversheets.
>
> Judy Brown, Associate Editor of *Finally Organized, Finally Free for the Office*

- **Do a little programming.** Take the time to read your fax user manual and program common phone numbers into your fax machine. Instead of having to remember and dial manually each time, your fax machine memory will remember for you and you can send rapidly.

- **Keep the manual nearby.** Keep your fax manual close to the fax machine for future trouble-shooting or for answers to questions. I recommend you tape your manual to the bottom of your fax machine—this way you'll always know where it is.

- **Confirm fax receipt.** Most of the time, your recipient won't be waiting by his or her fax machine for your fax to come through. When you send a fax, always be sure to call or email the recipient to be sure it was received— especially if you're faxing to a big office where there's a chance someone else may inadvertently pick up the fax you sent.

Michelle, a writer, faxed a printing order to her local printer before she left her office for vacation. When she returned two weeks later, she was surprised that her books were not delivered yet. She called up the printing company and was dismayed to learn they had never received her fax.

Customer orders had to be put on backorder due to the delay—all because Michelle never thought to call the printing company before she left for vacation to verify if they received it.

- **Leave at least a one-inch margin.** When sending a fax, be sure there's at least a one-inch margin on the top, bottom, left and right sides of your fax and don't write in the margins. Anything too close to the edge of the page may be chopped off by the time it reaches your recipient.

- **Use a dark pen or marker.** If you're writing on pages to be faxed, always use a black pen or marker. Don't use pencil or a colored pen, as they don't always reproduce well.

- **Don't fax red or orange paper.** Chances are, when your recipient receives your fax, it will be too dark to read.

- **Avoid underlining.** When creating a page to be faxed, avoid underlining. It decreases readability on your recipient's end.

- **Use regular paper.** If you still have an older fax machine that uses paper rolls, invest in a fax machine that uses regular plain paper. These faxes are more readable and easier to file and maintain. Plus they don't require a special paper order. Fax machines are relatively inexpensive these days, so it is worth the investment.

- **Keep it filled.** Keep your fax machine filled with an ample supply of paper to prevent it from running out. You may want to request that all fax users check the paper tray and fill it as needed.

---

### Organizing Clinic

**Question**

I don't have a lot of space in my office, but I could really use a fax machine. Right now, my telephone, computer, printer, answering machine and copy machine are taking up all the room I have. Do you have any suggestions to easily fit in a fax machine?

Wanda Nicholson

**Answer**

Dear Wanda,

You may consider one multi-function machine, rather than having several machines. Check your local office equipment store. Many sell machines that have printing, scanning, copying and faxing capabilities—all in one. My husband and I have a fax machine that also has answering machine capabilities. Purchasing a multi-function machine will help you better consolidate all of your equipment. Another option, if you choose not to do this, would be to add shelving to your office for your equipment.

---

- **Get one with memory.** When my fax machine is out of fax toner or if there is a fax transmission problem, whatever is being sent to me is not lost. My fax machine captures the data in its memory and it begins printing again as soon as the problem is taken care of. This way, there are no missing faxes.

- **Number your fax pages.** Be sure you always number your fax pages (i.e. Page 1 of 2, Page 2 of 2, etc.). If you're sending several pages and the transmission is interrupted, you'll be able to call your fax recipient and easily identify the pages that were received and those you still need to send.

- **Don't allow faxes to pile up.** Place the fax machine in the mailroom so that any incoming faxes can be placed in the mailboxes of intended recipients. If a mailroom is not available, put one person in charge of collecting and distributing incoming faxes. The faxes should not be allowed to pile up. One office took a harsh stance and threw away any printouts or faxes remaining on printers and faxes at the end of the day.

- **Fight unsolicited faxes.** If you are the victim of unsolicited faxes, do not call the 800 number listed on the fax to opt out. This will only place your fax number on a published list leading to more junk faxes!

There are call-screening gadgets available that request a numerical sequence to be entered before faxing. This will stop the unsolicited, automated faxes and only allow real faxes to get through. Just be sure that fax senders are aware of the required code before faxing. More information on how to stop junk faxes is available at: www.junkfaxes.org

### Great idea!

We used to use canary yellow paper for all faxes. It worked well to see it immediately. Due to the number of documents we have to copy onto white paper, we don't do that any longer. Most faxes fall into one category or another:

- Boss needs to review
- Boss needs to review, sign and return by fax.
- Case information which needs to be entered in the system (and then filed)
- FYI
- Form sample
- Junk/Sales

We make every attempt to have our boss sign documents ASAP and return to that party promptly, as it's too easy for it to blend in and get misplaced. If the document "requires action" or is an FYI, it is given to the person who needs to take the action and the paper is filed in the appropriate file. Form samples are 3-hole punched and stored in our "Form Book." Junk and Sales ads are filed in "file 13" (better known as "your trashcan.")

Jodi Arrowsmith, Associate Editor of *Finally Organized, Finally Free for the Office*

- **Use an Internet fax service.** You might consider using an Internet fax service. Incoming faxes are emailed to you. No more waiting at the fax machine. Plus, a electronic fax can be sent right from your email account. You can send using an Internet faxing service too, right from your computer. This is especially helpful because it gives you the ability to receive faxes even if you're out of the office.

- **Broadcast your message.** If you have a large number of opt-in faxes you need to send out, definitely consider a fax broadcasting service or software, this way you're not spending all day sending out faxes one at a time.

---

## Organizing Clinic

### Question

I have a home office, but can't afford to set up a second phone line for my fax machine. I'm not a technical person, so I don't want to send or retrieve faxes from my computer. Any ideas?

Dana Richards

### Answer

Dear Dana,

No problem. Just get a combination fax machine, telephone, answering machine system that can detect the difference between an incoming call and a fax. When someone calls, you can either pick up the telephone or let the call go to your answering machine. When someone faxes, the machine will automatically begin receiving. You only need one phone line to do this.

---

- **Preserve the environment.** Reuse paper by using the other side for fax transmissions. Since most fax machines only send one side of the paper, you can save lots of trees by doing this.

- **Don't make them squint.** Very tiny text could tend to get fuzzy on fax transmissions. Try to use a font that is at least 10 pt or higher.

- **Black out.** Avoid excess use of black, like using solid black borders. Even one small bit of black on a line requires that the entire line be transmitted and printed. It slows down transmission time considerably.

# Chapter 19

# Copying quick tips

- **Get a copy machine for your office.** Most large companies have one or more copy machines available, but many small businesses use a local copy shop for this purpose. Even small businesses though can benefit from a copy machine, especially for those days when you just need to make a copy or two. It's a lot quicker to do this in your office, than to have to run to your copy shop! Consider purchasing or leasing a small energy-efficient copy machine.

- **Don't make more than you need.** The copy machine has made the paper duplication process so quick and easy. Don't let this simplification result in copies that aren't really necessary. This wastes time and generates clutter.

- **Implement a "think before you copy" rule in your office.** Encourage co-workers to make sure they're only making the copies they need. Saving paper saves the company money and is good for the environment.

---

### Great idea!

When setting up a file or pile of photocopied forms, it helps to mark the original or master copy with a yellow highlighter dot in the upper-right hand corner of the page. This helps in several instances:

- When you come across it, you won't throw it away.

- You'll always use the best, most clear copy to fax or make more copies.

- If it is the last one left, you'll know not to use it or give it away.

Suzanne M. Keezel
The Organized Planet, Inc.
Organizing Solutions for Your World!
Located in Central Florida
www.theorganizedplanet.com

---

- **Print on both sides.** Some photocopy machines have a duplex feature, allowing you to print on both sides of the paper with no effort on your part. Post interesting reminders by the copy machine to encourage staff members to print on both sides, such as "2 Sides Are Better Than One" and "Make a Second Impression."

- **Always make a test copy.** If you have to run a large amount of copies, always make one test copy first. This will avoid problems such as the paper not being straight, too light or not choosing the correct settings.

Edward, a small business owner, went to Kinko's to make a bunch of copies of a packet for his customers. He was in a rush, so he chose the settings he wanted and then walked away to make a few calls from his cell phone. Upon his return, he realized that he inadvertently forgot to select the stapler setting. He wasted over an hour getting all of his packets stapled manually. A test copy would have eliminated this problem.

## Organizing Clinic

### Question

I have a crowded work area with several office machines and two computers. I would like to set up a copy center to help eliminate some of the traffic in and out of my area; however, I still need easy access to the copiers. Is there some place I can find this type of information?

R. Seward

### Answer

Dear R. Seward,

By your description, I can't tell if you have one large work area and you're thinking of putting the copy center to one side of it or if you're thinking of making the copy center in a completely separate area, like an empty office. Either way, I think it's an excellent idea that you want to stop some of the traffic coming in and out of your office by setting up a copy center.

It must be very difficult for you to get anything done, with so much traffic and noise. In fact, if at all possible, you might consider getting yourself a small copy machine that only you use. You'll always have access to your own copy machine, but everyone else will use the machine(s) you have set up in the copy center.

If this is not within your budget, try collecting all the papers you need to copy in a To Copy file and copying everything you need at the end of the day to avoid running back and forth to the copy center.

- **Duplicate common forms.** For those forms you use every day, instead of making one copy at a time, make a number of them. You won't waste time going to the copy machine a dozen times a day. Just be sure you're going to use them up.

Paperclip a 3" x 5" index card a few forms from the bottom that says: Time to run "x" more copies. Replace the "x" with the desired amount - 10, 50, 25 and you'll never run out of forms!

- **Distribute with caution.** Don't make a million copies and then freely distribute them to everyone without first determining if they really need them. You wouldn't want to contribute to someone else's paper clutter, would you?

- **Keep copy supplies in the copying area.** Store your copy supplies right near the copy machine so they're handy. Some common supplies include extra copy paper, toner, paper clips, a stapler and a staple remover. Keep extra supplies on hand so you don't run out unexpectedly.

- **Go for the gold.** If you happen to be buying a new copy machine soon, don't skimp on the features. Collating, stapling and duplex features can be truly worthwhile and excellent time savers. But certainly don't buy a machine with lots of bells and whistles you'll never use or that will need many servicing hours.

- **Keep the machine in good repair.** Let your copier maintenance person know when you experience any sort of difficulties with your copy machine. A simple tune-up may be all it needs. A copy machine that works well is less likely to jam and helps save paper and time.

- **Keep the copier closed.** Be sure to keep the copier top closed when not in use. This extends copier quality and life and results in less maintenance. Place a sign near the copier to remind employees to close the copier door when not in use.

- **Be sure there's a wastebasket.** Without a wastebasket in the copy room, papers, paper clips, staples and more have a tendency to end up on the machine, the floor, the shelves, and otherwise all over the place. Keep a wastebasket handy so you can immediately discard any trash.

- **Use a copy service.** Sometimes it's not worth your time to make your own copies. If you have a very large run, you might consider going to a copy shop and having someone else run your copies for you.

- **Check the glass.** The glass you lay your original on can easily be smudged. Be sure you always clean the glass before making any copies, to avoid the smudge image showing up on all your copies.

- **Have two machines available.** If many co-workers share one copy machine, there is bound to be lines of people waiting to use the copy machine—especially if one of the employees has to run a very large job. Consider getting a second copy machine—one to be used for quick copy jobs, the other to be used for more intense, time-consuming copy jobs.

- **Network it.** A copy machine can be networked into your company's internal operating system, so staff members can send copies to the copy machine right from their computers.

## Organizing Clinic

### Question

What are some tips for organizing a busy copy area? We don't have a lot of space.

Angie Berry

### Answer

Dear Angie,

Most offices have their copy areas set up in very small spaces, so you're not alone. With a little bit of creativity you can make the most out of the space you have. Here are some ideas:

- Consider adding shelving to your copy area, either free standing if you have the space or shelving that is attached to the wall(s). Very often, wall space is forgotten about. It's amazing what a few shelves can do to increase your available space. For example, with shelves you can store copy paper that might have been stored on the floor. Or you can also organize copy supplies in baskets on shelves, such as toner for your machine or paper clips.

- Install a flip-up/flip-down shelf and you'll have an instant work area where you or other staff members can temporarily set papers or files down. When it's in use, flip it up. When it's not in use, flip it down.

- Add plastic file pockets to the wall to hold items like copy machine manuals and instructions for changing the paper in the copy machine.

- Remove anything from the copy area that doesn't belong there. This may sound obvious, but just in case you're currently storing something other than copy supplies in this area, those items should be moved to another appropriate place to free up space.

- Consider using multi-purpose machines, such as a combination fax-copier. This may help to save space.

# Chapter 20

# Your briefcase

- **Do you need one?** Some people need a briefcase; some do not. Since I regularly work out of my office, I don't even own a briefcase. However, if you are normally on the road or you carry lots of papers back and forth between your home and office, then a briefcase may be ideal for you.

- **Think form and function.** When purchasing a briefcase, both function AND looks are important. You'll want a briefcase you're going to feel good carrying with you each day. It's basically going to be part of your everyday wardrobe. You'll also want a briefcase that is strong and big enough to fit the things you're going to be carrying around with you.

  Before shopping for one, write down the things that would make your briefcase ideal. Then, go shopping with an eye out for what you've written down.

---

### Organizing Clinic

**Question**

I'm planning to purchase a new briefcase, but how will I know what the proper size is for my needs?

Paul Mendez, New York, NY

**Answer**

Dear Paul,

You won't know if your briefcase will work for you, until you pack it up with the things you generally want to have with you each day.

However, do realize that the bigger your briefcase, the more you may tend to carry.

The first important thing is to determine exactly what you will be bringing back and forth with you each day. Once you know this, it will simply be a matter of choosing a briefcase that will fit those things, with a little bit of extra room to spare.

---

- **Get one with a shoulder strap.** Walking with your briefcase may be easier if you use one with a shoulder strap, especially if it's raining and you're using one hand to hold your umbrella and another to hold your coffee.

- **Look for one with lots of storage compartments.** Don't skimp. Buy a briefcase that will hold all of your things conveniently for you. Many briefcases today have cell phone and PDA pockets, a slot for your eyeglasses, zippered compartment dividers, key holders and so on.

  Some also include a mini, accordion file-folder section. These are ideal for holding valuable documents that you want to keep neat and flat and cuts down on the excess weight of having to carry document holders in your briefcase.

- **Do double duty.** If you're a woman, you may consider having your briefcase double as your purse, so you don't have to carry both.

- **Think color.** You may see a really fun looking bright red briefcase while you're shopping, but think twice. Basic black or basic brown will match with most anything you wear; this coordination won't always be possible with a wilder, brighter color.

- **Light as a feather.** If you plan to carry your briefcase every day, choose one that is not going to weigh you down. Look for a briefcase that is lightweight, but strong.

  Kathy, an Avon representative, wanted a briefcase to carry both her paperwork and her Avon samples to her prospective customers. Her leather briefcase was very stiff, heavy and not very roomy. This resulted in frustration and back pain.

  I advised her to switch to a canvas briefcase and this was the perfect solution for her. Her back pain vanished and the expandable material accommodated all of her paperwork and samples.

- **Don't over-organize.** Some briefcases today include a wallet/checkbook area, with places for credit cards, a calculator, etc. While this may be ideal if you plan on carrying your briefcase 24/7, you will waste a lot of time taking all of your cards out and transferring them to a wallet or purse each time you want to go somewhere that is not work related. Better to skip these features and keep a wallet that can be transferred from briefcase to pocket or purse.

- **Looks like it may rain.** Be sure your briefcase is weather-resistant to protect its contents and so it looks good for a long time.

  If possible, purchase a briefcase with reinforced strips on the bottom. This will save a lot of wear and tear if you actually have to set your briefcase down.

- **Carry what you need.** Evaluate how many supplies you have inside—you don't need ten pens and seven sticky note pads. If you only have time to read one or two magazines on your trip, don't carry along ten.

- **Compartmentalize.** Each paper, business card, magazine and so on in your briefcase, should have a specific home. Keep one accordion file folder with several slots to hold papers you need on the go. Get yourself a business card holder so they won't slide all over the place.

Hopefully, your briefcase has a few pockets—one for business magazines, another for travel documents. Keep supplies in one place with a slim plastic container that snaps shut or a zippered cosmetics bag.

### Great idea!

Be prepared for anything. For instance, in my briefcase I have film canisters where I have made emergency first aid kits and sewing kits and a small tin (like an Altoid's tin) where I have a mini office supply set up with staples, stapler, paperclips, tape, small scissors, a cloth/paper tape measure or anything you might need in a hurry.

Also compartmentalize your briefcase. One area for planner, another for emergency kits as well as extra writing supplies and folders.

Alphabetize your folders if you can. It makes locating and re-filing them easier.

Denise Williams, Associate Editor of *Finally Organized, Finally Free for the Office*

- **Clean it out regularly.** After you have your briefcase organized, maintain it! Clean it out every single day and restock supplies daily or weekly.

- **Consolidate.** Organize your papers in pocket folders and keep them in a three-ring binder or expandable file holder. Keep your pens, calculator, erasers, paperclips, rubber bands, envelopes, stamps, message pads and other small office supplies in a transparent pouch.

- **Get a computer briefcase.** If you regularly travel with a notebook computer (laptop), you may consider getting yourself a computer briefcase, which will double as your regular briefcase.

- **Wheel it.** Do you travel much? If so, you may consider a briefcase with wheels so you don't have to carry your briefcase along with your other luggage.

# Chapter 21

# Feng Shui in the workplace

- **Know the principle.** Feng Shui is an ancient Chinese art that embraces the idea of living in harmony with our environment. This art stretches all the way back over 7,000 years. Feng Shui literally means *wind and water*, both of which are fundamental forms of life's energy.

  Feng Shui teaches that there are subtle forces in our surroundings that can affect our everyday lives. In other words, if you're surrounded by chaos, your life will be chaotic. When surrounded by a peaceful, non-chaotic environment, your life will be stress-free, peaceful and happy.

- **Give your desk an about-face.** Place your desk facing your office entry door. This is known as the power position and will keep you alert, productive and aware of your surroundings. You will also be able to see who is coming into your office. This means you won't be surprised and you can offer your visitor a proper greeting.

- **Give yourself some space.** Keep some open space in front of you. If the space in front of your desk is too cramped, you're going to feel closed-in and frustrated.

- **Treat your files with respect.** Your file folders represent your past, present and future business. Be sure your files reflect your business goals. This means they shouldn't be ratty or torn. It also means they should be organized.

- **Your wealth and prosperity corner.** As you enter your office door or entryway, the far left corner is known as your wealth and prosperity corner. This is an excellent spot for something symbolizing financial goals, such as a photograph of something you may like to own in the future.

- **Bring the outdoors in.** Plants and flowers bring life into your office. Try including some large floor plants or perhaps a hanging plant.

- **Remove obstacles.** Remove clutter from your desk, your overall office and your briefcase. Keep wires and cords well hidden. Clutter is an obstacle that prevents you from being at peace.

- **Light up your life.** Avoid working or meeting in poor lighting. You may tire quickly and strain your eyes. Research shows that people are more motivated and lead healthier lives if they sit near open windows. Dark corners are lifeless areas that force you to use twice the energy to do a job. Keep these lights in mind:

  ❖ Desk lamps, floor lamps or portable lights for close work or reading

❖ Overall light, like a ceiling light, for those times when you need your office to be extra bright

❖ Mood lighting for meditation or relaxing

## Organizing Clinic

### Question

Got any tips for organizing messy art studios?

Jason

### Answer

I'm glad you're asking for organizing help, because I know that by getting organized your creative juices will flow even more. You'll be opening up your space, relieving stress and freeing your mind for new and exciting ideas.

First and foremost, only keep supplies in your studio that you regularly use.

Second, determine your main purposes for your art studio. This room shouldn't have more than four purposes. For instance, perhaps one area is for painting, another is for storing art supplies, another is for unfinished projects and the last is for finished projects.

Divide your room up accordingly so that each corner of the room you're in is only used for the purpose you've defined for that corner. This will help you stay focused and will keep the room well defined.

In addition, for an artist, I recommend open wall shelves. Don't allow wall space to go unused. The open-shelf concept allows you to quickly grab art supplies, as you need them. Of course, items should be categorized into plastic see-through containers and/or supply holders to keep similar items consolidated. This way you can find what you need when you need it.

- **Be inspired.** Inspirational pictures on your wall will help you take mini-vacations throughout your workday. For example, a picture of a mountain can be a reminder for achieving goals. A picture of a running stream can be relaxing.

- **Color your world.** Colors can energize, relax or oppress. Keep your office as bright as possible. If you have white walls, liven them up with bright pictures.

Green can create a serene environment.

Red symbolizes happiness and fame.

Avoid having too much of the same color in a room—a room in all white or all dark colors can lead to fatigue, lower productivity and reduce creativity.

- **Create good smells.** Surround yourself with good smells, such as the scent of flowers, a burning aromatic candle or scented room sprays. We're all greatly affected by scents.

  I particularly love the smell of fresh grass, so my window is always open right after the grass is mowed or in the morning, when the grass is fragrant and dewy.

  A friend of mine loves the smell of peppermint. She makes herself a fragrant cup of peppermint tea each morning to enjoy with her morning business reading.

- **Create good sounds.** Soothing sounds may help you increase your productivity and relieve stress. Try an indoor fountain or a soft music CD.

- **Go fish.** An aquarium or tabletop fountain filled with black or blue fish will be relaxing to look at and symbolizes business and career success.

# Home Office Feng Shui

By Vishal P. Rao

Whether you believe in the Oriental powers of Feng Shui or not, there are an increasingly large number of people who do. Feng Shui is said to make you more aware of how your environment affects your state of mind. Business people in Asia have considered work place Feng Shui to be a crucial contributor to personal and business success for centuries. Feng Shui helps you to stay focused by forcing you to store incomplete and future projects in a storage area so you won't be distracted by worrying over them every day. Feng Shui can:

* Increase your prosperity and abundance.
* Boost your health.
* Reduce insomnia and stress.
* Enhance your personal power.
* Ease family conflicts.
* Increase your concentration.
* Enhance financial security.
* Attract new customers to your business.
* Upgrade your life in many other ways.

Have a separate outside entrance to your office if possible. If you cannot, then choose a room that is near the front or back door of the house or apartment. Separate your home office from the rest of the living area in order to keep your business and personal lives separate. If your home office is part of a larger room, then partition the space with bookcases, screens or large plants. Place a picture of a lake, waterfall or any other water scene on one of the walls to represent the flow of energy. You can also use one of those desktop fountains or even an aquarium.

Keep your workspace clean and clutter-free. Stored items should be filed away or stored neatly in a cabinet or closet to allow the flow of Feng Shui energy. Place a green plant on a shelf in the corner or use an artificial plant if you are a known live plant killer.

Take a short walk before entering your office to work each day and another one at the end of your working day as another measure of separating your business life from your personal life. Leave seven to nine inches of space between each piece of office furniture. If you have views of harmful elements from your window, negate them by the strategic placement of wind chimes or plants.

There is a lot more to Feng Shui than we can possibly cover in this article. Even if you don't subscribe to the ancient Oriental ways, I'm sure you'll agree that an uncluttered office, with room to move around and pleasant decorations is much better than a cluttered dungeon that's stuffed to the ceiling with piles of paper and unwanted junk. Good luck and good health!

Reprinted with permission. Vishal P. Rao is the editor of Home Based Business Opportunities - A web site dedicated to opportunities, ideas and resources for starting a home based business. Visit: www.home-based-business-opportunities.com He also runs the Work at Home Forum - an online community of folks who work at home. Visit: www.work-at-home-forum.com

# Chapter 22

# Being productive on the telephone

- **Go long or go cordless.** Your telephone should be within arm's reach. Put the phone itself near you and get a long phone cord if necessary. The phone cord should be positioned against the wall on the floor—not stretched across the room where someone can trip over it. Better yet, get yourself a cordless phone.

- **To the right or to the left.** If you have your telephone on your desk, the best placement is usually the left side if you're a right-handed person. This way, you can answer the phone with your left hand and write with your right hand. The opposite is true if you're left handed. This is not a rule that's set in stone though. Put it on the side that's most comfortable for you.

## Great idea!

Email, document conversations, promises made, appointments and other information—with phone conversations it's easy to forget exactly what was promised and other details of what was said. Each morning the first thing I set up is a phone call log; a dated, lined pad with a column each for time of call, name of the person calling/called, a few key words and return phone number. Lengthy notes are not the idea here. A single line on the pad per call is sufficient.

This exercise goes a long way toward helping me feel in control of my day and the act of making these brief notes keeps me focused on the call and the caller. It requires so little effort. On the last day of each month, I clip the sheets together and put it in a file with the previous three months, purging the oldest monthly record.

Most calls will probably never need to be referenced. But for those that do, the notes can be priceless. Aside from being able to recall business information, being able to note that the caller is leaving on vacation or celebrating a personal event can win points when mentioned on a follow-up call.

Kathleen Luskus, Professional Organizer
Orderly Manor
Everything In Its Place
PO Box 201, Newtown Square, PA 19073
610-324-2445
orderlymanor@comcast.net
Member, NAPO

- **Hang it up.** If you're looking to create more workspace, you can always hang your telephone on the wall.

- **Hands free.** If you prefer not to hold the telephone handset during your conversation, get a telephone headset. The conversation is typically much clearer than it would be if you were using a speakerphone.

  Plus, you won't have to cradle the phone on your shoulder, which can be very uncomfortable with lengthy calls.

  Use a wireless headset and you'll not only be able to talk and write easier while on the phone, but you'll even be able to walk around your office without having to carry the phone or getting tangled up in your phone cord.

- **Speak up.** You may consider getting a telephone with a speakerphone so you don't have to hold the handset when you talk. Personally, I rarely use the speakerphone and I'm not too thrilled when someone on the other end of the line is using one. It almost always causes an annoying echo effect.

  However, speakerphones are ideal for conference calls when a group is taking a call together in the same room.

- **Place a time limit on your calls.** If you answer the telephone and the person on the other end is a long-winded conversationalist, start the conversation with, "I've only got 5 minutes to talk." This will give you an easier out when it's time to hang up.

- **Let people know when to reach you.** On your voicemail, state the times of day you are available. Tell your assistant when you're available to take calls. When you leave messages, let your call recipients know a good time to return your call.

- **Get to the point.** If you want to get on and off the phone quickly, get to the point of the call right away. Say, "Hi Jack, I have these two questions for you" or "Jill, did you get the Federal Express letter I sent you?"

- **Bring the other person to the point.** If your caller is very talkative and you don't have time for chitchat, immediately say, "I'm glad you called. What can I do for you today?" This type of question calls for an immediate response.

  If the person continues to get off subject, say something like, "Mary, I hate to interrupt you, but I only have a minute before an appointment. Let's wrap up the key points and we'll chat more later."

- **Business first, pleasure later.** If you do wish to socialize on your call, at least take care of the business items first. Then, socialize after those points have been addressed.

## Organizing Clinic

### Question

I recently invested in a cell phone for my business and now it seems like I'm always "on call." At first, I felt it gave me the opportunity to handle every call with a personal touch. Now, I get so many calls that I'm ready to toss the phone over my shoulder. What can I do to keep that personal touch, without losing my mind?

Jack Winston, Philadelphia, PA

### Answer

Dear Jack,

The first thing I suggest is that you be more judicious when it comes to giving out your cell phone number. You don't need every customer, vendor and associate to have that line. If you've already given your number to dozens of people, you may want to switch your number.

When you need people to call you, have them call your regular office line. If you're not there, they can leave a message on your voicemail or with your assistant. Then, call into your office regularly to get your messages.

At that point, you can determine whom you wish to call when you're on the road. In doing so, you've taken control over your calls. Plus, you can still manage to keep that personal touch.

- **Use an egg timer.** The majority of business calls can be completed in five minutes or less. Keep a timer in your office and set it for five minutes when you make or take a call. When the timer goes off, you'll know you should begin bringing most conversations to an end.

- **Have a clock visible.** When you're having a phone conversation, you will be reminded of how long the call is taking and if you need to end it soon.

- **Make use of your voicemail.** It's difficult to focus and concentrate when you have to stop everything you're doing every time the phone rings. Most telephone calls are not emergencies. If possible, have your answering machine or voicemail field your calls. Only pick up if it's absolutely necessary.

- **Ask someone to screen calls for you.** Hire a telephone answering service to field your calls or ask your administrative assistant to do so.

- **Get Caller ID.** Ask your telephone company if Caller ID is available in your area. Basically, it allows you to see the name and/or phone number of the person trying to reach you.

I never thought Caller ID would be worth it until my phone company asked me if I wanted to try it out for a free trial period. Now, I'd miss it desperately if I didn't have it.

When a call comes in, I just have to glance at the Caller ID readout. If it's someone I need to talk to right now, I pick it up. If it's someone I can call back or if it's a number I don't recognize, I allow my answering machine to take the message.

- **Redirect them.** If you are not the correct person to assist with a specific inquiry, direct callers to the individual that can help them. Provide them with the name and number of the individual and offer to transfer them.

  If you're not able to help someone, don't dawdle on the phone. Instead, find someone else who can assist the caller. Give regular callers names of people who can assist them when you are not available.

- **Give them all the info.** When transferring a caller, give her the name and extension of the person you're transferring her to. This way, if she gets cut off, she can call the other person directly, rather than interrupting you.

- **Make an "OK" list.** Help your administrative assistant or receptionist by letting him know which callers should be put through. Otherwise, ask your assistant to take messages.

- **Prioritize your calls.** Have a long list of people to call? Prioritize your list putting the most important calls at the top and the people who can wait a day or two towards the bottom. Then, make your calls in that order.

- **There's a time and place for everything.** Set aside at least an hour each day to make and return phone calls. You might set a morning hour, such as 10:00AM to 11:00AM or an afternoon hour such as 3:00PM to 4:00PM.

  Try to designate your chosen hour according to the time most people will be around to take your calls. In other words, setting your phone hour for lunchtime isn't a very good idea, since most people will be out to lunch.

- **Set up your telephone hour space.** Be sure that when you're ready to make your telephone calls during your telephone hour, you have a comfortable, equipped spot to do so. A comfortable chair, a telephone table, a writing tablet, a calendar and a timer are all must-have items.

- **Is it the best first step?** Ensure calling is the best first step. It may be more efficient to send out written materials, a fax or an email first. Plus, a written record is an excellent reference source for the future.

- **Be prepared.** Before you make any phone call, have a clear idea of what you need to say and have all materials pertinent to the call in front of you. Jot down any questions or comments you might have prior to the call so you don't forget anything. Whether you get the person or if you have to leave a message, you'll be able to express your thoughts intelligently and completely.

## Great idea!

One of the tools we can use to minimize telephone interruptions and maximize our efficiency is the Phone Log. "What is a Phone Log and why should I use one?" you may ask. The phone log is a repository for information and a valuable planning tool.

To begin with, you can use the phone log to record phone numbers, consolidate and prioritize your daily "to call" list and plan out an agenda for your business calls before you make them. Furthermore, it can be used for taking notes during your calls and recording the length of each call to help you plan your future calling sessions.

You can also use the phone log to keep down clutter in your office. Simply transfer the data from all those "While You Were Out" slips into your phone log then simply throw these slips away.

Finally, by dating the top of a new page in your phone log each day you will have a running record of when you made specific calls and the result of each call.

Jenifer Fox-Gerrits
Life Management Strategies, LLC
1516 Spruce Drive, Amelia OH 45102
jenifer@lifestrat.net
www.lifestrat.net

- **Have a goal.** For every business phone conversation you make, be sure you have a clear goal in mind of what you're trying to achieve. For instance, during a sales call, your goal may be to get an appointment. For a vendor call, your goal may be to determine when a particular supply can be shipped.

- **Prioritize calls.** Don't just answer calls in the order they were received. Put priority on calls that affect company sales or those that permit you or others to get started on tasks or projects.

- **Prioritize your points.** If you feel you may not be able to cover all of your points or questions in one phone call, list them out and prioritize them. Start with the most important and then if you can't cover everything, you can pick up on the less important points and questions during your next phone conversation.

- **Make a note of it.** Keep a spiral notebook right by your phone so you can take notes during your phone conversations. Write down the date, the person's name and the person's number. Then, jot down any specific points you wish to remember throughout your conversation.

A notebook will ensure all of your phone notes are in one place so you won't lose them like you might lose a loose scrap of paper or a sticky note. It will provide you with an excellent reference source for future conversations or for notes related to projects you're working on or an event you might be attending.

---

## Organizing Clinic

### Question

I have to make several cold calls during the day to grow my business, but I'm a bit uncomfortable trying to remember everything I have to say. I thought of using a script, but am afraid I'll sound unnatural and therefore unprofessional. Any ideas?

Barbara Emtec, Raleigh, NC

### Answer

Dear Barbara,

Many people who make cold calls use scripts and you're right—some sound very unnatural. To avoid this, why not simply make a list of the key points you have to make. This way, you can reference your list throughout the conversation, but you should still be able to sound fairly natural. Check off each point as you go and it should be an organized, productive, natural conversation.

---

- **Leave meaningful messages.** People won't always be ready to take your calls. You're bound to get some answering machines or voicemail messages when you call. This is why it's important to leave detailed messages.

  When leaving a message, include your name, company name, phone number and the time. If you require a call back, also tell the caller the best time to call you back or leave your email address to avoid playing telephone tag all day. Then, leave a brief but detailed message describing the nature of your call.

- **Speak slowly and clearly.** I'm sure you'll agree that it's pretty annoying to get a phone message and to have to listen to it ten times because the caller is speaking too low, too fast or is mumbling.

  If you're going to leave a message, always remember the words a) loud, b) clear and c) slow. The person getting your message is most likely writing down your contact information and any other details. She doesn't want to have to listen to your message over and over again.

- **Stop them.** If you get a call for a solicitation that you're not interested in, politely interrupt and tell the caller you're not interested and to take you off her call list. If she persists, say, "As I said, I'm not interested. I have to hang up now." If the person still persists, hang up.

  If your assistant fields your calls, have her head all solicitation calls off at the pass, so you're not burdened with them.

- **Keep a phone log.** Keep a log of people you speak to each day, along with any other contact information, the goal and result of each call. This will make future recall much easier and gives you a handy reference.

  Additionally, you should include calls that you need to make. You will then have a "To Call" list you can work with during your scheduled phone time.

- **Leave yourself a message.** When you're out on the road and you remember something you have to do when you return to the office, call your office voicemail and leave yourself a message. It will be on your machine when you get back to the office.

- **Take action after the call.** When you're finished with your phone conversations, take any necessary action. Transfer information to your calendar or To Do list. Put back any materials and file any important documents you pulled prior to the call. Delegate any projects.

- **Get accurate messages.** When someone else is answering the phone for you, be sure he has those pink message slips or a carbonless message book. Instruct that the message should be filled out completely with the caller's name, company name, number, best time to return the call and the nature of the call. In doing so, you will be better able to prioritize your phone messages.

  Make sure you also express the importance of message information being written neatly. The information is only useful to you if it is legible.

- **Delegate to electronics.** If you don't currently have a voicemail system in place, it is highly recommended. A voicemail system has three major advantages: 1) callers can leave messages 24 hours a day, 2) callers will never need to be annoyed with busy signals and 3) messages can easily be stored and retrieved. You can even combine certain voicemail systems with pagers and beepers.

- **Record helpful messages.** When people call in to your answering machine or voicemail system, most will expect you to call back that day or the next at the latest.

  If you're on vacation or will be out of the office for a prolonged period of time, be sure to say so on your message. It can also be helpful to redirect callers to someone else or give them another number where you can be reached.

---

## Create a visible phone message center

If it's visible, you'll always have a clear idea of your pending calls. You're probably familiar with the pink phone message slips people use to give phone messages to other people. When they're taped to the walls, attached to your bulletin board, stuck on your telephone or chair or tossed on your desk, they're bound to get lost pretty quickly.

The Phone Message Center solution can provide you and your staff members with an open, organized area to keep track of phone messages so you can act on them in a timely manner.

1. Hang a corkboard on your wall. Label it "Phone Message Center."

2. Divide the board into two with a strip of colored tape down the middle.

3. Label one section "Critical." Label the other section "Non-Critical."

4. Stick five pushpins in the "Critical" section and fifteen in the "Non-Critical" section. You're probably asking why there are only five in the Critical section. That's because most things are not critical. I repeat, most things are not critical. There should never be more than five messages, if that many, in the Critical section.

5. Provide your staff, co-workers, boss, assistants and anyone else who takes calls for you with pink phone message slips. Ask them to tack all phone messages to your Phone Message Center in the appropriate section. Make sure you tell them what constitutes critical. A critical message is only one that will affect you, a staff member, the company or a customer adversely if it's not responded to immediately.

6. Check your board regularly throughout the day and respond to your critical messages as soon as you see them on your board. Record any new phone data in your contact system. Toss these message slips out when the action is completed, but be sure to return the pushpin to the board.

7. Respond to your non-critical messages in the following manner:

   -- **Record:** Record any new contact data in your contact system.

   -- **Return the calls:** Use your phone hour to return the calls or have your assistant do so.

   -- **Toss:** Toss the pink phone message slips when the action(s) is completed.

---

- **Try pushing "O."** When calling a company, if you get caught up in infinite voicemail, try pushing "O" on your telephone keypad. Sometimes voicemail systems are set up so that you will get transferred to a human operator who may be better able to assist you.

- **Use a cell phone.** When out of the office, cell phone calls can come in handy. They're an excellent safety measure to have with you when traveling alone.

  You can take calls you need to take even when you're not in the office. Plus, since most cell phones have caller ID, you can see who is trying to reach you and decide whether or not to take the call.

  They're portable, which means you can make and take calls during idle time, such as when you're waiting in the airport for your flight.

  Always take proper safety precautions and never use a cell phone on the road when you're driving. If you must call someone during a car trip, pull over to the side of the road or better yet, pull into a rest stop.

- **Speed-dial.** Program frequently used numbers into your regular phone and cell phone, so you can make certain calls with the press of one button.

- **Make it unique.** Make your cell phone's tone unique, so you'll be able to distinguish your incoming calls from other cell phones around you. Some cell phones even allow you to make a call from a specific person unique, so you'll know if your wife or your boss is calling.

- **Get the vibe.** Turn your cell phone to "vibrate mode" when you're in a meeting or appointment. You will know a call is coming in, without everyone else in the room being disturbed.

- **Charge!** Charge your cell phone each night. This way, it will be fully charged each day. Bring your charger with you if you plan to be on the road for one night or more.

- **Schedule meetings by telephone.** Rather than driving across town or traveling to another state, some meetings can be handled with a simple conference call. This can end up saving you and your company both time and money.

- **Make telephone appointments.** If you plan to be on the phone with someone for fifteen minutes or more, you may want to schedule a phone appointment with that person. Whenever I'm being interviewed for a newspaper article, for instance, the interviewer usually calls or emails me to set up a date and time to speak. This makes it convenient for both of us.

- **Answer professionally.** If you answer your phone when a call comes in, always have a professional greeting ready. You might say, "Hello, this is Annie of the ABC company. How can I assist you?"

  I once called a restaurant and the person answered the phone, "Yeah?" When I asked if this was the Family Restaurant, the person responded, "Uh huh." As you can imagine, I was less than pleased.

# Chapter 23

# Your contacts

- **Choose your pleasure.** People have different methods for storing their contact information, ranging from the basic Rolodex system, to written name and address books, to computer databases, personal digital assistants or even more sophisticated systems. The key is to use a system that is easy for you to maintain and that you feel comfortable using. Here are some of the methods in which you can store your contacts:

  - **Paper-based Address Book:** Some people like to use paper-based address books. The only problem with most of these books is that once they get filled up or contact information changes, they tend to get a bit messy. Then, you have to spend time transferring information to a new address book.

    For personal use, paper-based address books are generally okay, but for business use, especially since contact information can change so frequently, I don't usually recommend them.

  - **Rolodex or 3x5 card box:** If you travel infrequently and need only basic information on your contacts such as name and number, a Rolodex or 3x5 card box should work fine for you. When you need to take a contact out, you just remove the card. Need to add a contact? Just insert a card. It's an easy system to use. Two drawbacks are 1) you can only fit a limited amount of information on a Rolodex card and 2) most are too bulky to be portable, so you can't have access to your contact information unless you are in the office.

  - **Business card organizers.** Many office supply stores carry business card organizers that contain plastic inserts for you to store business cards. If you use one of these, it is recommended that you designate no less than one plastic insert page per letter of the alphabet and use a label to label each page A, B, C, etc.

    If you don't organize your business card book this way, you're going to have to constantly move your business cards around to keep them in some sort of logical order.

  - **Computer-based address book:** If you use a regular computer and work in the office most of the time, a computer-based address book can be wonderful. The only thing is, you have to have your computer on all the time so that you can quickly look up contact information if necessary.

Many computer-based address books allow you to put in additional information, such as the person's email address, web site and birthday. Just be sure you back up your address book from time to time.

Remember, as discussed earlier in this book, it is important to have a back-up schedule for all the information on your computer. In the case of a computer crash, you won't lose all of your contacts.

Printing out your contact list is another way to save the information if your computer does crash.

Two major advantages of a computer-based system: 1) Many computer-based address book systems can be "synched "with a Personal Digital Assistant (PDA), which means you can copy all the contact information from your computer onto your PDA, giving you access to it anywhere at anytime. (Make sure you read your manual to find out how) and 2) If you have a computer network in your office, all the contact information (and all future changes) can easily be made available for use by everyone on the network.

- **Personal Digital Assistants:** If you travel frequently and don't like the idea of having to carry around a bulky book with all your contact information, you might look into getting yourself a PDA, also known as a Personal Digital Assistant.

  I was just talking to a business associate, who travels all the time and he is able to store over 700 of his business contacts on his PDA—and they're with him all the time. Again, just make sure you back up your contacts from time to time, in case something goes wrong with your PDA.

  Additionally, many PDA devices can communicate with the contact software you have on your PC, so the information on your PDA and your PC are consistent.

- **Contact Management Software:** If you have lots of contacts and need extensive information on each contact, it is recommended you invest in Contact Management Software such as ACT! Back up your information regularly. Better safe than sorry.

- **Reference it.** Within your contact system, you may wish to include reference pages or cards for airlines, hotels and restaurants. For instance, you might have one page or card that includes all of the airlines you use for making travel reservations. Your page or card entitled Airlines would be filed under Airlines and on that one page or card it would include the names and numbers of the major airlines such as American Airlines 800-433-7300, Delta Airlines 800-221-1212 and Midwest Express Airlines 800-452-2022.

**Great idea!**

Use an empty box that is business card size to collect business cards from meetings, shows and other events. Write the name of the event and date on the reverse side of the card before you include it in the box. Once a week, at a consistent time, add these cards to your database or mailing list.

Lillian Kaufman
When you think of jewelry, think of Diamond Lil
www.diastarjewelry.com

- **In case of emergency.** One very important card to keep in your contact system is a list of emergency numbers, such as 911 (if you live in the USA), Poison Control, and names of emergency contacts such as a spouse, parent, neighbor or friend. This information should be entitled "Emergency" and should be kept on the first page or first card, in your system, plus under "I" (labeled as ICE) for "In Case of Emergency".

- **Don't waste time rewriting if you don't have to.** If you use a Rolodex system and someone hands you a business card, don't waste time transferring the contact information from the business card to your Rolodex card. Instead, either tape the business card right on a Rolodex card, invest in a cardpunch for your business cards or purchase business card sleeves that fit in your Rolodex—the business cards slide right inside.

- **Don't start a collection of business cards.** If someone passes along his business card and you have absolutely no intention of contacting this person in the future, then by all means toss the card. Of course, don't do this in front of the person who just gave you the card.

  Once, when working with a client to help her organize her office, she showed me her business card collection. We played a little game called, "Who is this person?" I picked up each card one by one and asked my client, "Who is this person?" She was only able to answer about 40% of the time. Most of the time, she had no idea. In the end, it was pretty easy to weed out the unnecessary business cards.

- **Don't toss them in a shoebox.** For those business cards that you do keep, an organized system will help you locate them quickly later. Whatever you do, don't just collect your business cards and perpetually store them in a shoebox without doing anything with them. I once knew someone who did this. Every time she needed a number, she had to rummage through her shoebox for 30 minutes or more—obviously a big waste of time.

## Organizing Clinic

### Question

I work in a small, but very busy office. There have been five people in this position before me over the past 4 to 5 years. Our company does data research and I have two co-workers with opposing styles. One throws everything away; the other keeps every single piece of information.

If that weren't bad enough, the Rolodex is a hodgepodge of business cards and handwritten names, some filed by first name, others by business type and still others are bunched up together under one organization's name.

Help! What can I do to make it more uniform? Looking forward to your life-saving ideas.

Gary Zimmerman

### Answer

Dear Gary,

First, a staff member should not decide what gets kept and what gets tossed. The head of your department needs to come up with standard procedures that all staff members follow. This way, there is no question for current staff members and future employees will know exactly what to do.

As far as the Rolodex, it would be a lot more uniform if one person and one person only were in charge of this system. As far as how to organize the names and companies using the current Rolodex system, it's important to file the card in a way that the majority of people using the system will be able to find it.

If most people look for the ABC Company under ABC Company, that is how it should be filed. If most people look for Mike Smith under the category of Plumber, that is how it should be filed. And if most people search for Jean Anderson under Anderson, that's how that should be filed.

If necessary, file two cards in the Rolodex system, perhaps one for ABC Company and another for Jean Anderson. There is going to be duplication if you choose to use this system, but at least everyone will be able to find contact information when needed.

Another possibility would be to use a computer-based contact manager. All contact information would need to be input into the system, but you can later easily and quickly search by name or company name or category. This would eliminate the need for duplicate entries.

In order for all staff members to have access to this one contact manager, you would need to have a local area network set up between computers. Another option is to store the information on one person's computer, such as an administrative assistant, who can retrieve the information when needed.

- **Color code business and personal.** If you use your work Rolodex for both personal and business phone numbers, use one color Rolodex card for business and another color for personal. You'll then be able to easily distinguish between the two.

## Organizing Clinic

### Question

I do income taxes. From mid January to April 15, I'm really busy. I would like to continue to grow and add new customers, but I feel I am close to the limit of how many clients I can serve in this short amount of time. Any suggestions?

Karl Koch

### Answer

Dear Karl,

Having too many clients is certainly better than not enough clients, especially in a down economy. I'm assuming that you're using the computer to do the income taxes and not paper and pencil. If you are not using the computer, then this timesaving tool would help you help more customers in less time. Of course, you should also be using the latest tax software to make the job as quick and easy as possible.

Do you currently have very strict schedules when it comes to your current clients? For instance, you should be able to group your customers into three categories based on the amount of time you generally spend with them, such as 30 Minute Customers, 60 Minute Customers and 90 Minute Customers. It's important that you stick to the scheduled times for each customer, to ensure that you can maximize the number of customers you can serve on a daily basis. Double-check your time for possible time-wasters that can be eliminated during your busy season.

If you really want to grow your business, you may have to seriously consider hiring some help, even if the help is only temporary during the busy tax season months. Being able to delegate some of the work will free up your time to grow your business even more. Additionally, providing clients with a list of records they should bring with them will speed up the process and ensure the client is ready to work with you.

- **Cross-reference.** If you have to put Ralph Smith (your accountant) in your Rolodex and you're not sure you will remember his name, have a card for him under S for "Smith" and a cross-reference card under "A" for accountant.

- **Make an office directory.** If your office doesn't have one already, put together an office directory of all the people in your office and their phone extensions. Pass this directory out to everyone and keep one on your bulletin board or near your telephone.

- **Use the back for notes.** The next time you take a business card, use the back to jot down any quick notes about this person or her company—such as where you met her, the name of this person's spouse or an event this person may be celebrating. This information may help jog your memory at a later date.

### Great idea!

I use the program Act! to keep my contacts, to-do list and calendar. When creating a new contact, I put them into an appropriate group (client, prospect, networking group, etc.). If I want to send email to a group or do a mail merge for sending a letter to a particular group, it's done with a few clicks of the mouse.

When scheduling an appointment or a "to do" related to a client, a log of that item is stored in the contact's file so I can go back to see a history of what I've done with that client. I can also add notes to their file and set up reminders for each appointment, phone call or "to do." Act! also works in conjunction with Outlook, so it tracks email and can be synched with my PDA.

Jean Hanson
16212 Miles Circle, Brainerd, MN 56401
218-855-1854
jean@vaofficesolution.com
VA Office Solution, www.VAOfficeSolution.com
Virtualize Your Business, www.VirtualizeYourBiz.com

- **Highlight the Yellow Pages.** If the phone book is yours, feel free to highlight frequently called numbers with a fluorescent marker or tag certain pages with sticky notes so you can find numbers faster.

- **Go the sophisticated route.** If you have many contacts or plan to have many in the future, contact management software may be for you. One of the popular ones is ACT!, but there are several others. Look for features such as:
  - ❖ Ready to use database with searching features
  - ❖ Unlimited contacts
  - ❖ Mail, fax and email merge
  - ❖ Customer specific notes
  - ❖ Customizable fields
  - ❖ A calendar that links to contacts
  - ❖ Automatic Pop-up Reminders
  - ❖ Sales tools
  - ❖ Automated history entries
  - ❖ Autodial phone
  - ❖ Links to the Internet

# Chapter 24

# Leading a meeting or presentation

- **Is a meeting necessary?** The first question to always ask yourself is if a meeting is the best way to accomplish your goals. Sometimes a meeting can be avoided with a simple phone call or email communication.

- **Is it a good reason?** The top five reasons to hold a meeting are:
  - ❖ To give information
  - ❖ To get information
  - ❖ To brainstorm as a group
  - ❖ To make decisions as a group
  - ❖ To socialize

- **Out of town.** When possible, meet electronically with out-of-town staff members or customers. Instead of traveling out of town, hold a telephone conference or videoconference instead.

- **What's in a name?** If attendees don't know each other, prepare nametags for each. On the day of the meeting, arrange the tags alphabetically outside the meeting room for attendees to pick up and use.

- **Be prepared.** Lack of preparation by the meeting leader will waste everyone's time.

- **Plan meetings in advance.** If you don't know what you're going to say or do at a meeting, don't have one. Your attendees are expecting you to lead them.

- **Determine your budget.** You may have to think about expenses such as transportation, facility rental, equipment rental, accommodations and catering. You may want your presentation to be very posh, but you may not have the budget to do so. Also, always leave a little wiggle room to accommodate any unforeseen expenses.

- **Determine where.** It's important to decide whether you want your meeting to be offsite or onsite. Onsite may be excellent for a typical staff meeting, but offsite may be better for a large meeting that involves staff and customers. Plus, offsite prevents staff members from leaving the meeting to check on email, voicemail, and so on.

- **Check the room ahead of time.** Get to the presentation room well before your meeting to check and make sure it has everything you need. You should be there in enough time to handle any surprises. It will also give you ample time to practice.

- **What equipment will you need?** Sometimes, a simple pen and paper will do the trick. Other times, you might need things like a projector, laptop, Internet connection or video-conferencing tools. Make a list and check it twice.

- **Dress the part.** The leader of any meeting or presentation should be dressed one-notch up from the rest of the attendees. A well-dressed leader commands more respect.

---

### Great idea!

Always prepare and send out an agenda prior to the meeting to give people time to get prepared and to improve the productivity of the meeting. You can either insert the meeting agenda in your "meeting notice," or attach it as a file to the meeting notice.

A well-prepared agenda provides a tool for all to agree on the objectives and desired outcomes of the meeting, as well as to ensure that the group stays on track as the meeting progresses.

A follow-up message summarizing the meetings key points and action items also gives all attendees a chance to share the results of the meeting with other non-attendees who may be interested in the results, as well as a reminder for their action items.

Ilene Drexler
The Organizing Wiz
201 East 87th Street #11G, New York City, NY 10128
917-301-1981
OrganizingWiz@aol.com

---

- **Be on time.** You should arrive at meetings you're chairing well ahead of time, anywhere from 15 minutes to an hour, depending on how much equipment you have to set up and test.

Leandra, a government staff member, had to present the budget plan for her department. She arrived at the presentation a few minutes early. After exchanging some pleasantries with early arrivals, she still had to set up her projector, arrange seating and place handouts on chairs.

As it turned out, she was still setting up over ten minutes after the meeting should have started. In other words, she wasted everyone's time setting up while they waited for her, plus the meeting ran over into overtime.

- **Keep on top of things.** Regular staff meetings are important to keep on top of what's going on. However, if these meetings turn into gab sessions or "what did you do this weekend" sessions, they're going to be a waste of time. Keep staff meetings down to a half hour or less and be sure the important topics are discussed.

- **Pick wise dates.** Be careful about holding meetings or presentations when many people won't be able to make it, such as during religious observances, holidays or vacations.

- **Avoid Monday mornings.** If you hold meetings, avoid Monday morning meetings. People need time to start their week and tie up any loose ends from the previous week.

- **Avoid Friday meetings.** You can't stop people from dreaming about the weekend. Additionally, the information will be forgotten by the time everyone is back to work on Monday.

- **Schedule when they don't want to linger.** If you schedule a meeting right before lunch hour, there will be little chance of the meeting running into overtime, as people will want to stay on schedule so they can go to lunch on time.

- **Best meeting times.** Try early in the week, like Tuesday at around 10:30 or 11:00am. This will give people some time to get some tasks accomplished before the meeting. Also, most people are alert early in the week and early in the day—but not too early.

- **Invite only who is needed.** Before inviting people to a meeting, really think through who "must" attend and who doesn't really have to. You don't want to waste the time of people who really don't have to be there.

  On the other hand, be certain you do invite the people who are critical to the goals of the meeting. For instance, the sales people should be involved in meetings for computerized customer products—not just the computer design team.

  Necessary people generally include those who have the expertise required to meet the objectives, must approve or implement the decisions made, or will be significantly impacted by the decisions.

- **Use scheduling software.** If your company uses a program like Outlook, you can automatically schedule meetings and send out advisories to all necessary parties. This, however, requires people to be networked.

- **Give them a scheduled time.** If certain people are needed at the meeting, but only needed for a small period of time, don't ask them to attend the entire meeting. Have them come in at the beginning, middle or end of your meeting to do their part.

- **Prepare written agendas.** Always prepare written agendas for your meetings and distribute them to the attendees at the meeting so everyone is aware of what comes next.

  If this is a major meeting, you may wish to send copies of the agenda to all attendees ahead of time so they have time to prepare or so they know what is going to be reviewed or discussed.

  The agenda should include the purpose of the meeting, topics of discussion and possible presenters, if applicable.

- **Prepare standard agendas.** For staff meetings, it's generally not necessary to make a new agenda for each and every meeting, especially if typical items are discussed at each meeting. Make a standard agenda that can be used at all meetings that include consistent subjects. For example, meetings with your department managers might include items like employee issues, department budgets and pending projects.

- **Don't go into overtime.** Set a meeting start time, a meeting end time and time limits for each topic. Indicate this on the agenda. Avoid going into overtime, if possible, by sticking to the agenda.

- **Close the door.** If you're meeting in a conference room or office with a door, close it so everyone's attention is on the meeting and not what's happening outside the room. It will also deter people from coming late, as they clearly have to disturb the group to enter.

## Organizing Clinic

### Question

I use overheads in my classroom. I want to store them so I can find them. They fall out of my folders. Is there a better way?

Carmen Emmert

### Answer

Dear Carmen,

Here's a very simple system you can use which will guarantee a smooth and organized presentation.

- Insert your overhead transparencies into sheet protectors. Get a set of clear sheet protectors from any office supplies store. Be sure they are 3-hole punched. Insert each overhead into one of these sheet protectors.

- Insert the sheet protectors into a 3-ring binder for each of your presentations.

- Remove, present, replace. As you're presenting your material, remove one of the sheet protectors and lay it on your overhead projector. Since these are clear, there is no reason to remove the transparency from each. As you complete presenting the material on the first transparency, re-insert it into your binder. Then, go to your next transparency. By the time you're done presenting, all of your transparencies should already be in your binder and ready for your next presentation in the future.

- Note: You may choose to eliminate the sheet protectors and just 3-hole punch the actual transparency. However, sheet protectors protect the transparencies, especially if you're going to be using them over and over again.

---

- **Johnny come lately.** Don't wait for latecomers. Start without them, unless of course they're your supervisors or clients. They can catch up on anything they missed when the meeting is adjourned, so they're not wasting everyone's time.

- **Last one to arrive is a rotten egg.** To make sure everyone gets to your meetings on time, have the last person to arrive take the minutes. People generally hate to do this and will run to the meeting to ensure they're not the last one there.

- **Set the tone.** Immediately let everyone know what's going to be discussed and how long you expect each item to take. Stress the importance of keeping on schedule.

- **Set timers.** Set timers in meetings to stay on track. Kitchen timers work very well. Set the timer for 20 minutes or the amount of time needed to take care of the first topic.

  When the alarm goes off, it's time to move on to the next topic. Hopefully, you wrapped up your goals for the initial topic, but if not, write down where you left off so that you can pick up on it at the end of the meeting if you have time or at the next meeting.

- **Stay on track.** If someone gets off topic, say, "We can discuss that issue at another time or after the meeting. Let's get back to the scheduled topic." As the meeting leader, it's your responsibility to ensure the meeting stays on track.

- **Have a late afternoon coffee meeting.** If you like holding meetings at restaurants, but feel you are spending too much time at luncheon meetings, consider late afternoon coffee meetings instead. You'll have a nice break to briefly escape the phones and interruptions, without spending too much time out of the office. Another plus is that the restaurant will be empty making it a good forum to talk business.

- **Have a breakfast meeting.** The menu is always simple which makes ordering quick and easy. Also, people will usually not drink anything stronger than a cup of coffee this early in the day.

- **Luncheon meeting your only option?** If you must have a luncheon meeting, try to set it to start between 11:30 and 11:45AM before the lunch hour crowd hits. You'll avoid long waits.

- **Order in.** If you're having a meeting with staff members, why waste time going to a restaurant at all? Order in and save time.

- **Weekly meetings.** If you manage several departments in your company, hold weekly meetings with your department managers to keep informed about projects and goals in individual areas of your business. Always have a planned agenda with goals.

- **Assert yourself.** Speak loudly and clearly so you can be heard. Stand or sit where you can make good eye contact with everyone in the room.

- **Get feedback.** Don't be the only one talking through the entire meeting. Give others a chance to speak their minds and provide feedback. You'll give yourself a break to sip some water and take a breath, while giving others a chance to speak up.

- **Take control.** Don't allow meeting-hogs and ramblers to take control of your meetings. Some people simply like to hear the sound of their own voices. Ask those people kindly to bring up their points in writing or to see you at the end of the meeting privately.

## Organizing Clinic

### Question

As the head of my department, I feel it's necessary to hold weekly staff meetings. But, they almost always turn into "grief sessions" with everyone complaining about one thing or another. How can I make these meetings more productive?

Cheryl Anderson, Milwaukee, WI

### Answer

Dear Cheryl,

First, be sure you cover whatever you need to, without the interjection of your staff members unless you specifically ask them a question. Make it a rule that all staff questions and comments be addressed at the end of your meeting. Schedule a maximum of fifteen minutes at the end of your meetings for this purpose.

Stop the complaining immediately, by requiring anyone with a complaint or issue to have at least three possible solutions. This will stop most complaints immediately, because it's easy to complain, but much harder to come up with viable solutions.

Once that person presents his or her possible solutions, open other solutions up to the group. Who knows? You may actually be able to make some improvements. At minimum, at least you will be aware of what some of the issues are.

Better yet, you may wish to skip this part of the staff meeting and have staff members fill out Employee Suggestion forms that give them the opportunity to present the perceived problem, some possible solutions and specific information on how those solutions will save the company time, stress or money.

They can drop these off at a designated drop-box and you can get back to them individually, in an employee newsletter or you can bring it up at a staff meeting if you think it's worth the time.

- **Assign someone else to take notes.** If you can't take notes while you're speaking, have someone else take notes for you. If necessary, have someone write the "minutes" or details of the meeting. Rotate this responsibility if you have meetings with the same people each week. Or, have a tape recorder take minutes and have your assistant type the minutes up after each meeting.

- **You don't have to have all the answers.** When someone asks you a question that you can't answer right there and then, tell that person you will get back to her after the meeting. Be sure to jot yourself a note so you remember to follow up.

## Great idea!

**Before the meeting**

- Try to arrange the meeting to be at a central location.
- Have light refreshments, so that people feel comfortable.
- Arrange sitting with everyone facing each other.
- If the meeting is a weekly event, plan to make it the same time and place every week. This will allow for members to mark a whole year on their calendars.

**Make an agenda**

- Call to order.
- Approve the minutes from the last meeting.
- Announcements.
- Committee reports, if any.
- Unfinished business.
- New business.
- Discuss any special projects.
- Set up the next meeting.
- Adjourn.

Send out the agenda, well in advance, to the members. This will enable people to come prepared.

**During the meeting**

- Greet members individually.
- Start on time.
- End on time.
- Stick to the agenda.
- Encourage discussion, members will feel more involved, important and not bored.
- Keep minutes during the meeting.
- Praise members for their input.
- Keep members focused on the task at hand.
- Be flexible, not rigid.
- Take care of problems swiftly and confidently.
- Encourage attendees to see different perspectives.
- Help members work out conflicts.

**After the meeting**

- Type up the minutes.
- Write up the next agenda. Put in any unfinished business.

Diane Sullivan
The Organization Station
800 No. 4th St., Springfield, NE 68059
402-253-8145
www.organization-station.net

- **Don't cram it full.** Don't attempt to cover a million different things in a short meeting. People will be confused, bored and overwhelmed. Stick to a few topics per meeting.

- **If it ends early, adjourn.** If a meeting you had scheduled for 60 minutes ends 15 minutes early, adjourn the meeting. No sense wasting time sticking around for the entire hour.

- **Keep an action list.** At the end of each meeting, you should have a list of Action Items that need to be completed, who is responsible for completing them and when. Follow up on your Action Items later.

- **Schedule the Next Meeting.** If another meeting is required to follow up on issues or a project, schedule the next meeting while everyone is still in the room. This will allow everyone to check their schedules on the spot and quickly arrive at a good meeting date.

- **Stand up.** If a meeting should only take a few minutes, meet standing up. Doing so will reduce the chances of the meeting dragging on. When I managed my staff at Nielsen Media Research, I used to hold regular "update meetings" with my staff. Everyone would gather at the back of the department, standing up. Each staff member would give me a 1-minute update of any issues that needed to be addressed and I would give everyone a quick pep talk. These meetings were fast, productive and kept everyone updated.

- **Use a flip chart.** If you're going to be discussing a number of points, especially those involving numbers, use a flip chart or Powerpoint presentation so everyone gets a visual.

### Great idea!

The best way to lead a meeting is to make sure you engage your audience. Be succinct, logical in sequence and involve everyone there in the discussion.

Pamala J. Mielnicki, Associate Editor of *Finally Organized, Finally Free for the Office*

- **Point it out.** If you decide to use a pointer, point but don't touch the screen, which will cause it to sway and distract your audience. Better yet, use a laser pointer.

- **Be sure it's readable.** Use appropriate, straightforward colors, font types and font sizes on your charts.

I once attended a presentation at which the leader used red type on a purple background. Also, she used a very tiny, fancy font. None of the attendees could read the charts!

- **Include appropriate graphics and photographs.** Graphics and photographs on your charts can definitely help to make a point, but only include them if they have a definite purpose. Graphics and photographs merely meant to "decorate" can be very distracting.

- **Avoid busy backgrounds.** Keep the background of your presentation simple. Too much going on will make the text very hard to read.

- **Avoid using all caps.** Don't use all capital letters in your presentation. All capital letters represents SHOUTING and is very distracting to your audience.

- **Use a microphone.** If you're presenting to over 20 people, you may want to consider using a microphone. This way, even the people in the back of the room will be able to hear you.

- **Prepare for disaster.** When leading a meeting or giving a presentation, keep Murphy's Law in mind. Always have back-ups on hand in case of disaster. An extra light bulb will help if your projector light bulb goes out. A battery backup will be an enormous help in case of a power failure.

  Handouts for your audience are key, in case you happen to drop all of your slides on the floor—I once saw this happen to a poor soul. He spent half the presentation picking up his slides and attempting to put them back in order!

- **Rate your meetings.** Always rate your meetings for effectiveness on a scale of 1 to 10, with 10 being excellent and 1 being poor. Evaluate your results and make any necessary improvements at your next meeting.

  - Did it start on time?

  - Did you have a written agenda?

  - Did you follow the agenda?

  - Were there distractions or diversions?

  - Did you encourage participation and questions?

  - Was everyone clear on your goals at the end of the meeting?

  - Did the meeting end on time?

- **Hire a meeting planner.** If your event is much bigger than you can handle, consider hiring a meeting planner. This person will help you arrange invitations, seating, equipment, food and beverages, accommodations and more.

# Great idea!

When holding an effective meeting, come prepared with a clear agenda, a time frame and a goal. There is nothing more frustrating than attending a meeting that goes on and on, with no clear focus or intended result.

Plan your agenda in advance listing the people in attendance, the purpose of the meeting and who will speak on which topics at what time. Prioritize the agenda by putting the items of the most crucial importance first and allocating a bit more time for those, while slotting in the least important items at the end of the meeting.

Distribute the agenda prior to the meeting, so people will know what to expect when they arrive.

If you don't have a neutral facilitator, at the beginning of the meeting, establish yourself as the facilitator. Let attendees know that it is your job to keep the meeting focused and on-track, so that you can meet your goals.

At the same time, establish the "ground rules" for the meeting, which will help you control time-wasters, questions and those who try to derail your agenda by being disruptive.

Monica Ricci
Get Organized Now! Associate Editor of *Finally Organized, Finally Free for the Office*
Catalyst Organizing Solutions, 770-569-2642
Member and Past President, NAPO Georgia
To Receive Free Organizing and Simplifying Tips Just Click and Subscribe!
www.CatalystOrganizing.com

# Chapter 25

# Attending meetings and presentations

- **Dress appropriately.** At some business meetings and presentations, you will be expected to wear a suit. Sometimes, business casual will do. Sometimes, jeans and a t-shirt will do. It all depends on what you do for a living, what your company's dress code policy is and who is going to be there. To be on the safe side, always ask your boss or your manager when in doubt.

- **Take notes.** Jot down any necessary notes that concern you or your department. Don't try to remember everything that was discussed. You're bound to forget something.

- **Bring two pens.** Just in case the pen you're using runs out of ink, you'll have a spare without having to disturb your neighbor.

- **Bring address labels.** When asked to put your name and address on a card, like for a contest or mailing list, you can just peel and stick an address label. No more having to write out your mailing information.

---

### Great idea!

When attending a meeting, make sure you are alert and paying attention to the discussion. Participate by asking questions and offering constructive suggestions towards solving the issue(s) at hand. Take notes. This will refresh your memory and enable you to utilize the valuable information being shared.

Pamala J. Mielnicki, Associate Editor of *Finally Organized, Finally Free for the Office*

---

- **Bring business cards.** Meetings and presentations are perfect forums to get to know people. Be prepared with at least 15 business cards. Keep them in a business card holder in your suit pocket or your briefcase.

- **But not just for the sake of it.** The notes you take should be notes you plan to implement, delegate or file for future reference. Don't just take notes for the sake of taking notes.

Eliza, a receptionist at a cosmetics firm, attends a New Product Conference each year. During conference, she takes down notes. When she returns to the office, she immediately files the notes—and never looks at them again!

Obviously, this is a waste of filing cabinet space. When I brought this to her attention, she admitted she only took notes because others around her were taking notes.

Now, when she attends conference, she only takes notes of the points that directly affect her and that she plans to use when she's back at the office.

## Organizing Clinic

### Question

I have to attend staff meetings every Monday morning and I never arrive on time. It's so embarrassing! Any suggestions?

Helen Leukert, Munich, Germany

### Answer

Dear Helen,

If you're already in the office prior to your staff meetings, you are probably late due to distractions like phone calls, visitors or other projects. If you have a staff meeting first thing every Monday morning, don't take any calls, send visitors away until later and don't even start on your projects. Avoiding these things will keep you focused.

If the meeting is right down the hall, you can probably wait until five minutes prior to get there—a few minutes to walk down the hall and a few minutes to sit down and relax before the meeting begins.

If you have to take an elevator or the stairs to get to the meeting room, leave anywhere from ten to fifteen minutes early to ensure you make it on time.

Also, realize that if you have to stop in the restroom or grab a cup of coffee on the way, you'll have to leave a few minutes earlier to accommodate this extra stop.

If you're not in the office prior to your staff meetings, then you have to work on your morning wake up or commute. You may need to wake up a half hour earlier or take the earlier train.

Make it a point to get out of your house earlier on Mondays so you arrive at your staff meetings on time.

- **Come with ideas and questions.** If you already know what the meeting is about, think about it a bit before you attend. Perhaps you can come to the meeting prepared with any ideas or questions you can think of.

- **Reconfirm before you leave.** When you're going to a meeting outside the office, always reconfirm the time and place before you leave. You'll save time and embarrassment if for some reason the meeting was cancelled and nobody was able to reach you.

- **Be on time.** Give yourself plenty of time to arrive at the meeting or presentation. You should plan to arrive a minimum of five to ten minutes before it starts.

- **Get a good seat.** This is especially true if you have trouble seeing or hearing from the back of the room. Get there early to get your choice of seats. Or, move your chair closer to the front or out of the way of the obstruction.

- **Be prepared for meetings outside the office.** If you have plans to meet someone from out of town, ask them where they're staying. Request the phone number and name of the hotel. Jot the information into your planner so that you can contact them in case of cancellation, change of plans or to confirm.

- **Be courteous.** If you're running late for a meeting, call and inform the necessary people. Their time is valuable too and perhaps they can begin the meeting with a section that doesn't involve you being there.

- **No leader, no accomplishments.** If you're ever at a meeting with a group of people and nobody seems to be in charge, suggest that a meeting leader be appointed to keep the meeting on track. Without a leader at a meeting, it is nearly impossible to achieve anything.

- **Stay alert.** Avoid eating heavy meals or very sugary foods prior to meetings. They may drain your energy and reduce your focus. Get enough sleep the night before. Bring a cup of coffee. Stand up and stretch. Ask a buddy to nudge you if you start to nod off.

- **Bring something soothing.** Have throat lozenges and something to drink on hand. Whether you have a cold, get a tickle in your throat or simply get thirsty, these comfort items can help soothe you. Plus, you may disturb your neighbors if you have to constantly clear your throat or if you have a cough.

- **Should you be there?** If you feel that your presence is not really necessary at a particular meeting and you can get out of it, a lot of time will be saved and your day will be more productive. If you're only needed for a few minutes at the meeting, offer to come in at the very beginning and leave when your part is done or come in and leave at a scheduled interval.

- **Be prepared.** If you're going to be discussing an issue at a meeting you're attending, be certain you're prepared. Bring written notes, important dates and any other vital information so you're not wasting your time or anyone else's time.

- **Don't flip ahead.** If you're given handouts during a presentation, remain focused and avoid flipping the pages. First, flipping pages is extremely distracting to the speaker and other attendees. Second, you're bound to miss something being said if you're reading the handout, rather than listening.

- **Bring a tape recorder.** This is not always allowed, but it doesn't hurt to ask. If you record, you'll be able to review the presentation later at your leisure.

- **Ask questions.** When confused about a point just stated, raise your hand and ask for clarification. Or, if you prefer to wait until after the meeting, jot down your question(s) so you don't forget.

- **Use the telephone or written communication instead.** Sometimes a meeting might not be necessary. Determine if you can use the telephone or written communication to keep in close contact with the necessary people instead.

---

## Organizing Clinic

### Question

Do you have any ideas for easier note taking? I want to take notes, but I'm a slow writer. Before I'm finished writing down a thought, the speaker has generally moved on to the next subject and if I'm writing, I can't hear what he's saying. Please help.

Mike Daniels, San Diego, CA

### Answer

Dear Mike,

If you're allowed, bring a tape recorder with you. This way, you can listen to the presentation again later on at your own pace. You might also look into reading a book on shorthand, which will allow you to jot notes down in a fraction of the time it would take you to write longhand.

When taking notes, abbreviate whenever possible. Rather than writing "should be" for instance, use a code such as s/b. Rather than writing the word "representative," write "rep." Rather than writing the word "change," write "ch." You get the idea.

---

- **Delegating your attendance.** Can someone else attend the meeting for you? Sending someone in your place that is familiar with the subject(s) might be an option.

- **Talk to your boss.** If you're attending meetings that rarely involve your input or presence, ask your boss if you can forego the meeting to get other work done.

- **Bring something to do.** Just in case a meeting you're attending is delayed due to a speaker who does not arrive on time, etc., be sure you bring reading material or a task you can do in the meantime. Be in control of your waiting time.

## Great idea!

- Always attend meetings with a pen and paper. It communicates preparedness.

- Bring your calendar/personal organizer in case a follow up meeting is scheduled.

- Don't answer your cell phone. If you're expecting an important call, notify the meeting facilitator ahead of time and set your ringer to vibrate. Leave the room if you must answer a call.

- Regardless of whether you expect to take notes, have paper in front of you. In the top left-hand corner, write the date. Title the sheet with the name of the meeting. In the left-hand column, list the name of everyone in attendance. If you don't know every person's name, simply note his or her role. This information may become helpful later when remembering who was in attendance or who was present for key decisions.

- Don't rely on the minute taker to summarize the meeting outcomes for you. Write down all "To Dos" or "Take Aways" from the meeting; not only yours, but everyone's. List the "To Do" with a box to the left of it (to check off when complete) and the name of the person responsible to the right of it. This is helpful for keeping track of outcomes.

Brigitta Theleman
Organized Insight
919-302-0567
brigitta@organizedinsight.com
www.organizedinsight.com

- **Seek networking opportunities.** When attending a meeting or presentation, make it a point to network with other attendees. You never know whom you might meet—it may turn out to be someone really worth your while.

- **Keep an open mind.** If you attend a meeting or presentation, you are bound to hear some new ideas. Rather than immediately discounting them, try to think of at least 5 benefits of that new idea. Doing so will force you to focus on the good, rather than the negative. Perhaps the ideas that didn't sound very good at first, will be very effective after all!

# Chapter 26

# Dealing with the dreaded reading pile

- **Relax your reading ambitions.** Most people are overly ambitious when it comes to the amount of stuff they think they want to read. I've seen some reading piles over 4 feet high!

  You're busy. There's only so much time in any given day that you can dedicate to reading.

  Be reasonable. Pick and choose information that will help you learn something beneficial. Other reading can release stress by helping you relax.

- **If you want to read, make time to read.** If your idea is to read when you have the time to read, your reading pile may grow into Mount Everest. The only way to keep up is to set time aside to read each day.

  Choose a consistent time, like 9:00AM to 9:30AM each morning. Or, if it's tough for you to read for 30 minutes straight, you might want to set aside three 10-minute increments—10 minutes in the morning, 10 minutes after lunch and 10 minutes in the afternoon.

- **Highlight the important stuff.** If you're reading a newspaper or industry magazine, skim through it first, quickly scanning the headlines. When something interests you, highlight it in yellow fluorescent marker or tag it with a sticky note if the reading material is not yours to keep.

  You should be able to go through an average newspaper or magazine, skimming in this manner, in about ten minutes.

  Then, you'll be able to go back and read only those sections you've highlighted. This really helps if you're planning to read in short intervals throughout the day or if you decide to read while you're waiting.

- **Train someone to read for you.** If you're the boss, train an employee to scan and read for you. Teach her how to selectively deliver a final summation of articles and important points.

- **Read selectively.** Pick up a magazine and glance at the Table of Contents. Circle the articles you wish to read. Then go directly to those pages only.

- **Designate a reading area.** Make one place in your office your reading area. Be sure you have adequate lighting, a comfortable chair and your reading materials stored neatly in a basket.

## Organizing Clinic

### Question

I don't have a problem with finding the time to read. My problem is "remembering" what I've just read. I can read through an entire book in a few days, but when I'm done, I can hardly remember any of it.

Tracey Boyle, Kansas City, KS

### Answer

Dear Tracey,

First, are you truly reading or are you skimming? The only way to really comprehend what you're reading is to read each thought slowly and think about what you just read. Try to picture it in your mind. Ask yourself a question about what you just read. Really involve yourself.

Second, take notes as you're reading. When you come across a very important point, jot a note down in a notebook. Or, keep an index card in your book and note the page number and (T) for top of page, (M) for middle of page or (B) for bottom of page. This way, when you're done with your book, you can use your index card as a guide for those pages you wish to reference later.

- **Evaluate your subscriptions.** Don't automatically renew business subscriptions. Renew only those that are helpful to your business goals, those that you enjoy and most important—those you consistently read.

- **Rate your reading pile.** Using a pen and paper or your computer, jot down the names of all of the reading material you read. Include magazines, newspapers, email newsletters, professional journals and so on.

  Then rate each item's value to you on a scale of 1 to 5 (one being low and 5 being high). Discontinue any publication that scores lower than a 4. Also, if you have rated a magazine a 5, but you have three or more back issues you haven't yet read, you've rated it too high. If it were really important to you, you would be sure to get to it more regularly.

- **Designate a toss out date.** Whenever you receive a publication or report, immediately indicate a toss-out date on it, like one month from today. If you still haven't gotten to that report by your toss-out date, it will most likely be outdated by then and not worth your time to read.

- **Take a speed-reading course.** For getting through business reading quickly, speed-reading can be an enormous help. Check your local college or town listings for classes in your area.

- **Don't strain.** If you haven't been to the eye doctor lately, get a check-up. Eyestrain is often a cause of piled up reading. If you're uncomfortable reading, you're not going to read very often. A new pair of glasses or contact lenses may do the trick.

- **Give yourself mini reading goals.** Just looking at a huge pile of reading material may be overwhelming and discouraging. Make a goal to read just three to five pages at a sitting. If necessary, take those pages from your pile and read them somewhere else, so that huge pile isn't constantly staring you in the face.

## Organizing Clinic

### Question

My office routes industry magazines to my five co-workers and myself. But with all of my projects, the magazines sit in my inbox for weeks. My co-workers are always disturbed to get these publications so late. Any suggestions?

Lucy Campanoli, Hoboken, NJ

### Answer

Dear Lucy,

A very easy solution is to have your name placed last on the routing slip. This way, your co-workers will all get the magazines before you do and they can sit in your inbox until you're ready to read them without getting anyone upset.

However, I also recommend that when you do get these magazines, you set aside a mere 15 minutes to flip through them. While doing so, flag any pages that catch your interest. Then, walk over to the copy machine and make copies of those pages. Read those pages during your regular reading hour or even on your commute home from work if you take mass transportation.

- **Go somewhere quiet.** You won't be able to focus on your reading if the telephone is ringing or visitors are stopping by. Go into a quiet room and close the door. Or leave the office and read in a library, local park or a restaurant before or after the busy lunch hour.

- **Read with your ears.** Many business books are now available on tape or CD. These give you the opportunity to read with your ears.

Lance, a regional sales manager for a tool and die company, swears by books on tape. Since he is always on the road, he rarely has the opportunity to sit down and read a paper-based book. But, in the car, he just pops his book-on-tape in the tape player and he easily keeps up with his business reading.

## Great idea!

What amount of space have you allotted for your reading pile? Chances are, every square inch of space you've designated has been taken up. Your reading pile (or file) must be a realistic size. It should be small enough to set a boundary that you cannot exceed (by your own rules).

Never leave the office without something to read. The reading file will shrink much more quickly if you'll make a habit of grabbing something to read on your way out the door.

You may not want to make an appointment to read that magazine article, but you certainly don't want to be caught with nothing to read while you wait for one appointment or another. While you're reading, make notes in your planner or on your PDA as to any action or tasks that are required.

Tracy Wyman
The Clutter Buster
Tallahassee, Florida
850-205-5279
solutions@clutterbuster.org
www.clutterbuster.org

- **Read without reading the words.** Get through your reading pile faster, by reading faster. Try not to mouth each word one by one. See the words. Just don't read them outloud. No moving your lips! We all speak a lot slower than we're capable of reading.

- **Improve your vocabulary.** If you get stuck on a word you're not sure about and it's important for you to know what that word means to understand the point, look it up to become more familiar with it. Then practice using that word, so you don't get stuck on it again in the future.

- **Read more often.** The more often you read, the better you'll get at it and the faster you'll be able to plow through your pile.

- **Use an index card.** Some people read quicker by using an index card. Place the card below the line you're reading and as you finish a line, move the card down another line. The main premise is that you're hiding the rest of the words so you're able to keep your place. This is helpful if you are interrupted by a phone call. The index card will remind you where you left off.

# Chapter 27

# The art of scheduling

- **It's a fine art.** Scheduling is the fine art of packing every day "just full enough" of the most useful activities. "Too full" and you're liable to exhaust yourself. "Too loose" and you're wasting precious time that can be used to work towards your goals.

  A good rule of thumb is to schedule no more than 70% of your day. This way, you'll have some time to breathe, you'll allow time for interruptions and you will be giving yourself extra time for those projects that take longer to do than you originally thought they would.

- **What's your pleasure?** There are a plethora of calendars and planners on the market, some fancy, some not. Some are big and some are small. The color, style and size of calendar is going to depend on your personality and your needs. Here are some guidelines:

  - ❖ **Year-at-a-glance:** A year-at-a-glance calendar allows you to see the whole year at once, hence the name. You can see each month all on one page—January, February, March, etc.—with the days in each month. Most year-at-a-glance calendars do not give you the opportunity to fill in much information, if any.

    For the most part, they're used for reference purposes—to be able to glance and see all of the dates of the year quickly and easily.

  - ❖ **Month-at-a-glance:** This is the calendar I recommend for most people. Unless you're running around all day from one appointment or meeting to the next, a month-at-a-glance calendar should be sufficient. It shows you each individual month on a separate page with boxes for each day.

    I use month-at-a-glance calendars now and have used them for years. There's plenty of space to write in appointments, meetings and other events, even if there are two or three things happening on one particular day. Plus, I can always easily see what is coming up tomorrow, the next day and so on, without having to flip the page.

    Of course, I use this strictly as my calendar—not my planning and list system.

  - ❖ **Week-at-a-glance:** This calendar will allow you to see one single week on a page, generally Sunday through Saturday or Monday through Sunday—with enough space to jot down notes for each day. Some also list the times of day so you can jot each appointment down at exactly the time it is scheduled to happen. Although you have to keep flipping the pages forward to determine what's coming up next week, they're a great solution if you have lots of appointments each day.

❖ **Day-at-a-glance:** This calendar only allows you to see one single day at a time. I don't like these types of calendars at all and they're of little use to most people. You have to actually keep flipping ahead to see what's coming up and the majority of people don't remember to keep flipping the page the next day.

Jack, an insurance salesman, had his day-at-a-glance calendar displayed prominently on his desk. The date displayed was 4 months ago!

These day-at-a-glance calendars are sometimes novelty calendars that display a quote-a-day or a sports fact-a-day or a joke-a-day. If you really like these little ponderables, that's fine. Just know that day-at-a-glance calendars are generally insufficient scheduling tools.

❖ **Combination of two or more:** Some calendars have combinations of many different types of calendars. For example, my month-at-a-glance has a handy year-at-a-glance reference in the back. If you're mainly using one of the types of calendars for jotting things down and another type of calendar for referencing dates, that's fine.

I don't normally recommend that you jot some items in the month-at-a-glance and then jot other information in the week-at-a-glance or any two-calendar combinations for that matter. When you write things in two different places, chances are something is going to get lost or there's going to be a scheduling conflict.

- **Choose the right calendar.** If you have less than four appointments in any given day, a simple month-at-a-glance calendar should be sufficient for your needs. If you have four or more appointments in any given day, you may consider using a week-at-a-glance calendar with a number of slots in each day for appointments. Whether you use a paper calendar or an electronic calendar depends on your preferences.

- **One watch is enough.** There's an old saying that goes, "A man who wears two watches never knows the correct time." The same goes for calendars. If you use one calendar at work, another at home and yet another on your computer, something is going to be missed.

Jackie, a real estate agent, kept two calendars—one at home and one at work. On her home calendar, she jotted down her daughter's ballet recital on Monday, the 3rd at 3:00PM.

When she was at work the next day, obviously she didn't have her home calendar to reference and she never bothered to jot in her daughter's ballet recital on her work calendar. So, when she had to set a meeting with a homeowner, she set the meeting for Monday, the 3$^{rd}$ at 3:30PM. When the 3$^{rd}$ arrived, she glanced at her home calendar and determined she had to leave work at 2:30PM to make her daughter's recital on time.

When she got to work, to her dismay she discovered that she had a customer appointment at 3:30PM.

Luckily, Jackie's customer was sympathetic to the scheduling problem and was able to reschedule. However, Jackie was in a very uncomfortable position with her customer which looked unprofessional and disorganized.

The bottom line is that you have only one life that includes both business and home-related items—use one calendar. Carry it back and forth if you have to.

### Great idea!

Are you buried under scraps of paper, sticky notes and pink message slips? Is it impossible to keep track of the details of daily life?

Purchase a hardcover spiral notepad to use as an "action planner." It's a great reference tool that prevents memory loss. A 5x7 inch notepad fits conveniently into a purse, briefcase or date planner. Record daily details regarding phone conversations, messages, meeting notes and items requiring action by you.

Stay on top of family and business details and effortlessly find important numbers, directions, instructions and plans. This saves rewriting To Do lists since your list will evolve from it.

No need to use a page per day. Make the entries continuous, separated by a horizontal line. Highlight completed tasks with a vertical line along the margin. As you flip back you'll see at a glance anything that has fallen between the cracks.

Record items, that can't immediately be scheduled, into your date planner or PDA. Prioritize your time by taking care of a few of these items each day before they become urgent issues. You'll know if you are procrastinating when you have to flip back too many pages!

Karen Sencich, Owner of Sencich Solutions
Author of the "Havoc to Harmony" organizing series
128 Castlehill Road, Brampton, Ontario, L6X 4C2
905-452-7008
info@sencichsolutions.com
www.sencichsolutions.com

- **But someone else does my schedule.** If you're fortunate enough to have an administrative assistant schedule your day for you, be sure you're in good communication with this person on a daily basis.

If you use Outlook as your calendar system at the office and your office has a network setup, you should be able to easily see what appointments have been set up for you. You can even update your calendar so your assistant will be aware of any additions, deletions or changes.

If you use a paper calendar, it is suggested there be one calendar you share between yourself and your administrative assistant to avoid conflicts, otherwise you're going to have to be sure appointments are always written in both your calendar and your assistant's calendar.

- **Leave your calendar open.** Always leave your calendar open to the current month (or day/week) on your desk. You'll be able to see everything at a glance and you won't have to flip pages to jot in an appointment.

- **Schedule free time.** Especially if you have an assistant making your appointments, it's important to have some time in your day when appointments are not to be scheduled. You don't want to be squeezed with appointments all day long.

- **Wanted! $25 Reward for returning my life.** If you have everything written down on your calendar, then that calendar is a very valuable asset to you. Guard it and take care not to lose it. Just as a safety precaution, include a note inside the front cover that says:

**$25 Reward for Return:** If found, please return to (your name, address and phone number).

Twenty-five dollars is not very much when you consider how much data you could lose forever. In fact, I know people who have posted up to $100 for the return of their calendars if lost.

- **First thing, last thing.** Your calendar should be the very first thing you look at each morning and the very last thing you look at each night. Using this system, you'll always know what comes next.

- **Get it in there—quick.** The second you determine you have an event, task, appointment or anything that must be written on your calendar or in your planner, be sure to write it immediately. Don't delay and risk the chance of forgetting to write it in.

Jane, a restaurant operator in Dayton, Ohio once told me she missed her haircut appointment, even though her hairdresser scheduled the day way in advance and sent her an appointment card. The problem was that Jane didn't immediately jot the date and time in her calendar when the date was set. She waited to get the appointment card.

Once she did, she tossed the appointment card on her desk; the card slipped under papers and, of course, the appointment came and went. Don't let this happen to you.

- **Fill in all appointments—even recurring ones.** Chances are, if you have a meeting every single Wednesday, you will probably remember. But to be on the safe side, I always recommend you fill in ALL appointments—both one time and recurring appointments.

---

**Great idea!**

When I schedule an appointment in my planner, I mark off an hour. Then if the appointment only lasts for 30 minutes, I have time to finish paperwork/notes for that appointment as well as prepare for the next.

Denise Williams, Associate Editor of *Finally Organized, Finally Free for the Office*

---

- **Make a temporary note.** If for some reason you don't carry your calendar around with you, temporarily jot the information on a sheet of paper or call your voicemail and leave yourself a message with the necessary information. Then, as soon as you get back to the office, fill the information in on your calendar.

- **Write it in red.** On occasion, you will need to jot down something very important in your calendar or planner. Jot those one or two important things in red marker so they stand out.

- **Don't overload.** Avoid jamming your calendar full of a million things to do. When your calendar is this tight, one little thing that doesn't fall right on schedule can throw your entire day off balance.

- **Pad your time.** Most people underestimate the time it takes to do things. If you think it's going to take 15 minutes, schedule 30 minutes. If you think it might take 2 hours, schedule a minimum of 2.5 hours for this activity.

- **Make appointments with yourself.** Set aside time in your day to do business reading, make your calls or to have some quiet mental relaxation time. Jot these appointments on your calendar and keep them.

- **Abbreviate.** You can save time and space by abbreviating common events on your calendar. Here are some business-related abbreviations:

  - ❖ AP    Appointment
  - ❖ MT    Meeting
  - ❖ BR    Breakfast

- ❖ LU    Lunch
- ❖ DN    Dinner
- ❖ PH    Phone or Call
- ❖ EM    Email
- ❖ FX    Fax
- ❖ ML    Mail
- ❖ VC    Vacation
- ❖ DO    Day Off
- ❖ WK    Workshop
- ❖ SM    Seminar
- ❖ DS    Discuss
- ❖ WR    Write
- ❖ FU    Follow Up
- ❖ BD    Birthday
- ❖ AN    Anniversary
- ❖ PR    Presentation

Choose some of the above and add your own to make your own personal list. Tape this list to the front cover of your calendar and planner for easy reference. Make the abbreviations more specific by adding the details after the abbreviation. For example, AP-Mike would mean Appointment with Mike or WR-ABC Co. would mean you'd have to write a letter to ABC Company.

- **If you have to switch mid-year, that's ok.** Different jobs require different types of calendars. Perhaps you started off the year working at a job that required you to make very few appointments. Up to that point, using a simple month-at-a-glance calendar worked well for you. Then, maybe in mid-year you switched jobs and now need a calendar that allows for ten or more appointments each day. Just because it's mid-year, doesn't mean you can't switch calendars. Use the type of calendar based on your current needs.

- **Copy your calendar page.** If you're not going to be in the office for a few days, make a copy of your month-at-a-glance calendar page. You can then slip this one page into your briefcase or purse to ensure you don't make any appointments that conflict with another date you already have set.

- **Use a pencil.** Consider using a pencil—or an erasable pen—to write in your calendar or planner. As things change, you will be able to easily erase and re-write, without it getting messy.

- **Geographically schedule errands and appointments.** Try to schedule your errands and appointments geographically so you're not zigzagging back and forth across town. Each stop should be on the way to the next stop.

- **Be flexible.** Every so often, something is going to throw your schedule off. Don't let this alarm you. Just take a deep breath and reschedule whenever necessary.

## Organizing Clinic

### Question

I can't possibly schedule my workday. If the telephone rings, my boss requires me to pick it up. If an important project comes in, I have to drop what I'm doing and work on it. Visitors are constantly stopping by to chat and my boss doesn't allow me to close my office door. It's a nightmare. I can't get anything done.

Beckie Planter, Boise, ID

### Answer

Dear Beckie,

Just because your boss requires you to pick up the phone and work on important projects when they come up, doesn't mean you can't have a schedule. It just means your schedule has to be flexible.

Be sure you have a written schedule to use as a daily guide. When the phone rings, pick it up, but then get back to work on whatever is on your schedule. If an important project comes your way, reschedule whatever you're working on to a later date.

One tip is to keep your schedule on the light side. This way you're leaving plenty of room to take those phone calls and work on unforeseen projects without throwing your schedule off totally.

As far as those office visitors though, if you can't close your door, you'll have to be a bit more aggressive. Politely send your visitors away whenever they're only stopping by to chat. Simply tell them you'll stop by their office later when you're done with your project.

- **Use a grid.** When you have to make a schedule that involves many people, make yourself a grid. It may look something like this schedule which indicates weekly start times:

|        | Mo   | Tu    | We    | Th    | Fr    |
|--------|------|-------|-------|-------|-------|
| 09:00A | Judy | Ellen | Judy  | Ellen | Judy  |
| 10:00A | Kyle | Kyle  | Kyle  | Jack  | Jack  |
| 11:00A | Mike | Jayne | Jayne | Mike  | Jayne |

# Chapter 28

# Electronic or paper?

- **Match it to your personality.** Some people love technology and thrive when they use the latest innovative gadgets that just came out on the market. That's why some people have chosen to use PDAs—better known as Personal Digital Assistants.

  PDAs are basically tiny computers that fit in the palm of your hand. Others prefer to use a paper planner. Neither way is the right or wrong way. Either system can work beautifully if you enjoy it and you commit to using it correctly each day.

- **Paper people should use paper planners.** If you'd prefer to jot your tasks and appointments into your paper planner, rather than entering the data into a PDA and the paper system works well for you, then use it.

  You don't have to use a PDA to be organized. In fact, many people are much more organized using the tried and true paper method.

- **Digital people should use PDAs.** If you hate paper, hate the thought of carrying around a paper planner with you and hate the thought of physically writing things down, then a PDA might be your better choice.

- **Consider maintenance time.** The system that will be the most effective is the one that can be easily maintained. The easier it is to maintain your planning system, whatever your preference, the easier it will be to stay organized. The following lists outline the benefits of a paper planning system and a digital system.

  The key is to make sure that you adopt one system, which serves as a repository for all of your appointments, planning and note taking. Keeping your information centralized in one location is the key to staying organized.

- **Benefits of a paper planning system:**

  ❖ **It is always on.** When you want to jot something in, you can do so in a second without having to press any buttons.

  ❖ **Inexpensive.** You are not required to spend a small fortune on a paper planning system. $40-$50 will get you a system that should help you keep track of your events, appointments, tasks to do, important dates and so on. Most PDAs that are even worth looking at will cost a couple hundred dollars or more.

  ❖ **Quick and easy to fill in.** Rather than taking the time to enter data into a tiny electronic device, it only takes a few seconds to jot something into a paper planner. Note: I once watched someone enter a name and phone number into a PDA . . . and it took over 10 minutes!

❖ **It's always ready when you are.** You never have to worry about re-charging a battery or having the battery die on you while you're in the airport. The planner can be opened and used at any time—no power necessary.

❖ **It won't crash.** All electronic devices, no matter how good, have the possibility of crashing and losing all of your data. A paper planning system obviously doesn't have this type of problem, unless someone happens to erase all of your notes—highly unlikely.

❖ **Not worthy of stealing.** When was the last time you heard of a paper planning system theft-ring? You could probably leave your paper planning system on top of an office desk for a week and nobody would have the slightest interest in taking it.

❖ **It's not delicate.** If you drop a paper planning system, it won't break. However, if you drop a PDA, chances are it will. A colleague of mine dropped his PDA out of his shirt pocket and it broke immediately.

- **Benefits of a PDA planning system:**

  ❖ **No re-writing required.** With paper systems, you may spend a good deal of time re-writing. For instance, you may have ten tasks on your paper To Do list, but you complete five of them crossing those five out. You then have to either work with a messy crossed-off list or you re-write those five items you haven't yet done to a new list. With a PDA, there's no need to transfer. You can easily delete things you've already done, without harming any items you haven't yet completed.

  ❖ **Lightweight.** Many paper planning systems are bulky to carry around. If you're on the road a lot and need to constantly have your planning system with you, a lightweight PDA might be a better choice for you.

  ❖ **You'll look cool.** Don't laugh. Many people use digital devices just so they look cool to others around them. Heck, besides better communication, the coolness factor is the second reason why so many people have joined the cell phone revolution. In fact, it may be the first reason for some people.

  ❖ **There are bells and whistles.** Many PDA planning systems have built-in alarms, a warning system so appointments don't conflict with each other, search capabilities, ability to carry forward your To Do's, calculators, web browsers and more.

- ❖ **Easier to consolidate information.** When synching communications with other computers, it is much easier to incorporate information from other sources into your PDA. This is helpful if you use multiple computers or have an administrative assistant setting up appointments for you.

- **PIM or PDA?** When considering your electronic type organizer, determine if you would rather use a PIM (Personal Information Manager) or a PDA (Personal Digital Assistant.)

  A PIM is a very simple device that allows you to keep phone lists, appointments and addresses, but doesn't interface with a computer.

  A PDA is more sophisticated. It acts more like a personal computer. It can be hooked up to a fax or even linked to your computer in work. Many include word processing and spreadsheet capabilities.

  Of course, the more bells and whistles you get, the more expensive the unit will be.

- **In the market for a paper-based organizer?** Here are some criteria you should keep in mind when comparing paper organizers:

  - ❖ How heavy is the organizer? If you travel often, you will want a light model. If your model is heavy, is there a way for you to remove just the pages you need and transfer those pages to another binder when you're traveling?

  - ❖ What size are the pages? Some people prefer a large sheet of paper, such as 8" x 11." Others prefer a smaller size.

  - ❖ How expensive is the organizer? When you're on a budget, this is an important point to keep in mind. They can run anywhere from $20 to hundreds of dollars.

  - ❖ Do you need to regularly purchase refills? If so, this can really run your costs through the roof. Some organizers allow you to simply make copies of the pages you need to add to your binder.

  - ❖ Are the calendar pages perpetual? If not, you'll have to buy new calendar pages every year.

  - ❖ Is it attractive? Strong? Weatherproof?

  - ❖ Are there additional pages/forms for your contacts, taking notes, writing ideas or thinking about your goals?

  - ❖ Does it have all of the features, calendar pages and additional forms you need?

- **In the market for an electronic organizer?** Here are some criteria you should keep in mind when comparing electronic organizers:

  - ❖ How heavy is the unit? If you travel often, you will want a light model.

  - ❖ How big is the unit? Again, if you travel often, the smaller the unit is, the more convenient it will be to carry with you.

  - ❖ How expensive is the unit? When you're on a budget, this is an important point to keep in mind.

  - ❖ Can you type onto a small keyboard or will you write with a pen-device right on the screen? If you type onto a keyboard, is that a comfortable option for you? If a pen-device, is it a device that actually recognizes your handwriting?

  - ❖ Is the screen easy to read? Is it backlit?

  - ❖ How easy is it to back up your data?

  - ❖ How long will the power source last? Does it come with a battery back-up feature?

  - ❖ Does it have all of the features you need in an electronic device?

- **Final words of wisdom.** I must share the following quote said by Robyn Pearce, researcher, author, international speaker, businesswoman, time management specialist and founder of the TimeLogic Corporation www.gettingagripontime.com:

*"It's not the diary or planner that makes you organized—it's how you use it!"*

Excellent summary, Robyn! There is no system on the market that's going to organize you. Just like a golf club can't guarantee you'll play a great game of golf, a paper or digital planner can't guarantee you'll be well-scheduled. That is entirely up to you. The planning system can just help remind you of the schedule you've chosen, so you don't have to remember it in your head.

## 6 criteria for deciding if an electronic or paper calendar is best for you

As our lives speed up and become more complex, the common calendar system does not seem to be as effective as it once was. Or is it? If you are unsure about an upgrade, this article can help you decide between a mobile, electronic calendar system (MS Outlook and a PDA for example) or a paper-based system. There are six criteria you can use to decide which makes more sense to you.

- **Mobility**: A paper calendar system is excellent if you stay in one place whenever using it. Receptionists are legendary for having large, paper-based calendars. A paper-based system will become a challenge to tote if it is bulky and does not fit in your purse, briefcase or pocket.

On the other hand, a PDA, such as a Palm Pilot, is very portable and will fit in a pocket. The Palm Pilot is great if you go from meeting to meeting and are rarely in one place.

- **Technology Literacy**: If you are comfortable with computers, a Palm Pilot and Microsoft Outlook will be easy to start using. However, if you find computers to be daunting and you avoid using them, then it makes sense to stick with your paper calendar.

- **Frequency of Changes**: If you are using a paper-based system today, but have lots of scratch marks in it or need to carry correction fluid with you, it makes sense to change to an electronic system. The calendar will be easier to update and read. Conversely, if you seldom make changes to appointments, an electronic system may not be worth the money.

- **Shared Calendar**: The data in a Palm Pilot can be synchronized with any computer that contains a calendar program (Outlook, Act, Palm Calendar). Also, if you synchronize your PDA with your calendar program and you are connected to a network, others will be able to access your calendar with permission. This is helpful if others set appointments for you or when scheduling meetings or conference calls. If only you use your calendar, the paper-based system may be sufficient.

- **Additional Information**: Daily task lists, contacts and notes are some of the types of information typically carried with a calendar. A PDA makes it easy to keep all of this information in one place and share it. This reduces the effort required to set up a contact to call to confirm an appointment on your calendar. A paper-based system can also store the additional information. However, every piece of new information takes up extra space and causes your calendar to increase in size and weight. Think about how much information you store in your calendar, other than appointments, to make a decision on this point.

- **Price**: A basic, paper-based system is less expensive to get started. However, a Franklin Covey type planner can cost upwards of $100 initially. Also, there are annual refills to take into consideration. A small calendar will cost under $10 if that is all you need. Alternatively, a PDA is always over $100 and most people tend to buy more than they need, causing the price to be even higher. Look for a used one or purchase just the features you need to control the cost of getting started.

Now you can intelligently decide if a paper-based or electronic system coincides with your habits. By making the right decision, you can make the calendar work for you, increase your productivity and reduce stress at the same time. What could be better?

By Daniel Roth, Squared Away, Inc.
www.getsquaredaway.com
FREE Organizing Tip-Kit available at www.getsquaredaway.com.
Learn ways to organize your home, life, business, time, move, classroom and finances on this fun and interactive Web site.

# Chapter 29

# Master lists and To Do lists

- **The Master list.** A Master list is a running list of things you have or want to do. It does not have to be in any specific order and it can go on and on for pages if you'd like. It's nothing more than a holding place for all of your tasks, errands, ideas and so on.

- **The To Do list.** The "To Do" list is really a misnomer. That's why I've renamed it the "To Do Today" list. Each day you're going to be transferring tasks from your Master List to your To Do Today list and you're going to work on those items today.

  So that you don't get overwhelmed, I recommend you start off with transferring no more than 4 tasks each day. If that's too many for you, drop down to 2-3 tasks. If that is too little, increase to 5-7 tasks. The basic idea is to include enough to stay productive, but not list so much that you get overwhelmed or anxious with the number of tasks.

- **Include a variety.** Always include a variety of items on your list, this way you're working on the important stuff, but you're also ensuring the less important tasks get done too. Include some that are high priority, some that are medium priority and some that are lower priority.

  Be careful not to transfer only your low priority tasks. If you do, you'll never get any of the important stuff done even though you'll be exhausted from working all day long.

### Great idea!

I am a firm believer in having a checklist. When I meet with my supervisor on Monday mornings, I always have a pad of paper and pen in hand. When he gives me a task to perform, I immediately note it on the pad. If it's something that needs to be completed as soon as possible, I note this with an asterisk in the margin so I know it has to be done quickly. As each task is completed, I cross it off. At the end of the day, I begin a new checklist with those tasks that still need to be completed and any more that may have been added throughout the day.

Colleen V. Isaac
Executive Secretary
Loyola University Medical Center
2160 South First Avenue, Maywood, Illinois 60153
cisaac1@lumc.edu

- **Decide if you are a paper or computer person.** Some people like to write their Master lists and To Do lists out on paper. Some people prefer using the computer to do so. Either way is fine. Whatever you're most comfortable doing is the system you should use. The important thing is that you have a Master list and To Do Today list. Consider your preferences and the maintenance required.

## A simple but powerful time management system

A well-known, true story about the effectiveness of a To Do list concerns Charles Schwab when he was president of Bethlehem Steel. He called in Ivy Lee, a consultant and said, "Show me a way to get more things done with my time and the time of my employees and I'll pay you any fee within reason."

"Fine." Lee replied. "I'll give you something in twenty minutes that will step up your output by at least fifty percent."

With that, Lee handed Schwab a blank piece of paper and said, "Write down the six most important tasks that you have to do tomorrow and number them in order of their importance. Now put this paper in your pocket and the first thing tomorrow morning look at item one and start working on it until you finish it. Then do item two and so on.

Do this until quitting time and don't be concerned if you have finished only one or two. You'll be working on the most important ones first anyway. If you can't finish them all by this method, you couldn't have done it by any other method either and without this system, you probably wouldn't have decided which was the most important."

Then Lee said, "Try this system every working day. After you've convinced yourself of the value of the system, have your employees try it. Try it as long as you wish and then send me a check for what you think it's worth."

Several weeks later, Schwab sent Lee a check for $25,000 with a note proclaiming the advice the most profitable he had ever followed. This concept helped Charles Schwab earn $100 million and helped turn Bethlehem Steel into the biggest independent steel producer in the world at that time.

You may think Charles Schwab was foolish to pay $25,000 for such a simple idea. However, Schwab thought of that consulting fee as one of his best investments. "Sure it was a simple idea," Schwab said, "but what powerful ideas are not basically simple? For the first time, my entire team and myself are getting important things done first."

- **Check off or cross out as completed.** As you finish each of your tasks on your To Do Today list, cross those tasks out or check them off. You'll feel a sense of satisfaction since you'll have a "picture" of everything you've done.

  If you use a computerized To Do Today list, refrain from just deleting the tasks you've completed, at least for a day or two. Check them off instead. Otherwise, you're bound to forget how much you've done and it may leave you with a feeling of emptiness.

- **Add action on your To Do's.** Don't put anything on your To Do Today list without preceding it with a verb. If you just put the name "Kathy" on your list, it doesn't really have any sense of action. However, the verb "call" insists on some action.

  Some examples of using verbs on your To Do Today list are: <u>Call</u> Kathy regarding purchase, <u>Deliver</u> March invoices, <u>Write</u> Sally's recommendation letter to ABC company, <u>Train</u> Evelyn to use computer system and <u>Purchase</u> paper clips from Staples.

---

### Great idea!

The Master List is for your ongoing projects. Keep your Master List separate from the To Do List. Give yourself a time frame for completing the projects in order of priority.

The To Do List is your daily reminder of what you need to do for that day. Some of the items from your To Do List will come from your Master List. Every day sit down and plan for the next. Sometimes planning for the week will help you plan out daily To Do Lists. At the end of each day cross off the items you completed and add the ones left to another day in order of priority.

Without lists it is hard to plan ahead and complete the things we need to get done. The benefit of using lists is to know what you are going to do for that day, before the day begins. Without lists it becomes very difficult to remember all that we need to. Lists help keep you focused and motivated. After you complete an item from your list, it will give you the motivation to move on to the next. The key to lists is to allow time for the unexpected.

Michelle Morton
Clutter Control
43527 Kiplington Square, South Riding, VA 20152
703-327-2974
michelle@controlyourclutter.com

---

- **Know the difference between a task and a project.** Generally, a task on your To Do list should be something that can be completed in less than an hour. A project is actually a series of tasks.

Listing a goal or large responsibility, such as: "complete sales analysis" is bound to cause frustration because it may be too much to complete in one day.

If "completing sales analysis" is something that will take more than an hour, this is a project and not a task. Most people will dread starting this "huge project," making it a likely candidate for procrastination.

- **Break Projects into Tasks.** Instead of listing "complete sales analysis" as a task, this project can be broken up into smaller tasks, such as: 1) review trend data, 2) update graphs and 3) review presentation.

The individual tasks required for the project can be listed in the Master List and scheduled to your To Do Today list. Breaking up the project into tasks is a fundamental principle of Project Management. The smaller tasks will allow you to schedule, delegate and complete parts of a project easily and contribute to a greater sense of accomplishment each day.

A project will be completed on time and with less stress when measurable progress is made each day towards completion.

- **You're not in the list business.** Having a Master List and a To Do List is important. Remember though that having lists is not enough in itself. Actually "doing" the items on those lists is what really counts.

# Chapter 30

# Remembering

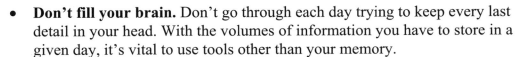

- **Don't fill your brain.** Don't go through each day trying to keep every last detail in your head. With the volumes of information you have to store in a given day, it's vital to use tools other than your memory.

One of the most basic memory tips is to write things down. If it's on paper, you don't have to remember it. The paper will do the remembering for you.

## Organizing Clinic

### Question

I can never remember names. This is a problem as I meet many people at networking seminars. It's so embarrassing when I see the person again later and her name has escaped me. Are there any systems for better remembering names?

Linda Ellis, Dunedin, FL

### Answer

Dear Linda,

Here are a few easy systems:

- **Pay attention and repeat.** When a person mentions his or her name to you, really listen. Then, try to say his or her name at least 3 times during your conversation. Then, end your conversation with the person's name: "It was nice meeting you, Angela."

- **Ask.** If it's a difficult name, ask how to spell it or ask if the name has a special meaning.

- **Make an association.** If a person's name is Michael Monroe, associate him with Marilyn Monroe. If the person's name is Mr. Campbell, associate him with Campbell's soup.

- **Make notes.** As soon as you walk away from the person you meet, jot notes about her on a business card or in a notepad. Notes such as Jackie Jones, blonde hair, thin, raised eyebrows and glasses will all help.

- **Don't sweat it.** After using some of the basic techniques, if you still can't remember the person's name when you see him or her again simply say, "I'm sorry. I remember you well, although I can't remember your name." Most likely, the person will be more than happy to remind you.

- **Record it.** You've probably run into many situations when a potentially useful idea occurs, but you can't easily write it down. For example, when you're driving, you certainly can't pull out a pen/paper and begin taking notes—at least, not while ensuring the safety of yourself and others on the road. Perhaps a terrific idea pops into your head while you're resting in bed.

  Fumbling for writing material in the dark is not the way to go. Hand-held recorders eliminate the loss of these great thoughts. Here are some hints for making the best use of your hand-held recorder:

  - ❖ **Have it with you.** Carry your hand-held recorder at all times in your briefcase or purse. At night, leave it on your nightstand. At the office, keep it on your desk. As long as it's with you, you can record your thoughts at any time.

  - ❖ **Transfer your thoughts.** If you record something and you don't play it back within a reasonable amount of time—a day or two—you're liable to forget you even recorded it. Each night or at a scheduled time each day, transfer your thoughts to paper or to your computer. Or ask your assistant to do this for you.

  - ❖ **Power up.** Keep an extra set of batteries on hand at all times, just in case you begin to lose power.

  - ❖ **Test your voice.** Test your voice level by recording and playing back. You want to be sure you can hear yourself later.

### Great idea!

Let paper remember it all for you. Write everything you need and want to do down on paper and make sure it's in one place. Keep only one calendar and one place that contains all your to do lists and refer to them often. This not only gives you an excellent reference and reminder, but the literal act of committing goals to paper actually helps make them happen.

Pamala J. Mielnicki, Associate Editor of *Finally Organized, Finally Free for the Office*

- **Act on your ideas.** It's not enough just to have ideas. Reference your ideas each day. If one turns out to be one you'd like to try, act on it. If not, delete it from your list. Ideas are a dime-a-dozen. But good ideas that are acted on can be worth the world.

- **Read and remember.** When you're reading a book, if you come across something you wish to reference in the future, jot down the page number and the idea on a 3" x 5" card that you use as a bookmark.

My husband likes to keep his index card bookmarks tucked into the front covers of his business books so he always has a ready-reference of important points without having to flip through the entire book to find something of interest.

- **Write down your questions.** Need to remember to ask questions? Write them down and you won't have to clutter your brain with them. Bring them to your interviews, appointments and so on.

- **You've got to see it.** Have something to remember? An old-fashioned system is to put a string around your finger and it still works today. Or, stick a note on your office door, telephone, mirror or car steering wheel.

Of course, this shouldn't be your main form of helping yourself remember everything you have to do, otherwise you'll end up with strings on each finger or notes covering every inch of your office. But, it can be very helpful to give yourself a quick reminder for a thing or two you have to remember such as picking up milk on the way home from work.

### Great idea!

I like to leave "visual cues" for myself to remind me of what needs to be done. Sometimes the cue is a sticky note in the middle of my computer screen, though I don't recommend gathering too many of those at one time.

Sometimes when a package needs to be taken out of my apartment or office, I'll put it in the doorway so that it blocks my path and reminds me to pick it up when I leave.

Having a place for everything at home and at work has also been useful. This helps me not to forget where I've put stuff and saves me time and frustration by avoiding searches for missing items.

Those searches still happen on occasion, even when I'm careful to put things in their place, but they're not very frequent.

Mike Logan
Logan's Logic
256-348-7485

- **Tickle your brain.** The Tickler File System or the 31-Day Reminder System is perfect for planning, helping you remember to start projects on scheduled days, reminding you to send out letters and greeting cards and more. You'll find an easy system for setting up your Tickler File System in this book.

Bob, a web hosting technician, works on dozens of customer projects—some that require his immediate attention and others that have to be completed within a few months. He uses his Tickler System religiously.

When Bob learns about a new project, he uses a standard form to jot down the customer's name, phone number and project details. He then slips each form into a day or month, in his Tickler System.

Each morning when Bob arrives at work, he checks his Tickler System and gets to work on his projects. Nothing is ever forgotten.

- **Use an alarm.** To ensure you call that customer when you said you would or to leave for your meeting on time, set an alarm to go off. It's easy to get caught up in a project or conversation and lose track of time. Once the alarm sounds, you will be reminded.

  Some computers have nifty alarm systems you can use or simply use an alarm clock.

- **Choose consistent days and times.** A trick for remembering to do recurring tasks is to always do them on the same day(s) at the same time(s). Just like you brush your teeth each morning, your other recurring tasks will become a habit too.

- **Hire someone with a good memory.** If possible, hire an assistant to help you remember those details. The President of the United States would probably be lost without all those assistants.

- **Yahoo!** Go onto the Internet and go to Yahoo's web site: www.yahoo.com. When you get there, click on the Calendar link. The Yahoo Calendar service will allow you to enter everything you wish to remember. Then, you set it up to send you an email reminding you of the event or task. It's free and very useful!

  My husband, Joe, uses the Yahoo! calendar all the time, for both business reasons and personal use. Events like business meetings, birthdays, haircuts, and recycling pick-up days all are input into the Yahoo! calendar. Then Yahoo sends Joe an email the day prior to the event.

  It's an excellent system and can even be used as a backup to your regular paper-based calendar system.

- **Leave yourself a message.** Want to remember something at the office or at home? Leave yourself a message on your answering machine or voicemail and listen to your messages each day.

- **Put a tote bag on your doorknob.** This tote bag should be used for whatever you need to take with you when you leave your office. Hang it on your doorknob. As you think of items you wish to take, just put them in the tote bag. When you're ready to leave, just grab the bag and go.

---

### Great idea!

I rely heavily on my electronic planner to keep my schedule and I do schedule almost everything into it.

The planner has audible alarms that remind me of upcoming meetings or tasks. The audible alarms are also terrific for reminding my clients that I have another appointment.

When a client hears my planner's alarm, I say, "That's my planner reminding me of my next appointment." This is a great way to transition into wrapping up our session.

I also love the electronic planner because it allows me to automatically schedule recurring tasks, which means I don't have to worry that I'll forget a standing appointment or meeting each month. It automatically gets entered into the calendar according to the frequency that I choose.

The bottom line is that if I rely on my memory to keep my schedule, I fail every time. I learned that the more I get my ideas and appointments out of my head, the more at ease I feel and the more I can use my brain for important things such as marketing, being creative and problem solving for my clients.

Monica Ricci, Get Organized Now! Associate Editor of *Finally Organized, Finally Free for the Office*
Catalyst Organizing Solutions, 770-569-2642
Member and Past President, NAPO Georgia
To Receive Free Organizing and Simplifying Tips Just Click and Subscribe!
www.CatalystOrganizing.com

---

- **Use a checklist.** Whenever you have to remember a bunch of items or a recurring process, make a checklist. You'll have a handy reference to use.

- **Take a memory course.** Sharpen your memory by taking a memory course. There are proven tricks you can use such as pneumonics and associations that can boost your memory power. There are excellent systems to remember names, stories and so on.

- **Choose the best method.** Charlie Parks, a salesman in a new home development, has to remember each day to turn on the lawn sprinkler of the model homes. However, Charlie would be much better off simply installing some timers so the water sprinkles automatically.

Before forcing yourself to remember, see if there is something you can do so you don't have to remember!

## Great idea!

Many of us use visual reminders as cues for tasks.

These cues can include putting the insurance agent's business card next to the phone as a reminder to call during business hours or setting outgoing packages near your car keys so you remember to mail them during your next trip out.

Visual cues can be a good reminder system but please keep these pitfalls in mind:

**Short Timeframes Only:** Visual cues work best for tasks that need to be completed within a short timeframe, say, a day or two. After a couple of days, they become invisible to us and don't grab our attention anymore.

**Avoid Visual Clutter**: Visual cues only work when they are isolated. If you have three business cards next to the phone, no single cue will grab your attention.

**Choose the Right Cue:** In most cases it is better to skip the visual cue entirely and go straight to the calendar, action file or daily to-do list. For instance, if your paper shredder has shredded its last document, don't leave it next to your desk as a visual cue. Instead, write that item down on your office supply shopping list immediately.

Kerry Crocker, Professional Organizer
Space Cadette
Chapel Hill, NC
919-928-9825
kerry@space-cadette.com
www.space-cadette.com

- **Put a checklist on your fridge.** If there are always things you need to do before you leave for work in the morning, put a checklist on your fridge that lists things like:

  - ❖ Take umbrella

  - ❖ Bring brown-bag lunch

  - ❖ Be sure kids have their lunches

  - ❖ Bring change of shoes (especially helpful if you work in the city, but wear sneakers to make the trek back and forth from work)

  You might even consider a wipe-on/wipe-off board so you can add/remove/change things as needed.

- **Repeat, repeat and repeat.** When reading something you want to remember, read the information. Then read it again, look away and try to write the information down. Practice remembering on your way to work by reviewing the information in your mind over and over again. This is how we were taught to learn in school—by repetition.

### Great idea!

When you are short on time or under a great deal of stress, it is easy to forget. If you create a routine to help you remember specific information, under those circumstances, you will remember more and be less stressed.

- **Use Association through Placement**: Remembering where you have put something important will be easier if you can associate the item with where it has been placed. Example: FEDEX envelopes to wall pocket by door.

- **Use a Code**: To remember to bring items to a meeting, use a coding system in your calendar, planner or Palm. Example: use C for confirmed meeting time/date and B for bring along as in important files or printouts.

- **Use a Symbol and a Marker**: To remember where you took a break in an online project file, add a symbol %% into the text of your word processing document. Symbol example: Use the menu command: "edit," "go to ," "find" and type in that symbol %%. Marker example: To remember where you pulled a file from in a filing cabinet, insert a brightly colored tall cardboard card. It will help you locate the space easily. When working in teams in the office, add first names to the card.

Elizabeth Early Sheehan
Organizational Solutions
Nine Old County Road, Deering, NH 03244
603-464-3080
elizabeth@eesheehan.com
www.eesheehan.com

- **Think healthy.** Excessive sugar intake can affect your memory and cause you to lose focus. Sugary snacks like soda and candy bars are big culprits. Lack of sleep is also bad for remembering. Get a minimum of eight to ten hours of sleep whenever possible.

# Chapter 31

# Staying focused

- **Set an alarm.** If you have a tendency to get off track when working on a project, set an alarm to sound in fifteen minutes. When the alarm goes off, check and see if you're working on the project you intended to when you first set the alarm.

  If so, wonderful! Set the timer for the next fifteen minutes and repeat the process again. If not, that's okay. Just go back to your original project. The alarm makes sure you get back on track if you get diverted.

---

### Great idea!

Good planning is essential, figure out the time or date your project must be completed and give yourself plenty of time to plan it, prepare it and process it.

When working on difficult projects, schedule them during the time of day you are most alert or energetic. Break the work down into manageable steps and allow yourself a break as you progress. Between steps, do something totally unrelated for a while.

Judy Brown, Associate Editor of *Finally Organized, Finally Free for the Office*

---

- **Eliminate distractions.** If you're having trouble staying on track with what you're doing due to distractions, you have to do what you can to eliminate them.

  ❖ Close your office door.

  ❖ Leave your office and work in an empty conference room or the library.

  ❖ Let your voicemail field your calls.

  ❖ Turn the volume down on your email indicator on your computer. Better yet, log off email for a while.

  ❖ Ask the mail person to leave your mail outside your office instead of bringing it inside.

  ❖ Turn off the radio if you can't work with it on, until you're done with your project.

  ❖ Turn off the television if you're working at home.

- **Work in smaller increments.** Some people get bored working on one project for a long period of time. If this sounds like you, commit to working on your project for 15 minutes without stopping. At the end of that time period, stop and work on something else for 15 minutes. The rule is you must come back to your original project when those 15 minutes are up. This will ensure you work on more of a variety, but you still get your original project completed.

- **Get someone to remind you.** Ask your office assistant or a co-worker to help you stay on track. Ask him to come into your office every half hour to be sure you're still working on your task or project. Of course, you can't bother someone else every time you need to get something done, but this system works well for a very important project.

- **Don't go hungry or thirsty.** It may sound silly, but if you don't eat a nutritious lunch or breakfast or you miss that needed snack, it may be terribly difficult for you to remain focused. Don't eat a big bowl of pasta or a candy bar before an important project, as it's bound to make you feel very sleepy afterwards. Before making a meal or snack choice, always consider how focused you need to be and make your decision based on the complexity or detail of your project.

- **Let in some air.** A very warm room tends to make people very sleepy. If possible, open the window and let in some cool air or at minimum turn down the heat.

### Great idea!

I keep my desk clear of any other paperwork or projects. If an email comes in, I check to see who the sender is. If it is not company-related or doesn't apply to a project I am working on, I save it for later to read.

Lynne Poindexter, Associate Editor of *Finally Organized, Finally Free for the Office*

- **Know why you're struggling to focus.** Sometimes we lose focus if we concentrate on the wrong things. For instance, if you want to grow your business, but you're always thinking of the obstacles of doing so, it will be hard to focus on growing. Instead, you can focus on how to eliminate those obstacles one by one.

- **Take a day off or take a vacation.** Every once in awhile, everyone needs a break. If you're feeling overtired and overworked, it may be time for a vacation. Use that vacation time to relax and rejuvenate, so when you return to work, you'll feel more energized and focused.

- **What time is it?** Know what time of the day you begin to lose some of your focus. Use that time for more mundane tasks and your more focused times for your important projects and tasks.

- **Work on positive self-talk.** Sometimes you just have to remind yourself that you're loosing focus and to get back on track. Stay positive. Use cue words to remind you to re-focus. Use a visual to remind you of your original goal.

- **Hour of Power.** Most people can maintain their attention for an hour. After this, most attention spans starts to fade. When working on projects, be sure to take a break after an hour to regroup and recharge. You will be able to work more efficiently because your ability to maintain your attention will not be jeopardized.

## Great idea!

"I can't seem to get focused," is the number one comment I've been hearing from clients and colleagues recently. There are some excellent reasons we don't get focused or stay focused on what is most important to us. Some of these are:

a) We have lots of interests
b) We don't like to say no to projects or favors
c) We are easily distracted
d) We haven't thought through what we want to focus on
e) We are so busy that we stay on the surface of life, just trying to get through the day

Why don't you feel focused on what you most care about? Do any of the above possibilities resonate with you? Or are there reasons I haven't listed that are what allow your energy to be scattered? I have found that when someone makes the decision to get focused, there are several things that make the shift easier and more lasting. It can make a difference when...

- **You want to live your life with more of a purpose.** When you turn toward something positive, as opposed to only turning away from the negative, you quickly build up momentum. The usual distractions and other elements that drain your energy will still be there, but you will have a reason to stay focused. This makes it easier to ignore the distractions.

- **You work to gain some insight into why you struggle to focus.** Knowing yourself allows you to identify what gets in your way and then you can step back and look at these issues in a more detached and objective way. Instead of getting frustrated that there isn't enough time in your day or getting swept up in the flood of your activities, you can keep a healthy perspective on what is pulling you in and how you would like to respond.

- **You pay attention to how you spend your time and stop allowing yourself to waste time on unworthy projects.** If your teenager had a big test tomorrow and you saw her doing everything but study, you'd probably share some words of wisdom with her about planning to use her time properly and your concern that she is wasting the time she needs to use to study. How can you make sure that you first take care of what you most need to do? What advice would you give your daughter or best friend? Contrary to popular belief, downtime is not wasted time. But spending your most valuable resource (time) on something that is not extremely important to you is a waste of time.

- **You stand for something.** Getting focused has a lot to do with your mission. Your mission should be the foundation of your various intentions and actions. If you spend your time, attention and other resources on what furthers your mission, you will feel productive and you will feel that you are spending your time well.

- **You create conditions in your life to allow you to focus on what you most care about:**

**Eliminate unnecessary activities**

- Reduce your overhead

- Learn to enjoy down-time without feeling "unproductive"

- Don't do projects simply because you feel obligated to do them

- Don't say yes to anything right away (You'll really thank me for this tip!)

- Let others know what your mission is so they can send opportunities your way

- And most importantly, know what your priorities are so that you can make them your focus

If you try these tips, you should notice some changes right away. But if you follow this method for three months, you will feel more productive, energized and focused!

Leslie Godwin, MFCC is a Career & Life-Transition Coach, Writer and Speaker. She publishes a free email newsletter on career and life transition. For information, email godwinpss@aol.com and mention that you'd like to be on the email newsletter list.

- **Go outside.** In the spring, summer and fall, I take many of my business reading and writing projects outside. The fresh air and sounds of nature are soothing to me. I am able to think more clearly and creatively. I enjoy the work more. Plus, I always feel good that I'm taking advantage of the gorgeous weather, while getting things done at the same time.

# Chapter 32

# Conquering procrastination

- **Reasons you may procrastinate.** There are several reasons why one might procrastinate, but the top reasons are:

  ❖ **You don't know what to do.** More information is needed and questions need to be answered, but you're not sure where to turn.

  ❖ **You feel overwhelmed.** Rather than seeing a project as a series of small steps, you look at it as if it's so big that you don't even know where to start.

  ❖ **You don't know where to start.** You feel that if you don't know where to start, you shouldn't start at all.

  ❖ **You are a perfectionist.** You feel you don't have the time right now to do the job perfectly, so you're waiting for a more opportune time.

  ❖ **You would rather do something else.** You feel that if you just do the things you want to do, maybe the thing you don't want to do will just "go away."

  ❖ **You feel you can do it later.** Unfortunately, this often results in a big, last minute rush to finish the task or project by the deadline, instead of a comfortable pace.

  ❖ **You feel uneasy about doing it.** Why are you feeling uneasy about it? Is this something you really don't want to do because it may hurt you or someone else emotionally? If so, procrastinating on it can sometimes make the situation even worse.

- **Make a "Procrastination Log."** Make a log of all the items you are procrastinating on. Keeping these types of tasks hidden will not make them go away. Instead, getting them "out in the open" will give you a visual to start working on.

- **Make sure you really have to do it.** Ask yourself if it's really necessary to do that task or make that decision or read that book. Some things are not worth doing at all.

- **Don't string yourself along.** If you really don't intend to do something, it is better to take it off your To Do list.

- **Are trivial tasks causing your procrastination?** It's very easy to use trivial tasks as excuses for procrastinating on the important stuff.

One executive once told me he couldn't get to his marketing because he was always too busy with administrative tasks. Once I had a look at the other tasks he claimed were holding him back it was easy to identify this executive was just using those other less important tasks as excuses to avoid doing his marketing.

- **Start somewhere.** Make it a point to choose one of the items on your Procrastination Log each day and work on it first thing in the morning, before you start anything else, even if you can only dedicate 10-15 minutes at a time.

- **Break it down.** When you realize you're procrastinating on something very important, it helps to break whatever you have to do into smaller increments.

Often a job is never started because as a whole it seems enormous and overwhelming. But broken down into 15-minute chunks, it is almost always easier to get started and work towards accomplishing your project or task.

## Great idea!

Getting started on a difficult project or task is often the hardest part. We procrastinate for every reason, but once we actually get started, it's much easier to complete the task.

Here is a secret weapon that has always worked for me, whether it's a huge project or just an unpleasant one.

Just commit to 10 minutes anywhere in your day to start your project. Anyone can find 10 minutes.

Why does this work? Because you're taking action. In 10 minutes, you can do any number of things that will motivate you to keep going. Set a timer. You can:

1. Break down the project into small steps.
2. Gather materials or tools you might need.
3. Write a few words or one page.
4. Unclutter three or more things and see the results.
5. Make one telephone call.

You get the idea. Do whatever it is that will get you started. Then commit to 10 minutes every day. The best part is that once you're engaged in your task, you'll want to continue and 10 minutes may turn into 15 or 30 minutes. So you're way ahead of your commitment of only 10 minutes and you'll feel great! You'll be done in no time.

Patsy Murray, Life Coach
SimpleLife Coaching
Simplifying the lives of Mid-Life Professional Women
617-923-1158
patsmur@rcn.com

- **Set specific deadlines for each mini-goal.** Post a note on your office door that says, "Do not leave until you do _____." Since each mini-goal is only going to take fifteen minutes, you can certainly do it before you leave without having to worry that you're going to be in the office all night.

- **Gather the information.** Perhaps you're procrastinating because you don't have all the information you need to do the project or to make a good decision. Begin collecting what you need or ask a friend or associate to assist you, or at least find out who, where and/or how to obtain information.

- **Announce your intentions publicly.** Tell your friends, co-workers, employees or spouse. Telling the world is an excellent way to help ensure completion of your project, task or decision.

- **Team up.** Get a partner to support your goal and to help encourage you to keep pushing ahead. Ask her to nudge you every time she notices you procrastinating.

- **Make them attractive.** When you look at your tasks as chores, it is easy to put them off and do something else. Rather than write "make 10 sales calls," write "make 10 calls to increase my income."

- **Make it more pleasurable.** While working on an unpleasant task, turn on the radio and listen to your favorite music radio station at the same time or sip your favorite, soothing herbal tea. This may help to ease your boredom or frustration, while you progress on your task or project.

- **Make it a game.** Make a game out of unpleasant tasks. Come up with rewards based on point values. Give yourself points for each completed item and when you build enough points, trade them in for your rewards. For example:

  ❖ Task One=5 points

  ❖ Task Two=10 points

  ❖ Task Three=7 points

    ➢ 20 points=10 minute lemonade or coffee break

    ➢ 40 points=buy that new paperback you've been meaning to read

    ➢ 60 points=half hour reading break

- **Apply the "more than 1 month" rule.** If an item has been on your Master List more than one month, either a) do it now, b) delegate it to someone else or c) cross it out—if it's still there after all this time, it's obviously not that important to you.

- **Don't give yourself more to procrastinate on.** Handle routine items—mail, correspondence, email and phone calls—each day. Toss papers you don't need immediately. Don't allow junk to pile up on your desk. The more you handle right away, the less you'll have to procrastinate about.

## Organizing Clinic

### Question

I tend to procrastinate when it comes to making my follow-up calls. I understand and believe how important it is to make those calls to prospective customers, but I guess I'm finding difficulty making the time to do so. Any ideas?

Jimmy Nader, Queens, NY

### Answer

Dear Jimmy,

I doubt the procrastination problem is with your time. I would bet my bottom dollar it is the fact that you don't like making follow-up calls, so you choose to do something else more comfortable and less difficult.

One of the fears of follow-up calls is fear of rejection. Another may be that you feel you are annoying someone with your call. I recommend that first you are sure you're offering your prospective customers something very compelling when you call. This way, you won't feel like you're a bother. Instead, you'll feel that you're helping them and it would be sad for them if they didn't hear from you.

Second, realize that you can't secure a customer with every follow-up call. Just realizing you have to get so many "No's" before you get a "Yes" can be a big help to getting over any fear of rejection. If you really and truly believe that making follow-up calls is important, you will do so at all costs. Set aside a specific hour or 30 minutes each day for this purpose. Put this priority ahead of other administrative or less important tasks.

- **Start with the most difficult.** If you find you are always procrastinating on your more difficult tasks, do them first thing in the morning. Once they are out of the way, the rest of your day will be smooth sailing. Same thing when it comes to doing projects. Start with the most difficult step first. The rest will then seem like a piece of cake.

- **Come in early or stay late.** Come in thirty minutes earlier or stay thirty minutes later, specifically for the purpose of working on those items you've been procrastinating on. Only work on these items. Don't be tempted to work on something else more attractive or less difficult.

- **Use the "Decision Assistant."** Procrastination definitely can apply to making decisions. To help overcome decision procrastination, grab a sheet of paper and draw a line down the middle of the page. Write PROs at the top of the left hand column and CONs at the top of the right hand column. Then, fill in the pros and cons of a particular decision. Your answers in each column will help you decide which option is going to be the most beneficial.

- **Flip a coin.** If you've done everything you possibly can and still can't make a decision, flip a coin. Making a decision is better than not making one at all. Control your own destiny.

- **Commit to a time frame.** Many people procrastinate because they have an exaggerated sense of how long something will take or how difficult the job will be. To jump-start something you have been dreading, commit to a specific timeframe, whether the task is completed or not.

  Maribel, a freelance writer, commits to working on an article for one hour, when she has trouble getting motivated to start. The fact that she has an hour gives her a way out and lets her know that she will not be working on the article all night. She is usually amazed at the amount of work she can accomplish in one hour and it spurs her to the finish line.

- **Lower your standards.** Some people procrastinate because they are perfectionists and fear they will never finish the task at hand. Determine whether a higher level of accuracy or detail is really needed. By lowering your standards, you can accomplish what is needed to get the job done, instead of trying to make it perfect and never finishing it.

- **Delegate.** Can a task or project be delegated to someone else, like an employee or co-worker? Can you outsource the task? Can the task be delegated to a system that is more automatic, like an email autoresponder or a voicemail message? Keep your possibilities open and look outside the box.

- **Swap tasks.** Rather than procrastinating, can you swap a task you don't enjoy doing with someone else? You do something for the other person, while he does something for you.

- **Streamline your tasks.** Sometimes you may procrastinate on something because there are so many tedious steps involved. Think through what you're doing to determine if any of those steps can be skipped or consolidated. There is almost always a better, more efficient way to do something.

- **Expect the inevitable.** You might use the excuse that you have all of next week to start on a task or that you'll get to that task during a holiday week as the phone won't be ringing as much. There are always going to be other priorities that come up. Don't delay a task based on speculation that things will be better at another time.

- **Consider the consequences.** What will happen if you don't finish this task or project by the deadline? If the answer is "nothing bad will happen" then the task probably doesn't have to be done at all. If the answer is that your boss will be furious with you or you won't make your sales projections or that you could lose business, this may be reason enough to get you going on it.

- **Banish perfectionist tendencies.** If you feel you can't start something because you only start projects you can complete, then don't give yourself anything too big to start on in the first place. Take a project that requires two hours and vow to work on just one part of that project; perhaps a part that will only require 15 minutes. You should then have no problem at all completing what you started . . . perfectly.

- **Lower your expectations.** While some projects are worthy of your perfectionist tendencies, some things are just not worth the time and effort you're putting into them.

  For instance, if you're spending hours just trying to decide what color to make the employee newsletter this month, that's probably going overboard. Just pick a color and move on. Few people will care. Save your perfectionist tendencies for things that truly matter.

- **You will get over it.** Sometimes you may procrastinate on doing something you really dread, like making a return phone call to an irate customer or putting an employee on probation for insubordination. But as you know, the problem will not go away on its own.

  What is the worse thing that could happen? If the customer is going to yell at you, let him vent his anger. You'll be upset, but you will get over it. If you fear the employee may get violent when you reveal he is being put on probation, have the meeting along with a human resources representative or one of your company managers.

  Think of what you can do to deal with or make the situation easier for yourself. And just think—the second it is done you will most likely feel relieved that it is over with.

- **Last-minute Louie.** You might be the type of person who gets a high from doing tasks at the last minute and finishing them up right before your deadline. This can result in more errors. In addition, what if some other project comes up that you didn't anticipate? Try to get the majority of your project done ahead of time and leave the last minute high for reviewing it.

# Chapter 33

## Organizing ideas

- **Make idea files.** So many ideas. They come to you out of the blue. You find them in magazines. You read them in books or hear them on television. You can probably use these ideas for something you're doing in the office—perhaps a future project or an idea for a company newsletter or a motivational tidbit for an employee.

  The problem is, how do you store all of these ideas so they're easily retrievable in the future? Your best bet is to create a few categorized "Idea Files."

  I have idea files for marketing, motivation, customer service, goals, writing reference, new organizing thoughts and more. Yours can be tailored to whatever work you do. These files can be paper files or you can create one on your computer.

> ### Great idea!
>
> All of my notes and ideas are kept in my Palm Pilot. I used to use sticky notes, but I didn't like the mess of papers.
>
> My Palm is small enough to fit in my pocket and has memory large enough to hold tons of information. It offers me quick recording and quick retrieval of ideas.
>
> Jason Michael Gracia
> www.motivation123.com

- **Random ideas.** Get yourself a spiral notebook and capture your random ideas inside. Use this only for your ideas and you'll be creating your own personalized "Idea Notebook" that you can constantly refer to for inspiration and as a reminder for you to begin taking action on some of those ideas.

- **Record them.** As ideas come to mind, record them on a tape recorder. This is an excellent way to capture great ideas while you're driving or lying down in bed. Listen to your tape the next day and transfer your thoughts to paper—or ask your assistant to do this for you.

- **Use index cards.** Put each idea you have on an index card. Lay the completed cards out on your desk or place them on a bulletin board so you have a good visual of all your ideas. Add, change and eliminate as needed. Put them in order.

- **Take notes.** Whenever you have to come up with ideas for a particular subject and you're researching magazines, the Net, and so on, be sure you take notes. Sometimes a simple note can spark an amazing idea. Keep all of your notes in a notebook or binder so they can be referenced quickly and easily.

- **Highlight it.** Whenever I see an idea I like in a magazine or newspaper, I highlight it with a florescent marker. Before I recycle the publication, I transfer those ideas to my idea files.

## Organizing Clinic

### Question

I am a freelance writer and have lots of wonderful ideas for future stories to submit to magazine editors. I religiously write them down in my idea notebook. The problem is, I never get around to implementing them. I sit around waiting for editors to contact me. I guess I'm just lazy. How can I be more motivated to use my ideas?

Renee Dockety
Scottsdale, AZ

### Answer

Renee,

Since you're a freelance writer, I'm guessing your bread and butter comes from the volume of articles you're able to produce and sell to magazines. Taking the reactive approach that you're currently taking—waiting for editors to contact you—will minimize the money you can make at freelance writing.

The question here seems to be, do you wish to make more money from your freelance writing? If so, the only way to do so is to take a more proactive approach.

How about setting a goal each month to look through your idea notebook and come up with just two query letters each month to editors based on those ideas? This way, you'll be making use of all those wonderful ideas, you'll be exposing your writing to editors at the same time and you will give yourself the highest chances of bringing in cash each month.

- **Use a flipchart.** When you're trying to organize ideas from a group of people, use a flipchart. Encourage everyone to share ideas, no matter how silly, bizarre or difficult they may seem to be. Write each idea on a flipchart. This visual shown to the group may help spur other ideas and may result in one or two you can actually use.

- **Don't reinvent the wheel.** In grade school, we were all told never to copy someone else's work. We had to start from scratch and come up with our own brilliant ideas. So, we stayed up all hours of the night, struggling to think of an idea for the perfect essay or the most unique shadowbox.

  Well, here's a new concept for you. Copy the best and discard the rest. Did Burger King go out and come up with a completely new food concept? Not at all! They decided to sell hamburgers, just like McDonald's. So, if it's good enough for Burger King, it's good enough for you.

  This certainly doesn't mean you should go out and begin plagiarizing someone else's work. But it does mean that if something has already been done, like another company's employee evaluation forms or customer surveys and that system works beautifully, then copy that system if it's not copyrighted or use that system as a guide.

  Enhance it if your creative juices are flowing, but don't struggle from the ground up.

  The work has already been done. Why would you want to do it over?

### Great idea!

Whenever an existing system is causing frustration, it is not working. Many times it is hardest to fix the problems we're "closest" to, for just that reason. We're too close to get a clear focus.

Sometimes the best place to resolve a system problem or paper control problem with your office, is away from the office. Take time while on vacation perhaps or on a Saturday while relaxing by the pool.

Have a pen and legal pad in hand and ask yourself, "What is not working smoothly?" List all the areas you can think of and pick just one to focus on for a few minutes. Why isn't it working? What arrangement would make this system run more efficiently?

Make a bulleted list and perhaps even a drawing of the ideas you come up with. When you're back at the office, get ready for a fresh start and put that one new idea to work. Then keep "tweaking" it until it's perfect. It may take a few weeks to get it right, but it will be well worth it.

Tracy Wyman
The Clutter Buster
Tallahassee, Florida
850-205-5279
solutions@clutterbuster.org
www.clutterbuster.org

- **Make an outline.** Remember how you used to outline in school to write a book report or thesis? You can use the same method for keeping track of your ideas. This is especially helpful when you have to write a report or a sales letter.

- **Tell someone.** Sometimes the best way to work out an idea is to tell someone about it. Have this person counter your idea or add onto it. It's a wonderful way to work out the glitches and enhance your original thoughts.

- **Send out a survey.** Send out a paper survey to your customers and/or employees to generate ideas. Once you begin to receive the surveys back, you'll have a better idea of what people are looking for.

- **Start a discussion forum.** If your company has a web site, see if your boss is willing to have a discussion forum installed on your server. A discussion forum is interactive software that allows people to post messages to an online "board" visible to a group of people. This is a wonderful way to generate ideas from staff members and customers.

- **Save the site.** While surfing on the web, you may come up with sites that have excellent ideas for your business or office. But sometimes you don't have the time to read the entire site that very second.

  The best thing to do is either save the site address in your Favorites or Bookmarks in a virtual folder called "Ideas." Once each week, check your virtual folder and re-visit those sites. Second best thing to do is write the site addresses down in an "Idea Log" so you don't forget about them.

- **Flag the page.** When you find a good idea in a book, magazine or other publication, flag the page with a sticky note. Be sure the note is sticking out so you can see it. When you're finished with the publication, revisit the page you flagged. In your planner or Tickler file, schedule time to research or implement that idea.

- **Start an expanding folder.** Sometimes it can be effective to store your ideas in an expandable file folder with compartments. For instance, perhaps you're researching ideas for a new home office. One section might be for business furniture, another for business equipment, another for décor and so on.

- **An idea a week.** A great idea can be worth millions. Make it a point to check your idea file(s) once a week and act on at least one of those ideas.

# Chapter 34

# Organizing your business writing

- **Plan before your write.** When I was in grammar school, I remember my teachers encouraging all of the students to first make an outline before writing a book report. An outline is nothing more than an organized guide to follow through the writing process. Outlines also work very well for business writing.

  What I like to do is get a set of index cards and write down one specific thought on each. I then organize my business cards in a logical order. From there, I can make a very nice outline and proceed with my writing—whether I'm writing a letter, memo, report or book.

- **Choose clear words.** When writing for business, your goal should not be to dazzle them with the great American novel. Instead, your writing should be very easy for the reader to read and understand. Steer clear of jargon, huge words, slang and foreign languages.

- **Proofread with and without your computer.** It's very easy and convenient to use spell check and grammar check on your computer, but it should not replace human proofreading. Do both.

- **Number your points.** If you have a number of points to make in your letter or report, number them. This way, it's very clear where one point starts and ends and the next begins. It's also easier if you need to reference a specific point later on.

- **Use subheadings.** If you have a lot to say about your subject, separate your thoughts with subheadings—generally a few words in bold. If your reader needs to find a section quickly, he or she should be able to do so easily.

- **Keep your sentences short.** Remember run on sentences? They keep going, with no commas, periods or pauses for that matter. Run on sentences are difficult to follow. If your sentences are going beyond two to three lines, they're probably too long.

- **Keep paragraphs short.** As a rule of thumb, try keeping paragraphs to no more than five to seven lines each. This will give your reader a break and allow him to comfortably move on to the next paragraph.

- **Use appropriate graphics.** Graphics are wonderful, as long as they relate to what you're writing about. Don't use graphics just for the purpose of decorating a page or filling in a section you don't have much to say about.

# Great idea!

You've got something to say. You know it. Your associates know it. But you don't regard yourself as "a writer." How are you going to express your wisdom? How will you communicate your thoughts?

Yes, you can follow the path of J.Paul Getty, Lee Iaccocoa and Donald Trump and hire someone to write your words. That works. But there is an easier way. I call this the "two step" because that's all there is to it. Here's the secret in a nutshell: Step one is state your principle. Step two is illustrating it.

Pretty simple dance routine, right? Yet you can use this method to write ANY type of nonfiction--- whether it's your life story, a school paper, an executive brief or a full-length scholarly book. (Actually, the scholars sorely need this method. They're too stuffy!)

I was reminded of this method while reading a book from the 1940's. I noticed that throughout the book the author would make a statement and then illustrate it with a story. The more I thought about it, I felt this was the easiest way to write anything. Here's how it works:

1. Make a list of the ideas you want to communicate. Pretend these are laws, rules, insights, commandments, theories or whatever will work for you. What you're looking for is a list of messages.

For example, I was working with a Houston body-mind therapist and I told him about this method. I said, "One of your messages is that people can have whatever they want, as long as they aren't attached to how they get it." He nodded.

"Another message of yours is that the energy we put out is the result we get." He nodded again.

"Those are your key points," I explained. "Write those down. That's easy. All you do is pull out a sheet of paper or turn on your laptop and just jot down the ideas you want to get across."

2. Now all you do is illustrate every point with three stories.

This is what I liked about that book from the forties. The author made a statement, then illustrated it with a story that made the statement come to life.

"You have all kinds of stories to share," I reminded my therapist friend. "For every point you make, support it with a story. Maybe tell how someone achieved a breakthrough following your main point. This reinforces your point and makes it easier to understand."

That's it!

Principle-story, principle-story, principle-story.

You can take ANY subject and break it down this way. You're making it easier on the readers, too. They don't have to wade through a long involved tale. With this method, you cut right to the point. You say, "Here's what I believe," and then you use a story to explain why you believe it.

The book from the forties that I'm referring to was "How to Develop Your Executive Ability" by Daniel Starch. I'm using it as an example of this two-step formula and not necessarily urging you to run out and find a copy (it's out of print, anyway).

I just pulled the book off the shelf and opened it at random. I'm looking at the chapter titled "Putting New Ideas to Work." It begins with a statement: "Write them down at the time they come to you."

It then spends four paragraphs giving lively quotes from Tolstoy, Darwin and Robert Louis Stevenson about the importance of writing down your ideas when they come to you.

If you just write down your message or key point, it will sit on the page in a lifeless, very un-hypnotic way. If you want people to remember the message, if you want them to install the message in their skull, then tell a story that illustrates it.

Your stories don't have to be classics of literature. A relevant quote can bring a statement to life. Stories from other people can bring your message to life. But most powerful and memorable of all are the stories from your own experience. I just flipped open Starch's book to chapter twenty-four, on "Turning Bad Breaks Into Opportunities." Right off the bat there's a statement: "Resolve not to be downed by failure."

And then follows a page and half of stories about people who were in accidents and went on with their lives, including a quote from Cervantes and John Bunyan. This supportive material awakens your message in the reader's mind.

You might notice that I just used this very technique to write this chapter. I told you there was a two-step formula for writing anything. Then I illustrated the two steps with stories from my clients and with a story about the book that gave me the idea. This "two-step" works!

The next time you have to write something, remember: principle-story, principle-story, principle-story. It's the easiest way to write anything!

Joe "Mr. Fire!" Vitale, regarded as one of the world's most powerful copywriters, is a best-selling author of marketing books and courses, including "The AMA Complete Guide to Small Business Advertising," Nightingale-Conant's audio program, "The Power of Outrageous Marketing!" and "Create Advertising That Sells." Visit: www.mrfire.com/

- **Keep abbreviations to a minimum.** If you're writing an internal memo, product abbreviations may be fine to a point. But avoid using them all the time or you'll run the risk of someone not knowing what it means. This is especially true when writing letters to customers.

- **Use the thesaurus.** Find you're using the same word over and over again? Get some ideas using a printed or electronic thesaurus. But again, use words that most people understand without having to go to a dictionary.

- **Find a quiet place.** It's difficult to write well when there's a lot of noise and activity. Close your office door or bring your laptop to the library when you're writing something that requires a lot of focus.

- **Work in small blocks of time.** Someone once asked my husband Joe and I how we write our books and we responded, "A chapter at a time." I like to choose a subject or a chapter and spend about 15-20 minutes at a time on it. This gives me a chance to think about one thing at a time. In between, I take short breaks and then continue.

- **Avoid writer's block.** Many people, when asked to write something, stare at a blank page for hours. You don't have to start at the beginning. Start writing anything. You can even start in the middle. You can always organize your thoughts later (more easily done if you are using a computer to compose).

- **List your reader's questions.** When writing a letter or report, always keep your readers in mind. What questions will they want answered by reading your material?

- **Talk into a recorder.** For some people, it's easier to talk than to write. If this sounds like you, no problem! Just record what you want to say into a tape recorder. Later, type up your thoughts or have your assistant do so for you. When the typing is done, just adjust and proofread as necessary.

- **Take a break.** If you can't think of what you want to write, walk away and take a short break. Sometimes, just relaxing for a moment is all you need to let those words slip off your tongue.

- **Schedule time to write.** If you're finding you don't have the time to write, you have to actually schedule a definite time for this activity. If you write often, schedule a day and time of the week to do all your writing, like Tuesdays from 2:00 to 5:00PM. And keep that appointment, just as you would any other.

- **Edit on the computer.** If you use a word processing program to write, you can actually have someone else read and edit it for you. You can set the software up to track any edits the other person makes. Edits are usually marked in red right on your computer monitor. You can then decide later to accept the edits or leave as is. It sure beats making marks on hard copy printouts.

- **Cite your sources.** Give credit where credit is due. Keep a running list of your sources on an index card or in a typed word processing document. Then, include a reference box or page with your article or publication.

# Chapter 35

# Getting there on time

- **Mark the time you have to leave.** You have a meeting in a few minutes, but decide to take just one more call. The call takes a little longer than expected. Now you're stressed because you realize you have to run to the meeting to avoid being late.

  In the future, rather than just jotting the actual time of your appointment on your calendar, mark the time you have to leave instead. Consider the time it's going to take you to get there and then pad that time generously.

---

### Great idea!

Use a sport watch chronograph (stop watch function) to time how long it takes you once you leave your office to travel somewhere else or how long to travel from home to the office. Be sure to include time gathering your purse/briefcase, walking out to the car; the drive time, finding a parking place at your destination, getting out of your car and walking into building, getting on the elevator, walking down the hall to the office and so forth.

People oftentimes only consider the actual time on the road and forget to add in these other factors that often cause a person to be late.

Also, use an answering machine to screen calls within fifteen minutes of a planned departure time. Many people are made late by taking last minute calls, but most of them can be called back later at a more convenient time.

Linda Richards
Organize and More
352-373-1086
Linda@organizeandmore.net
www.organizeandmore.net

---

- **Take advice from the coach.** A famous football coach had a simple rule that ensured everyone was always on time. Everyone was expected to be present at team meetings fifteen minutes before the scheduled time. That meant players had to arrive for a 1:00PM meeting at 12:45PM.

  You can use this very same concept when scheduling your meetings and appointments. Give yourself a minimum fifteen-minute cushion and take the pressure off.

- **Be prepared ahead of time.** At least 24 hours prior to the time you must leave your home or office, make a list of everything you must do before you leave.

  Make sure you have enough gas in the car. Go to the ATM or bank and get the pocket money you'll need. Put your briefcase or purse right near the door. Gather what you're going to wear, so you can grab everything and get dressed quickly. Jot yourself any reminders on sticky notes and stick them to the inside of your front door, such as things to pick up, things to bring or things to do.

  You'll save lots of precious time if you have everything organized and ready to go, you won't have to rush, and you'll get to your destination without stress.

## Organizing Clinic

### Question

I'm supposed to be in work by 8:30AM, but no matter what I do, I'm always late. I wake up at 6:30AM, take a shower, eat breakfast, walk the dog and then drive the 20 minutes or so it takes to get to work.

Since I don't get to bed until almost midnight (I work a second job and I don't get home until 11:00PM), I can't possibly get up any earlier. I'm in jeopardy of losing my primary job. Please help!

Alan Sothman, Minneapolis, MN

### Answer

Dear Alan,

You said you always arrive at work late, but you didn't mention how late. 5 minutes? 15 minutes? 30 minutes?

I'm sure you already know that you have to leave for work earlier to get there on time. If you're arriving late, you're leaving too late.

To prevent waking up any earlier, try taking a shower at night instead of in the morning. That should give you at least another 15 to 20 minutes.

- **Prepare your family.** If you have to send your kids off to school in the morning before you leave for the office, be sure their belongings are prepared the night before.

Lay out their outfits. Be sure their books are in book bags and sitting by the door. Make lunches the evening before. Be sure they wake up so there's ample time to get dressed and eat breakfast.

- **Leave early.** If you have to be somewhere at a certain time, be sure you leave early enough. Pad your time. This way if there is traffic, you'll still be on time. In other words, if it takes you a half hour to get there, leave at least forty-five minutes early or more.

- **Avoid obstacles.** If construction is scheduled on the interstate, take an alternate route. Avoid rush hour. Read your local papers and listen to local radio stations so you're prepared.

### Great idea!

- Get directions well in advance either from the client, associate or an Internet-based map service. Don't do a search as you're headed out the door.

- If time permits, do a practice run, preferably around the same time of day you'll be traveling. This is very helpful before appointments like job interviews or sales presentations, when it's possible you'll be nervous and thinking of other things. It also gives you a good idea of what potential challenges the area might present that will impact the time you'll need to arrive on time (e.g., one-way streets, long traffic light cycles, no left-hand turn lanes, limited parking, heavily traveled railroad tracks, school bus routes).

- Get gas the day before a morning meeting.

- Pack your briefcase the night before a morning meeting.

- Always expect traffic, accidents and long red lights. Pad your travel time by at least 20 minutes.

- Lastly, if being late cannot be avoided, always call the client or associate to say so. Showing up late with no forewarning is discourteous and does not present a professional image, regardless of the reason.

Brigitta Theleman
Organized Insight
919-302-0567
brigitta@organizedinsight.com
www.organizedinsight.com

- **Know how to get there.** When you're not really sure how to get to your destination, such as when you're visiting a customer for the first time, allow for extra time.

If possible, drive to that destination prior to your appointment. This way, you'll know exactly how to get there on your scheduled day. If that isn't possible, call someone at your destination. Ask for specific directions and write them down. You can also use a map service on the Internet, such as Mapquest, to get directions: www.mapquest.com

- **Avoid unnecessary distractions.** If the phone rings right as you're leaving your home or office, let your answering machine screen the call. Unless it's someone calling about the particular destination you're about to leave for, then that message can probably wait until later on. It will still be waiting for you on your answering machine when you return. Believe me, if you pick up that phone, you're going to be late!

- **Keep an eye on the time.** Always wear a watch or have clocks in the rooms you're constantly in. And if you have to, set an alarm clock or timer to go off at the time you must leave. When the alarm sounds, it's time to get going.

- **Early bird?** Some people are just not morning people. Are you one of them? If so, try to schedule important meetings for later in the day if at all possible. You'll be more alert and you shouldn't have to rush to get there.

- **Set two alarm clocks.** Never rely on only one alarm clock when it's imperative to wake up on time, especially if you hit the snooze button the second your alarm goes off. Place a second alarm clock on the opposite side of your bedroom, so you have to actually get up and walk across the room to shut it off. That second alarm should be set at your final wake-up warning time. Once you're up, stay up.

- **Same time each day and night.** Go to bed at the same time each night and wake up at the same time each day, including weekends. Your body clock will get into a rhythm and you may start waking up even before the alarm sounds.

- **Use scheduled transport.** You're more likely to get to the train or ferry if you know it's leaving at a set time.

- **Watch your diet.** I know that if I eat a lot of sugar like an ice cream sundae, right before bed, I tend to wake up very tired in the morning. If you must be somewhere important the next day, don't eat anything that may slow you down. Keep a food diary to determine what those foods are if necessary.

- **Change your hours.** If you have so much going on in the morning—have to get the kids to school, have to walk the dog, have to shovel snow—you may consider switching your work hours if this is possible. Tony, a web designer, asked his boss if he could get to work at 10:00AM instead of 9:00AM. He would work until 6:00PM instead of 5:00PM. His boss was agreeable to the idea and Tony was never late for work again.

# Chapter 36

# Productivity

- **Same place, same time.** Plan to do similar tasks at the same time each day or the same day each week. With a consistent schedule, you will always know what has to be done well ahead of time.

    For instance, if you make sales calls, plan to make all of them each day at 3:00PM. If you work on a weekly report, plan to do so every Wednesday at 9:00AM.

> ## Remember the woodsman
>
> *There was a woodsman who had a new ax. The first day, he was able to chop down twenty trees. With each passing day he worked longer and harder, while chopping down fewer and fewer trees. A friend wandered by and suggested, "Why don't you sharpen your ax?" The woodsman replied, "I'm too busy. I've got to chop down more trees."*
>
> Working longer and harder will not help you find more time. It will make the problem worse. The only way to save time is to waste less time. Stop chopping with a dull ax. Sharpen your ax. In other words, take the time to collect your thoughts and re-evaluate how you can work smarter—not harder.

- **Let in some light.** Good lighting is a must. If your eyes are strained, you're going to be less productive. Increase the lighting in your office by installing a stronger light bulb, getting more lamps or opening your window blinds.

- **Comfort counts.** Sit in a comfortable chair without slouching. Ensure the items you use often are located within close range so you don't have to strain yourself to reach them. Tune your radio to a relaxing station. Keep comfort in mind. It really counts towards high productivity.

- **Keep your essentials nearby.** Avoid having to get up and down every minute to reach for frequently used items.

- **Make packages ahead of time.** If you send the same letters, brochures and price lists to prospects and clients when they make a request, make your packages ahead of time.

    Enclose all necessary information in your packets and store them away until you need them. When somebody asks for your materials, the packets will be ready to go.

- **Email standard responses.** Many email programs give you the option of storing standard responses in email folders. When you type a response to a question you're likely to be asked again, save that letter in your email folder.

  The next time someone asks you that same question, you insert the response (or highlight and copy the information and then paste the information) into a new email.

  Finally, personalize the email with the person's name and any additional information and send. No need to retype it all again.

> ## Great idea!
>
> When writing email, I like to include promotional messages to my readers after my salutation. These are commonly called "sig lines" or signature lines. I use about 40 sig lines, sometimes more, including standard responses that I use frequently.
>
> So, I send an email to myself with the appropriate subject and store it in an email folder. When I want to include a sig in an email, I just go to my folder and select the appropriate one. I then copy and paste it into my email.
>
> This eliminates the need to recall my sig lines by memory, eliminates the need to retype them and helps to keep them in a handy file so that I can retrieve them in an instant without having to retype.
>
> Marilyn Butz, BizCard Pro
> Color, price and foil all show, your card was made by BizCardPro
> www.bizcardpro.com

- **Other standard responses.** If your email software doesn't have email folders or if you're just interested in saving a letter you just typed, store these responses in a standard word processing file. You can then open, copy and paste part or all of the information easily, from one computer file to another.

- **Create standard "Reminder Forms."** Create standard Reminder Forms to send to clients and customers when a scheduled appointment is coming up or when the product they purchased is due for service.

- **Reply on the same note.** When someone sends you a memo or other correspondence that requires a response, rather than getting another sheet of paper, respond right on that person's original note, such as in the margins.

- **Handwrite it.** A handwritten note or reply can sometimes save a lot more time than typing it up, especially if it's just a short note. It may not look as pretty, but for the majority of situations it's okay to do so.

- **Dictate and have someone else type.** If you're good at dictating into a tape recorder or to a stenographer, you might choose this option for your correspondence. Then, have an office assistant type it.

- **Color code.** Distinguish your drafts from your final forms of written materials by using colored paper—perhaps yellow for your first drafts, pink for your second and white for your final. You can also use colored circular stickers to color code.

- **Create a template.** Have to type similar letters or forms over and over again? Don't reinvent the wheel. Instead, create a template.

  A template is a file that you create once and use over and over again. For instance, you might have a regular letter that you send to all customers when payment is past due. There's no need to type a new letter for each customer each time. You type a letter once and save it as your master file.

  Each time you have to send a letter out, open this file, type the customer information in the name/address space and print. All you ever have to change is the name and addresses.

  You might even want to get fancy and do a word processing mail merge.

- **Read instructions.** You just received that brand new media storage cabinet you've been waiting for. It needs some assembly, but looks pretty simple. So, while glancing at the photo on the box, you begin putting it together and work for two hours straight.

  Tired, you sit down to take a break, look across your office and a sickening feeling suddenly sets in. You realize that you've missed an entire assembly section and there's no way you can correct your mistake without starting over again.

  Very often, people feel that reading through instructions for assembly, computer software, projects and tasks is a waste of time. They figure they can just jump right in. Unfortunately, this almost always results in mistakes and hours of wasted time.

  One of the best tips for being organized: Always read the instructions first.

- **Early bird or night owl?** Do your highest priority work during your most energetic portion of the day.

- **ABE.** Always Be Evaluating. Don't do something the same way you did it the last time just because that's the way you've always done it. Always evaluate how you can do the task with fewer steps, in less time or with less effort.

## Organizing Clinic

### Question

How can I ensure my employees are more productive?

Kim Miller, Cherryville, NC

### Answer

Dear Kim,

That's really a management question, more than an organizing question. However, I can tell you that it's important to ensure the "systems" your employees are using are productive. Take a look at how things are being done and see if you can streamline any of the processes.

For example, you may think an employee is very slow in filling out daily forms. However, if you take a look at those daily forms, you may find that much of the information this employee is filling out each day isn't really necessary.

Another employee who assembles products takes his time, because he is paid by the hour. Bad system. If you pay this employee by the number of products he is able to assemble, you can be almost certain he's going to get more done.

Most employees aren't trying to do a bad job. Most want to be respected and rewarded for doing well. Looking at your systems may increase employee productivity dramatically.

---

- **Pace yourself.** Don't set yourself up to work at top speed all day long. After doing something that has been physically or mentally taxing, do something that is less demanding. Sandwich easier tasks in between more difficult ones.

- **Get an early start.** Arrive at the office 20 to 30 minutes before everyone else does and you will have quiet time to get some tasks accomplished or do strategic planning.

- **Keep small projects handy.** You're going to have idle time throughout your day, like when you're on telephone hold. Keep small projects handy that you can tend to during that time, like reading an article or weeding out your Rolodex.

- **Keep a time log.** What have you been doing all day long? Most people can't easily answer this.

A great way to determine where all the time is going is to keep a time log for a period of two weeks. Don't do less, otherwise it will not be a representative sample.

A time log can help you determine where your time is going, what time wasters occur on a regular basis, if you're spending too much time on low priority tasks, what priorities you're getting to, what priorities you may be neglecting and how time wasters are affecting your productivity.

Write down everything you're spending your time on, as you're doing it. Don't wait until the end of the day to fill this out. Fill it out continuously throughout your day.

Every time you do something, write the starting time and a description of the time spent. For example, if Bob just interrupted you to talk about the football game at 9:00AM, you should indicate this.

When you stop doing something, indicate the end time. At the end of the day, highlight all high priority items in yellow, medium priority in blue and low priority in pink.

Add up your total minutes spent for each category. Divide the time for each category by the total minutes in your workday to determine the correct percent of your workday spent on each category.

After the two-week period is up, analyze your log. See where your time is going. See if you're spending enough time on your priorities. Begin developing systems to eliminate the time wasters and to get the most out of each day.

- **Take a breather.** A bit of time off for relaxation can actually make you more productive. Always leave some time in your day to relax your eyes or to walk away from your office to take a break.

- **Focus on one thing at a time.** Multi-tasking is fine when you are working on tasks that don't require too much concentration. When you're working on something that is very important and brain-heavy, focus on that one task only.

- **Consolidate similar projects.** Make all of your office appointments in the morning, so you can take care of them one after the other and have the rest of the afternoon available for in-office projects. Consolidate all of your outgoing phone calls.

- **Use voice recognition software.** If you hate to type or can't type very fast, you might consider using voice recognition software. With this type of software, you speak into a microphone on your computer, while the computer types what you just said—automatically.

While you may have to spend a few minutes correcting errors (most voice recognition software according to the experts is about 90% accurate these days), it may be well worth the time you'll save actually doing the typing.

- **Upgrade your computer equipment.** If you're using old, slow computer equipment, chances are you can increase your productivity dramatically. Give your computer system an overhaul. Get more hard drive space, more memory, a faster printer and so on.

- **Get your plan on paper.** It's difficult to be productive when you're working randomly or trying to remember everything that needs to get done. Get your thoughts on paper and put them in a logical sequence. Work on each thought one by one.

- **Determine if it's the best way.** One time, I watched someone use an enormous sheet of graph paper to add columns of numbers, instead of simply using a computer spreadsheet.

  Another time, I watched someone writing out business invitations one by one, instead of simply setting up the copy and running them through her printer.

  Just because you've been doing something the way you've always done it, doesn't necessarily mean it's the best way.

  Always consider if there's a faster, easier or smarter way of doing something.

- **United we stand.** When leading a large group of people working on a project, be sure you monitor the project's progress each step of the way. If even one person out of twenty isn't pulling his weight or producing at a fast enough pace, the entire project may come to a standstill.

- **Communicate effectively.** Nothing puts an obstacle in the way of productivity quite like a lack of communication. Be sure everyone involved understands exactly what is to be done and by when.

- **Get rid of the clutter.** Clutter is an obstacle to productivity. Cluttered space leads to a cluttered mind. Clear the clutter and pave the road clear for a more productive day.

- **Create easy access.** Be sure it's easy for you to get to machinery and office equipment, without having to struggle, reach and stretch.

  If it's difficult to get to, you're going to get irritated and your productivity is going to suffer.

  Benita, a manager at a bank, had to step over her calculator cord every time she needed to access her filing cabinet. Because of this obstacle, she rarely filed.

  Needless to say, her To Be Filed pile was a mountain! We traded in her electric calculator for a solar one—no cord required. Problem solved.

# Organizing Clinic

## Question

How can one multi-task and keep a clear head and desk? It's so much easier to keep an organized desk or work area when you only work on one thing at a time. In my current line of work, being an assistant to a busy child and adult psychiatrist, I am often doing more than one thing at a time. I am on the computer entering data about a therapy session presently taking place and have the appointment book nearby. In the meantime, I may receive a phone call from another patient making a new appointment or changing one, get another call from a patient asking for a prescription renewal, greet the next patient coming in and then give a message to the patient coming out that her husband called and will meet her at a particular place. Phew! All this happened one day, one minute after another.

By the time I get the chance to catch my breath, I have files and papers all over the desk that I have to sort through and put away, before my boss comes out with a personal request (get coffee or lunch) or the next patient calls or comes in. Any suggestions? My boss rarely has to do more than one thing at a time.

Yvonne Fitz

## Answer

Dear Yvonne,

You might think you're working on more than one thing at a time, but you're really not. If you're entering data into your computer and the phone rings, you will stop entering data and take the phone call. What's really happening is that you can't actually "complete" a project without being interrupted, due to the nature of your job. This is fine. It just takes some fancy footwork.

Keep a spiral-bound notebook to write down some notes. Yes, you might then have to transfer notes to patient files or make a phone call pertaining to a note, but at least your notes will be in one place and not on several sheets of loose paper. Keep a file sorter on your desk. This way, if you have to temporarily pull a file and you get interrupted, the file can be temporarily stored in your file sorter until you can get back to it. At the end of the day, all of these files can be filed back at once.

Take care not to just toss papers on your desk with each and every task that you have to do. When you're done taking notes, put your notebook back in the corner of your desk. Keep all of the file folders you pulled in the file sorter until you're ready to work on them or they're ready to be re-filed. Keep mail in an In Basket until you're ready to go through it. A patient will wait a moment if you ask him, if it's necessary for you to clear your desk before you speak to him.

The trick is to be calm as a cucumber. Even though your day may be chaotic, YOU don't have to be chaotic. Just work calmly and little by little, you'll complete everything you have to, even if you must come back to the same project two or three times before you finish it.

- **Don't just stand (or sit) there.** While you're making copies at the copy machine, don't just stand there and wait. Do something else. Read a business article or jot down some notes for a call you have to make later on.

  The same goes for when you're waiting for a file to download on your computer. Don't allow the day to waste away because of a slow Internet connection or a large file download.

- **On hold, doesn't mean everything is on hold.** Every once in awhile, you're going to be put on telephone hold. While waiting, type up a quick email, organize the top of your desk or purge the outdated cards in your Rolodex.

- **Does it need to be done?** I once worked with Terry, a customer who worked at a local custard stand. For years, she worked on the computer filling in a product cost database for her business.

  When I asked her what she did with all this information after it was filled in each month, she didn't have a good answer for me. Basically, she told me this database has been updated for years, but nobody ever even looked at the information.

  We determined that this report was probably used for something years ago, but not any more. Needless to say, the report was eliminated and she saved over 3 hours each week!

- **To multi-task or not.** In some cases, multi-tasking may not be the best way to go. Newly released results of scientific studies in multitasking indicate that carrying on several duties at once may, in fact, reduce productivity, not increase it.

  The research, published in the *American Psychological Association's Journal of Experimental Psychology: Human Perception and Performance*, determined that for various types of tasks, subjects lost time when they had to switch from one task to another.

  This is especially true if you're working on something complicated that requires your full attention. For example, working on your budgeting plan while you're handling phone calls may result in mistakes in the budget plan and annoyed people on the phone.

  But multi-tasking does work very well, when you're *waiting* for something else to happen.

# Chapter 37

# Reducing interruptions

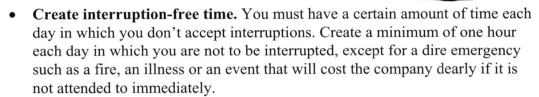

- **Create interruption-free time.** You must have a certain amount of time each day in which you don't accept interruptions. Create a minimum of one hour each day in which you are not to be interrupted, except for a dire emergency such as a fire, an illness or an event that will cost the company dearly if it is not attended to immediately.

  Utilize the same exact block of time each day for something specific, rather than looking for a free hour here and there.

### Great idea!

It's easy to turn the ringer off the phone or quiet the email notification on your computer, but how do you stop "people interruptions?" In struggling to maintain correct office politics, how do you politely get people to leave you alone when you have work to do? It's as simple as a sign.

A sign on your desk that says "Work In Progress, Please Do Not Disturb" is a subtle way to let people know that you do not wish to be interrupted.

As long as the sign is not overused, people will typically respect your need to not be interrupted and come back at a more appropriate time.

Susan Bailey
Susan's Organizing Service
PO Box 578, Redmond, OR 97756
541-350-4449
suznb@oregontrail.net
www.susansorganizingservice.com

- **Write it on your calendar.** Always write your interruption-free time on your calendar and be sure it's also noted on your assistant's calendar if she uses a separate one.

- **Know what interruptions cost.** On average, each interruption costs a minimum of ten to twenty minutes of precious time by the time you can get back on track with what you were originally doing before the interruption. That's a high price to pay.

- **Learn to recognize them.** You're all revved up and set to go on that important project. You are prepared and the energy is flowing. Your pencil hits paper and then it happens—someone stops by your office to ask you a question or to discuss last night's football game.

Learn to recognize interruptions for what most of them are—time robbers. While the occasional interruption might be an emergency, most can be avoided.

- **Be aware of who is interrupting.** Very often, interruptions come from the same people each and every time. Determine why these people are constantly interrupting you and work on a system to eliminate this problem.

- **Make an interruption log.** Keep a log of interruptions stating what the interruption was, whether it was necessary, the day and time of the interruption, how long the interruption was and if you have a solution to prevent this type of interruption in the future. This will give you a good picture of what is happening and will be an excellent tool to help you reduce interruptions in the future.

- **Create people time.** Establish specific periods of time when you're available to speak with people in your office. Let them know what your schedule is so they know when you'll be ready to talk. If you're the boss, this should not be a problem.

  If you're not the boss, then speak to your boss about the importance of undisturbed, quality time—even for an hour or two a day, so you can give your projects the time and attention they deserve. If your boss is reasonable, he or she will agree.

- **Close your door.** If you're lucky enough to work in an office with a door, close it when you need time to focus on a task or project. Put up a DO NOT DISTURB sign if necessary.

- **Catch up with them later.** If you work in a cubicle, you may have to personally send people away. Try saying, "I'm sorry, I'm tied up right now. I'll get back to you at 3:00 this afternoon," or "Is it all right with you if I stop by your office in the morning? I'm working on a project that I have to finish ASAP."

- **Stand up and stretch.** When someone unexpectedly stops by your office or cubicle, stand up. If you do, the other person will be discouraged from sitting down. Then, you can briefly say hello and ask the person if he or she can come back later in the day once you've had a chance to work on your To Do list for a little while.

- **Give your visitor chair the heave-ho.** Visitor chairs encourage people to stop in, lounge and shoot the breeze. Temporarily remove the visitor chair until you have a legitimate appointment.

If the chair can't be removed, put some decorative pillows or a plant on it. This should help discourage people from taking everything off of your chair and sitting down.

## Organizing Clinic

### Question

My husband and I run a small campground without staff. Interruptions are part of our business. Visitors coming in and telephone calls make the business run, but we still need to accomplish things like maintenance, bookkeeping and advertising. How can we more effectively complete these tasks and make our visitors welcome?

Ellyn Kern, Bennington, IN

### Answer

Dear Ellyn,

Here are a few ideas that can help you manage and grow your business, while still maintaining a friendly atmosphere, both for new visitors and current camp members.

- You mentioned you and your husband run your campground without any staff. However, hiring a part-time receptionist to help you manage the day-to-day phone calls and visitors might be in your best interest. This way, you and your husband can work on growing your business. If you can't afford to hire someone right now, check for volunteer workers at a local high school or college. Many schools provide internship programs that may help.

- To alleviate some of the phone calls, set up a company voicemail system that gives callers recorded information. For example, it may tell them to press 1 for directions to the campground, press 2 for registration information and so on. Of course, you should also give them an opportunity to leave a message or speak to someone live, but it will reduce the number of calls you have to personally answer.

- Do some of your administrative work, marketing and so on before business hours and after business hours. For instance, your business hours may be from 10:00am to 4:00pm. Then, you can use the hours of 9:00AM to 10:00AM and 4:00PM to 5:00PM for your administrative and marketing projects.

- Schedule a few orientation sessions throughout the day, to orient new members as a group, rather than personally addressing each person one-by-one. Perhaps have a group orientation at 10:00AM, 12:00N and 2:00PM. It will save you time if you can give all necessary information to a group, rather than randomly throughout the day.

- Keep brochures and a booklet of Frequently Asked Questions on hand. If current members or prospective members have questions, you can give them the information you have available and they can read through it at their own leisure. If you have a Web site with information, provide the Web site link in your informational pieces.

- Assign camp leaders to your current camp members. These leaders should be able to run their groups independently. Meet with your camp leaders weekly to address any questions they may have. Ask them to limit their questions to those meeting times, unless there is an emergency situation.

- Use technology to simplify your administrative and bookkeeping tasks as much as possible. This way, you spend as little time on these tasks as possible. Spreadsheets, simple databases and accounting programs can greatly simplify processes and they're no longer limited to large companies. Small companies can benefit greatly from technology as well.

- **Take yourself elsewhere.** If possible, bring your project to a quieter spot where you're less likely to be interrupted, such as an empty office or conference room.

  If your job allows, you might even decide to leave the office entirely to work on your project in a local library, a coffee shop or on your laptop at a local park.

- **Don't be the cause of the interruption.** If your staff or co-workers or customers are always interrupting you with the same questions again and again, you might be the cause of all these interruptions.

  Make a written manual for your staff that they can reference on their own. Give co-workers a typed list of frequently asked questions and answers. Put customer questions and answers on your company web site, so they can get the information they need quickly and easily without interrupting you.

- **Prevent self-interruptions.** If you find you're always distracted by your own thoughts when you're working through a project, keep a "Hold That Thought" log.

  As you're working on a task, if a thought comes to mind about something you have to do later like stopping by an associate's office or making a phone call, don't do it now. Instead, jot the thought down on your "Hold That Thought" log, rather than dropping everything you're doing.

- **Put up a visual barrier.** If someone easily catches your eye while walking past your desk or cubicle, that may entice them to just drop by for a visit. Put up a visual barrier like a tall plant in the direct line of a door or window. If they don't see you and you don't see them, you'll reduce casual drop-ins.

- **Work earlier or later.** Arrive at the office before everyone else does or stay later to minimize interruptions. The fewer people there are around, the less chance you'll be interrupted.

- **Use your assistant as a liaison.** During time you cannot be interrupted, ask your assistant to tell visitors or callers that you're not available at the moment, but any notes or messages can be passed on as soon as you're free. Have her keep a phone log, so you're aware of what has been happening in your absence.

  If she can handle a request, give her permission to handle it without interaction from you. If there are some visitors or callers you do need to be interrupted by, give your assistant a list of the names of these people so she knows it's okay to interrupt.

---

### Great idea!

My office sits right in front of "Grand Central Station" (the reception area) in the building where I work.

Everyone on the staff passes my door on their way to the mail table and copy room, often socializing as they come and go. Though I'm glad for the chance to have frequent contact with my co-workers, distractions are plentiful.

Fortunately, we have a receptionist on duty almost all of the time who is able to handle the phone calls and direct visitors to the right places.

I leave my door open most of the time, but have found that closing it has been helpful in blocking out unnecessary disruptions when I'm on a project that demands high concentration. Closing the door has been a simple but effective way to stay on task.

I rarely close the door completely so that people who need to see me can push it open and come in after they've knocked.

Mike Logan
Logan's Logic
256-348-7485

---

- **Use the rule of 3.** Wait until you need to return at least three phone calls before calling others back. You'll be able to get back to people fairly quick, without allowing the telephone to constantly interrupt every single job you're working on.

- **Morning, afternoon and evening.** If you are traveling, check voicemail three times: once in the morning, once at lunch and once at the end of the day. This will allow you to be responsive, but not be at the mercy of voicemail.

- **Screen your calls.** Don't allow your phone to interrupt you every five minutes. Use your answering machine or voicemail to field your calls until later.

> ## Great idea!
>
> STOP people from controlling your time.
>
> **S**tep away from the situation. Just ask: Can I get back to you on that? Or, let me think about that.
>
> **T**hink about what is being asked or demanded of you.
>
> **O**utcome: Determine the outcome if you do it or the outcome if you don't do it.
>
> **P**roceed: Put off, Purge the thought - Do one of the three and move on.
>
> Yvonne Surrey
> Y.E.S. Surrey Office Services
> 181 Hawthorne Street, Suite 1H, Brooklyn, NY 11225
> www.sos-organizing.com

- **Let people know when to reach you.** On your answering machine message, leave the time of day that is best to reach you. Try to answer your calls during this time. This should alleviate some people calling you during those times you do not wish to be interrupted.

- **Jot down where you left off.** If you do get sidetracked while you're working on something or in the middle of a thought, jot down where you left off. You can then get back to it easily when the interruption has passed.

- **Some interruptions are valid.** If you are interrupted and it's a valid interruption, ask yourself whether it is important enough to drop everything you are working on right this second or if it can wait until later in the day.

- **Don't prolong it.** When responding to a valid interruption, don't prolong it by asking how the person's vacation was or what happened at the latest conference. Save these questions for later and get back to what you are working on.

- **Make your work area less inviting.** For instance, if your desk always holds a big bowl of candy that you share with everyone, consider removing it. First, it's not your job to provide the entire office with snacks. Second, it may significantly reduce the amount of walk-by traffic causing you to be interrupted.

# Chapter 38

# Putting out fires

- **Are you putting out fires?** One of your best customers just called frantically wondering where her merchandise was. You think to yourself, "Jan was supposed to mail it a week ago." When you ask Jan, she says, "I was leaving for vacation and figured I'd just take care of it when I returned." You drop everything to get this customer's order together for mailing.

  Shortly after, Mike stops by to tell you the copy machine is jammed—again. You drop everything and begin working on that problem.

  You're just catching up, when your daughter calls crying because you were supposed to be home at 5:30 to take her to cheerleading practice. You leave in a rush.

  When you finally get to bed tonight, you realize you didn't accomplish any of your planned projects. You've been spending all day running around and tending to emergencies. In other words, you've been putting out brush fires. Below are just a few ideas to help you manage your time better by reducing those brushfires.

- **Start or suggest a training program in your company.** Lack of training is one of the biggest culprits when it comes to time wasted on brush fires. Thousands of problems can be easily avoided when staff members are properly trained.

  An effective training program involves a number of criteria, including showing someone how to do something, giving them a detailed checklist to follow and refer to, making sure the trainee can do the work independently and allowing the person ample time for practice.

- **Make procedure-related checklists.** People will make fewer mistakes and be less likely to forget important steps, if there are specific work procedures that must be adhered to.

  Think about the customer I just described, who didn't receive her merchandise. Obviously, Jan did not have a checklist. If she did, she would have known that all orders should be taken care of and mailed out every single night. She would not have left for vacation before the package was mailed and you would not have a frantic client on your hands.

- **Make equipment related checklists.** If you do, you won't have to deal with every equipment breakdown on your own. For example, when the copy machine jammed, Mike could have easily pulled out a checklist and fixed the problem, rather than wasting your time with it.

- **Eliminate the excess.** Eliminate all activities that don't support your plans for achieving your goals. Prioritize everything you need to do. Determine your highest priorities (things that have to be done), establish a time limit and do them first.

## How to go from putting out fires to solving interesting problems

"It's one thing after another," says Judy, a freelance graphic designer. I solve one problem and another one is there waiting for me. I feel as if I'll never stop solving problems in my business."

Most people think that problems in their business are signs that something is awry and dream, like Judy, that someday they'll wake up and have no more business problems. (This can apply to your career even if you don't have your own business.)

I see it differently. I think that our goal shouldn't be to get rid of our business problems once and for all. Instead, we should resolve BORING problems so we can get to the INTERESTING problems that intrigued us when we started our business or chose our career.

What were some of the interesting problems you hoped to solve with your business? Maybe you thought it would be fun to choose the newest style of clothing to carry in your boutique each season. Or maybe you fantasized about creating delicious menu items for your restaurant. You may have looked forward to adding interesting articles and creating unique features for your web site.

Instead, you may be struggling to pay the bills during the "off-peak" season in the retail clothing industry. Or your waiters keep leaving to go back to college so you're bussing tables and taking orders while trying to fill those positions. Or you're spending most of your time calling your ISP about server problems so that your web site (with it's outdated content) can be seen at all.

In other words, instead of solving interesting problems, you're solving boring problems.

One of my role models, Peter Drucker (who Warren Bennis called "the most important management thinker of our time") recommends the following to reduce the amount of boring problems we're faced with regularly: "The first task here is to identify the time-wasters which follow from lack of system or foresight. The symptom to look for is the recurrent "crisis," the crisis that comes back year after year. A crisis that recurs a second time is a crisis that must not occur again." (The Effective Executive, page 41)

Do you scramble every quarter to get your taxes in on time? Do you "forget" about marketing when business is coming in and then "remember" when you have a slow period? Does the phrase "putting out fires" come up in conversation with colleagues more than once a year? These are crises you could have resolved by creating a routine.

Here's more on routines:

Drucker describes routine as a system "that makes unskilled people without judgment capable of doing what it took near-genius to do before; for a routine puts down in systematic, step-by-step form what a very able man learned in surmounting yesterday's crisis."

So how can you spend more time on interesting problems: What are some of the interesting problems you fantasized you'd be working on when you first started your business? List them here:

What else would you like to be doing in your business if you had more time? Write down whatever comes to mind here:

What are some of the boring business problems you are stuck handling either from day-to-day, month-to-month or annually? You don't have to come up with solutions to them now, but try to identify where you spend your time that is NOT rewarding or interesting.

List your four top recurring problems:

1.
2.
3.
4.

Plan to take some time each week for the next four or five weeks to figure out how to create a system where before you had to solve a crisis. I recommend that you do a little each week because it's unrealistic to tackle all of your crises at once. Schedule the time now, maybe an hour twice a week for four weeks.

Pretty soon you'll be spending your valuable time on what you find interesting and challenging about your business!

Leslie Godwin, MFCC, is a Career & Life-Transition Coach specializing in helping people put their families, values and principles first when making career and life choices. Her book, *From Burned Out to Fired Up: A Woman's Guide to Rekindling the Passion and Meaning in Work and Life* (Published by Health Communications, Inc.) is available at all bookstores or go to www.lesliegodwin.com for more information.

- **Don't be a Super Hero.** Many people spend the entire day putting out brushfires because it makes them feel important or because they think it proves to others how busy they are. You know—the damsel is in distress and the knight has come riding in on his white horse to save her. This may be an ego-booster, but it is also a huge time waster.

- **Create Process Flow Diagrams.** These diagrams, also known as decision trees, can help a person identify the next point of a process and the next step. Rather than describing the process in words, the flow diagrams provide a graphical representation that can clearly show the next step based on one or more options or conditions.

If it's good enough for a car mechanic to troubleshoot a complex car problem, it's good enough to describe any complex or multi-level process. Sometimes, creating a process flow diagram helps to define a process that has not been adequately defined or is currently done haphazardly. This can result in streamlined solutions that make it easier on everyone.

- **Delegate it!** If you are not the "expert" of the subject matter at hand, refer the person to the "subject matter expert." This is especially important if you are a manager and a question can be handled more effectively by one of your employees.

- **Make company maps.** New employees will keep asking you where so and so is located or where the restrooms are or where the cafeteria is. That is, unless you've already provided them with a company map the very first day they were hired.

  New employees should be able to find most typical areas, staff members, files and reference books without your assistance. A company map helps to ensure this. This is also a wonderful reference for your current employees. Rather than having to come to their rescue because they can't find something, help them upfront and you won't have to spend time saving them.

- **Put the monkey back where it belongs.** Jeff's staff comes to him with problems to solve each day. They come to him with dilemmas and Jeff offers them solutions. But this is a problem. Because Jeff always takes the monkey off staff members' shoulders, they never bother to try to solve a problem on their own.

  If this sounds like you, it's time to put the monkey back where it belongs—on their shoulders. This certainly doesn't mean you abandon people, but it does mean you need to give them an opportunity to figure out what to do, especially when it's not that difficult a problem.

  If a staff member can't program his answering machine, don't do it for him. Instead, give him the manual. If someone can't find the graphics department, don't take her. Give her a company map. You get the picture.

- **You already have a job. Do you want to be a firefighter too?** Realize when you're truly needed versus when you're simply putting out a brushfire. Always ask yourself if the problem could have been handled without your intervention, with a tool (checklist) or by another person. Get a handle on this problem and you won't have to play firefighter all day long. You may even get some real work done!

# Chapter 39

# Delegation

- **The art of delegation.** Are you one of those people who say, "But I'm the only person that can do this job." That thinking is the kiss of death—to your valuable time.

  Many people fear delegation because they feel nobody can do the work as well as they can. Others fear it because they feel they don't have the time to teach someone else. They feel that by the time they teach another person how to do it, they could have already done it themselves.

  If you never delegate and you have people to delegate to, then it's time to re-adjust your thinking. Delegation can be wonderful if it's done well.

  I used to manage the Data Analysis Department at Dun and Bradstreet's Nielsen Media Research in New York. Believe me, I had a ton of work on my desk and if I had decided to do it all instead of delegating, I would have had to pitch a tent and stay at the office for the rest of my life!

  Once you master the art of effective delegation, you'll have more time for yourself and the things you love to do. While it may be hard for you to give up work at first, I can practically guarantee that when you know how to delegate well, you'll love it.

- **Get yourself a promotion.** A supervisor or manager must be able to delegate effectively. If you're able to delegate well, this skill may help you get promoted to a higher position in your company. It also makes you more desirable to companies that may consider hiring you.

- **It's not a hand off.** Delegation does not mean you give a project to someone else and then it's out of your hands forever. Delegation is the art of effectively relaying what you need done and tracking its progress regularly to make sure it's getting done properly.

  Delegation is an excellent way to free up some of your time now. Plus, in the future you will be able to easily delegate a similar project to the same person who will already be familiar with many of the project details.

- **Know it yourself first.** Never give a person a task that you're unfamiliar with. In other words, if a strange and detailed project lands on your desk, don't just pass it off to one of your employees or co-workers. Delegating is not about ducking out. Instead, delegate tasks you do regularly so that your time is free to think about the unfamiliar projects.

- **Figure out what you can delegate.** Knowing "what" to delegate is one of the first steps towards mastering the art of delegation. If you're not sure what you can delegate, keep a log of all your tasks and projects for the next week or so.

  At the end of the week, choose at least two of those tasks to delegate. Do this system, until you feel that you've delegated as much as you possibly can.

## Organizing Clinic

### Question

I own an insurance business. Each year, I hire college interns to assist me. I have no problem delegating routine phone calls, typing, copying and other tasks I really don't like to do. But I feel guilty for delegating what I consider "grunt work."

Lorraine Vaupel, Eau Claire, WI

### Answer

Lorraine,

Good for you on making use of the college internship programs in your area. College interns are wonderful resources.

First, routine phone calls, typing, making copies and other tasks have to be done by a person who chooses to work in an insurance business. So, by delegating these tasks, you are giving your interns a feel for what to expect in this business.

Consider also that what you consider to be "grunt work" may be tasks that your interns actually enjoy.

However, you would be doing your interns a better service by also delegating work that is a bit more challenging in addition to the other tasks. You can act as a mentor. This way you're likely to feel good about delegating.

- **Don't only delegate the monotonous.** While it's fine to delegate some work that you simply find to be boring, try your hand at delegating some more challenging tasks. It will help to stimulate the minds of the people you're delegating to and it will give you practice at delegating more difficult tasks.

- **Pick the right person.** When delegating, it's important to choose the right person for the job. For instance, if you delegate a project that takes a detailed-eye, you don't want to pass it along to someone who is not detail-oriented. If you delegate a project that takes a bit of physical strength, don't delegate it to the skinniest guy in the office. Match your project to the right person.

- **On the other hand, don't underestimate.** Don't underestimate a person's potential. Your perception may be significantly less than what the actual performance level can be. Give him a touch more than you think he can handle. He may do just fine and you may be pleasantly surprised in the end.

- **Make it clear.** Make sure the person you're delegating to, is clear on the aspects of the assignment, including desired results, time frames and how you'll be tracking his or her progress. Encourage questions before and during the project. Don't assume the person knows what you want him to do or knows where to find necessary information to do the task.

- **Give bits and pieces.** While it's a good idea for you to express the general idea of the entire project to the person helping out, don't delegate the entire project at once. Make a list of all the project steps, organize them into parts and then delegate one part at a time.

  If you're delegating to several people, have each person work on one aspect of the project. The main idea is to get your project done little by little without overwhelming the people assisting you.

- **Keep track of who is doing what.** It's vital to keep track of what you're delegating, to whom and when you need it done. Keep a list and check it regularly. When an item is complete, mark is as complete or cross it off your list.

- **Keep an open mind.** The way something has always been done may not be the best way to do it. If a staff member suggests a different method and it's clear the method is a more productive one, then go with the new way.

- **Define the limits of authority.** Can the person you delegate to ask other staff members for help? Can she hire outside help? What are her spending limits for the project? Be sure you go over these details in your own head and with the person you're delegating to.

- **Set realistic and firm deadlines.** Always let the people you're delegating to know exactly when you expect each portion of the project to be completed and tell them to tell you if that deadline is in jeopardy of not being met on time. Remind them when deadlines are approaching. "As soon as possible" is not a deadline. The deadline should be a specific date and time.

- **Give yourself a cushion.** Ask them to complete things a few days before you really need them. This cushion will allow for unexpected last minute problems.

- **Ask for feedback.** To ensure the person understands the assignment and is able to complete it by the deadline, ask for feedback from the person along the way. Find out what he has done so far and determine if the project is on track.

## Great idea!

Give full credit and recognition to the person who gets the job done. Don't take the credit yourself. If the person you've delegated to is unsuccessful, take the brunt of the blame yourself rather than using him/her as a scapegoat. If the person has not developed their skills fully enough to accomplish the task, you as the manager can assume the responsibility for that. Learn from the experience so you can more effectively delegate the next time.

Kathy Paauw, a certified business/personal coach and organizing/productivity consultant, specializes in helping busy executives, professionals and entrepreneurs de-clutter their schedules, spaces and minds. Contact her at orgcoach@gte.net or visit her web site at www.orgcoach.net and learn how you can Find ANYTHING in 5 Seconds --Guaranteed!

- **Make yourself available.** The person you're delegating to should be aware you are available for questions. Don't make the person feel abandoned.

- **Answer questions quickly.** Answer any questions in a timely manner so the person can complete what he has to do within the expected timeframe.

- **Be there for them.** Give support and direction throughout the project as needed, but don't fall into the trap of doing the work. You're there for guidance. Also, don't hang over their shoulders every second. Give them space and time to complete the project.

- **But don't do it for them.** While you should be available for questions, you might consider giving your staff some authority in trying to figure out a problem on their own. Or, ask them for suggestions on how the problem should be handled and assist them in working through it. Give them the opportunity and give yourself a break.

- **Praise can go a long way.** When the project has been completed, don't forget to thank the person for a job well done. A small gift or handwritten note goes a long way in showing your appreciation. If this was a major project, you might wish to take your assistant(s) out to lunch or have a pizza party.

- **Give me the money.** You may want to award financial bonuses for jobs well done. If so, be sure to define the criteria and the bonus amounts in writing. For instance, $100 bonus for creating 50 widgets by Friday, June 13th.

- **Don't jump ship.** If you delegate a project and something goes wrong, don't immediately take the project away from the person assigned to it without giving her a chance to right the wrong. Give the person a chance, explain where the project went astray and try to guide it back in the right direction.

- **Ask them to ask.** Let staff members know they can ask you if there's anything else they can help you with, when they're experiencing some down time. They may be waiting on a phone call or report pertaining to the part of the project you've delegated to them, but perhaps they can work on another part in the meantime.

- **Put it on paper.** If you plan to delegate a similar job over and over to different people, write out the instructions. This way, any person you delegate to will have a reference.

- **Mix it up.** Don't always delegate to the same person if you have several people available that can help.

- **Delegate to an outside service.** If someone internally can't handle your project, perhaps someone outside your office can. Delegate to fulfillment services, web design services, answering services, and more.

- **Delegate to technology.** Many people think of delegation as giving something to *someone* else to do, but you can also delegate to your computer or your answering machine.

Instead of responding to requests for information for your web site, delegate this responsibility to an autoresponder. Rather than picking up every telephone call that comes in, delegate this responsibility to your answering machine or voicemail.

When I first started generating book and product orders from my web site, I was spending over an hour each day manually entering orders into my customer database. My husband, Joe, discovered software that actually works with our merchant account and shopping cart. I now go on the web once each day and download my orders—automatically—into my new customer database software. An hour a day was transformed into 2 minutes each day. Now that's an excellent benefit of delegating to technology, wouldn't you say?

# Chapter 40

# Outsourcing

- **Do you really have to do it yourself?** Are you spending hours working on things that someone else could easily be helping you with? Are these things constantly taking up your time and getting in the way of your goal achievement? If so, you may consider outsourcing all or part of these tasks and projects.

For example, when I first began writing books, every time I got an order my husband and I would pack and ship to each customer—from our basement. After a while, especially when we began getting upwards of over 100 boxes that needed to be shipped each week, we decided that all of this packing and mailing was very time consuming—so much so that it was difficult to get anything else done. At this time we decided that our time would be better spent otherwise and we hired a fulfillment service. It was one of the best things we ever did and our company has grown enormously because of this decision.

### Great idea!

Some people try to save money and time by attempting to manage all aspects of home and business life. This technique works for some people, but not for all.

While it is a good idea to learn how to do things on your own, if you really don't know how to do something, you are having difficulty understanding how to carry it out or if you just don't have the time to provide quality results, you really should hire someone qualified to do it.

This will allow you time to focus on what you are good at, thus optimizing your results. You can still continue to educate yourself about the task so that you can do it on your own in the future. But your time and effort will be used to accomplish quality work on what you already know. In the meantime, the person you outsourced the tasks to is providing first-class results for you.

Although it may be tough to let go of some of the responsibility at first, once you see the benefits of your outsourcing partner, you will wonder how you did it without them!

Linda M. DePaz
Be Clutter-Free
PO Box 335, Ellington, NY 14732
www.BeClutter-Free.com

- **Leave it to the specialists and save time.** Specialists can always accomplish more in less time, since they have the knowledge, skill, equipment and experience. You can outsource printing, telephone answering, direct mailing, fulfillment and more for your business.

### Great idea!

According to the International Virtual Assistants Association, "a Virtual Assist (VA) is an independent entrepreneur providing administrative, creative and/or technical services. Utilizing advanced technological modes of communication and data delivery, a professional VA assists clients in his/her area of expertise from his/her own office on a contractual basis."

Working with a virtual assistant (VA) is a great way to outsource administrative work that you may not have time for or may not have an expertise in. A virtual assistant can take over many tasks: newsletters, web site maintenance, mailings, email management, travel planning, document formatting, scheduling and much, much more.

Virtual assistants who specialize in working with solo entrepreneurs like professional organizers are also great at brainstorming ideas for your business. By freeing up your time from these administrative tasks, you gain more time for working with clients, networking and marketing your business.

Plus it's a very simple way to work. You only pay for the time the VA works on your business so her time is totally productive. In addition, you don't need to worry about all the hassles of having an employee. You only need to pay one check per month to your VA.

Jean Hanson
16212 Miles Circle, Brainerd, MN 56401
218-855-1854
jean@vaofficesolution.com
VA Office Solution, www.VAOfficeSolution.com
Virtualize Your Business!, www.VirtualizeYourBiz.com

- **"If I outsource this job, I'm going to make $3.00 less profit on each unit."** You really have to determine what your time is worth. How much more money could you make if you weren't spending your time doing data entry or answering your telephone or typesetting your own newsletter? Very often, outsourcing is well worth it saving you time and making you even more money.

- **"If I want the job done right, I have to do it myself."** If you continue to think like this, you'll never get the important things done. Help the person or company that is helping you, by making a checklist of things to be done and how to do them. Build in an accuracy check. Be available for questions. You have to let go of some things, in order to work on the more important stuff.

- **"I have nobody to outsource to."** The company you outsource to doesn't even necessarily have to be located in your state. I outsource to many organizations throughout the United States. Other options include outsourcing to students at local high schools and colleges. Many schools have internship programs that are free of charge or low-cost, to you. Call your local university and ask about their internship program or you can always ask if you are allowed to post a project opportunity on their bulletin board.

- **Advertise.** Advertise a project opportunity in your community or church bulletin. Instead of hiring someone permanently, you can hire someone temporarily to get a one-time-only or short-term project completed.

- **Check on them.** When you evaluate proposals from service providers, don't hesitate to ask questions and check references. The more you know about a particular company, the more comfortable you'll feel.

## Organizing Clinic

### Question

I spend a good deal of time fulfilling orders for my Internet business. I would love to outsource this service to a fulfillment company, but I'm concerned about how I would be able to pay them. The ones I've checked charge at least $4.00 per box for inserting just one item inside. Many of my orders are for multiple products and they charge an additional fee for everything I add to the box. In addition, I've researched and they usually require approximately three month's worth of inventory on their shelves. I'm not sure I can purchase that much inventory ahead of time.

Another problem is I have no idea how I would get my customer orders over to them. When I receive an Internet order, I get individual email. Do I forward every single order I get? Do I consolidate orders in a spreadsheet—of course that would mean that I would then have to spend time typing. Is there any hope?

MaryAnn Lipshaw, West Richland, VA

### Answer

MaryAnn,

You have to build the fulfillment costs into your shipping and handling charges to the customer or these costs will have to come out of your profit. Although most charge a per product fee as you've mentioned, the price for inserting additional items into a box is usually minimal. If it's taking you hours to fulfill your orders, you're probably not spending a whole lot of time marketing. Marketing is what you have to do to grow your business. Packing and shipping orders is probably not the best use of your time. You have to take that fact into consideration.

Regarding the inventory these services require, they have these requirements to safeguard you. They want to be sure that when you ask them to fulfill an order, that they have inventory on the shelves all the time. You're going to have to buy product anyway, so why not buy a little bit ahead? If you only anticipate ten orders per month for any particular product, three month's worth would be 30 orders. You can determine what you can expect by your past sales.

Also, you may not have to use a traditional fulfillment service at first. You may be able to get a local secretarial company to assist you with your mailing for a fee. They may be less strict regarding the amount of inventory you're required to stock.

Regarding getting orders over to the fulfillment service, you'll have to check with them to determine what your options are. Some will accept individual order emails. Others may require you to provide a spreadsheet. I use software from Stone Edge Technologies called Order Manager. Orders are automatically downloaded into my Order Manager software each day and I can automatically generate spreadsheets with customer name, address and products to email to my fulfillment service.

- **Put it in writing.** Whenever possible, put exactly what you want in writing. I can't stress this enough. Doing this gives you protection. The person or company you outsource to then can't say you didn't tell them about something important.

  Since I do a lot of writing, getting proper instructions to book printers, cover designers, editors, and other vendors is a must. Typing up a one-page list of numbered instructions allows me to think through the project and gives the companies I'm outsourcing to clear guidelines concerning what I need done.

- **Get it in writing.** When you outsource a job, get the agreed upon conditions, prices, details, and everything else in writing. Keep copies of any correspondence between you and the company you're outsourcing to. This is to safeguard you, so you get what you asked for at the price promised to you.

- **If you're not sure, ask.** Don't assume the company you're outsourcing to will be able to perform all the services you need. If you're not sure what their services, policies and fees are, don't be afraid to ask.

- **Choose wisely.** Although it may be tempting, never select a vendor based solely on price. Select the vendor that offers the best balance of good value and quality results.

- **Expect problems.** Sometimes you'll be able to outsource and experience no problems at all, but every once in awhile, there's going to be a hiccup. If you expect there to be problems along the way, you won't become overly stressed and annoyed when they happen.

Try to anticipate problems whenever possible, so you can alleviate them upfront. But when unexpected problems do arise, take a deep breath and begin listing solutions. Keep a clear head and the problem(s) will be resolved more productively.

- **Do you need support later?** Determine if you'll need support from the company you outsource to after the initial project is completed. This is especially true if you outsource someone to create something technical, like a company network or database.

  You may need training support or troubleshooting support for quite some time. Consider this when you're making your decision.

- **Start small.** When dealing with a service provider for the first time, start with a project that is relatively small and simple. This will give you a better idea of the provider's style and capabilities before you entrust them with a critical project.

- **Price is not the only factor.** When choosing a vendor, never choose solely on price. Just because a bidder is the highest bidder, doesn't necessarily mean that company is the best for your job. Choose based on experience, references, personalities, time frames, etc. in addition to price.

- **Tie payment to results.** Never pay for the entire project upfront. Pay your outsourcing service as each part of the project is completed.

  Janis, a building manager, outsourced a painting job to a local company. The painting job involved painting several offices in the office building she worked in. The painter asked for full payment upfront and Janis paid him. Unfortunately, the painter dragged his feet on the project. What should have taken three weeks to finish turned into 4 months!

  Since the painter was already paid, he didn't really care how long it took to complete the project. If Janis would have paid the painter a deposit to start with and then paid him as he completed each office, she may not have run into this problem.

# Chapter 41

# Working as a team

- **Choose a leader.** A team without a leader is like a body without a head. It simply doesn't work. Someone has to be in charge of keeping the team together, keeping track of goals, deadlines and progress.

- **Listen to others.** When you're working as a team, listen to team members' questions and ideas. Being on a team means that everyone is working together to reach a common goal.

- **Know what's expected.** Always know exactly what's expected of you. If you don't understand something, bring it up. Be perfectly clear on what needs to be done and by when.

- **Pull your weight.** If even one member of a team isn't pulling her weight, the entire project can come to a grinding halt. Be sure you're not the one holding everyone back.

- **Don't be afraid to speak up.** If you have a question or any concern about an idea, a complaint, or about someone not pulling his weight, be sure to bring it up. If you feel something should be done another way, say so. Everybody on the team should have equal say, but the leader has the final say.

- **Don't hold a grudge.** Even if you don't agree, sometimes it's necessary to "bite the bullet" and do what is asked of you anyway. Holding a grudge isn't going to get you anywhere.

- **If it's too challenging, say so.** If the part of the project that has been assigned to you is beyond your grasp or capabilities, speak up. Perhaps someone can assist you or responsibilities can be shifted around.

- **Express your time commitments.** If you can only give so much time to the particular project you're working on, make sure everyone on the team knows. Otherwise, you may get someone complaining that you're not pulling your weight.

- **Don't blame.** If someone on the team makes a mistake, don't waste time blaming him. Instead, work together to correct the error.

- **Compromise.** When people are working together, sometimes it's necessary to compromise. In doing so, there are no losers. Everybody wins and at least you'll get part of what you wanted rather than nothing.

- **Recognize achievements and success.** Be sure to praise the team and also recognize individual efforts. Recognition can be anything from a simple positive verbal reinforcement of a job well done to a lucrative cash bonus.

**Great idea!**

I find it helpful to schedule 5-minute "progress sessions" with the others in my group. If the project is due in a month, the progress sessions can be weekly or every third day depending on your schedule or group setup.

By doing this, we have regular updates to see how far each of us has come and to see if the others need help. We can all sleep well knowing that we're on task or realizing where we need to dig in a little deeper.

While we need to let others do their part of the project, the important thing is that we all contribute and have no excuses as to why something isn't getting done. After all, we are all in it together.

Lynne Poindexter, Associate Editor of *Finally Organized, Finally Free for the Office*

- **Tell them you love them.** When new ideas are successful, generously, sincerely and openly compliment the team members who made the initial suggestions, as well as those who implemented them.

  It's also very important to make it clear that no one will ever be penalized for taking planned and carefully considered risks, regardless of the results.

- **Avoid playing favorites.** It is important, especially if you are the leader of a project team, that you assign work equally. If someone perceives that he is getting more of the work, he may feel resentful.

  Deal quickly with team members that are not keeping up their end of the project, by giving them training, helping them identify roadblocks or clarifying requirements.

- **Have periodic meetings to review progress.** Based on the timeline of the project, it may be suitable to have weekly or monthly meetings. In either case, the group should determine the meeting frequency so that progress can be monitored continuously. If there are many members involved, have meetings with team leaders to keep the meetings short and sweet.

- **Record project details.** Be sure to document project status and action items required. This will keep everyone apprised of progress and ensure that no area falls behind. Be sure to specify who is responsible for completing an action item and when it is due.

- **Decide on decision-making.** If the team encounters a snag, there may be delays in getting the project done. Decide early on how the group will accept decision-making. Will it be by consensus? Majority vote? Review with higher-level management?

Each method of decision-making has advantages and disadvantages. Have the team agree on the method and you can avoid long, dragged out thinking in which nothing is accomplished.

- **Have a cross-functional team.** Many ideas succeed because team members from different departments were involved early on in the project. By involving people from other departments, the team has access to a variety of experts to provide different viewpoints and to generate more ideas and solutions than one department with one focus.

- **Get out of the conference room.** Sitting in a conference room with a group of people can be stifling. Once in awhile, meet on the golf course or at the company picnic tables outside.

Jenny, Peter and Kit were responsible for coming up with a new company logo. They sat in the office for hours trying to come up with creative ideas. When half the day had passed, Kit suggested they have a change of scenery.

They all left the office to sit outside near a pretty outdoor water fountain. The peacefulness and fresh air really paid off. The team returned with three possible logos that the management team loved.

- **Work out a schedule.** If team members are going to be sharing certain tools and equipment, work out a schedule so one person isn't waiting for the other.

- **Meet regularly.** Teams that meet regularly are always better informed of project progress and delays. The project leader should set consistent days and times to meet and bring everyone up to date.

- **Get excited together.** Increase the momentum of the group by celebrating together. Go out to a group lunch when a project is completed or have smaller rewards in between project milestones.

- **Laughter required.** To keep your team happy and motivated, encourage laughter and fun. In between project sessions, share a funny story, play a bloopers video or read some clips from a funny book out loud.

- **Cheer each other on.** If you ever attend a professional baseball game, you'll notice team members cheering each other on. When someone is at bat and gets on base, the team cheers. If someone strikes out, generally that person gets a "that's okay, shake it off" pat on the back. A team that works together, motivates each other and pulls together during good times and bad, is a strong, committed, productive team.

# Chapter 42

# Keeping organized when others are not

- **Divide the room.** If you share an office with a messy co-worker, chances are she's destroying your organizing efforts. If she's not interested in being organized, chances are you won't be able to change her. But, you can add a strip of colored tape right down the middle of the room. Ask her to keep her mess on her side. If possible, add a folding screen to further divide you.

- **Put one person in charge.** When several people are responsible for keeping an area organized, the chances of it staying organized are pretty slim. But when one person is in charge, there's a much better chance of staying organized. Put one person in charge of retrieving office supplies, one person in charge of the central filing area, one person in charge of the central computer database, and so on.

## Organizing Clinic

### Question

I work for 5 different people and they all demand my immediate assistance. They make my job very stressful, so every morning I wake up full of anger and hatred that I have to go to work there.

Stressed Out

### Answer

Dear Stressed,

First and foremost, going to work full of anger and hatred every day is not only extremely stressful, but detrimental to your health. You need to address these emotions in order to move on. One solution is speaking with each of the five people you work for and describing your situation. Perhaps they might have empathy and try to work things out with you. Be sure you are calm when approaching them and keep your emotions in check.

They might hire additional help or perhaps they will agree to you taking a maximum number of requests from each person each day. If you speak with them, do so in a professional, non-complaining, solution-oriented manner. Be ready to offer possible solutions for your concerns.

Otherwise, perhaps it's time for you to look for a job better suited to your tastes and energy levels— something that you can truly enjoy doing each day.

- **Work elsewhere.** With telephones ringing, meetings going on, training sessions in place and so on, some offices can seem pretty chaotic. This is especially true if you're working in a cubicle. No doors, no walls, lots of noise. When working on a project that requires your full attention, move to an empty office or conference room, close the door and work on your project in peace and quiet.

- **Develop "one" system.** If some people give others phone messages using the pink phone message slips, others write on scraps of paper and still others just tell people verbally, there's going to be a problem with messages getting lost.

  A consistent system in this case would be to require everyone at the office to *only* use the pink phone slips and to place them in a specific area. Being consistent applies to all systems throughout your company such as your communication system, your customer service system and your employee evaluation system. The more consistent the systems, the smoother everything will run.

- **Provide visual aids.** Some people may appear to be disorganized, but in reality, it's the system. For instance, if people don't know where to put files and other office items, they may tend to just put them "anywhere."

  Because many people may be using common areas, label areas clearly or provide diagrams for items and their assigned homes. This will allow anyone to find things and also to identify when things are out of place.

- **The disorganized boss.** When your boss is disorganized, it can be very frustrating, especially when she expects everyone around her to be organized.

  Ellen, a department manager in a research company, had an office that constantly looked like a tornado hit it. There were piles of paper everywhere, scrap notes all over her desk and trade magazines stacked to the ceiling. As projects came in, they would find their way to the bottom of Ellen's desk, often getting lost for days. Once she found projects, she would run out to a staff member's desk and urge them to complete that project by the deadline.

  Of course, by the time Ellen found and distributed most projects, the deadlines were completely unreasonable. Worst of all, Ellen would then blame the late projects on her "unproductive" staff.

  If this is a problem in your company, something has to be done. It's difficult to go over the head of your manager to talk to her boss, but if someone does not, the insanity will continue. If you're not willing to do this, you may have to find another job. You should not be blamed for someone else's disorganization.

# Chapter 43

# The cubicle factor

- **Privacy please.** Most cubicle walls are less than five feet in height and there's rarely a noise barrier. Unfortunately, privacy is not always that easy when working in a cubicle setting. But with a little bit of ingenuity, you can still be organized and maintain your sanity in this type of open work environment.

- **Space is a premium.** When you're working in a cubicle, your space is almost always pretty limited. Be judicious when it comes to displaying personal items. Hang your effects on your cubicle walls, instead of keeping them on your desk. Attach wire trays to your cubicle walls to save on space. Don't store anything extraneous.

- **Face your desk away.** If possible, face your desk away from the opening of your cubicle. This will help to prevent distractions. Put a mirror in front of you, so you can see if someone is standing behind you.

- **Remove the guest chair.** If you have a guest chair in your cubicle and you don't have regular appointments with others, remove it. You can use that space for a filing cabinet or scanner table. When you have an appointment, meet in a conference room.

- **Stagger lunch hours.** To get some peace and quiet, work while others are taking their lunch break. You can then take your lunch break while the others are working.

- **Speak quietly.** It's easy to eavesdrop on your neighbor in a cubicle setting. Just the same, it's easy for a neighbor to eavesdrop you. Remember to always speak quietly and never to say anything you wouldn't want your co-workers to hear.

- **Find a quiet spot.** When you're working on a project that requires focused concentration, consider leaving your cubicle and working in an empty office or a conference room.

- **Turn them away.** Just because you work in an open setting doesn't mean that you have to accept visitors every time they decide to stop by and chat. If you're working on something and can't be disturbed, say so. You have to respect your own time, before others will.

- **Add some white noise.** White noise machines are very effective when trying to get some privacy. They drown out conversation around you and prevent others from hearing everything you say.

- **Do not disturb.** Just like Do Not Disturb signs work on an office door, they also work if you hang them prominently at the entrance of your cubicle. When you have the sign up, don't allow interruptions—unless it's your boss, of course.

- **Go wireless.** If your cubicle is not equipped with enough outlets for your equipment, consider going wireless whenever possible. Or, ask your boss if it's possible to have a few extra outlets installed.

- **Brighten things up.** Dark cubicles can be pretty depressing and hard on your eyes. If you don't have good overhead lighting, add some lamps. They will help ease the tension in your eyes, give you more energy, help you work more efficiently and add a nice homey touch to your area.

- **Go compact.** When filling an empty cubicle, don't get anything too big for the space. Otherwise you're going to feel cramped. Think flat-screen monitors and narrow desk chairs without arm rests.

- **Put it near the entryway.** If staff members regularly pick up/drop off paperwork in your cubicle, hang in-baskets and out-baskets right near your entryway. This way, papers can be delivered and picked up without the need to disturb you.

- **Lock it up.** Don't ever leave anything valuable or confidential out in the open in a cubicle setting. Lock these types of things in your desk, a locking file cabinet or in a safe.

- **Got a hangover?** When you're shopping for office accessories for your cubicle, look for those designed to hang over the cube wall.

- **Get rid of the clutter.** Small spaces can get even smaller when they're filled with clutter. There should be no papers piled on the floor or on top of your desk.

- **Post a note.** If you're going to be in a meeting away from your cubicle, post a note outside saying when you'll be back. This way, if someone needs to bring a project to you. he will know when to return. This also works well if you're on vacation. Let them know when you'll be back.

- **Slide them under.** Don't forget about the space under your cubicle desk. This area is perfect for a slide-under keyboard tray. If you can fit a filing cabinet under your desk without taking up all your legroom, you will have the perfect filing area. Put wheels on your 2-drawer filing cabinet so you can easily slide it in and out when needed.

# Chapter 44

# Organizing communication

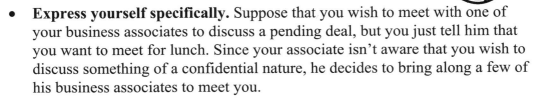

- **Express yourself specifically.** Suppose that you wish to meet with one of your business associates to discuss a pending deal, but you just tell him that you want to meet for lunch. Since your associate isn't aware that you wish to discuss something of a confidential nature, he decides to bring along a few of his business associates to meet you.

  Once you arrive at the restaurant, you soon realize that because you didn't communicate your intentions to your associate, you are now wasting your time at a meeting that cannot address your original goal. Plus, now you have to schedule another meeting.

  The moral of this story: Always be very, very specific. Communicate exactly what you expect or deal with the consequences of getting exactly what you *didn't* want.

- **Driving directions.** Create and print out directions to your location, coming from north, south, east and west. Leave these instructions right by your telephone to verbally read to anyone visiting. Also, make a few copies and keep in a file, ready to send to anyone who needs them. If your company has a web site, it's a good idea to have this information, along with your business hours, right on the site.

- **Give them both.** Have a job for someone to do? Give them your verbal and written instructions. Then have them repeat the vital details back to you. This is a great way to clear up any confusion and make sure the person understands what you want.

- **Checklists are powerful tools.** Instead of telling employees and co-workers what to do and leaving the completion of those tasks to their memories, you are sure to get what you need without question if you give them detailed checklists describing exactly what you want. As they complete each step, they check it off the list. So many successful companies do it this way. Imagine NASA, airlines or hospitals running smoothly without checklists!

- **Create standard letters.** Come up with standard form letters that answer common questions or relay standard information. When the need arises, make a copy of your standard answer and send it on its way. No extra work.

- **Will a simple call do?** Writing a formal letter may not be necessary to communicate your point. A simple phone call may be all it takes.

## Organizing Clinic

### Question

I am a manager in a fast food establishment with fifty employees under my belt. I write an employee newsletter to keep everyone abreast of policy changes, customer comments, employee birthdays, staff member promotions and company events.

I try to include as much information in the newsletter as possible, so employees don't waste my time asking questions I've already answered in the newsletter.

The problem lies in the fact that only a select few of my employees actually read the newsletter. How can I encourage more of them to read, so I spend less time repeating what I took so much time to write in the newsletter?

Kaye Caswell, Lowell, NY

### Answer

Dear Kaye,

I have a very easy suggestion. When an employee asks you something that can be found in the newsletter, don't answer her question. Re-direct her to read it in the newsletter herself. If you do this all the time, your employees will soon understand that you will not allow them to waste your time. I do recommend, however, that you don't include important things like company policies in the newsletter alone. Important company policy changes should be addressed in a memo or a meeting.

The problem with many company newsletters is that they are boring. I'm certainly not saying that yours is boring, but a newsletter with a fun look, a fun feel and interesting content will be more likely to attract more eyes.

---

- **The 3-step system for communicating a task.** If you're training someone to do a task, such as changing the paper in the copy machine, follow this plan of action:

1. Tell them how to do it.

2. Show them how to do it.

3. Ask them to show you how it is done.

- **Don't just ask if he understands.** He may say "yes," but how will you really know if he truly understands it? After all, something you said may have been misunderstood. Heed the old saying, "Tell me and I'll forget. Show me and I might remember. Involve me and I'll learn."

- **Create two company newsletters.** Company newsletters are excellent for keeping people abreast and motivated. Create one for staff members and another for customers:

  - **An employee newsletter will:**
    - ❖ Provide employees with current company information
    - ❖ Alert employees to company events and contests
    - ❖ Motivate employees by congratulating them for accomplishments and promotions

  - **A customer newsletter will:**
    - ❖ Provide customers with current company information
    - ❖ Alert customers to special offers and discounts
    - ❖ Keep your company fresh in your customers' minds

- **Your company newsletter can't do it all.** Don't expect to communicate solely through your company newsletter or a memo and assume everyone will be up-to-date and abreast. Unfortunately it doesn't work that way. You have to follow up with people to make sure they read and understand new company policies and other changes.

- **Create maps.** Create department and company layout maps so new employees won't have to keep asking where people and things are.

- **Put it on their shoulders.** Have each staff member keep a 3-ring binder containing answers to their most frequently asked questions such as, "How do I change the copy machine toner?" or "How do I program my telephone."

- **Storyboard.** Storyboarding is a great way to communicate and plan when a team is responsible for achieving something. It keeps everyone involved, is an excellent visual and will save an enormous amount of time.

  1. Give everyone a thick, felt-tip marker and index cards.
  2. Post the problem, project and outcome you expect.
  3. Ask each person to write a one to five word description giving their ideas on their cards.
  4. Give them a time limit. Collect and post the cards on the wall.
  5. Group the cards into categories and discard duplicates.
  6. Create category headings and with input from the team, arrange the ideas into a workable plan.
  7. Assign responsibilities.

8. Transfer the plan to paper and distribute copies to everyone to implement.

9. Follow up, meet with your team regularly and adjust the plan whenever necessary.

- **Tell them when it's due.** When you write letters that require a reply, don't forget to specify your required due date. Include a line such as, "Please reply by July 7" or "Response required by May 5."

- **Stamp it on.** Get a rubber stamp with your signature at your local office supply store or local print shop. Stamp the signature on any appropriate correspondence. However, please keep your stamp locked up so nobody will ever have access to it.

- **Create a Responsibility List.** One office had a quick list of contacts with responsibilities posted in common areas. The list included who to contact for parking passes, printer supplies, fax machine, keys, badges, beverage services and other administrative functions.

- **Follow up with a call.** Sometimes it's not enough to send a fax or email. If you're trying to communicate something really important, send a fax, email or letter, but be sure to follow up with a phone call.

- **Don't expect everyone to be a techie.** Just because you may be technically astute, others, like other staff members, customers, associates and vendors may not be the same way. Organized communication means that you can communicate with others and that others can understand your communication. Use methods that the people you call regularly are comfortable with.

Jack liked to use his pager instead of his cell phone. With a pager, when a call came in he didn't have to take it right away. The number was there when he was ready to call back.

Unfortunately, Jack later found out that the majority of his customers, non-techies, didn't know how to call Jack on his pager. They didn't realize they wouldn't be able to "talk" to the pager or leave a voice message. So, rather than punching in their phone number, they would just hang up. Jack lost tons of business and now uses his cell phone instead.

# Chapter 45

# Three cheers for the checklist

- **What is a checklist?** Many tasks in the average business day are composed of a number of sequential steps. Just like you can't drive a car without first opening the door, getting in, turning the key and so on, you can't perform any task without following a series of steps.

  While the steps for driving a car may be easy to memorize for the average person, there are other tasks that are a bit more involved or are unfamiliar to many people.

  For example, if you just purchased a brand new, souped-up voicemail system for the office, chances are that most people won't be familiar with its available features and how it works. Equipment manufacturers know this and therefore they generally include instruction manuals—which are nothing more than a series of checklists.

  In a nutshell, a checklist is a series of instructional steps in sequential order that a person follows to complete a task or project. When using a checklist, the results should be consistent each time, no matter who uses it.

## Great idea!

As the owner and manager of a call and receptionist center, I used to get upset when tasks like refilling the fax and copy machine were not completed. It's easy for employees to adopt the attitude, "It's not my job" or "I thought she did it."

Instead we developed a checklist of duties for each desk in our office. As we rotated workstations for a week at a time, everyone got the opportunity to do all of the tasks on an equal basis. What's great is that after this change, I never heard anyone complaining that "the copy machine was empty" or "I filled it yesterday. It's her turn." The completed checklists were turned in at the end of the week. In addition, a place for special projects completed was on the lists. It gave my employees a chance to note completed tasks that I may not have known about. Completing the checklists also gave each employee a chance to be recognized for her accomplishments.

I've since sold that business and started another. Now that I'm a personal chef, I've carried these organizing concepts I've learned over to my new business, and they still work like a charm!

Louise Block, Personal Chef
Cuisine at Home, Mequon, WI
ChefLblock@aol.com
www.uspca.net/wi/whatachef/

- **The benefits.** Determine what tasks in your office require checklists and create one for each procedure. You're guaranteed to end up with a set of wonderful resources that will:

    ❖ Ensure all steps are remembered, whether you do the task or you delegate it to someone else.

    ❖ Help you train others to do a variety of tasks easily. Since they have a written guide, they won't be asking you the same questions over and over again.

    ❖ Eliminate the "I didn't know I had to do that" or "you never told me that" excuses that occur often after oral training sessions.

    ❖ Ensure that if someone else is training a person on how to perform a task, they train using the exact steps and the exact sequence required.

    ❖ Ensure that everyone performs tasks in the most efficient and most effective way.

## Organizing Clinic

### Question

I already have training checklists for my staff, but how do I organize them? Right now, they're just individual sheets of papers in a huge file folder!

Elizabeth Gray, Boca Raton, FL

### Answer

Dear Elizabeth,

Good for you that you already have training checklists. To organize them, I recommend keeping them in a 3-ring binder, organized by subject or job responsibility. Separate by subject or job responsibility with index tabs.

You can insert the checklists in the binder in either the order you plan to teach each task, in the order the tasks are completed or by the importance of each task. I suggest you keep an index in the front of the binder, so you know what section/page each checklist is at a glance. This way, you won't have to flip through the entire binder every time you're trying to find something.

You may want to put each checklist in a sheet protector to be sure it always looks like new. When you're training an employee, make a copy of that particular checklist and give it to him to use. It's important that as the employee is being trained, he physically checks off each step he completes.

- **How to make a checklist.** Once you know what procedure you wish to make a checklist for, you can set up a checklist format on your computer. Then, perform the task—physically or mentally—step by step, making sure to type each step as you do it.

  Here is an example of a checklist for changing the paper in a copy machine:

  __ 1.  Get a batch of copy machine paper in the supply cabinet, approximately ½" thick.
  __ 2.  Fan the paper like a deck of cards to ensure the sheets don't stick together.
  __ 3.  Slide open the printer drawer.
  __ 4.  Insert the paper being sure it is secured under the metal tabs.
  __ 5.  Slide the printer drawer closed.

- **Don't combine two or more.** Write "one" checklist for each task. Include a task title on it, such as "Updating the date and time on your computer," or "Sending a fax transmission."

## Great idea!

When learning a new job or task, I take detailed step-by-step notes, on how to perform each task. While offices have similar routines, each office has their own unique procedures and different equipment and computer systems.

I place these handwritten notes in a 3-ring binder with A-Z colored tabs, by subject in alphabetical order. Among other things, such tasks would include:

\* Processing different types of invoices

\* Calendaring events and who to email for particular meetings

\* Operating all aspects of the database

\* Reimbursement steps for work-related conferences and meetings

\* Copies of sample forms for routine office procedures

This binder becomes a quick reference tool. Over time I use it less and less as I learn and become more confident on the job.

Using this principle of learning, my task binder (when the notes were typed) "became" the foundation of our office procedure manual, which I also wrote. This method of learning increases my efficiency and productivity on the job, while operating more independently and confidently. Best of all, I don't have to continually seek out a manager or co-worker for routine tasks.

Denise Turcotte
Creatively Organized
6641 Green Ash Drive, Springfield, VA 22152
703-644-7484
creatively_organized@hotmail.com

- **Make each point short and easy.** Never write up a checklist in paragraph format. Each step should be short and specific.

- **Number it.** Each step should be numbered, with a small line preceding the instructions, so you or others can check off steps as they are completed.

- **Make copies or laminate.** Make copies of checklists if you will be using them to train others. Or, to save on paper, laminate each checklist. Employees can still check off items with an erasable marker and you can then wipe the slate clean for the next employee to use and check off.

- **Don't just give her the checklist.** When someone is following your checklist for the very first time, go through it with her step-by-step, ensuring that she performs the steps properly. Assist if necessary. Be aware that you can't just give someone a checklist and expect her to perform all the steps without your help the first time around.

As you show her the procedure, have the person check off the steps on the checklist. Track her progress and supervise this person until she completes all the steps correctly and no longer needs supervision.

# Chapter 46

# Prioritizing

- **Know what's important.** Before you even attempt to prioritize, you'll have to be able to distinguish the very important (this will cost the company dearly if I don't do it) versus the not very important.

- **Use your A-B-C's.** Priority A should always be your most important work, Priority B is of medium importance and Priority C is of least importance. An example of each might be:

  - ❖ Priority A:     Work on design project for company's biggest customer
  - ❖ Priority B:     Write memo to employees regarding next month's staff meeting time change
  - ❖ Priority C:     Weed out old contacts from Rolodex

- **Is it an A, B or C?** This is the most difficult part of prioritizing for many people. People may give a task an A priority just because it can be done quickly. But it's not the amount of time a task will take, but rather the importance of the task, that should be used as the criteria for determining the appropriate priority code.

  It's not a good idea to only work on your Priority A tasks, because you'll then fall way behind in your Priority B and C tasks. The bigger problem is those people who only work on Priority C tasks, because they're generally easier to do.

  Beware of this or your day will be taken over by so many Priority C tasks that you'll never begin working on the important things.

- **Allocate properly.** Give 70% of your day to Priority A's, 20% of your day to Priority B's and 10% of your day to Priority C's.

- **Explain your dilemma.** If your boss gives you an "urgent project" today and you haven't yet finished an "urgent project" from yesterday, explain your dilemma to your boss. Determine together which project holds the higher priority.

- **Help others prioritize.** If you're a manager or boss, it will be part of your job to both prioritize yourself and to assist your staff with determining their priorities. What a staff member thinks is a priority and what you consider a priority may be two different animals.

- **Mark the proper code on your Master List and To Do List.** When you add a task to your Master List, be sure you code it Priority A, B or C. This way, when you're ready to transfer tasks to your To Do List, you'll be able to allocate an appropriate percentage of each. Keep the code on your To Do List also, so you have a visual.

- **The difference between Urgent and Important.** Most people spend their time completing urgent tasks. However, there may be many tasks that are important and should be done, but are not as time sensitive. This is the main difference between Urgent and Important.

  Urgent is usually based on a deadline, but Important is more in line with your long-range goals. Be sure to make time to complete important tasks as well as urgent tasks.

  If need be, schedule deadlines for your important tasks and break them down so they can be accomplished in a reasonable amount of time. Otherwise, your important tasks, which may not have a hard deadline, will never get accomplished.

- **It's a balancing act.** More often than not, you'll probably end up with two or three Priority A tasks on your list. Hopefully, you won't have more Priority A tasks than two or three in a single day.

  You will have to determine which Priority A task of the two or three on your To Do List, must be started first. If you can delegate any of these tasks, definitely do so.

  Balance your time between your Priority A's. For instance, maybe you can work on each for an hour or so. This way, you'll have a good head start on all of them.

  Or, since Priority A tasks are generally more difficult, you may want to sandwich some Priority B and C tasks in between them, as long as those lower priority tasks aren't going to take hours to complete.

  On a typical day, you might try:

  | 9:00A–10:00A | Priority A task |
  | 10:00A-10:15A | Priority B task |
  | 10:15A-11:15A | Priority A task |
  | 11:15A-11:45A | Priority B task |
  | 11:45A-12:00N | Priority C task  etc. |

  Your boss or manager may let you know the Priority A task you should be working on first.

# Organizing Clinic

## Question

What is the best way to prioritize the in box for the boss? Some items are time sensitive, some creep up suddenly and need to be done right away, some are for review and some require a signature.

We've tried "urgent," "signature only," and "review," but after a while the inevitable happens and everyone puts things in "urgent" since they know it will get looked at.

We've tried, "review immediately," "today," and "within three days." Same thing; everybody ends up putting their work in the fastest moving box. Help!

Mitch Michael

## Answer

Dear Mitch,

- First, it is imperative that staff members understand what is meant by "urgent." To most people, everything is urgent in their own minds, but in most cases, there are in fact very few urgent items.

- Be sure to explain to staff members what you mean when you say Urgent, such as a) a customer is irate due to this problem or b) your company is going to lose a dire amount of money if this problem isn't handled immediately.

- Second, list the types of papers that should go in each box, right on the box itself so the staff member can easily remember. Identify the specific types of correspondence that can be put in the Review in 3 Days Box (Employee ideas, Customer Suggestions, etc., those that can be Reviewed in 2 Days (Product Inquiries, Catalog Requests) and those that must be answered that day (Customer Questions, etc.) The more specific you are, the better. The last thing you want to do is have staff members making their own decisions about what is important and what is not important. Your boss has to make that decision based on the typical correspondence that comes in and out of your office.

- Third, if the staff member is promised that his or her correspondence in the Review in 2 Days Box will be reviewed in two days, then be sure that correspondence is actually reviewed in two days as promised.

- Finally, once all of the above is handled, the boss must make it perfectly clear to the staff members, which papers should go in which box. They have to be told, in writing and verbally, that if they put the papers in the wrong box, they're going to be re-routed back to the person who put them there, unanswered. Under no circumstances should some people get away with putting the papers in the wrong boxes, while others are following the proper system.

# Chapter 47

# Getting projects done

- **Start with the end in mind.** Start your projects with the end in mind. Take the time to determine the desired end result, rather than jumping right in. A little bit of upfront planning goes a long way. Close your eyes and picture the best outcome. You can then work backwards to determine exactly what you have to do to achieve that outcome.

- **There are major goals in each project.** Each project entails a series of major goals, also known as milestones. Each major goal accomplished will help you make a giant leap towards project completion.

- **There are mini goals in each major goal.** Breaking down your major goals into bite-sized mini goals will help your team clearly see the individual steps to be completed. This results in a less daunting perspective of the major goal and a more frequent sense of accomplishment. Just as in football, each ten yards advanced equals another mini goal met.

- **Shoot for deadlines.** Assign specific deadlines to each major and mini goal. When you have a specific date you are targeting, you can then determine approximately how much time each project goal is going to entail and how long it will be before the entire project can realistically be completed.

- **Pad it dude.** Generously pad your projected completion dates. For instance, if you're targeting that the project will be completed by February 20th, schedule your projected completion date for February 4th.

  It's rare for a project to be completed without any setbacks at all. There's always the possibility that you may actually get the project done early, but better to be early than late.

- **Make it visible.** Write down everything you are trying to accomplish. Don't try to keep it in your head because there is too much you have to remember.

  If you work in a large company, you may choose to use reliable, user-friendly project management software to help you organize and present your project steps, goals, deadlines, time, costs and team member responsibilities.

  This may be overkill for small businesses, but for large businesses with very involved tasks, project management software can be an enormous help.

- **Get rid of the clutter.** Disorganized, messy work areas and productivity don't go hand in hand. Clear your desk of all papers, except for the project you're working on right now.

# Organizing Clinic

## Question

I am always shuffling papers for multiple projects and have tried boxes, file cabinets and colored file folders. Nothing seems to keep the papers organized efficiently. Also, the myriad of notes in paperclips, sticky notes and cutouts are here in a pile under my monitor. How can I organize these?

White Owl

## Answer

Dear White Owl,

Organizing products will help you organize your papers, but you have to be sure you're using the best system so that you're helping those products to help you.

Just like an oven won't cook your food properly without you turning the dial to the right temperature and taking proper steps, your project filing system won't work without you following a tried and true system for keeping your papers organized.

You might plan on working on five projects in a day, but you can only work on one thing at any one moment. This means that the only project out of your system at any one time, should be the one project you're working on right now. As you stop working on any particular project, all papers related to that project should immediately be filed back into your filing system, before you pull papers out for another project.

One of my favorite systems for keeping multiple projects organized is a Project Binder. Simply get yourself a 2-inch binder and insert ten 3-hole punched, pocket folders inside your binder. Get yourself a package of removable file folder labels. Stick a file folder label on each of the pocket folders and write a different project name down on each label. You now have one consistent place to keep all of your ongoing projects.

Once a particular project is finished, all of the papers in that pocket folder can be moved into your filing cabinet for future reference. Finally, just remove the old label from the project folder and apply a new, blank label to be used for your next project.

- **Priorities please.** Very often, you're not working on any one project, but rather a series of different projects. Prioritizing is important. Each project cannot be deemed top-priority. There are always some that are going to take higher precedence over others and working 24 hours a day is not an option. You'll run yourself ragged.

- **Get your beauty sleep.** To ensure maximum productivity, most people need seven to eight hours of sleep at the very least. Lack of sleep causes insufficient concentration, poor decision-making ability, mistakes and missed deadlines.

- **Don't skip lunch.** A study conducted by the Productivity Institute in Huntington, Connecticut found that 60% of business professionals regularly skip lunch.

  Food gives you both physical and mental energy. Without energy, productivity suffers. Take a break for a healthy lunch each day. You're not too busy for lunch. After all, you do care about your health and well-being, right?

- **Eat your veggies first.** There are always going to be tasks on your To Do list that are less desirable than others. The sooner you get them off your plate, the quicker you can move on to more fun tasks. Think about it. You wouldn't eat your dessert before your veggies would you? What in the world would you have to look forward to?

- **Early bird or night owl?** Do your most productive work at your most productive time of the day. Some people are early birds and some are night owls. If it takes you a little while to get going in the morning, take care of your mindless tasks first. This way, you can do tasks that require a great deal of concentration later in the day.

  On the other hand, if you're the rare bird who is ready to go-go-go the second you wake up, then focus on your most intricate tasks first thing in the day and take care of your more mindless tasks in the afternoon.

### Great idea!

I try to take a particular time each day to work on a task or project until it is completed. By making an appointment each day, the task or project gets completed quickly.

Diana Romagnano, Associate Editor of *Finally Organized, Finally Free for the Office*

- **Make an appointment with yourself.** Schedule appointments in your day for creative thinking and to catch your breath. When that time rolls around, keep that appointment with yourself just as you would any other important appointment.

- **Reward yourself and your team.** Designate rewards for each goal achieved within the projected timeframe. Bonuses, time off, free pizza and other incentives are great motivators.

- **Create a project binder.** Many people have a number of different projects going on at the same time. But it's not practical or productive to keep all of the papers associated with all projects on top of your desk in piles. A great way to keep it all organized is to create a project binder. See the Paper Clutter and Paper Flow Management chapter in this book.

- **Track it on the wall.** Track multiple or large projects on a wall chart, especially if there are a number of different people involved. Be sure it's at a height that makes it easy to make changes and at a distance so it can be read without having to squint.

- **Use technology.** A woman I used to work with spent hours using graph paper, calculator and pen to add up huge columns of numbers, rather than a computer spreadsheet that would help her do the same task in minutes. Always think about the possibility of using an automated system, rather than doing something by hand.

- **Start somewhere.** Not sure what project to even start on? That's okay. Just start somewhere. Anywhere. Don't get bogged down in delayed decision making.

- **Choose from a hat.** Get yourself a set of index cards and jot down one project task on each. Put all the cards in a hat and pull one out. Then, do the task on that one card. Repeat the same process tomorrow, the next day, and so on, until the hat is empty.

- **Just say no.** When you're working on getting a project done, you can't say yes to every other request for your time. Practice saying no in a friendly, but firm fashion, such as "I would really love to help you out, but prior commitments will not allow me to do so at this time. Perhaps Jim or Andy could give you a hand?"

- **Delegate.** You don't necessarily have to do the entire project by yourself. Consider delegating to someone else in your company, or outsourcing part of the project.

- **Switch between left and right brained activities.** For instance, work on a detailed, number-heavy report first thing in the morning, and then switch off later to a more creative project such as the design of your web site or company brochure.

# Chapter 48

# Business trip smarts

- **Prepare a detailed itinerary.** Include contact information for your business appointments and your overnight stays. Give a copy of your itinerary to the appropriate people in your office and your family members so they know how to reach you—especially in case of an emergency.

- **Make a packing checklist.** Create a general packing checklist that includes everything you normally need to go on a business trip. Simply pull out the checklist and use it to pack your luggage, checking off items as you place each in your bags.

  Bring the checklist with you so when you're ready to return from your trip, you can ensure that everything that must come back with you gets packed.

- **Keep toll money in your vehicle.** If you always use the same vehicle for business travel, keep extra change in a cup holder or pouch for tolls and parking meters. If you generally rent, the same idea can work. Just keep a small change pouch in a travel bag you always use.

- **Get an expandable file folder with several sections.** You'll be able to keep many items you'll need for your trip categorized within each section. Some sections might include:

  - ❖ Directions, maps, rental car information, passenger tickets, local restaurant information, phone numbers

  - ❖ Receipts and expenses

  - ❖ Work related information, reports, charts, notes, computer disks

  - ❖ Contingency section with items you haven't had time to complete, so you can work on them during airline delays or in the cab

  - ❖ Things to read—business or personal

  - ❖ Things you'll need to follow up on when you return

  - ❖ Things you'll need to file when you return

- **Keep track of your expenses.** For tax-related reasons or for reimbursements, it is very important to keep track of travel related expenses. When you receive a receipt, jot the date, place, dollar amount and any other necessary notes regarding that particular expense, on the back of the receipt.

Then, store it in an envelope or in your expandable file folder in the appropriate section. When you return to the office, if you have to make out an expense report, do it right away.

## Organizing Clinic

### Question

I am heading an expedition to Philmont Scout Ranch in two years. Do you have any ideas on how I can organize the immense flow of information that will have to be kept up with (money/receipts, health forms, travel forms, expedition info, tickets, etc.?

Seth

### Answer

Dear Seth,

A great way to keep all of this information organized is with an expanding file with a flap. These are generally 10" x 15" or so and have anywhere from 10 to 31 pockets. Just assign receipts to pocket 1, health forms to pocket 2, travel forms to pocket 3 and so on.

I would also recommend you keep a simple log of everything in a format that keeps everything categorized. Since this is an expedition, you will need a master list of all the participants names with columns to check off for money received, health forms and travel forms.

---

- **Pad your time.** Allow plenty of time in between meetings and appointments so you're not rushing from place to place. It's going to take you longer to get to your destination if you're in an unfamiliar city or if you experience traffic delays.

- **Book everything in advance.** Whatever you do, don't wait until you get to your destination to make reservations. Book everything you possibly can before you leave—as far in advance as possible. This will save tons of time and ensure you won't be stranded without necessities, like a hotel room or rental car.

- **Utilize communications devices.** Bring your laptop and your cellular phone on your trips. Take advantage of airline or hotel business amenities, such as using their computers to send faxes, receive stock prices, make phone calls and to check and write email.

If you rent a car and are unfamiliar with the area, request a computerized navigational system if your rental company has this available.

- **Get motivated.** Listen to motivational or business enhancement audiotapes when driving to your destination.

---

# Power Wheels: 10 steps to organizing your mobile life

by Debbie Williams

Some of my clients literally live from their cars. That is not to say that they camp out with sleeping bag, pillow and a lantern, but rather LIVE from their cars. Many of us spend more time in our cars than at corporate headquarters or in our home office, creating the need for product storage, a compact filing system and organized desk space. Car organizing is not limited to those working outside the home either; many a soccer mom dreams of a leisurely commute without library books and sports gear rolling around in the back of the minivan.

Use some of the tips listed below to create a mini-filing system, store product literature and product samples, stash groceries and organize all those items needing to be mended or returned during your daily outings.

- **What's your hang up?** Store important papers in hanging files in a portable crate. These come in all sizes, open or with lids. To prevent the crate from sliding around during travel, place a fluffy towel underneath or place it on the floorboard where it cannot tip over. It's a great way to organize the kids' permission slips, contracts for clients or memos. (Be sure to keep business and personal records separate so there are no surprises in the boardroom.)

- **Read between the lines.** Carry a To Be Read folder with you for review during stopped traffic or while waiting for an appointment. This is one of my favorite time-savers and reduces stress at the same time.

- **It's all in the system.** Create a follow-up system using a notebook with pocketed dividers, a recipe box or an accordion file. Number the dividers 1-31 and file documents (or note cards) behind the appropriate date of the month for future action.

- **What's on the agenda?** Consolidate important notes into a daily planner, spiral notebook, calendar or small wipe-off board. If you keep a master-planning calendar at home or in your office, carry a spare in your car for taking notes. Remember to consolidate these each day to eliminate overlooked appointments and special days.

- **Mobile desk.** For bills and other correspondence, buy a 3-ring binder and fill with twelve pocketed dividers, one for each month of the year. On the front of each folder, list the birthdays, anniversaries and billing due dates. Then fill with correspondence. The binder can be used as a portable desk or can be stored at your work area. Don't forget to stick your favorite writing pen in the front pocket.

- **Improved storage space.** Keep a large sturdy crate or laundry basket in your car to contain product samples, grocery bags, clothes headed to the dry cleaners, library books and rented videos. Invest in two so that you can carry a full one into the house, saving wasted trips from car to kitchen or office. My all-time favorite is a collapsible plastic crate that takes up very little space when not in use.

- **It's the little things that count.** There are a number of visor and glove compartment organizers available to hold pens, paper, sunglasses and loose change. Make a habit of putting your small items here after each use so you can easily find them.

- **More legroom.** Expand limited floor space by using pocketed organizers that hang on the back of the car seat to hold maps, brochures, product literature, umbrellas, business cards, kids' tape players and even snacks for those long days away from home.

- **A compact model.** Create a compact office-on-the-go by filling a zippered pencil case with office supplies for your briefcase, tote bag or car. Store basic desk drawer items such as letterhead and envelopes, business cards, brochures, postage stamps, calculator, pads of paper, pens, pencils, stapler and staple remover, scissors, tape dispenser, sticky notes, rubber bands, paper clips and change for parking or tolls.

- **Emergency road care.** Assemble first-aid supplies, a small fire extinguisher, a large towel or blanket, jumper cables, basic toolkit, rain poncho and a change of clothes. If this sounds like someone's mother telling you to always be prepared, you're right! Experienced parents realize the value of a change of clothes for their kids, but seasoned travelers know how miserable it can be delivering a speech while in wet clothes from a downpour.

Last but not least, don't forget the stress ball you picked up at your last tradeshow—keep that one in your cup holder so you can grab it during heavy (or stopped) traffic. Mini-kits come in all forms and purposes: diaper bags for baby, activity kits for older children, busy boxes for adults (which brings us back to that reading folder again, but stash some fiction and hobby magazines in there as well.) Using everyday items to organize our briefcases, cars and offices on the go will not only improve our effectiveness on the job, but will reduce much of the stress we encounter along the way. Happy trails!

Reprinted with permission. Debbie Williams is an organizing strategist and parent educator who offers tools and training to help you put your house in order. She is the author of *Put Your House In Order*. Learn more at www.organizedtimes.com

- **Check and return email/voicemail during your trip.** Don't wait until you return or you'll end up with a ton of catch-up work after your trip. Return email from the hotel room. Return phone calls while you're waiting for your flight.

- **Make a traveling filing system.** If you're on the road often with your own vehicle, create a traveling filing system to keep in your back seat at all times. Office supply stores sell file boxes that hold hanging file folders. You'll always be prepared whenever you're on the road.

- **Goals first.** Never leave on a business trip without first clearly defining your goals. Write them down and refer to them during your trip to ensure you're staying on track and covering all ground.

- **Double duty.** If you're visiting one client, determine if you can visit another client during the same trip. This is a great way to save time and money.

- **Contact the necessary people prior to leaving.** Make plane, hotel and car reservations well ahead of time. Confirm all appointments. Discuss what materials you need to bring along with you. Ask about presentation rooms.

  Determine if your hotel has a fax center, copy center, desk, additional hook-up for your phone line and other amenities that will make your life easier while on the road.

- **Change your voicemail message.** If you don't plan on checking your voicemail for a few days, be sure to change your voicemail message so callers will know when to expect a return phone call or so they can be directed to someone else who can help them.

- **Set up an email autoresponder.** When you know you're not going to have access to email for a few days, set up an email autoresponder. When someone emails you, they will automatically receive your email autoresponder message back. Set it up to say you're on vacation or on the road. Tell them when you'll be back or how they can reach you.

- **Develop a relationship with a good travel agent.** Using a reliable travel agent to make your travel arrangements will eliminate the time it takes to research and book trips. Plus, you may get some excellent travel deals.

- **Use the same rental car company all the time.** Your information will be in their computers so it's a great time saver and you'll be able to build traveling points. Additionally, if you belong to rental car clubs, you won't have to wait on long lines when you are ready to pick up your rental car.

- **Don't forget electronic gadgets.**
  - ❖ Cell Phone
  - ❖ Cell phone charger
  - ❖ Extra batteries
  - ❖ Extra CDs
  - ❖ Extra diskettes
  - ❖ Headphones
  - ❖ Laptop (with appropriate cable, phone cord and battery pack)

- ❖ PDA
- ❖ Portable surge protector
- ❖ Portable recorder for on-the-road dictation

- **Don't just toss everything in your briefcase.** Otherwise, when you open it later you're bound to have a big, disorganized mess. Organize papers in pocket folders. Keep all of your pocket folders in a 3-ring binder or an expandable file holder. Keep your calculator, pens and other small items in a small, see-through pouch.

- **Always bring reading material.** Carry reading material with you in an expanding file folder, tucked into your briefcase or travel bag. Or have your administrative assistant scan some reading material into your laptop for you prior to your trip. Whenever you're waiting in line or awaiting your car rental, you'll have something productive or enjoyable to do.

- **Bring your laptop.** You'll be able to catch up on email, write letters and work on projects during your travels. Plus, if you have to give a presentation, it can be stored right on your laptop.

- **Organize for airline metal detectors.** When going through airline security checkpoints, make things easier on yourself and the security person by having everything organized before you place your belongings on the conveyor belt and before you walk through the metal detector.

  For instance, rather than waiting to be asked, take your shoes and coat off and put them in the bin provided by the airlines. If you don't do this and security personnel detects metal, you're going to be pulled from the line and checked from head to toe—unnecessary time wasted.

  Keep your airline tickets and your driver's license safe, but easily accessible, as you'll need to pull them out several times in the airport.

  In addition, take your laptop out of its case and put that in the bin, along with items such as your cell phone and pocket change. Try to keep all of your belongings in one bin so that when the bin comes out at the other end, everything will be together.

- **Join airline lounge clubs.** If you travel frequently and if your budget allows, you might consider joining an airline lounge club. It will make your airport waiting time more comfortable and productive. It will also eliminate time waiting in lines.

- **Fly direct.** Time is more valuable than money. Flying with stopovers may save a few bucks, but it's going to soak up your time quicker than you can imagine. Whenever possible, fly direct.

- **Avoid checking baggage.** If you're going on a long trip, checking baggage might be a necessity. But if you're only traveling for a day or two, pack lightly and avoid checking baggage. This will save you time departing for and returning from your destination.

### Great idea!

Your health and well-being during a business trip are paramount. Nothing kills productivity like feeling unwell. There are a few air travel essentials besides your tickets and itineraries that will easily fit in your briefcase.

**Water**: Always carry a bottle of water. During a business trip, your normal eating and more importantly, drinking schedules, are disrupted. Proper hydration is essential for productivity and health.

**Sleeping Mask**: It takes a little extra effort to relax when flying so tune out the other people crammed inside the airborne tin can. You might even be able to catch a nap on the plane.

**Inflatable Neck Pillow**: Give your neck some extra support, especially if you are able to sleep on the plane.

**Lavender Essential Oil**: Dab a little around your mouth and nose. Not only does the scent help you relax, some experts say it can clean germs from the recycled air you are breathing. And it is safe to apply directly to your skin.

Kerry Crocker, Professional Organizer
Space Cadette
Chapel Hill, NC
(919) 928-9825
kerry@space-cadette.com
www.space-cadette.com

- **Make a travel bag.** There's no sense packing and re-packing the things you always bring with you when you travel. Keep your travel bag pre-filled with toothpaste, deodorant, hairspray, shampoo and lotion. When you're ready to go on a trip, most of your necessities will already be packed.

- **Take a travel alarm.** Consider your travel alarm your primary alarm. Then use a wake up call or room clock as a backup.

- **Don't pack the kitchen sink.** Most people pack way more than they need and then end up lugging around tons of clothes, toiletries, business materials and more that they never use during their trip. Bring mix and match clothes, so you don't need to bring a complete outfit for each day.

- **Limit your colors.** By limiting the number of colors in your wardrobe, you will be able to mix and match separates, requiring less clothing. Additionally, keeping footwear and accessories in neutral tones will allow you to do more with less.

- **Don't rely solely on your electronic gadgets.** Always be prepared for something to go wrong. For instance, bring along a paper copy of your entire presentation. Just in case something goes wrong, you'll at least have the paper presentation ready to be copied and handed out. This will prevent your trip from becoming a waste of time.

- **Be prepared for lost luggage.** If you're flying, there's a chance your luggage may be lost. Rather than checking in all of your clothes, pack a few light outfits, underwear, sleepwear, cosmetics, medication and necessary toiletries in your carry-on bag.

- **Evaluate.** When you return, take a look at your original goals. Did you accomplish everything you wanted to? What follow up calls do you need to make? Do you have to do a write-up? What follow-up materials do you have to send?

- **Charge your battery.** If you plan to use your laptop while flying, be sure you fully charge your battery before boarding the plane. Some planes actually have power outlets, but are generally only available to those people flying in first class.

- **Carry rations.** Many airlines are no longer offering meals onboard flights. The ones that do charge a nice sum of money, for a little bit of food. Arrive at the airport ahead of time so you can pick up a sandwich to bring on board. Bring some non-perishables too, like trail mix, just in case you are on board for more time than expected.

- **Stay fit while on the road.** Many hotels have exercise facilities and swimming pools available. There's no need to skip your workouts when on a business trip.

- **Send it ahead.** Mail any heavy materials to your destination ahead of time. Why carry it with you when it can be delivered? Sure, it may cost a few bucks, but your back and shoulders will thank you later.

- **Use the same.** Use the same airline, car rental company and hotel chain when you travel. If you're a regular, chances are service will be quicker, you'll get better deals, you may not have to wait in long lines and you'll know what to expect each time.

- **Go high speed.** If you plan to use your laptop to access email or the Internet during your trip, consider choosing a hotel that offers high-speed Internet access in your room.

- **Relax.** There are often going to be minor problems, but don't fret. For example, if your flight is delayed, use that time to read or do some work.

    Try to look on the bright side. For instance, in the case of a flight delay, tell yourself that you're safer on the ground if there is a weather-related problem.

    Be positive and relax—you'll be amazed at how much better you feel and you may even be able to get a bunch of additional work completed.

- **Forget anything?** After the trip, determine if there was something you didn't do or bring on this trip that you wished you had. Write it down so you don't forget about it on your next trip.

### Great idea!

I have typed on my computer a packing list that has everything that I may need for a business trip. It is in Microsoft Word and ready to print. It has blank spaces with day headings so that I can write in what clothes I will be wearing each day. This way if I take a black business suit, I make sure that I check off that I also have my black shoes as well.

I write down everything I may need, even down to sunscreen and just cross it off if I don't need it on that particular trip. The list is checked right before I walk out the door so I don't accidentally walk out without my laptop!

Nicole Bickett, MBA
Organize to Optimize, LLC
5116 Puffin Place, Carmel, IN 46033
317-409-3607 Phone
317- 815-1677 Fax
nicole@organize2optimize.com
www.organize2optimize.com

# Chapter 49

# Achieving your goals

- **Dream a little.** What would make your life perfect? Make a wish list of everything you'd like in life that would make you happy. Don't worry if some of it sounds corny. Just be honest with yourself and list everything. This list is something you should be referencing every single day. It should be your inspiration.

- **Keep your eyes on the prize.** Make your goal visible. When many charity organizations want to reach goals, they draw a picture of a thermometer or a mountain as a symbol of their progress.

  Numerical mini-goals are designated on the picture to display completion of that mini-goal. Every time a goal is met, the thermometer or mountain is filled in with red, so everyone knows the current results.

  You can do the same thing with your business goals. Having a visual to look at each day should motivate you to continue to work towards reaching that goal.

- **Make them mini.** Don't get overwhelmed by big goals. Rome wasn't built in a day. Instead, break your goals down into SMART mini goals.

- **Be S.M.A.R.T.** Translate your dreams into SMART goals by being sure each one meets the SMART criteria: Specific, Measurable, Attainable, Realistic and Timely.

  - ❖ **Specific:** Your goals should not be vague. Saying you want to increase current sales is vague. Saying you want to increase current sales by 25% is specific.

  - ❖ **Measurable:** If your goal isn't measurable, how will you know how far along you are in completing it? How much extra money do you wish to make by next month? How many steps have you completed to be promoted? How many business books do you want to read this year?

  - ❖ **Attainable:** Sometimes goals can be overwhelming. Break up your goals into small, attainable mini-goals. Get a set of at least 10 index cards and write a mini-goal on each of them.

  - ❖ **Realistic:** When setting your goals, it's important to be realistic. You can't grow a multi-million dollar business in a week, no matter how enthusiastic you are. When setting goals, always ask yourself if it's possible. It's wonderful to be optimistic. It's another to be totally unreasonable.

- ❖ **Timely:** Set a deadline for your main goal and for all your mini-goals. Saying "someday" or "eventually" is too vague. Set a specific date, like September 13th or June 5th.

- **Can do.** Always keep a positive "Can do" attitude. If you tell yourself you can't do something because you don't have enough time, enough energy or enough money, you probably won't reach that goal.

- **Write them down.** Goals that are written down and posted somewhere prominent are a lot more concrete than vague goals floating around in your head. Sales legend Tom Hopkins once said, "If it's not in writing, it's not a goal. An unwritten want is a wish, a dream, a never-happen. If it's in writing, it's a commitment."

- **Know your obstacles.** Write down any obstacles that may be preventing you from reaching your goals. Once you know what they are, you can work on getting rid of them.

- **Ready, set, go.** Schedule time each day to work on your mini-goals. Whether you can set aside an hour or ten minutes each day, if you just work on your goals a little bit at a time you will eventually reach them.

- **Get bored easily?** Rather than working on certain tasks for long stretches of time, work on them in shorter increments. The task will seem less boring if you know you only have to work on it for 15 or 20 minutes at a time, but at the same time, you'll be moving towards its completion.

- **Never lose sight of your goals.** In 1952, Florence Chadwick attempted to swim the English Channel. After swimming for more than 15 hours, all she could see was fog and in spite of encouragement from her trainer, she quit— only one half mile from her goal. Later she said, "I'm not excusing myself, but if I could have seen the land, I might have made it." Many of us fall short of our expectations, because we lose sight of our goals.

- **Make your goals concrete.** Each year, list the top five business goals you'd like to achieve that year. These should be goals you'd be proud to accomplish. Hang them in a prominent place where you'll see them every single day and make it a point that at least one item on your To Do list each day is something that will get you closer to one of your five goals.

- **Make your best estimate.** When you have to do something, always estimate approximately how long it will take you. Then, take that figure and multiply it by two. Most people underestimate how long it will take to complete a task or project.

- **Hooray!** Shooting for goals is even more exciting when you have someone to cheer you on. Tell someone about your business goals, whether it be your spouse, your boss, your secretary or anyone you trust who will cheer you on throughout the process.

## Great idea!

Look long, act short. My philosophy about meeting your goals is to have a long-term focus, but short-term objectives. It is the little steps that keep us going, those little victories that stop us from becoming frustrated by the short-term setbacks that will occur from time to time.

Do not be afraid of taking a few steps backwards sometimes. That is okay. As long as you are also taking steps forward, ultimately heading in the direction where you want to go.

You will get to where you want to be in the end. Trust me. You can never be a winner in life unless you have the courage to face the obstacles that will appear.

Charles Marcus is an international speaker and trainer. To subscribe to his FREE personal and professional development newsletter, please send an email to charles@cmarcus.com with the word SUBSCRIBE. For more information on how Charles and his programs can benefit your group, please call 416-490-6744, email charles@cmarcus.com or visit his web site: www.cmarcus.com

- **Choose one or two.** No doubt, you have several goals. But trying to work on them all at once almost guarantees lots of unfinished goals. Choose one or two for now and focus on them.

- **15 Minutes each day.** Schedule a minimum of 15 minutes each day to work on your most important goal. Don't allow your goal to be sidetracked by less important work.

- **Never give up.** My husband Joe is one of the most persistent people I know. When he has a goal, he stops at nothing to reach it. Since I've known him, I've never, ever seen him give up—on anything. That's why he's reached so many goals in his life. He's an inspiration to me.

  If you have it in your mind that you're going to reach your goals, no matter how difficult, no matter how many problems you run into, no matter who is against you reaching those goals, you will succeed at each one.

- **Start today.** Forget starting tomorrow or at the beginning of next month or two weeks from now. Start today. There's no better time than the present.

- **Learn to refuse.** While it would be nice if we could say "Yes" to every single request for help, if you're trying to reach some goals in life, it's impossible to accommodate every request.

- **Deal with setbacks.** Realize that anything worth reaching for is often met with bumps along the road. Leave setbacks behind you. Learn from them, but keep pressing on.

### Great idea!

Write a paragraph or two describing exactly why you absolutely must attain your goal. Write down all the reasons why you are committed to attaining your goal. Feel the emotion stir up inside of you. Feel the passion and drive. This will bring the goal to life!

How would you feel one year from now if you were to attain all your goals? How would that make you feel about yourself? Would your feel proud? Would your self-esteem be increased? Would you feel unstoppable?

Would you feel more confident in your ability? What results would you get from reaching your goals? Would you have greater job security? Would you be up for a promotion? Would you be earning more money? Would your family and friends be proud of you? How would that make you feel?

Glen Hopkins owns Motivational-Messages.com, your Free resource for daily motivation and inspiration, including quotes, tips and stories to help you lead a successful life. To join the Free mailing list, send an email to motivationalmessages-subscribe@listbot.com or visit www.motivational-messages.com today.

- **Always have another goal.** Once you reach one of your goals, set a new one immediately. Always having something to work towards can help you increase your knowledge and productivity.

- **High or low?** While you certainly don't want to set goals that are unrealistically high, you also don't want to set goals that are very low. When you set goals, set them so they're just slightly out of your immediate grasp. This will challenge you, but will also help ensure you meet your goal.

- **Involve others.** Involve your loved ones in the goals you set. Tell at least three people about them. Let these people know that your goals are very important to you and you'd appreciate any motivation they could send your way. Also, ask them to check up on you and to help you stay on track. Just telling others about your plans may give you the incentive to actually work towards achieving them.

# Chapter 50

# Working at home

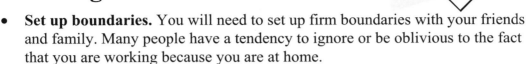

- **Set up boundaries.** You will need to set up firm boundaries with your friends and family. Many people have a tendency to ignore or be oblivious to the fact that you are working because you are at home.

  It is very important to set expectations early. Perhaps it is a closed door to your office if you are able to have it in a separate room.

- **Work is work—whether it's at home or the office.** You will also need to set your own expectations and to discipline yourself to continue to function just as you would as if you were driving into your normal place of business.

  This means showering and dressing just as though you were going to be in the office. The temptation to work in pajamas is very high when working out of the home, but discipline will help to maintain a professional demeanor, even if you are at home by yourself.

- **Get additional outlets.** Many homes do not have sufficient outlets for computer equipment, fax machines, copy machines and other necessary equipment. Call your electrician to get more outlets installed as needed. The same is true for your phone or cable jacks.

- **Get a separate line.** Consider getting a separate line for your business calls. This way, you can "close for the weekend." If you're always answering your phone, you may find yourself working around the clock. In addition, you probably don't want your young children—if you have any—picking up your business calls.

- **Get surge protectors.** For the minimal amount of money it costs, surge protectors can protect your electronic computerized equipment from damage due to power surges or outages.

- **Don't allow household chores to take over.** Working at home does allow a bit more freedom than going into the office. You have the ability to throw in a load of wash or to do a myriad of other small, non-labor intensive chores. Just be careful not to let the chores become the focus of your day.

- **Observe normal work hours.** Because your office is at home, there is also a temptation to check the work email in the evening or to work on a document or any number of things that should be attended to during normal work hours. This is another part of setting careful boundaries. It is important to stick to a work schedule and a non-work schedule.

## Great idea!

I've recently started a new scrapbooking business and have had to revamp my office to accommodate what I now do. Since I am working at home, I think one of the most important aspects of my office is its "home-i-ness." The challenge has been to keep this atmosphere and yet still have a sense of professionalism.

Here are some things I've done. I've added curtains to the windows rather than blinds. I've put hooks and holders on the wall for easy access to tools I use all the time like software and paper. I've placed a loveseat under the window for clients to relax on. My next move is to install a row of cupboards along one wall to store office materials with shelving above them to organize everyday needs. Color (and color coordination) adds to the personality of the room.

A "bulletin board" is made with folded fabric layers over a corkboard base to hold current paperwork and/or pictures can be pretty, functional and yet not the "same old" thing. Mine adds a splash of color and serves my needs as well as expresses my personality.

Bonnie Lewis-Watts
Dream Makers
8644 Parkhouse Drive, Mt Brydges, ON N0L1W0 Canada
bddlw@sympatico.ca

- **Take breaks.** Just because you're working at home, doesn't mean you can't take energy or relaxation breaks. Go for a power walk in the middle of the afternoon or sip a cup of tea while reading a motivational book. Two ten to fifteen minute breaks may be all you need to be at your best each day.

- **Separate personal files from work files.** Another thing to consider when setting up your office is where you are going to store your work files. A separate file cabinet is best rather than using the same cabinet for your personal files. At minimum, use different file drawers.

- **Open a separate checking account and credit card.** Don't ever mix your personal expenses and your business expenses. If you're running a business from home, you need a business checking account and a business credit card.

  If you plan to put aside money for taxes, social security and so on, you may also wish to open a business savings account.

- **Feeling isolated?** Many people who work at home begin to feel isolated and therefore have a tough time getting things done. Avoid this syndrome by attending meetings outside the office and by joining professional organizations such as your local Chamber of Commerce.

## Great idea!

The foremost key to setting up an office that is organized and stays organized is good lighting and the space you choose. I have seen people spend much time and money planning and designing the "perfect" office with all of the right bins, file systems and shelving only to find that they never go into their office! The reason they choose to load up their dining room table with papers instead of their new office in their dark, damp basement is because there is not enough lighting and they do not love the space.

In setting up your office, take the time to find a space in your home that you love and you know is a good fit. If you have bad knees, don't put your office upstairs. If your office is outside of your home, take the time to splash your personal style all over your workspace. Allow as much sunlight to shine through as possible.

So go ahead and enjoy your new office. Now that you have the right essentials, any of the organizing tips in this book are bound to help you get organized and STAY that way.

Rebekah Slatkin
A Professional Organizer
410-764-TIME
www.AProfessionalOrganizer.com
Creating Organized, Simplified, Balanced and Beautiful space

- **Set up a separate area.** You may not have the luxury of a separate room for your home office. However, you can set up separate areas within a room. Even if your work computer shares a desk or table top with your personal computer, keep them separate.

  Bonnie, a colleague of mine, has a home office which shares space with her personal computer, sewing machine, craft items and the bed her granddaughter sleeps in when she stays over, but she is sure to keep each area separated.

- **Store everything related to your business in your office.** Don't have office things scattered throughout your home. If your office is bursting at the seams with papers, supplies and products, designate a specific closet or portion of your home for storage. This will help you avoid wasting time searching for things.

- **Clients in your home.** Will clients or customers be coming to your home for business reasons? If so, try to set up your work area in non-obtrusive spaces in your home. For instance, you probably don't want to be right near bedrooms or play areas. Or you may consider blocking off views of certain rooms with folding screens for privacy. Another idea would be to meet clients in restaurants rather than in your home.

## Great idea!

Working at home can be especially difficult because your friends and family members feel that you are always available. One way to address this issue is to use creative scheduling.

Begin by establishing office hours: pre-determined blocks of time when you are available to anyone who may need to contact you. These blocks of time may change from day to day depending on your schedule, but if you are consistent in using them, it won't take long for people to get accustomed to your new system.

Just as you schedule and announce office hours as times when you are available to be interrupted, you also need to schedule and announce your interruption-free times. Write these in your planner the same way you would any other important event.

Try to identify your "peak times" and use them as your interruption-free times. During this time, you can maximize the use of your voice mail. Use your outgoing message to explain that you will be "in a meeting" during your interruption-free time. Then announce when your office hours are so the caller will know when they can reach you.

Jenifer Fox-Gerrits
Life Management Strategies, LLC
1516 Spruce Drive, Amelia OH 45102
jenifer@lifestrat.net
www.lifestrat.net

- **Establish a phone rule.** Strongly consider not accepting personal phone calls during working hours. Otherwise, you may find your time dwindling away as you talk on the phone with family and friends.

- **Hire a babysitter.** If you have very young children and you're finding it difficult to get any work done, consider hiring a babysitter—even if just for a few hours each day. This person can watch your kids at her home or even at your home while you work.

- **Get yourself a computer expert.** If you're not very computer savvy and your home business requires your computer to be in tip top shape, find yourself a computer expert who can assist you if your computer goes down or if you need computer upgrades.

Don't wait for your computer to give you problems to find this person. Look ahead of time and have his card easily accessible so you can call in a moment's notice. Be sure the person is reliable and can assist you very quickly.

## Great idea!

Be sure your home office has sufficient light and feels inspiring. If you don't have an inspiring view from your window, hang a painting across your desk that will give you an uplifting feeling.

Locate your home office closer to the front door if you have clients, associates or employees visiting you.

Blend your office in by using furniture that serves double purpose if you do not have the luxury of an extra room exclusively for your office. An attractive credenza can serve as storage for your office supplies. An antique trunk used as a coffee table can store your current projects.

Avoid setting up an office in your bedroom. It may interfere with your restful sleep. If you have absolutely no choice, at least separate the work area from your bed by using a partition or build an office into the closet and close it at the end of the working day.

Make use of the wall space all the way to the ceiling. Install shelves, hang wall pockets.

Use attractive boxes for putting away your unfinished projects. Leave the boxes in an accessible place for the next working phase.

Stania Rensberger
Stania's Organizing Systems
5645 Friars Rd. #368, San Diego, CA. 92110
Tel: (619) 296-3910
stania@bigplanet.com
www.staniarensberger.com
Reprinted with permission from Stania's booklets: "107 Ideas to Organize Your Home-Based Business" and "Secrets to Organizing Small Spaces."

- **Hire a cleaning service.** Many people think residential cleaning services are cost-prohibitive, but when you're working at home—or even if you work outside of the home—they can be an amazing help.

  Many residential cleaning services charge approximately $70 per cleaning session. If it is within your budget to have a cleaning service come in twice each month, I highly recommend it. You'll be amazed at how much time you can save.

- **Handy investments.** Utilize resources and tools available at office supply stores to allow your home office to function as an office. A speakerphone can be a great investment in a home office. Office supplies are not just for the corporate office.

### Great idea!

- Handle your mail one time. When you bring it in, look through it immediately, toss the junk and file the important stuff in your family center. If you do this every day, you will completely eliminate the clutter of junk mail and papers.

- Give each person in your family their own file. As you are cleaning, put all mail and paper related items into that person's file.

- Create storage for the things that you need to keep easily accessible such as bills to pay, filing, and things to do. Here again, you can use clear plastic shoeboxes. Label each one and store on a shelf in your home office.

- For storing office supplies that you need at reach, try using a wire, 3-shelf unit that is on wheels. It will hold all your supplies and be easy to move around your office.

- Always have an inbox, so that family members will know where you want all items for your office to go. If you are not home to sort the mail, have them make sure they place anything necessary in your inbox for you to handle later.

Lynn Herrin is the owner of Organize Easy, a professional organizer and freelance writer. You can get free organizing tips and a free newsletter with thousands of tips and tricks, ideas and tools by simply visiting her web site at www.organizeeasy.com

---

- **Baby oh baby.** Working from home while caring for a baby or two at the same time can be challenging, but it's definitely not impossible. I did it and I managed quite well.

Naptimes are crucial. Your young infants should be getting at least three naps each day, up to around six months or so. Afterwards, your infant through the toddler years should get at least one 2-hour nap or two 1-hour naps. Doing this curtails fussiness and gives you a *quiet* chance to get some of your work done.

Waking up an hour before the baby is awake and working an hour after the baby is asleep for the evening, will also grab you some extra work time. You can even work a bit while the baby is awake. You should be able to get around 30 minutes or so, while the baby plays in her bungee bouncer, baby saucer or on a blanket on the carpet rolling around with her toys.

# Chapter 51

# Hiring, orientation and separation

- **Know what you're looking for.** Before you set up any interviews, have a clear idea of what qualities and skills you would like your applicants to possess. Type up a list of these qualities and skills and have it handy to give to hiring agencies or to write up your advertisement.

- **Rate them.** Rate each candidate from zero to five (0=poor, 5=excellent) on each quality or skill during the interview. This will be a great reminder of each candidate's qualities and skills.

- **Give a student a chance.** If you don't need a full time employee, you might consider college internship programs. This is wonderful preparation for the student before he enters the workforce and can be of great benefit to you. Some interns work for salary, others work for school credits.

- **Make job descriptions.** Come up with standard job descriptions for every position in your company. When another staff member leaves, you won't have to frantically try to put one together.

- **Set a deadline.** Don't leave your hiring open ended. Set a deadline for filling the open position so you have a date to shoot for. If you have to hire very quickly, be sure to set up sufficient interviewing time each day.

- **Have a staff member talk to them.** If your time is very limited, you may wish to have a trusted staff member do the interviewing for you and recommend his or her favorite candidate based on your criteria.

- **Make a list of interview questions.** Don't just wing your interviews. Make up a standard list of interview questions and ask the same questions of each applicant.

- **Take notes.** If you plan to meet with several job applicants, take notes on each person you meet. Jot down the answers to your interview questions, write things you want to remember (i.e. extra friendly, a bit nervous, etc.). Keep each applicant's application and notes in one file until you're ready to make your decision.

- **Don't make them wait.** If you are interviewing someone at 10:00AM, be ready to interview him at exactly 10:00AM. Many people seeking employment have to be back at their current jobs that day. To make them wait is unprofessional and not very thoughtful.

- **Set up second interviews.** Very often, the first round of interviews is simply to eliminate those candidates who definitely will not do and to give you candidates to interview again. Set aside time in your schedule for both first and second interviews.

- **Screen them first.** If you have a human resources department in your company, you may be able to get them to initially screen all of your candidates first. This way, the only ones you end up interviewing are those that have the qualifications you've determined they should have.

- **Don't trust resumes alone.** Resumes rarely give an accurate picture of your applicants. Use the resumes as guides only, but use your one-on-one interview and your instinct to actually hire. Of course, the only way to truly tell if someone is going to work out is to test him out for a few weeks. Put him on a trial period and if it turns out to be a good fit make a permanent hire.

- **Check references.** It's always a good idea to check references. Normally, job applicants only list people that are willing to give them good references, but it pays to make those calls anyhow.

  Kevin, a small business owner, was trying to decide which of two applicants to hire. He decided to check references. The first person received wonderful references from everyone listed—including three past employers.

  Kevin discovered some red flags on the other applicant, however. When he called one of this applicant's past employers, the employer stated, "Sorry, but I only give good references." When he called another reference, Kevin discovered the applicant's relationship to this reference was a sibling. Needless to say, Kevin gave the first person the job. This was the safer bet.

- **Have two canned letters on hand.** One canned letter should be a "Yes, you've been hired," letter. On this one there should be a space where you can fill in the person's start date/time and where/to whom they should report. The other canned letter should be a "We're sorry, but we've filled the position," letter.

  The only other possibility is a "For now we've put you on our waiting list," letter. These letters should be handy in your files and sent shortly after you've made your decision on that particular position.

- **Have hiring packets made up.** Once you hire someone, she should immediately be given a hiring packet. It should contain information such as data about your company, her training schedule, an internal company map, and any tax forms that need to be filled out.

- **Clean out the person's office or cubicle.** Don't let a new candidate come to work on his first day and be placed in a cluttered, dirty office. Let him start fresh in a clean, organized environment. Clean out his office or cubicle before his first day or get staff members to do so.

- **Introduce them.** Make new employees comfortable with their new surroundings. Introduce them to fellow staff members, managers, and others they will be working with. Also show them where the restrooms, cafeteria, fire escapes and other important areas are located.

## Organizing Clinic

### Question

I have no problem interviewing, but how do I find applicants? The only way I know of is to run an ad in our local paper. Are there other ways?

Caroline Deluca, Staten Island, NY

### Answer

Dear Caroline,

There are several ways to get the word out. An ad is only one of the ways and I generally recommend you give that method a try.

Some other ways include private employment agencies, government employment services, the Internet (like through www.monster.com or www.careerbuilder.com), flyers to local churches, schools, senior citizen centers and the local Chamber, ads in industry publications, job fairs and referrals.

Private employment agencies screen applicants, so you generally get someone a bit more qualified. But, there can be an expensive initial investment that will pay off later if the applicant works out. Flyers to local churches, schools and other organizations are a very inexpensive method, but the qualifying process will be completely up to you. Give each of these methods a try to determine those that work out best for you.

- **Give them a company policy manual.** Hopefully, you have company policy manuals made up, detailing any uniform guidelines, time off, vacation, insurance and other company policies. If you do not, it is highly recommended that you create one. Go through your policy manual with all new employees page-by-page, answer any questions and then give them a copy for their records.

- **Get them trained.** Make a training schedule for your new employees. Either you will be solely training them or various staff members will be doing so. If you have written checklists for your company systems, training will go a lot smoother and you will ensure that all of your company's systems are performed in a consistent and professional manner. The trainer can just go through the checklists with the person until he feels good about what he's doing. The checklists will then be left with the new person for reference.

- **Keep records.** Keep accurate records for all employees during their employment period, especially negative behavior or major mistakes. This will be of benefit to you if you have to let someone go later on.

- **Don't ignore orientation.** An employee's first few days on the job are critical for both you and the employee. A new employee who feels ignored or abandoned may quickly lose respect for you and the company.

- **Hey buddy!** Give new employees an experienced person to buddy up with on his first few days on the job. This will make the new employee feel at ease and will help ensure the person has a support system.

- **Don't overwhelm.** People can only absorb so much information in any given day. Space out introductions to people, projects and policies over the course of a few weeks.

- **Give employee reviews.** Give each employee regular reviews and feedback. If action needs to be taken to correct something, a review or feedback will give your employees an opportunity to fix it. Nobody likes to be stunned to find out they're doing a bad job, especially if they've been working for you for months and have never heard anything negative.

- **Have a box of tissues ready.** Nobody with a heart enjoys firing someone and most employees don't like being fired. While some employees may get angry when they learn of their termination and others may not react at all, still others may actually weep in your office. Be sympathetic and have those tissues ready so the person can compose herself before leaving your office.

- **Fire in private.** When it comes time to fire someone, do it very quietly behind closed doors. The last thing you want to do is embarrass the person.

- **Get assistance.** If you're concerned for your safety when you need to fire someone, have someone from human resources sit in on the process with you. Or hire an outside human resources firm to assist you.

- **Back up files.** Prior to firing a key employee, back up any computer files and take steps to lock them out of the computer system. One disgruntled person can wipe out important files very quickly and this can cost you dearly in time and expense later.

- **Hold an exit interview.** If the employee you're terminating doesn't storm out, it's a good idea to hold an exit interview. During the interview you would tell the person why she's being terminated, give her the reason(s) for dismissal in writing, present the final paycheck—or tell her it will be mailed to her—discuss severance pay if any and instructions on leaving the premises. Document any details.

- **Offer assistance.** It is both professional and good-hearted to offer the person you're firing any outplacement assistance or counseling needed. Have a sheet of paper on hand that lists available services.

- **Keep other employees informed.** Rather than taking the chance of rumors spreading, gather all employees and let them know that Jack or Sue is no longer with the company. You don't have to give them all the gory details. Just tell them it wasn't a good fit or that the reasons are confidential.

# Chapter 52

# Managing a winning, organized team

- **Be sure they're well trained.** A winning, organized team is one that is well-trained. If you're responsible for people, be sure you have a structured training system in place—one complete with instructional checklists, personal guidance and practice time.

- **Be a good example.** Your staff will look to you for inspiration and motivation. If you have a cluttered office or a cluttered desk, your chaos will reflect in your staff.

- **Handle problem situations quickly.** If you have someone on staff that gossips, tries to avoid work or is an otherwise bad example for the rest of your staff, deal with that problem situation immediately. Bad morale can bring down a winning, organized team quicker than you can imagine.

  Confront the person involved impressing the need for an improvement. If the person refuses, don't keep him on your team. If the person accepts, watch him closely to be sure the problem does not recur.

- **Give them feedback.** Schedule time in your day for regular feedback sessions. Quarterly reviews are fine, but there is usually too much time in between for an employee to hear how she's doing and to learn if there's something she's doing that needs improvement.

  Give feedback daily or weekly at minimum. Your employees will always know where they stand. And you won't have to worry about not having kept your employees abreast.

- **Give deadlines and follow up.** When you give a staff member a project, it's imperative for you to give her a reasonable deadline. Follow up with her before the deadline to see how she's doing and to answer any questions.

  Encourage staff members to complete projects by their deadlines, by offering special incentives such as project bonuses, pizza parties or simply a pat on the back. A little bit of recognition can go a long way.

  If any particular staff member continuously misses deadlines, there has to be a consequence. Be fair, but firm.

- **Keep track of projects.** If you have a large staff, keeping on top of every project may seem overwhelming. But if you keep a log of all projects in progress, along with deadlines and the people responsible, it's not as difficult as it may seem.

One very important point is if you're facilitating projects, it's important for you not to jump in and start working on one of those projects. If you're involved in the meat of the project, it is extremely difficult to effectively manage the project.

---

## Organizing Clinic

### Question

Sara, one of my employees doesn't see the importance of organizing her cubicle area. She has papers piled on the floor. Her desk is a disaster of office supplies, magazines and paperwork. She even waits all week to begin tossing out empty cans of soda! It's so frustrating.

The funny thing is, she's a really good employee and I don't want to get rid of her. She's sweet and always finishes her projects on time. Unfortunately, she is setting a bad example for the rest of the staff and an unprofessional atmosphere for visiting customers. Can you help?

Reva McKenna, Jacksonville, FL

### Answer

Dear Reva,

By telling me you know she's setting a bad example for both staff and customers, I'm happy to know you realize Sara's disorganized environment is not a healthy one for your company.

Since she's a good employee, schedule a private meeting with her to tell her what a wonderful job she's doing. In the middle of the meeting, tell her that there is one area she needs improvement on and that is organizing her cubicle. Tell her you're happy to provide her with any assistance she needs, whether it's you helping her, getting another staff member to help her or hiring a professional organizer to assist.

At the end of the meeting, close with how thrilled you are to have her on staff, thank her for all her hard work and tell her you'll be following up to be sure she's receiving all of the assistance and instruction she needs to make her cubicle both productive and professional.

If after ample encouragement and assistance, she still does not conform to your requests, you may have to resort to replacing her with someone who possesses the organized qualities you want.

---

- **What do they know?** Keep an up-to-date log that details every company task/project and who is trained on those particular tasks and projects. You shouldn't have to spend time trying to figure out who knows what.

- **Two is better than one.** Never have only one person who knows a particular system in your company. If that person leaves and doesn't leave on a good note, you're not going to have anyone who knows that system.

Abby, a data analyst in a financial company, manages a staff of 20. Each person is proficient in a particular aspect of the department. During the busy tax season, one of those staff members got into an argument with Abby and quit unexpectedly.

Abby was really in a bind. The staff member that quit was the only person who knew how to do an ongoing monthly project for a major client. In the end, she had to learn the project herself, through trial and error. The client's project wasn't done on time and he didn't want to pay full price. Abby's manager was furious.

Always have at least two people, preferably three, fully trained on all systems in your department or company.

- **Don't be surprised.** People move on. If you realize that a staff member can leave at any time, you won't be caught off guard. Be prepared. Most people don't stay with companies forever, especially if they're young.

- **Be a good listener.** It may sound simple to just listen to your employees, but it's one of the most important things you can do as a boss, manager or supervisor. If you want happy, productive employees, you have to show them they're important. One of the best ways to do that is to really listen to their concerns, ideas and questions.

- **Be consistent.** Inconsistency can really affect employees—in a bad way. This often happens when there are several trainers on staff. Each may have his own way of training or doing a particular task. What you end up with is lots of confused, frustrated employees and lost productivity.

Don't allow your trainers to come up with their own systems without consulting you first. Your employees should be trained how to do the task the way YOU want it to be done. Not the way someone else wants it to be done.

- **Don't expect. Inspect.** Don't expect your employees to do the right thing. Inspect regularly and determine if they're doing the right thing. If so, great. If not, you now have the opportunity to help them make an improvement.

- **Be a continuous improvement advocate.** Just because you've always done something one way, doesn't necessarily mean it's the best way. If one of your staff members has an idea that can make money, save money, increase productivity or reduce stress, allow him to present it to you.

To save time and screen out the ideas that really won't work, have employees fill out employee suggestion forms. Be sure the forms are designed well so the employee can fill out his idea, the probable amount of money that can be increased or saved or how this idea can increase productivity.

Don't accept ideas that haven't been well thought out. An idea is only a good one if it can benefit the company.

- **Tell them upfront.** Tell your staff what you expect of them. This way, there won't be any confusion along the way. It's a good idea to put this in writing and have the employee sign it, so she can't say, "You didn't tell me that."

- **Tell them what comes first.** While some staff members may be able to prioritize very well, others may not have mastered this skill. Help staff members prioritize. Tell them which tasks/projects should always take top priority and which are generally lower priority.

- **Praise in public, criticize in private.** When an employee does something above and beyond, always acknowledge that effort, both privately and publicly. But, when you need to bring up an issue to an employee that involves something she needs to improve on, do so in private. Never criticize staff members in front of others.

- **There's always a margin of error.** Nobody's perfect—therefore, there will be errors. If you are aware of this fact, you shouldn't be surprised or caught off guard when an error occurs. Being organized will help you handle the situation in a calm, stress-free manner.

- **Give them a life.** Just like you probably want a life outside work, so do your employees. While asking employees to work a bit of overtime occasionally is okay, try not to ask them to do so often.

- **Pay for performance.** Realize that if you pay by the hour, some employees are going to work a lot slower than others. In essence, to some employees it doesn't really matter how hard they work—in their minds, they're still getting the same $8.00 or $9.00 as everyone else, regardless of their effort.

Most companies pay hourly rates. Some actually pay their staff members when a project has been completed. For instance, a fast food operator may pay his employees $9.00 per hour, but a basement remodeler may pay his employees $1000 upon the completion of a finished basement.

You may want to pay an hourly rate or a salary, but then pay bonuses based on certifications received or employees they trained or on something simple like excellent attendance records or job performance.

Come up with an organized, consistent plan. The key is to make sure you're getting what you want out of your employees. It doesn't hurt so much to reach into your wallet when someone is doing an excellent job for you.

# Chapter 53

# Organizing your marketing efforts

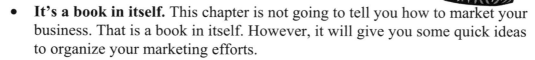

- **It's a book in itself.** This chapter is not going to tell you how to market your business. That is a book in itself. However, it will give you some quick ideas to organize your marketing efforts.

  I would like to take this opportunity to introduce you to my husband Joe's marketing web site. The name is Give to Get Marketing and you'll find it on the following link: www.givetogetmarketing.com

  If you're a small business owner, this site is for you. Stop by today and get a free marketing idea kit. While you're at it, pick up a copy of Joe's *Give to Get Marketing Solution.*

  If you want to grow your business, this is the route to take. I use all of my husband's concepts and we have been able to grow the Get Organized Now! site to well over a million visitors a year and hundreds of thousands of dollars in sales because of them.

- **Come up with a solid strategy.** Knowing a few marketing tips will not help you grow your business. You need a solid strategy, like the one you'll find in the *Give to Get Marketing Solution.*

  You can do a whole lot of work—print business cards, get a web site created, come up with sales letters, hire a sales staff and so on—but if you don't have a solid marketing strategy, you'll just be wasting energy, time and money.

- **Schedule your marketing activities.** Don't just randomly hop from one marketing activity to the next. It's best to have a schedule. For instance, maybe you might schedule an ad campaign for the first week in January, media appearances the 3rd week in January, a press release campaign in early February and so on.

- **Know your numbers.** There's nothing more important in marketing than knowing your numbers. Know how many prospects, how many appointments, how many first-time sales and how many repeat sales and other vital numbers.

- **Don't break the bank.** You don't have to spend wads of money to get your marketing activities off the ground. Start small. Work from a home office, instead of renting one. Do free talks at your local Chamber of Commerce. Send out free press releases, rather than initially spending money on ads. Don't get the most expensive stationery there is. You can always upgrade later.

# Great idea!

So many people ask me, "What is the best way to market my business?" It doesn't matter what kind of business you are trying to grow, the way to market it successfully is always the same:

1) Create a product or service that an extremely large number of people already want to buy.

2) Make sure you have a reliable way to reach those people.

3) Make sure your product or service is profitably priced.

4) Make sure your chosen product or service delivers exactly what your customers expect it to—or even a little more than expected.

5) Make sure your customers are very satisfied and happy with your product or service. Strive for "raving fans" of your product or service.

6) Attract unlimited numbers of people who have a genuine interest in the benefits that your product or service provides. These are called Prospects. Do this at the lowest cost possible.

7) Convert a percentage of those Prospects into First-Time Customers by making them special offers that they can't refuse.

8) Convert those First-Time Customers into loyal, Lifetime customers by offering special preferred customer offers or additional back-end products or services.

9) Organize and systemize all the steps so they become a smooth and consistent process.

There isn't a quick and easy answer to marketing a business effectively. You must accomplish the above steps. And, of course, that takes work and commitment and a lot more detail than I can mention here. In addition to the "what" to do listed above, you also need the "how" to do it. You need to know the exact steps to be taken to accomplish each of the above goals. You can't guess at how to market your business. Honestly, the easiest way to grow your business is to learn from someone who has already done it instead of blindly trying this and that with little or no results.

There are many different ways available to you for carrying out your marketing objectives. Some are low-cost, many are actually no cost. Which ones you choose to use are dependent upon your circumstances, your personality and your comfort level with each method. Once you learn exactly what your options are in a step-by-step guide like our Give to Get Marketing Solution, you will easily be able to select the marketing options that are just right for you. Only then will you know the answer to the question, "What's the best way to grow my particular business?"

Joe Gracia, Owner and President of The Give to Get Marketing Web Site
Get hundreds of marketing tips, ideas and articles for growing your business at the Give to Get Marketing Web site. A free Marketing Idea-Kit is also available. Visit:
www.givetogetmarketing.com

- **Come up with your offers.** Make a list of compelling offers, such as offering a free catalog or a discounted service. Then schedule time to test your prospects' and customers' interest in them.

- **Take creative time.** Each day, schedule at least 15 minutes for creative time. This is the time to think about your marketing systems, what needs to be improved, new product ideas and so on.

- **So and so told me about you.** Create a list of contacts that can provide your business with a good reference when needed. Be sure you ask the contacts if it's okay if prospects call them for references. Make copies of this list and bring them with you when you go out on sales calls.

- **I'll scratch your back.** Make a list of other companies you may be able to do a joint venture with and make a point to contact each of them—perhaps contact one of these companies each month.

  For instance, if you are a newsletter designer and you know of a local printing company, you may be able to send out a mailing to companies who might be interested in having a newsletter designed and printed. You'll both be able to split the mailing expense.

- **Marketing should be Priority A.** Since you must market to grow a business or to increase sales, marketing should always be an A Priority on your To Do list. So many people say they don't have time for marketing. That's like saying that you have no time for food and water. If you stop marketing, sales will suffer and business will begin to decline rapidly.

- **What do you like to drive?** Decide what marketing vehicles you plan to utilize. A marketing vehicle is something you use to get your message across, like an ad, press release, workshop or a joint venture with another company.

- **Test your ads.** In each ad you run (local newspaper, magazine, radio, TV spot, etc.) include a fictitious extension code. For instance, when you give your phone number in the ad, use 555-5555 ext. 22 for your local newspaper ad, 555-5555 ext. 32 for your radio ad and 555-5555 ext. 71 for your TV spot.

  As customers call you, you simply ask them what extension number is in the ad. When they tell you, you'll know exactly where that prospect came from.

  This is very useful to determine which ads are pulling for you and which are not. For instance, if you get 15 calls from ext. 22, but only 4 calls from ext. 32, then you may determine radio ads (or whatever vehicle is assigned to that code) is not worth further investment.

- **Be a media maven.** One way to market your business is to write helpful articles and submit them to publications. For instance, I regularly write articles on getting organized such as organizing your kids, organizing your home, time management, goal setting and organizing your basement. I then submit those articles for publication. I don't take pay for these articles. I simply allow reprint if my name, company name and web site is mentioned at the end of each article. This is one of the ways I generate traffic to my web site and sales for my business.

Since I do this often, it's important to have writing listed as one of my daily tasks on my To Do Today list. I schedule an hour each day, strictly for writing.

- **Designate a phone hour.** Most businesses require phone time in order to make sales calls. If you have to make several phone calls for your business, designating a phone hour may work very well for you.

  If you plan to make calls whenever, you probably won't end up making many at all because the day will be eaten up by other activities.

- **Never guess.** Never guess at how well a marketing activity is going to do for you. The only way to determine how good that activity is, is to test it. That means, you do the marketing activity and then count the results.

  Prior to doing that activity, set up some goals. For instance,

  1 to 3 calls = poor

  4 to 6 calls = fair

  7 to 10 calls = good

  more than 10 calls = excellent

  This way, you'll know if that marketing activity was successful or not according to your original goals.

- **Keep track.** The only way for you to improve your marketing systems is for you to keep track of your results. Keep a log of each marketing activity you do, the date(s) you did it, how much you invested, your minimum, expected and outstanding goals, your response rate and your prospect to customer ratio.

  Later when you do this same marketing activity again, you can tweak your system and then compare results. You'll be able to tell whether it's worth doing that marketing activity again or not.

- **Do business online.** If you have a business, a web site can be an invaluable tool. Prospects and current customers will be able to browse at their leisure and without pressure. Common questions can be answered on your site without you having to interact or devote additional time. If you sell a product on your site, with the proper pieces set up, the money can go right into your bank account. With a web site, you can do business even if you're on vacation.

# Chapter 54

# Staying in touch from your web site

- **How can I reach you?** Always include a contact form on your web site. This way, people can contact you with questions, comments and ideas and you can respond at your leisure—within a reasonable timeframe, of course.

  This will also reduce the amount of people who will get on the phone and call you. Phone calls can tend to be very time consuming.

- **Keep it clean.** Keep your web site clutter free. The only links and graphics on it should be those that specifically pertain somehow to your service or product.

- **Design for easy reading.** Make your backgrounds light and never put text over a graphic. Keep line lengths short—around 70 characters or so per line. People are not going to work to read your site. If they can't easily read it, they'll leave.

- **Just the fAQs m'am.** Include a page on your web site for frequently asked questions. Set it up in question/answer format so visitors can find what they're looking for in a jiffy. This will reduce email and phone questions. Do the work once and benefit from it endlessly.

- **Use autoresponders.** Use autoresponders for answers to common site visitor questions. When someone clicks on an autoresponder link, they automatically get a response emailed to them—no work on your part, except for the initial setup.

- **No broken links.** Check your site weekly for broken links—links to sites or areas that no longer exist. Just as you have to weed out outdated papers, you also have to weed out outdated links.

- **No waiting time.** Keep your web site as simple as possible so the pages load very quickly. Large photographs and intricate graphics can take forever to load, which is a timewaster for others.

- **Keep the site fresh.** Nobody will want to return to your web site if you never change the content and then all of that initial setup work will be for nothing. We update the www.getorganizednow.com web site once each week.

  We do the work ourselves as we enjoy the freedom to change something when we want to, how we want to. But if you prefer, you can hire a web designer.

- **Accept credit cards.** If you're selling products or services from your web site, set it up to accept credit cards. You'll increase your sales significantly and all funds you collect will go directly into your bank account, without you doing a thing—except for the initial setup.

- **Make it easy for them to buy.** Make it easy for site visitors to find your products and easy for them to buy your products. Otherwise, you're going to get bogged down with questions and lose sales.

## Great idea!

Many people will not do business with people on the Internet unless they have a phone number. Are you scaring people away by not having a phone number readily available?

It's a proven fact. If your web site does not offer information like telephone numbers, street addresses or more, people will shy away feeling that you are not reputable. Unfortunately, many scammers on the Internet have made people leery.

It is understandable that you don't want to receive phone calls, especially if your web site does not require that you do. But the phone number eases peoples' fears and you'll honestly see business improve if you don't appear to be so aloof. 99% of the web surfers won't call. They just like to know that they can.

I have tried to even email many web sites with a question and some don't even have email addresses or any way to contact them. This is hard to believe, but true.

We just attempted to add our ezine to an ezine list site, but the site had no email or phone numbers listed and we could not ask a question, so we passed them up. It appeared to us that all they were interested in was harvesting email addresses. This may not be so, but who knows. They didn't appear reputable to me without even so much as an email link—the number one way to communicate on the web. Guess they didn't want to be bothered. Well neither did I, so I just clicked off their site.

We get calls all the time at our online printing company from people who just want to "see if we are real." They actually say that on the phone. Then they hang up and place their order at our site. True fact.

So one little 20-second phone call reaps us lots of business in the long run.

Try it. Add your phone number today. See what happens.

Tom Falco is editor of XpectMore.com eZine and also owns: www.thediscountprinter.com
To subscribe to XpectMore.com Marketing eZine send an email to ezine@xpectmore.com with the word "subscribe" in the subject line or visit: www.xpectmore.com

- **Create a navigational menu.** People should be able to get to any page on your web site, from any other page on your web site. Include a navigational menu on every page and be sure it's the same on each page.

- **Use an order manager.** Most web businesses copy and paste customer information into an offline database. This is okay if you only have a few customers each week. But if you have hundreds each week like the Get Organized Now! web site, you may wish to invest in order management software.

  We use Stoneedge Order Manager and it's wonderful. With the click of a button, all of our orders are downloaded from the Internet into our offline database. We can then use that database to search customer data and to run our reports.

- **Send out an ezine.** An ezine or email newsletter, is the perfect way to keep in touch with your customers. Basically, you include a link on your site so the person can sign up. Then, each week or month, you send your newsletter to these people who have opted to receive it.

  Sign up with a list serv service, such as Aweber, Sparklist or Topica. People can subscribe and unsubscribe automatically. And when you're ready to send out a newsletter or announcement, you can do so with the push of a button—to a list as small as 10 subscribers or one with millions of subscribers.

- **The hostess with the mostess.** Web hosts sell virtual space on the web that you rent to store your web site pages. When deciding on a web host, choose one that is reliable. Your site should be up and running 99.9999% of the time. If it's not, it's time to switch web hosts. Otherwise, you're going to lose site visitors and you're going to be spending tons of time on the phone arguing with your web hosting provider.

- **What's in a name?** Make the name of your web site and your domain name as easy to remember and spell as possible. You want people to type in your domain name and to be able to find you.

- **Promote it.** Just because you have a site on the web, doesn't mean people are going to flock to or even be able to find it for that matter. If you want people to visit, you have to do some promotional work. The more promotional work you do, the more people you'll have coming to your site.

  Each week, I hand out business cards with my site on it, publish articles with bylines after each that lead to my site, do radio and TV interviews to give helpful tips and mention my site, send out press releases that mention my site—this is just a brief list. There are many, many things you can do and should do, to get the word out about your web site.

- **Avoid "site under construction" signs.** If your site is under construction, don't lead people to it until it's back in service. Otherwise, you're going to look disorganized. If you have pages under construction, simply don't upload them until they're done.

- **Respond quickly.** Web site contacts should be handled like telephone contacts. If someone inquires via email or an email form on your web site, try to respond within 24 hours or 48 hours at the very latest. Set up a consistent time each day to respond.

- **Start a discussion group.** Discussion groups are wonderful for keeping lots of people in touch with each other, without having to take the time to travel. You can have a private discussion group for your customers and a public discussion group for your prospects. Basically, one person posts a message and others can reply to it.

  If you do decide to have a discussion forum however, organizing it well is key. Otherwise you're going to end up with lists and lists of various questions on various topics and it's going to be impossible to find anything.

  You'll notice on the Get Organized Now! Discussion Forum, that we have many different topics, such as Organizing Your Home, Organizing Your Office and Organizing Your Time, just to name a few.

- **Increase your ranking.** Many people use search engines to find sites. If yours is nowhere to be found in the top search engines, you're going to lose a lot of visitors and sales.

  While it is very time-consuming to determine how to get your site ranked high and how to maintain that ranking with the ever-changing search engines, if you wish to have a high ranking, it is necessary.

  Schedule time in your day to research search engine information sites, such as www.searchenginewatch.com

- **Offer print and digital.** If you offer informational products for sale on your web site, such as books, offer them in both printed and digital format. We get about fifty percent of our customers ordering print and the other fifty percent ordering digital.

  Digital downloadable versions are more profitable as there are no printing costs or mailing costs involved. Customers can get them instantaneously, instead of having to wait for the post office or a courier to deliver them. And you don't have to spend your time shipping anything—the computer does it automatically for you.

# Chapter 55

# Balancing work and home life

- **Plan your agenda ahead of time.** Plan out your weekly agendas on Sunday for the upcoming week, both for work and home. List each day's items separately. This will be easier than looking at a long list and won't overwhelm you.

- **Use a few weekend minutes.** On the weekend, cook the entrees for the evening meals. All that will be needed to be prepared will be the side dishes. If possible, while the entrees are cooking, put a cake in the oven—Sara Lee or Pepperidge Farm frozen choices are fine—or make Jello or pudding.

- **Plan for tomorrow, today.** Each evening, before retiring, set up your briefcase with items needed for the next day at the office. Plan your dinner for the next day. There may be some items the children can start to prepare for you, like setting the table or making a salad.

- **Reduce last minute requests.** Check the children's book bags. See if all papers needed are packed and anything needing signing is done. No last minute hunting for the morning's exit!

- **A time for work and a time for play.** When you leave work, leave work! You need to get into the "home and family" mode on the ride home. There is nothing as important as your family and the items at work can wait until the morning. Make sure you include time for fun, reading together and cuddles.

- **Make it a routine.** Establish a routine so your kids know what to expect and so that everything gets done. Put that routine in writing so you can refer to it while you are learning it. Adjust it until it works for your family. Make sure you build in time for you and your children to relax and unwind from the day.

- **Make dinner as easy as possible.** Make meals that take no more than thirty minutes to prepare. It helps to prepare double recipes on the weekends; eat one and freeze one. This provides you with a few meals in the freezer that can be defrosted and cooked.

  The crock-pot can also be your best friend for dinnertime. Put in your favorite crock-pot friendly recipe together in the morning and a hot meal will be ready when you come home.

- **Keep breakfast simple.** Set out the bowls, glasses, silverware and cereal boxes the night before. Then, all the kids have to do in the morning is take out the milk and juice and help themselves.

## Organizing Clinic

### Question

My wife is always angry when I work late. My boss is always angry when I don't put in overtime. How can I make both my wife and my boss happy, so I don't always feel so frustrated?

Ben Granier, Pittsburgh, PA

### Answer

Ben,

First, have a heart-to-heart with both your wife and your boss. Explain to your wife that you will sometimes have to put in some overtime to ensure your job security. Tell her you'll do your very best to see to it that this only happens once or twice each week at most. Explain to your boss that you'll be a lot less stressed and a lot more productive at work if you have a happy home life. Try to work something out, so you only have to work overtime at night a few nights each week. A compromise may be all it takes to give you a break.

Is there a reason for all the extra overtime? Is it because you can't get your work done during regular working hours? If so, you may want to consider if there's any way to streamline what you're doing.

In the end, however, I'm assuming it's more important to you that you're happy at home. So, if the overtime at your job really begins to put a damper on your marriage, you may want to seek another job that pays more and requires less overtime.

- **Turn off the tube.** Turn off the television and discuss your day during dinner. Dinner can be a wonderful way to have quality time with your family.

- **Get up first.** Get up before your kids do and take care of yourself. Shower and have a quiet cup of coffee, tea or juice.

- **Have babysitters on hand.** Line up several babysitters who can care for your child/children on short notice.

- **Talk to your spouse about responsibilities.** Decide in advance how you and your spouse will share household and family responsibilities, such as taking turns or splitting days. Make a plan and write it down.

- **Work from home.** Work from home if you can. Make arrangements with your employer in advance for this possibility.

- **Keep in touch.** Communicate with family during the workday via email, telephone and instant messages.

## Great idea!

If you work from home it's important to keep yourself and your family organized, in order to stay focused on your priorities and maintain a proper balance.

Start by getting up at the same time each day and following a morning routine that includes when to start work. Remember to dress for success. This may be casual and comfortable, but it should not be too relaxed.

Planning meals in advance will also help you stay organized and avoid last minute trips to the store for missing ingredients. Start by preparing a weekly meal plan and list grocery items accordingly. At mealtime you can stop work and make dinner effortlessly.

Think of your work schedule when preparing your meal plan and choose fast and easy dishes for the days when you have less flexibility in your day to prepare dinner.

Planning is essential in order to balance home and work life while working from home.

Evelyn Page, Professional Organizer
evelyn.page@sympatico.ca
Brampton, ON Canada (serving the GTA)

- **Set reasonable bedtimes.** Set reasonable bedtimes for your children so you have more time for you. They need the sleep and you need the time. Happy couples make happy parents. One of the best things you can do for your children is to take care of your relationship with your spouse.

- **Go to bed early sometimes.** Turn off the phone. Decline some social invitations. Make your family relationships a priority.

- **Schedule fun time.** Make sure you include some personal time for you. Actually schedule time for yourself. Make an appointment with yourself and keep it. A leisurely 20-minute bubble bath, some light reading or a fifteen-minute walk in the fresh air can all do wonders for your mood.

- **Use personal waiting time.** Use waiting time at the dentist or doctor's office, while waiting for dinner to cook or most anytime you find yourself with time on your hands, to catch up on reading, planning, writing thank-you notes or cards and/or addressing envelopes. Keep a list or file of things on hand that you can do during these minutes so they are not wasted.

- **Change your clothes.** Upon arriving home from work, never remain dressed in your work clothes. Change into your casual attire so your mind and body switch from work mode to home mode.

- **A batch in the morning and a batch in the evening.** Try and wash a batch or two of laundry each day. Wash a batch in the morning and when you return from work you can put that batch into the dryer. Fold clothing and put away before bed.

  You can eliminate laundry on the weekends this way, except bedding which can be put right back on the beds. Also, your work clothes will always be in the process of being cleaned and ready for the next time you plan to wear them.

### Great idea!

When working at home it is essential to establish and maintain boundaries between home and work life.

A great part of working at home is having flexible time. But if your time is too flexible and unregimented, your productivity will sharply drop off.

Establish a work schedule and stick to it as much as possible. It's too easy to go run a few errands in the morning and find yourself getting home after lunch, leaving you only a half day to work.

Schedule which hours of which days are for in-office work and which are for work and home-related activities out of the house. Make this schedule known to your family members so they can coordinate their plans with yours, making everyone more organized.

Your physical workspace should be as self-contained as possible. Choose a workspace as isolated as possible from family-centric spaces.

This will minimize audible interruptions and be off the beaten path of family members. Minimize reasons to leave the office by having a small refrigerator or coffee pot in the room.

Finally, keep the door closed and tell your family that a closed door means "do not disturb."

Kerry Crocker, Professional Organizer
Space Cadette
Chapel Hill, NC
(919) 928-9825
kerry@space-cadette.com
www.space-cadette.com

- **When you go on vacation, go all the way.** When you go on vacation, try not to take your work along with you. You're supposed to be going away to relax and enjoy yourself.

  If you absolutely must check your email and phone calls while you're away, at least limit yourself to no more than thirty minutes daily.

## Great idea!

If you typically work from home during school hours, summer and holiday vacations can present some challenges. Here is a tip for staying productive with your home business while being a full-time mom and chauffeur.

I pack two lightweight briefcases for the road, one for my home business and one for personal and family matters. In the first, I pack business related books, articles, magazines, notes, paper, tape recorder and any small office supplies needed to "work on the road." In the second, I include all paperwork, mail, bills I need to review, activity/sport schedules and personal reading that I would really like to get to.

I pack each of these at night and put them right in the car. Then when I find myself waiting for any reason, I pull something out and start on it. It is amazing how many little things you can take care of with just a few minutes here and there. You can become very efficient with your waiting time after a little practice. Try making it a habit and soon you will feel a lot more organized.

Erin Nield
It's About Time Organizing Service
6N859 Brierwood Drive, St. Charles, IL 60175
www.homeorganizeit.com

- **Make a cleaning schedule.** Whenever you can, clean as you go. This way, you won't have to spend hours deep cleaning. Schedule a cleaning session each day to dust, vacuum or clean the bathroom. This can be before, in between or after work.

- **Schedule time for home projects.** Dedicate one to two nights each week when you don't work overtime at your job to doing your home-related projects. This may include building a deck, organizing the basement, getting your files in order or any number of other projects.

- **Set personal goals.** Goal setting is a requirement for business success. Why not use it for personal success? Set up family goals and share your dreams. Make time to make those dreams a reality. Manage these goals just as you would a business project, plan it and do it! You can even write a Family Mission Statement.

# Chapter 56

# When to hire a professional organizer and what to expect

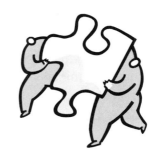

- **You can't get started.** In the event you're too overwhelmed to start getting organized, are not physically able to get organized or don't have the time to figure out productive, efficient systems, you may consider hiring a professional to assist you. There are actually people who will come to your office and work with you to get it organized. These people are called professional organizers.

    To find a professional organizer in your area, you can first look on my web site, as I have a pretty comprehensive listing available by area of the United States, Canada, Mexico and abroad. The direct link is www.getorganizednow.com/po-dir-index.html

    Or, you can check out the National Association of Professional Organizers on the following link: www.napo.net

- **You have to be there.** A good professional organizer will always request you work with her (or him) side by side. She will not usually do the job alone, especially because you will have to assist in the decisions regarding what gets kept and what gets tossed.

    Plus, the professional organizer will determine those systems that best meet your personality and needs and will train you on how to use these systems well into the future.

- **Invest in tomorrow.** Since professional organizers are independent contractors, they set the price and it can range anywhere from $15 per hour to $250 per hour, depending on the organizer's education, skill, experience, and expertise. Typically, you will spend around $50-$65 per hour if you need your office surroundings and filing system organized.

    On average, it usually takes about 10 hours or so to organize the typical office, so you'll end up investing approximately $500 to $700 total.

    If that amount seems high, just imagine how wonderful you're going to feel when the clutter is gone or your schedule is worked out or your stress has vanished. It's an investment in your future.

- **What about the future?** Many people acknowledge that a professional organizer can probably help them today. But what about tomorrow? What if they can't keep it up, after spending all that money?

Your investment should be a bit of an incentive to keep organized. In addition, some organizers offer follow-up assistance or follow-up service at a reduced rate.

## Great idea!

I have found that one of the most important things I can do as an Organizer when faced with a new client is to bend, adapt and go with the flow of the person I am working with.

Every professional organizer must realize that it takes both time and practice for clients to fine tune his or her organizing abilities.

We must learn to get the client organized in a functional and more productive manner than when we came on the scene and to not get hung up on perfection. This will not only be difficult to achieve but, most likely, will just set up the client for failure and frustration, particularly when dealing with someone who is chronically disorganized.

My experience has been that, once the client feels comfortable and not overwhelmed by my actions and realizes that they are working with someone who "gets them," a pattern of trust and understanding is established.

The result is the creation of a useable organizing system that works for the client and can be easily maintained by the client. If necessary, the client will feel comfortable with periodic maintenance visits from the Professional Organizer.

Richard Barbalato
Bee Organized
P.O. Box 289, Hawthorne, NY 10532
914-772-8361
b.drbee@verizon.net

- **Weekend warriors.** Some professional organizers are willing to work with you on weekends. Others may come in early in the morning and still others may work late at night. You'll have to work it out with the person you hire.

  If you decide to work with the organizer during your regular workday, it will be a lot more productive if you eliminate any possible interruptions. Allow your voicemail to take calls for you. Close your office door. Put a "Do Not Enter" sign on your office door so staff members know you should not be disturbed.

  If the organizer keeps getting interrupted, the job is going to take much longer and it's going to end up costing you more money.

- **Get quotes.** Get quotes from several professional organizers in your area. Meet with them to determine who can best meet your needs and budget. Don't only use cost as a factor. Use years of experience, references, the person's portfolio and personality to make your decision.

- **Is everything included?** When a professional organizer quotes you, it's generally just the organizer's time and expertise in that figure. If you need file folders, containers, computer disks, or other supplies, that's usually extra. Sometimes the organizer will assist you in getting these extras. Other organizers require you to pick up these items prior to your first session.

### Great idea!

People who hire professional organizers are not always disorganized people. You can know how to organize and be organized in many aspects of your life, but perhaps you're having trouble conquering a certain area.

Whether it's a closet, a paper-flow problem, a garage or your desk, there's bound to be one area that's a bit out of control.

If it's causing stress and frustration and if you're too busy to focus on the solution, call in a pro. You may just be too close to the problem to see the best solution.

Tracy Wyman
The Clutter Buster
Tallahassee, Florida
850-205-5279
solutions@clutterbuster.org
www.clutterbuster.org

- **Ask them to consult.** If it's just a little bit of advice you need and not necessarily organizing sessions, ask a professional organizer what he charges to simply consult with you. Many charge an hourly consulting fee and maybe that's all you need to get going.

- **Just call me bashful.** Please, don't be embarrassed about having to contact a professional organizer. Believe me when I say your office or home is most likely *not* the most disorganized office they've seen.

And even if it is, professional organizers are known for being kind, understanding, gentle and more helpful that you can imagine.

If you feel you need the help of a professional organizer to start getting organized, do yourself a favor and hire one today.

# Chapter 57

# Reducing stress

- **Stop and breathe.** Give your eyes and brain a little creative breathing room by stopping all activity for 30 to 60 seconds every half hour. Take a mini-mental vacation. Allow your eyes to wander away from the task at hand—which will ease eye strain! Be very conscious of your breathing, taking long, slow, deep breaths.

  Let your thoughts wander to happy memories or plans for the weekend. You'll be amazed at how much those few seconds can give you increased momentum, energy, brainpower and reduced stress.

- **Clear your workspace.** There is nothing more discouraging than leaving work with a desk piled high with papers. Consequently, there is nothing more stressful than encountering that same impossible pile the next morning.

  Plan to take a few moments each night to clear your workspace. If tasks are unfinished, put them away in a special basket or folder. Better yet, dedicate a portion of a file or desk drawer as a work saver.

  When you dedicate a place to put those unfinished tasks, there will be no frantic searching through random piles because all your work is still in order and easily accessible.

  You can create a stress free environment to return to in the morning by spending a few extra moments at night.

- **Accept responsibility.** It is important to remember you made a conscious choice to be where you are at this particular time. While very often you are not responsible for the circumstances you are in or for the actions of others, you are responsible for how you choose to react.

  Every time you're tempted to explode, stop, breathe and count to ten. If you can prevent becoming angry or frustrated, you will not only alleviate stress. You will find yourself able to more calmly and rationally deal with the source of your frustration.

- **Soothing influences.** If allowed, have something familiar on your desk, such as a picture of a family member or pet, a postcard of a favorite place or a little knick-knack with special meaning. If you can't have something visible in your work area, slip something into a drawer.

  It should be small enough to hold in your hand when the going gets tough. This momentary connection with a familiar object can produce a calming and soothing effect, allowing you to let stress slip away before it begins.

## Organizing Clinic

### Question

I'm so stressed out. Between my crazy schedule, deadlines and responsibilities at work and my suffering marriage and defiant teenage boys at home, I really feel like I'm about to go off the deep end. The last time I went to the doctor, my blood pressure was through the roof. What can I do to begin to calm down?

Name Withheld, Princeton, NJ

### Answer

Dear friend,

As you're probably already aware, stress can cause severe health problems. Your blood pressure is already elevated and it's clear you're not headed in a good direction. However, recognizing that you have to do something about your stress is an excellent start.

Take a deep breath. You can't work on everything that is stressing you out at once. Get a sheet of paper and write down three things that you'd like to work on over the next month or two.

Perhaps those things might be talking to your boss about extending your deadlines, delegating some work responsibilities, switching jobs, having a "date night" with your wife each week, fishing with your sons or concentrating on eating and exercise habits to bring your blood pressure down.

In addition, I also recommend that you talk to a qualified doctor about your stress problem, as related to both your physical and mental health. It's important that you take the time to step back and begin working on alleviating your stress. You only have one life to live and it's time for you to begin enjoying it.

- **Smile!** Remember the old saying, "Smile and the world will wonder what you've been up to?" A sense of humor banishes stress quickly and effectively.

  If you can remain pleasant throughout the workday, you will not only improve your own mood, but the moods of others.

  With a little attitude adjustment you can quickly learn to see the humor in situations, thereby eliminating stress.

- **Feed your brain.** Skipping meals can be tempting when you're on overload and facing too many deadlines. Proper nutrition, however, is essential to keep you focused, alert and on task. Trying to get by on a soda and a candy bar will only result in making you feel sluggish, ineffective and stressed out. Always have some trail mix or a bag of granola in your drawer for those days you find yourself chained to your desk. Cut back on your caffeine intake and drink bottled water instead. A healthy lifestyle inhibits stress.

- **Vary your routine.** Stress can occur from having to follow the same routine day after day until just going to work becomes a chore. Varying your routine in even a small way can bring you much needed relief.

  Drive or walk to work via a different route if you're close enough and if it's practical. Try riding your bike on nice days. Swap elevators for stairs. Spend your break outside the building getting a little fresh air.

  If you usually pack a meal, treat yourself by occasionally visiting a restaurant or bring a lunch if you generally eat out. If music is allowed in your office, change the radio station. If you're allowed to personalize your work area, change the photos or pictures.

  Pick up a snazzy looking ballpoint to write with instead of that same, drab, dull, stick pen. Pick out sticky notes in bright, vibrant colors instead of yellow or pastel.

  Change is good for the soul when it helps reduce stress.

- **Change out of your work clothes as soon as you get home.** This helps your mind and body make the transition. Find a few minutes to be quiet, whether sitting in a chair or lying down on your bed, rather than rushing into dealing with everyone and everything.

- **Establish reassuring, flexible routines that work for you.** People with high stress levels tend to be surrounded by mental and physical chaos. Establishing routines can help prevent and reduce stress by saving time.

  It can be a comfort factor in times of stress when predictability and certainty reassure us that no matter how bad circumstances get, some things remain constant and reliable.

- **Get it on paper and off of your mind.** Create a daily written list of what you expect to do. Making a list will help you become more realistic about your schedule and remind you of tasks you don't want to forget.

  By listing a task when you think of it, you also relieve stress by removing the thought from your mind, which helps to lessen mental overload.

- **Set aside time for yourself.** Your need for relaxation and recreation is vital to your happiness. Make time each day to do something for yourself. Identify something healthy that makes you feel good. Do it regularly.

  Whether you enjoy yourself indoors or out, alone or with others, do what's satisfying. Certain activities provide creative outlets, reduce fatigue and refresh your mind, body and spirit.

- **Exercise.** Exercise is a great way to work away your tension and fortify yourself against the negative physical effects of stress. Exercise brings pleasurable relaxation naturally. Choose any activity that appeals to you to give you the best chance of sticking with it.

- **Sleep.** Getting the right amount of rest will help ensure you can meet each day's challenges with energy and alertness. It's also important to get sufficient sleep.

  Good sleep habits include having a set bedtime and a set waking time. Following a pattern and establishing a rhythm for yourself and your body help you become more relaxed and less stressed during the day.

## Organizing Clinic

### Question

My husband and I work side-by-side. It's a medium size one-room office. We can't afford anything bigger and we can't afford a second office. We're both accountants.

Usually, we work really well together, but sometimes it's stressful working with each other all day in a tight space. We find that sometimes we get on each other's nerves.

What can be done to reduce this occasional stress?

Bob and Cindy Stewart, Boulder City, NV

### Answer

Dear Bob and Cindy,

Is it possible for you to put a partition in the middle of your office, so you really can't see each other all day long? This partition would be your privacy wall.

Another option would be to work different hours a few days each week. Perhaps Cindy can work in the mornings at the office and spend her afternoons doing work at home and vice versa for Bob.

- **Take A Break!** Take a break from what you're doing once in a while, so you'll feel refreshed and relaxed. When approaching difficult tasks make sure to schedule time for breaks. Try to take a 10 to 15-minute break for every hour of work.

  Take a walk, get some fresh air or call a friend. All work and no play can make you tense, irritable and less efficient. Schedule time for rest and relaxation.

# Organizing Clinic

## Question

Hello, I've been running a computer business for five years now. Lately it seems as though I've lost steam and am putting off acquiring new business more and more. I know I am burned out, but just can't seem to get out of this rut. I don't want to answer the phone when it rings, my office hours keep getting shorter and shorter and I even hung up on a customer for no good reason! The idea of finding a job with the least responsibility seems more attractive every day. Short of seeing a shrink for clinical depression, what do you recommend? Thanks.

Tom

## Answer

Dear Tom,

Running your own business can be very taxing, since you are responsible for everything. Have you taken a vacation lately? If not, it is recommended you do so. You need to take the time to rest and have some enjoyment. While finding an easy, lower-responsibility job may seem palatable now, it may not be the best choice for you and your personality.

I'm not sure if you're a computer programmer or if you do computer repairs, but most likely you work by yourself most of the day. In between your work projects, you might reward yourself by getting out into the world and being with people, like going for a walk in a populated park or having lunch in a busy restaurant. Sometimes people who typically work alone, get a bit stir-crazy if they don't surround themselves with people more often.

Do you set goals and then strive to reach them? Having goals and working to achieve them can be both energizing and satisfying. Does your business require you to work long-hours? Perhaps you can get back to a 9 to 5 schedule and work on something different each day so you don't get into a monotonous routine. Don't work weekends. Use your weekends to do something enjoyable like spending time with your family or going fishing with some friends.

Presently, you are at a crossroad. You have to determine whether you wish to continue in your current career or move on and do something else. If you choose to remain in your current career, you have to list the things that are currently bothering you each day and then you have to work on making adjustments to these things. Think of what you can do to alleviate the stress and perhaps even make your day more fun.

Do you have a spouse or close friend you can speak to about this situation? Speaking to a professional isn't really a bad idea either. Sometimes just talking to someone and getting your frustrations off your chest can help you release your frustration.

- **Delegate.** Learn to delegate so you don't become overloaded with unfinished tasks. Otherwise you will be more stressed and less productive.

- **Share more time with friends.** Social support is an important factor in lowering stress. Family and friends can give you the opportunity to talk and share. Talking with a trusted friend can go a long way toward putting your problems in perspective. Talking with others will allow you to vent your frustrations and concerns, making you feel better both physically and mentally. Make the effort to keep in regular contact with your friends and family.

- **Make mistakes and learn from them.** Perfectionism is destructive and often leads to procrastination. Trying to be perfect at everything you do is very stressful. Be gentle with yourself when things don't go as planned. Give yourself the same courtesy you would extend to a loved one. There are some things that you can't control, no matter how much you want to. Love yourself for who you are right now at this very moment.

- **Manage your time wisely.** Procrastination is one of your worst enemies. One of the most important things you can do to help reduce stress levels in your life is to develop a good time management plan. This will allow you to keep track of tasks that need to be completed and will also allow you to schedule fun activities too.

- **Just say no.** From time to time, you may be asked to volunteer your time in one way or another. Say yes when you can, but if you feel you're already stressed with your workload, it's okay to say no. You can't say yes to everything without getting overwhelmed.

- **Laughter is the best medicine.** Laughter is one of the best antidotes to stress. When we laugh and smile, blood flow to the brain is increased, endorphins are released and levels of stress hormones drop.

- **Get pampered.** A massage, facial, manicure, pedicure or other spa treatment can be very relaxing and enjoyable. You deserve to give yourself this gift at least 8-10 times a year.

- **Go out socially.** Try to go out with your spouse or friends at least once each week and have a good time. Just doing a couples or group activity, such as having dinner, dancing or bowling, may be all you need to relax and unwind.

# Chapter 58

# Staying motivated and organized

- **Accentuate the positive.** You have to go to work every day, so why not make the experience pleasant, productive and satisfying? Keep a positive, "can do" attitude. Keep your head up high and don't beat yourself up for temporary setbacks.

- **Don't skip lunch.** The Productivity Institute in Huntington, CT found in their studies that 60% of business people do not take lunch breaks on a regular basis. But, taking a break and getting some fuel is actually energizing and results in higher productivity. Stopping to eat lunch is not a waste of time. It's a necessary mini-vacation that allows you to rejuvenate.

## Organizing Clinic

### Question

I clean my desk on Saturday AM and by Monday PM it is back where I started. What is happening?

Dr. Jim

### Answer

Dear Dr. Jim,

Here are three quick ideas to keep your desk clear:

- When you're finished with any project, that project should immediately be placed in a file folder so that your desk is cleared for the next project.

- If people are constantly leaving papers on your desk throughout the day, eliminate that practice. Have a special area in your office where people can place incoming papers, such as trays or wall pockets.

- Don't wait until Saturday morning to clear your desk of all papers that have accumulated all week. Clear your desk every single day, as soon as you're finished with the day's work.

- It's very important for you to determine what is causing the papers to accumulate on your desk so quickly. Once you know the problem, the solution is usually a matter of tweaking your current system so that papers land in a file folder or tray rather than your desk and so that papers are constantly being cleared from your desk throughout the day.

- **Fun, fun, fun.** Schedule some fun things to do throughout your day. Read passages from an inspirational book or take a break to sip a cup of herbal tea while resting your brain.

- **Make it a game.** Set mini-goals throughout each day and reward yourself for every one you reach.

## Great idea!

There are schedules and there are "schedules." Sometimes those of us who are mothers (and we have enough to do as it is) tend to feel like we are the rope in a game of Multi-Tasking Tug-O-War. Yet when it comes to recharging ourselves, professional development is one of those options that we often leave by the wayside of our business mission. But just like in the traditional workplace, professional development is as necessary as being available for our clientele.

There are a number of ways to get professional development on a tight budget. For starters, check out freebies with the research staff in the local library or a college or university that has a list of special self-development events.

Volunteer and civic organizations, even churches, have access to many different kinds of activities that do not cost hundreds of dollars to attend. Better than that, check out a network marketing company and see if guests are welcome to attend various personal development seminars to add value to your service.

The local Chamber of Commerce may also offer community development for small business entrepreneurs. And don't forget friends and acquaintances that attend seminars. That way your training can be done in tandem and there is always a person to go to for feedback while running your own business. The possibilities are all around you. All you need to do is simply ask.

Regardless of whether we consider ourselves part-timers or full-timers in business, home or office, the most important thing to prioritize is planning time for your own personal development. It is guaranteed to be refreshing and often creates wellsprings of new ideas for your business endeavors. Make sure to attend seminars, learn and grow at least three to four times a year to keep a fresh outlook on helping you get to the next level!

Cynth'ya Lewis Reed
Gifts and Incentives Consultant
Accord Gifts and Incentive Services
P.O. Box 723, Muncie, IN 47308-0723
765-288-4084
accord@proalliance.net
www.proalliance.net
(Guest Entry Code 822084)

- **Set the mood.** If you hate your office or your work area, it's going to be awfully difficult to remain in a good mood. If possible, paint your office with a color you really like. If that's not possible, surround yourself with pictures or objects you enjoy looking at—anything fun and motivational. Try to make your environment as pleasant as possible so you enjoy being there.

- **Add some tunes.** If you enjoy listening to music, put a CD player or radio in your office. Play it at a background music level—so you don't disturb anyone around you and so it's not distracting. For some people, music can greatly enhance productivity and decrease stress.

- **Create compelling goals.** If you have goals you're looking forward to achieving, you'll be naturally energized along the way. Make your goals fun. Set goals and delight in rewards for all your achievements.

- **Form a support group.** There's nothing more motivating than a group of people cheering you on. Form your own support group and ask them to motivate you. Be a member of their support group too.

- **Steer clear of naysayers.** Why would you want to hang around someone who always puts you down? Surround yourself with people who lift you up, are confident in your abilities and make you feel wonderful.

- **Chart your progress on paper.** You'll be able to visualize how far you've come if you chart your progress on paper. Write down where you started on the left side of the paper and your goal on the right hand side of the paper. Then, in between, indicate all milestones reached.

- **Keep a motivation file.** Every time you find a motivational quote, story or article, copy or tear it out and include it in a "Motivational File." Whenever you need a little bit of inspiration, open your file and read.

- **Free yourself.** Give yourself a free day to rest, relax and rejuvenate. This may be all you need to get yourself re-energized.

- **Line yourself up with a mentor.** Hook up with someone you truly admire and be inspired. Meet with this person weekly or monthly for a dose of inspiration.

- **Further your knowledge.** Get ahead in your career by learning more about your field. Perhaps there's a promotion on the horizon or maybe you might be happier in another position or in another company. The more knowledge you have, the more confident and motivated you're going to be.

- **Log your disappointments.** Things may not always go as well as planned. Keep these disappointments in a log and work on how you can avoid those disappointments in the future. The best thing about making mistakes is that there's usually a lesson to be learned.

- **Log your accomplishments.** Keep every single accomplishment in a log. This written record will always serve as a source of motivation. You probably accomplish a whole lot more than what you think. Start writing your accomplishments down and you're bound to end up with a long, long list.

- **Stay healthy and fit.** It's better to look good *and* to feel good. When you know you look good and you feel energetic, you're starting the day off motivated and ready to take on whatever you need to.

- **Keep a testimonial file.** Whenever you get a congratulatory note from a customer, a thank you note from your boss or any other complimentary personal correspondence, save it in a folder. Open this folder whenever you need a pick-me-up.

- **15 Minutes each day.** To maintain your organizing efforts, dedicate 15 minutes at the end of each day to tie up any loose ends. Be sure your inbox is emptied out, your voicemail box is empty, your email inbox is clear, your desk doesn't have any loose papers, you've looked in your daily Tickler file and you have created tomorrow's To Do list. A few minutes at the end of each day is all it takes to be prepared for tomorrow.

- **Tweak.** The organizing systems you've set up for yourself may not necessarily work perfectly the first time around. Try using an organizing system for 21 days. At the end of the 21 days, if you haven't gotten used to that particular system or you feel it can be improved, tweak it and try your new system for the next 21 days. Always think "continuous improvement."

- **Have a ball.** Remember, being organized is going to free you, so that you can spend your time doing exactly what you want to do, whether that's leaving work earlier to spend time with your family or freeing your time to market and grow your business or better yourself financially or simply to be just a little happier. Have fun getting organized. Make it a game. And for all of your efforts, always remember to reap your rewards!

- **Keep visiting Get Organized Now!** As you're taking your organizing journey, at Get Organized Now! I'm here to help you every step of the way. Read my free weekly newsletter, filled with fresh ideas every single week. Browse my site for articles, e-courses, quick tips, inspiration, checklists and more. Hang out in my discussion forum. While there, ask questions and share your ideas in this amazing community of people trying to get organized and sharing their success stories.

  You CAN get organized! I believe in you. And remember, "there's no better time to get organized, than to Get Organized Now!"

# Chapter 59

# Final words

I hope you have enjoyed this journey we've taken together. Please let me know how you're doing in your efforts to get and stay organized. Write to me with your success stories. I would love to hear from you.

Keep this book handy for future reference. Whenever you need a brush-up, just read a few chapters.

If you have ideas or tips that are not in this book, please submit them to us. We'll consider printing them in a future edition. You will find a web form when you visit this page on our site:

www.getorganizednow.com/readertip.html

Visit the Get Organized Now! web site each day. You'll find new ideas, tips, articles, checklists, e-courses, recipes, motivation and more. Hang out in our free discussion forum, frequented by thousands of people from around the world, to ask questions, share ideas or simply to get a dose of motivation.

I wish you the best of luck and success on your path to a stress-free, pleasant, fun, exciting, productive, organized life.

In the final chapter of this book, I leave you with the 10 Commandments of *Finally Organized, Finally Free.*

Maria Gracia
Get Organized Now!
www.getorganizednow.com

# Chapter 60

# The 10 Commandments of Finally Organized, Finally Free

I _____
                                    (your name)

on this date _____
                                    (date)

do hereby solemnly swear to accept and abide by the following 10 Commandments so that I can be *Finally Organized, Finally Free.*

I.   Thou shalt not get overwhelmed, but shall go forth and be organized with baby steps.

II.  Thou shalt not give yourself the disadvantage of generating clutter, physical, virtual or mental, for it will trap you into living a life of chaos.

III. Thou shalt always have a place for everything and thou shalt always put everything back in its place immediately.

IV.  Thou shalt always write it down and never commit details to memory alone.

V.   Thou shalt banish obstacles barring you from reaching your dreams. Thou shalt achieve your dreams by always working with a vision, a goal and a deadline.

VI.  Thou shalt not attempt to do everything yourself, lest you exhaust yourself. Seek help from family members, friends, associates and professionals.

VII. Thou shalt spend a minimum of ten minutes each day organizing, tidying, planning and scheduling.

VIII. Thou shalt not procrastinate. Do what you say you're going to do, when you say you're going to do it. Control your destiny.

IX.  Thou shalt take care of yourself and your health. Thou shalt make time for yourself and your loved ones. Thou shalt strive to have a positive "Can Do" outlook on life. Thou shalt have fun by designating and enjoying rewards for all your effort.

X.   Thou shalt respect your time, by not allowing unnecessary interruptions and not accepting every request for your precious time.

# Contributors

The following people have been instrumental in the writing and editing of this book.

- **Reader Contributions.** We have a special area on our web site where web site visitors can contribute their own organizing tips and ideas. We have thousands of excellent, truly unique, ones in our archives. We are thrilled to print many of these tips in our books and publications.

  A big "Thanks," to all contributors. Your personal insights have greatly enhanced *Finally Organized, Finally Free for the Office*.

- **Joe Gracia: Senior Executive Editor.** Joe Gracia began his marketing career over 30 years ago. He is an expert in both traditional offline marketing as well as marketing on the Web. Over the past 13 years, he has made his clients literally millions of dollars in increased sales and profits with his unique approach to small business marketing and management techniques.

  After receiving his degree in Marketing and Advertising Design in 1976, Joe entered broadcast media; first with Public Television (PBS), and then, through the years, with both ABC and CBS television affiliates. As an advertising designer and then Director of Advertising Design for 14 years, Joe learned some tremendous marketing lessons by working with thousands of small business owners on their marketing strategies and advertising.

  In 1990 Joe left broadcasting to start Effective Business Systems, a small business consulting firm, specializing in helping small business owners develop simple, but effective, low-cost and profitable marketing systems to replace the costly and wasteful systems commonly in use. Joe's consulting practice quickly grew as word spread about the dramatic sales increases his strategies were producing for his clients.

  When Joe asked one new client to set a sales goal for her $300,000 business, she said, "I would love to grow my business to one million dollars in annual sales within the next four years." Just 24 months later, Joe's client celebrated the achievement of her goal—two years ahead of schedule! By the fourth year, she was fast approaching two million in annual sales, and still growing.

  Another client wanted to double her sales, and then sell her business for a healthy profit. In 1999, her goal of doubling her business was achieved, and in January of 2000 she signed the papers for the sale of her business. All achieved with the help of the marketing techniques Joe shared with her.

  In 1997 Joe set a goal to make his marketing expertise available and affordable for all business owners, no matter how big or small their budget.

His plan was to put all of his marketing expertise, and effective marketing methods—the same simple marketing methods he was using to help grow his current clients' businesses—into written form.

In 1999 the project was completed. He called it *The Give to Get Marketing Solution*. Finally, Joe was able to share his "tested and proven," low-cost techniques for attracting customers not just with hundreds of business owners, but with literally thousands across the country, and around the world.

In 1997 Joe and his wife, Maria, brought their business and marketing experience to the Internet by co-creating the Get Organized Now! Web site.

Joe applied his marketing expertise to the design of the site, as well as the overall marketing strategy of the site. Maria actively hosts the site and with the help of Joe's marketing strategy has grown the site into one of the most popular and successful organizing web sites on the Internet.

On October 1, 2000, Joe founded a new company division called Give to Get Marketing. His Give to Get Marketing Web site is designed to educate small business owners in a wide variety of marketing principles including effective strategies and proven marketing systems. Visit his Give to Get Marketing Web site at: www.givetogetmarketing.com

When he's not working, Joe enjoys spending quality time with his wife and daughter, playing guitar and reading—especially anything with historical significance.

- **Laura Sherman: Senior Executive Editor.** Laura Sherman: Executive Editor. Laura, a freelance editor, has an excellent "eye for detail". She lives in Watertown, WI with her husband, Alan, and three wonderful children, Abby, Emma and Jack.

Laura graduated from the University of Wisconsin-Madison in 1989 with a degree in English. Active in her community, Laura has served on the board of the Watertown Newcomers and Neighbors Club in positions including Treasurer and Social Coordinator.

She enjoys being outdoors in the warm weather and you'll frequently see her gardening or reading, while enjoying the company of her kids. She plays violin, attends monthly book chats and plays a mean game of Bunco!

Laura understands the great benefits of clutter control, and holds regular rummage sales throughout the year to "lighten up."

- **Maribel Ibrahim: Executive Editor.** Maribel C. Ibrahim is a freelance writer and stay-at-home mom residing in Severna Park, Maryland. After thirteen years as an Industrial Engineer for two Fortune 500 companies, she traded in her briefcase for a diaper bag.

Maribel and her husband Omar recently welcomed their first-born son Aidan. Sampson, their iguana, is very jealous, but is gradually making the adjustment to the new addition.

Maribel is a lifetime member of Weight Watchers, a La Leche League member and a vocalist for the Magothy United Methodist Church Praise Band. Maribel's monthly column, MomTalk, featured in the Severna Park Voice, provides moms with tips on organizing, finances, fitness, home management and family resources available in the Severna Park area. You can visit Maribel online at www.abundantlivingnow.net or via email at MomTalk@abundantlivingnow.net

- **Pamala Mielnicki: Associate Editor.** Pamala J. Mielnicki has been a resident of Irwin, Pennsylvania—a suburb of Pittsburgh—her entire life. She lives in her home with her wonderful and loving husband, Stephen, their three terrific sons, Alexander, Brandon and Ryan along with their sweet yellow Labrador retriever, Spencer, who still acts like he's a puppy even though he's all grown up.

Pamala has been an administrative assistant to the owner of a commercial and residential real estate development and management company for almost two decades. She also started her own thriving business, in partnership with her father, a year ago—a greeting and information service for new residents called "Welcome New Neighbors." www.NorwinCommunityGuide.com

She also loves volunteering for her local Lions Club and PTA, spending time with friends, reading, singing and collecting model horses. Pamala is able to maintain and enjoy her very busy schedule thanks to the amazing teamwork and support from her husband. Together, they work to prioritize, organize and balance responsibilities.

- **Jodi Arrowsmith: Associate Editor.** Jodi Arrowsmith is a lifelong resident of Bay City, Michigan. She has been married to her husband, Rob, since 1993 and they have two boys, Evan and Adam. Jodi has worked for a Bankruptcy Attorney and Trustee as a "Trustee Administrator," since 1993. Her job consists of reviewing all Trustee cases in her bosses care to be sure that they are actively administering all assets of each file in a timely manner. Jodi processes all documents, does her own filing, maintains dates to follow up, as well as updates all case records with all banking transactions.

Much of Jodi's volunteer time is spent at her parochial school and church. She listens to children read, monitors various lessons in the computer lab on Fridays, is a PowerPoint Multimedia Projection System technician for her church service and serves on several committees at the church/school. She also served as a volunteer bookkeeper for her children's school daycare.

Jodi has been a Moderator on the Get Organized Now! forum, since 2002. She enjoys seeing new friends progress from chaos toward peace of mind. As Jodi says, it's a work in progress!

- **Jane Ellen: Associate Editor.** Jane Ellen is a freelance composer, lecturer and web designer, currently living in Albuquerque, NM. A national-award winning member of the American Society of Composers, Authors and Publishers (ASCAP), she has more than 40 published works to her credit and has recently produced two piano solo CDs of original compositions.

  Her works have been performed internationally and she has been the recipient of several prestigious commissions. She is a popular speaker for educational, social and religious groups and she also serves as webmaster, worksheet editor and occasional script assistant for the national award-winning children's radio show "Boombox Classroom."

  Jane's overwhelming schedule and desire to find methods of organizing that would fit her lifestyle as well as her "creative personality" in general led her to the Get Organized Now! web site where she served as a moderator for several years. She has also written articles on becoming organized specifically for right-brain individuals. When not involved in music, web design or her ongoing quest for organization, Jane enjoys watching old movies, reading classic adventure novels and studying Italian. You can visit Jane on the Internet at www.janeellen.com

- **Diana Romagnano: Associate Editor.** Diana lives in Elgin, IL. She has four kids, Louis Jr., Sam, Lucy and Sabina and four grandsons, Louie, Rudy, Andrew and Nathan. She also has two grandkitties, Lynde and Sylvester. Diana is retired and enjoying things she put off when her children were home and she was a busy working mom and wife.

  Her hobbies and interests include a love of organizing, cross stitching, card making, crocheting, reading and going out to lunch with friends. She was born in Chicago and loves the city, but has moved to the country and loves that also.

  Diana retired shortly after her husband Lou died and her Mother moved in with her. She enjoys having her mom and her daughter living with her. They call themselves the "Golden Girls" minus one!

  Diana enjoys working as a moderator on the Get Organized Now! forum and helping people. She loves when they start to see an improvement in their lives. She says the forum has helped her through a very devastating time in her life and changed her into the person she is today. Diana says she could not have done it without Get Organized Now! and the wonderful people involved with the site. The other thing she has learned over the years is to take time for herself each and every day. It changes one's entire outlook—reading, stitching or just sitting and thinking. She says that we all deserve it and definitely need it in our lives.

- **Lynne Poindexter: Associate Editor.** Lynne Poindexter was born and raised in Philadelphia, Pennsylvania. She is a corporate paralegal for a satellite television communications corporation. Lynne is a member of her church's choir. She is a big movie buff with a movie library of over 1,000 films.

  She moderates the Get Organized Now! forum and enjoys her ongoing quest of getting organized. Lynne enjoys line dancing and has been taking classes for over two years. She is a member of a line dance and social club. Her other interests include, sewing, cross-stitch and miniature dollhouse building.

- **Denise Williams: Associate Editor.** Denise Williams lives in Tampa, FL. She has two wonderful children and three special grandchildren. Her daughter April, blessed her with two granddaughters, Hallie and Taylor. Her son, Keith, and his wife Erica, brought her grandson, Dustin, into her life. Denise also has a calico cat named Princess Patches—who thinks she's a Queen!

  She currently works for a major credit card company assisting customers with Internet support, as well as a part-time start-up organizing company. She also volunteers her time as a moderator for the Get Organized Now! forum. Her hobbies include organizing, scrap booking, reading, swimming and spending time with the family.

- **Judy Brown: Associate Editor.** Judy Brown is the owner of Organized Forever. She believes that the hardest part of getting organized is getting started. Judy is a freelance writer and Professional Organizing consultant in Yale, British Columbia, Canada. Using skills she acquired as a mother of five and foster mother to many, she helps young mothers get a handle on organizing the family. A former librarian, Clerk of the Court and Justice of the Peace, Judy uses all her skills and training experience to help others get organized at home and at work. Home business owners are her specialty.

  As a Professional Organizer, she assesses each clients' personal organizing and decision-making style. She then develops customized methods that will work best for them. She says that when clients work with techniques that fit their own style, they are better able to maintain new organizing habits.

  Judy coaches her clients to work on one small project at a time and shows them how to make a difference in lifestyle and thinking to enable them to continue being organized long after the consultations are over. Visit her website: www.organizedforever.com and be sure to check out her online organizing workshops.

- **Monica Ricci: Associate Editor.** Monica Ricci has been an organizing and productivity specialist since 1999. She helps her clients streamline and organize their time, space, paper and processes in both the home and workplace. Her web site is www.CatalystOrganizing.com As a motivational speaker, Monica presents workshops on time and action management, overcoming procrastination, simplifying life, as well as getting and staying organized.

  Monica is immediate past president of The National Association of Professional Organizers, Georgia Chapter. She publishes a monthly newsletter, Simplicity News, as well as writes for several newsletters and magazines. She has also been the source of organizing advice for many magazine and newspaper articles, has been an expert guest on radio and television, including the nationally syndicated Clark Howard show and was named to Forbes Magazine's "Organizing Elite" in 2003.

  Monica enjoys entertaining, cooking, travel, competitive pistol shooting, board games and baseball. She lives with her husband, Ed King and their two cats in Atlanta, Georgia.

- **Tina Peters: Associate Editor.** Tina Peters lives in Watertown, WI and shares her busy, yet organized lifestyle, with her loving husband and two wonderful sons, Jacob and Ryan. She earned a bachelor's degree in journalism from the University of Wisconsin-Milwaukee and has worked for years designing employee newsletters, writing resumes for family and friends and co-managing a small printing business.

  Now a stay-at-home mom, Tina challenges herself daily with the tasks of managing a household, scheduling play dates, driving her children to school and making feeble attempts at creating the perfect layout for her son's train table. She is active in her community and has served on the board of the Watertown Newcomers Club as newsletter chairperson and president. Her hobbies include gardening, singing and spending time with family and friends.

- **Lea Schneider.** A professional organizer in Jackson, Tennessee, Lea is the owner of Organize & More. She brings solutions to home, office and life as she consults with time-crunched small businesses and homeowners to manage their environments and simplify their lives. Lea offers presentations on a variety of organizational topics.

  She has been a professional journalist for many years and her feature stories appear weekly in The Jackson Sun. A mother of three, she has a B.S. in Business from Florida Southern College and is a member of the Association of Food Journalists and the National Association of Professional Organizers (NAPO).

# About the author

Maria Gracia, founder of Get Organized Now!, specializes in helping people get better organized to live the kind of stress-free life they've always dreamed of.

During Maria's ten years with Dun and Bradstreet's Nielsen Media Research in New York, Maria worked as a marketing, organizing and management specialist.

Throughout her tenure, she managed the data analysis department, worked with hundreds of television stations and advertising agencies and developed effective, productive systems for her clients and staff.

Today, Maria, her husband, Joe, and their beautiful daughter Amanda Grace, live in Watertown, Wisconsin. Joe and Maria own and operate their company, Effective Business Systems. Maria founded Get Organized Now! as a division of the company in 1996.

The Get Organized Now! Web site is currently visited by over a million people per year. Maria has hundreds of thousands of people on her Get Organized Now! newsletter list.

Specializing in peak time and space management, Maria has over 20 years of organizational experience. Her broad range of skills covers clutter control, planning, scheduling, peak productivity, records management, space planning, time and paper management, filing systems, computer oriented-organizational systems and more.

Maria Gracia has appeared at, wrote for, or has been interviewed by hundreds of international, national and local media and organizations such as Woman's Day Magazine, Country Living Magazine, Access Magazine, USA Today, Staples and hundreds of television and radio stations.

Maria is the author of the *Finally Organized, Finally Free* series. Her books have been read by thousands of people all over the world. In addition, she has created a variety of other helpful organizing products, sold worldwide, which can be found in her Get Organized Now! Store on her web site: www.getorganizednow.com

On the homefront, Maria is a huge proponent of family time and enjoys as much time as possible with her husband Joe and daughter Amanda. She has served on the board of the Watertown Newcomers Club in a number of positions including President, is an avid scrapbooker, attends monthly book chats and enjoys cooking, traveling and entertaining.

# Other Products Available from Get Organized Now!

### Finally Organized, Finally Free – For the Home
If you loved Finally Organized, Finally Free – For the Office, you will definitely love Finally Organized, Finally Free – for the Home. You'll discover tons of tips and ideas to help you get your home and your life organized, including how to banish clutter, better manage your time, get more done and so much more!

### The Easy Organizer
It's not just a planner. It's much, much more! Loaded with easy-to-use forms to help you eliminate those notorious scraps of paper and consolidate all of your home-related data into one place so you can find your info when you need it.

### The Easy Bill Paying System
Pay your home-related bills on time, easily organize your statements and conveniently keep track of your expenses with this simple, but powerful, system.

### The Ultimate Guide for Professional Organizers
This comprehensive guide contains everything you need to know about starting, running and growing your professional organizing business, while making a great profit! If you've ever dreamed of owning your own professional organizing business, this guide is the only one you'll need.

### Give to Get Marketing Solution
Have a small to medium-sized business or thinking of starting one? Kick start your marketing program into overdrive with this all-encompassing guide that will help you develop a solid strategy for attracting customers to your business.

### The Christmas Holiday Planner
A must-have planner to help you get and stay organized for a stress-free, enjoyable holiday season.

### FileWISE®
This is the new, revolutionary, easy and time-saving way to file, organize and find all your documents and files within seconds! This pre-categorized filing system makes the job of setting up either your home or business filing systems a breeze.

### TuffBaggs®
Tired of heavy purses weighing you down? TuffBaggs® are strong, but they're light as a feather. As the name indicates, TuffBaggs® are constructed with durable materials which provide superior strength. Best of all, the many compartments can help you stay organized.

*For more information about any of these products, please visit: www.getorganizednow.com and click on the STORE link.*

# Your Tips, Ideas and Comments

## Write to Us

Do you have an organizing tip, success story or comment you'd like to share? We'd love to hear from you. Feel free to write to us at:

Get Organized Now!
611 Arlington Way
Watertown WI 53094

Please include your name and full mailing address on all correspondence. If you send an organizing tip or a success story, we may publish it, along with your name, city and state as the contributor, on our web site, in our newsletter, in a media press release or in one of our future products.

## Spelling or Link Corrections

While careful care has gone into the writing and editing of this book, there's always the possibility that we may have missed something. In light of this, if you happen to notice a spelling error or a web site link that no longer works, please feel free to write to us at the above address. We'll then have the opportunity to correct it in future printings. Please be sure to include the page number where you located the error.

## Grammatical Corrections

As far as grammatical errors, Maria Gracia has always said, "I write the way I speak. If I followed every grammatical rule there was, my writing would be awfully stiff and stuffy. My main concern is that I get my point across." But feel free to write to us about any grammatical error that truly bothers you and we'll bring it to Maria's attention for consideration.

## Correspondence

Although we do respond personally to some of our mail, due to the thousands of email messages we receive each week, we regret that we can't respond personally to every single one we receive. However, please be assured that we do read and consider all correspondence.

# Index

## A

Abbreviations, 217–218, 252

ABE (Always Be Evaluating), 260

Accessibility, 263

Accessories, 28, 39

Accomplishment log, 361

Accordion files, 115

Accountants, 101–102

Accounting knowledge, 104

Accounts payable representatives, 106

Acrobat Reader, 83

ACT!, 71, 188, 192

Action files, 131

Activity stations, 28

Address books, 187–188

Addresses, 156

Address labels, 204

Advertising, testing, 338

Agendas, 194, 196, 200, 203, 310

Air, 237, 239

Airline lounge clubs, 313

Airline metal detectors, 313

Airline mileage credit, 101

Air space, 52

Alarm clocks, 257, 314

Alarm systems, 232, 233, 236

Alburger, Claudette, 97

Align text feature, 73

Alphabetical filing system, 123

Alphabetical sorter book, 37

Alphabetizing, 67–68

Alternate between applications (shortcut), 66

ALT-TAB, 66

Always Be Evaluating (ABE), 260

Amenities, 31

American Psychological Association, 265

Answering machines, 184–185, 232, 254, 257

Anti-virus programs, 70, 72, 74

AOL, 85

Applications, computer, 66, 72

Appointments, 186, 216–217, 217, 306

Aquariums, 176

Archive files, 22, 45, 46, 132, 135

Arrangement of office, 26

Arrowsmith, Jodi, 37, 165, 366

Articles, 142

Artificial plants, 27

Art studio, 175

Assertiveness, 198

Assistants, 268, 270

Association, remembering by, 229, 235

Asterisks, 68

Attachments, email, 74, 83

Audiotapes, 211–212, 310

Audits, 115

Authority, defining limits of, 278

Automatic bill payment, 98, 107

Autoresponders, 340

Availability, 271, 279, 324

Aweber, 342

## B

Babies, 326

Babysitters, 324, 345